This Day
IN
CIVIL RIGHTS HISTORY

Horace Randall Williams and Ben Beard

NewSouth Books
Montgomery | Louisville

In memory of
Harry T. Moore, Medgar Evers, and Robert Kennedy,
whose lives were cut short because of what they believed;
and of E. D. Nixon, C. G. Gomillion, Fannie Lou Hamer, Daisy Bates, Myles Horton,
Septima Clark, and Ruby Hurley, who spent their lives working in the movement;
and of attorneys Thurgood Marshall, Charles Hamilton Houston, Constance Baker Motley,
William Kunstler, and many others whose belief in the law changed the law;
and of Judges J. Waites Waring, Frank M. Johnson Jr., Elbert P. Tuttle
John Minor Wisdom, Richard T. Rives, John R. Brown, and Hugo L. Black,
whose belief in the Constitution restored it;
and in tribute to Fred D. Gray, C. T. Vivian, Robert Moses, Diane Nash, Jack Greenberg,
John Lewis, and scores of others who made a revolution and are still trying to improve on it.

ERRATA: The December 5 (1955) entry states that on that afternoon black leaders reconvened in the basement of the Dexter Avenue Baptist Church and organized the Montgomery Improvement Association. That meeting was actually held in the Mt. Zion A.M.E. Church.

Copyright © 2009 by NewSouth Books, 105 South Court Street, Montgomery, AL 36104. All rights reserved under International and Pan-American Copyright Conventions. Published in the United States by NewSouth Books, a division of NewSouth, Inc., Montgomery, Alabama.

Library of Congress Cataloging-in-Publication Data

Williams, Randall, 1951–
This day in civil rights history / Horace Randall Williams and Ben Beard.
p. cm.
Originally published: Cincinnati, OH : Emmis Books, c2005. Includes index.
ISBN-13: 978-1-58838-241-2 • ISBN-10: 1-58838-241-9
1. African Americans—Civil rights—History—Chronology. 2. African Americans—Civil rights—History—Miscellanea. 3. Civil rights movements—United States—History—Chronology. 4. Civil rights movements—United States—History—Miscellanea. 5. United States—Race relations—History—Chronology. 6. United States—Race relations—History—Miscellanea. I. Beard, Ben, 1977– II. Title.
E185.61.W7375 2009
323.1196'073—dc22
2009014643

Cover photos copyright Governor George ... Martin Luther King (middle left) courtesy of POPPERFOTO/Alamy; Detroit Riot (middle right) courtesy of Library of Congress; "I Ain't Afraid of Your Jail", Kelly Ingram Park (top right) courtesy of Travis Bryant; Freedom March, Washington DC, August 29, 1963 (bottom left) courtesy of POPPERFOTO/Alamy.

IN
CIVIL RIGHTS HISTORY

Horace Randall Williams and Ben Beard

emmis
books

- TABLE OF CONTENTS -

*"We claim for ourselves every single right
that belongs to a freeborn American,
political, civil and social;
and until we get these rights
we will never cease to protest and assail
the ears of America. The battle we wage
is not for ourselves alone but for all true Americans."*
— *W. E. B. Du Bois, 1906*

— INTRODUCTION —

Of the many issues that can be debated about the American civil rights movement, one that always comes up early in the discussion is how to define its scope. On the timeline of history, where do you put the movement's start and, if you assume it is over, what date do you use for its end?

One common answer is to use the 1955 Montgomery bus boycott as the beginning and the 1968 assassination of the Rev. Dr. Martin Luther King Jr. as the close. This view has been summed up as: "Rosa sat down, Martin stood up, and the world moved." Satisfying, tidy . . . and wrong.

Back up just a year and you get the 1954 U.S. Supreme Court ruling in *Brown v. Board of Education,* which definitively overturned the "separate but equal" doctrine that had kept African Americans in legalized Jim Crow segregation since the late 1800s. Or go back six more years to President Harry Truman's 1948 executive order desegregating the U.S. armed forces, thus ending the hypocrisy of a nation that sent black soldiers overseas to die for democracy while denying it to them at home. Or consider the 1944 U.S. Supreme Court ruling in *Smith v. Allwright,* which gave Lonnie Smith, a black man, the right to vote in the previously all-white Democratic primary elections—the only game in town at the time—in Texas. Or move back along the timeline to the 1920s when Congressman Leonidas Dyer tried every year to get a law passed that would make lynchings a federal crime so as to end the horrific Southern harvest of "strange fruit" of which Billie Holiday so hauntingly sang. Keep moving back and you come to the 1909 founding of the NAACP, the group that more than any other in the 20th century organized the collective energies and passions of blacks and whites who dreamed of real democracy and real justice. Before that was the Niagara Movement of 1905. And the futile protests against the "black codes" and disenfranchising constitutions adopted at the turn of the 19th century, and the establishment of black churches, schools, and fraternal orders in the post–Civil War years. Even earlier were Emancipation, the Civil War, slave revolts, and the abolition movement.

The point is that a direct line extends from the moment the first African slaves were brought to North America to the 1963 March on Washington for Jobs and Freedom some four centuries later. One can't tell the story of the civil rights movement of the 1950s and 1960s without also telling about the earlier history of Reconstruction and Civil War and slavery, because the civil rights story is about a long journey from bondage through segregation and on to equality under the law.

Nor is the story even close to being finished. Although it is true that by the time of Martin King's murder in Memphis the civil rights movement had defeated Jim Crow, many substantial battles remained. Although the law no longer keeps white and black kids apart, there are still schools that are just as segregated in 2005 as they were in 1954. Although fair-housing laws no longer allow blacks to be legally kept out of certain subdivisions, the rate of home ownership for African Americans remains lower than that for whites. Although African Americans now register to vote without restrictions, somehow in the 2000 Bush–Gore presidential election there still were more procedural problems in Florida's black precincts than there were in wealthier white precincts. Even racially motivated violence, although minuscule compared with that of the past, still happens, as we saw in the horrific 1998 Texas case in which white thugs tied a chain to a black man and dragged him to death behind a pickup truck.

This book thus takes the long view that the civil rights movement began with slavery and continues to the present day. The 1965 Selma-to-Montgomery March is here, of course, but so is the 1917 parade organized by the NAACP of 10,000 persons silently tramping down New York City's Fifth Avenue to protest the St. Louis race riot. Rosa Parks is here, of course, but so is freedman David Ruggles, who filed a lawsuit in 1841 after being dragged out of a whites-only railroad car. The famous Tuskegee Airmen of World War II fame are here, but so is Robert Smalls, a slave who commandeered a Confederate ship in 1862 and sailed it out of Charleston Harbor and turned it over to the Union navy. The 1664 passage of the nation's first miscegenation law is here, but so is the 2003 announcement by a biracial South Carolina woman that she was the daughter of Strom Thurmond.

As these few examples illustrate, the book traverses the whole span of African American history. What makes the book a civil rights history rather than a general African American history is that all its entries show—in ways large and small—the striving of blacks and their white allies for equal rights. Thus, great as he was, there is no entry on George Washington Carver. His contribution to history was of a different nature; that Carver was African American is almost incidental to what he accomplished as a scientist and inventor. But John H. Johnson, on the other hand, was not simply a black publisher: He was the publisher of magazines that entertained, yes, but that also gave voice to the issues and struggles of the civil rights movement.

That said, this book is no definitive history. Rather, it is 366 minichapters plucked somewhat at random from within the history of the movement. It is based not on any original scholarship but on wholesale assimilation of information from books, newspapers, magazines, encyclopedias, and other published works. Assembling all this information to fit the format of the *This Day in History* series presented a number of research and editorial challenges. First, larger events that had unfolded over time often had to be broken into several dates that didn't always fall consecutively within the calendar. In the Montgomery bus boycott, for example, the judges began hearing the case in May 1956, but Mrs. Parks was arrested in December 1955. So the story of the bus boycott, like some others, could not be told linearly as it would be in most histories; instead, each piece of each story had to stand alone. We don't recommend this approach to writing about complex events, but it's what had to be done.

In addition, the calendar doesn't always cooperate with the "day in ..." format. On any given day, several significant events may have occurred in different years, but we could write about only one. On some days, however, we could find nothing of significance to civil rights history. We balanced those two problems with some creative date-juggling, and we ask in advance for the reader's understanding when we occasionally open an entry by noting that on a particular day some person or some situation "continued" in whatever had been happening a day or two days earlier.

Although no book organized this way could be definitive, we have tried to be faithful to the major themes and events of the civil rights movement. As we've said, we reached back to the establishment of slavery, to the abolition movement and the Underground Railroad, to Civil War and Emancipation, to Reconstruction and then the successful white effort to overturn the gains of the 1865–1877 period, and to the gradual codification of white supremacy into Jim Crow segregation in the late 1800s and early 1900s. Then we sought to give snapshots of the first stirrings of what scholars now identify as the modern civil rights movement: the debate over strategy personified by the rivalry between Booker T. Washington and W. E. B. Du Bois—remarkable giants each believing his way was the best way forward for his people; the births of the Niagara Movement and then the NAACP; the Great Migration from the sharecropping South to the industrial but often no-less-brutal North; the heartrending race riots and the protests against them of the early 1900s; the antilynching and suffrage campaigns of the 1920s; the joblessness and abject poverty—for whites and blacks—of the Great Depression in the 1930s; and then the eagerness of blacks to add their effort and blood to the worldwide fight against fascism from 1941 to 1945.

Reading back over the events of U.S. history, one can almost hear the collective voice of black America crying, "Let us in. Let us do our part. We are Americans too. Give us a chance, and then treat us like men and women." That in a nutshell is what the civil rights movement was about. That the plea could be ignored for so long by so many now seems—a half century after the movement began winning its victories over Jim Crow segregation—both a great mystery and a great tragedy, and a colossal waste of human potential. And of course the bills for the past negligence are still coming due and must be paid, one way or another.

In the years right after World War II, the civil rights movement picked up steam. Again, a book such as this one can give only quick glimpses of the forces that were coalescing. But we have tried to include highlights of all the major campaigns, from the NAACP's brilliant legal strategy to overturn school segregation, which played out in *Brown v. Board* at Little Rock's Central High School, in George Wallace's grandstanding at the schoolhouse door in Alabama, and on to the furious antibusing protests in Charlotte and Boston in the 1970s; to the Montgomery bus boycott and the later freedom rides that ended segregated public transportation; to the hundreds of sit-ins and swim-ins and sleep-ins that desegregated public accommodations; to the heroism of the black and white SNCC workers who joined Mississippians like Medgar Evers, Aaron Henry, Fannie Lou Hamer, Ed King, and Will Campbell in confronting the most extreme white-supremacist violence; to the creation of the various organizations like SCLC, COFO, CORE, AFSC, ACLU, NLG, CCR, etc., each of which owned a piece of the civil rights turf; to the sustained protests in cities like Albany, Birmingham, Selma, and Chicago; to the voting rights campaigns in Mississippi and especially in Selma; to the significant legislation that resulted from the undeniable moral force of the movement; to the emergence of the black-power, free-speech, and antiwar movements as the issues began to move beyond mere segregation; and on to the gradual splintering of the civil rights movement.

In the pages to follow, the reader will find brief accounts of the events, organizations, and people of the civil rights movement. Our hope as we researched and wrote the entries was that they collectively would bring some understanding of the remarkable achievement of the movement, along with some recognition of its limits and of the challenges still ahead. We regret that many events and many people had to be left out. We did try to balance big events with smaller ones, and household names with the largely unremembered—those who are now called the footsoldiers or the unsung heroes.

Earlier we mentioned the white allies of the civil rights movement, and it is worth pointing out that even though the book is populated by plenty of white villains—from segregationist demagogues like Strom Thurmond, Orval Faubus, and George Wallace, to stone-cold killers like Byron de la Beckwith and "Dynamite Bob" Chambliss—many Southern whites recognized the rightness of the movement cause. True, few white Southerners had the courage of Will Campbell, H. L. Mitchell, Virginia Durr, Chuck Morgan Jr., and others to go against the grain of white opinion in the 1950s and 1960s, to risk being ostracized and punished economically for believing in brotherhood. But some did, because they saw at the time what is now obvious: that the yoke of discrimination was holding back the entire nation, not just the nation's African American citizens. Slavery and segregation were morally evil, and ending them freed not only the bodies and ambitions of black people but also the souls of white people. Young people who read this book and other histories of the movement must understand that.

The authors of this book worked together for several years in the publishing offices of NewSouth Books in downtown Montgomery. Still an overgrown small town, Montgomery is famous for two things: civil war and civil rights. A hundred yards from our office door, one can see the spot where African Americans were bought and sold like cattle on the auction block. Right across the street from that spot, in 1861 on the day before he was to be sworn in as president of the Confederacy, Jefferson Davis smiled and waved from a hotel balcony to admiring throngs of white Southerners. A few feet from that spot, the telegraph was sent to fire on Fort Sumter, touching off the Civil War, the ruinous end of which also ended those slave auctions. In 1955, just a hundred yards from where Jefferson Davis smiled, Rosa Parks boarded a bus for a two-block ride that made her famous and, in the end, let her smile, too.

Montgomery's coincidence of history and place juxtaposes people and events. It seemed to us a fitting metaphor for how a book such as this one—admittedly a peculiar type of history book—moves from one page to another back and forth through different eras of the African American struggle, first against slavery and then against segregation.

This book mentions frequently many organizations with long names that are commonly referred to by their initials. Below is a list of these acronyms.

ACLU	American Civil Liberties Union	NAACP	National Association for the Advancement of Colored People
ADL	Anti-Defamation League		
AFL	American Federation of Labor	NOI	Nation of Islam
AFSC	American Friends Service Committee	NCC	National Council of Churches
		NCNW	National Council of Negro Women
BPP	Black Panther Party		
BSCP	Brotherhood of Sleeping Car Porters	NLG	National Lawyers Guild
		NUL	National Urban League
CBC	Congressional Black Caucus	PUSH	People United to Serve Humanity
CCR	Center for Constitutional Rights		
CIO	Congress of Industrial Organizations	SCEF	Southern Conference Education Fund
CORE	Congress of Racial Equality	SCOPE	Summer Community Organization and Political Education
CCCO	Coordinating Council of Community Organizations		
COFO	Council of Federated Organizations	SCLC	Southern Christian Leadership Conference
DCVL	Dallas County Voters League	SDS	Students for a Democratic Society
DNC	Democratic National Convention		
FBI	Federal Bureau of Investigation	SNCC	Student Nonviolent Coordinating Committee
FOR	Fellowship of Reconciliation		
ICC	Interstate Commerce Commission	SPLC	Southern Poverty Law Center
		SRC	Southern Regional Council
JOR	Journey of Reconciliation	STFU	Southern Tenant Farmers Union
KKK	Ku Klux Klan	UAW	United Auto Workers
LCFDP	Lowndes County Freedom Democratic Party	UNCF	United Negro College Fund
		UNIA	Universal Negro Improvement Association
LDF	NAACP Legal Defense Fund		
MFDP	Mississippi Freedom Democratic Party	VEP	Voter Education Project
		WCC	White Citizens Council
MIA	Montgomery Improvement Association		

This day in

January

— JANUARY 1 —

1863

PRESIDENT LINCOLN ISSUES EMANCIPATION PROCLAMATION

On this day in civil rights history, President Abraham Lincoln formally issued an executive order, commonly known as the Emancipation Proclamation, declaring that "all persons held as slaves . . . are, and henceforward shall be free."

But, there was a catch. The edict applied only to slaves who lived in rebellious territories—in other words, in Confederate states—and not even to slaves in those parts of the Confederacy already in Union control at the end of 1862.

President Lincoln so worded the Proclamation because he didn't want to alienate key border states that were loyal to the Union. So in reality no slaves were immediately emancipated by Lincoln's action. Nonetheless, the Proclamation was symbolically significant, and it did help the Union win support abroad, especially in England.

The Proclamation also changed the nature of the war. Up to then, the war often had been seen as a struggle between nationalism and states' rights. After Lincoln's Proclamation, the issue became more clearly one of human liberty and freedom. Slaves and abolitionists had insisted from the beginning that the war was about slavery; Lincoln's Proclamation confirmed this assertion, and added a powerful moral dimension to the North's war effort.

The Proclamation also had the effect of steadily widening the gap between the North's and the South's manpower resources. Whenever Union forces captured

Abraham Lincoln

new rebel territories, the slave labor within immediately became unavailable to the South. In addition, the Proclamation invited freed slaves into the Union army and navy. Ultimately, some 200,000 African Americans took up arms against their former masters.

The end of the war and actual emancipation ended slavery; still ahead were the long battles against segregation, discrimination, and racism. But Lincoln's Proclamation was the first step, and January 1 thus became one of the most important anniversaries for African Americans. Throughout the civil rights movement and up to the present day, Emancipation Proclamation ceremonies have been held annually on New Year's day in communities throughout the nation.

— JANUARY 2 —
1965
SNCC INTENSIFIES VOTER REGISTRATION IN SELMA

On this day in civil rights history, Martin Luther King Jr. addressed a mass meeting in Selma and announced the beginning of a renewed campaign to register black voters in Dallas County. A registration campaign, under the leadership of the Dallas County Voters League and the Student Nonviolent Coordinating Committee (SNCC), had been underway in this small city in the center of Alabama's Black Belt for two years, but the effort had faltered in the face of a July 1964 injunction by a local judge that had barred activists and organizations from picketing, marching, parading, or even having the mass meetings which were a hallmark of community-organizing for civil rights.

This injunction was appealed to federal court, but no ruling would be issued until April 1965. Meanwhile, arrests and other intimidation by Dallas County Sheriff Jim Clark slowed registration activities significantly. In early July 1964, almost 100 blacks applied to register, though only six were successful. But for the rest of the year, only about 50 more blacks tried to register, with only another six succeeding.

So King's speech on January 2 set the stage for the activities that would lead up to the Bloody Sunday confrontation at the Edmund Pettus Bridge on March 7, and the subsequent Selma-to-Montgomery March two weeks later, all of which focused the attention of the nation on Selma and led directly to the passage of the Voting Rights Act in August.

Also in January, white-owned restaurants in Selma yielded to Justice Department pressure and agreed to desegregate. Further, Selma police chief Wilson Baker, reacting in part to a more moderate mood among local white business leaders, had worked out an agreement to keep the defiantly segregationist Sheriff Clark out of law enforcement activities within downtown Selma except at the county courthouse.

All of these developments were encouraging to King and other black leaders, but unfortunately the worst was yet to come. Because the point of the black protests and marches was to seek voter registration at the county courthouse, all demonstrations ended in a confrontation with Clark on the courthouse steps. On January 18, 64 blacks attempting to enter the front door of the courthouse were arrested by Clark on charges of unlawful assembly. Over the next two months, more than 2,000 persons were arrested while attempting to register or while encouraging others to register.

The Justice Department and the federal courts, meanwhile, were steadily showing mounting impatience with the obstructionist tactics of Sheriff Clark and other local officials.

— January 3 —
1949
First Black Heads Congressional Committee

On this day in civil rights history, U.S. Representative William Levi Dawson of Chicago became the first African American to chair a regular committee of the House of Representatives.

Born on April 26, 1886, in Albany, Georgia, Dawson graduated *magna cum laude* from Fisk University in Nashville in 1912. He then studied law at Northwestern University in Chicago, and after graduation remained there to make his home and to begin his legal career. He also entered into the rough-and-tumble Democratic ward politics of Chicago and was elected to the city council.

In 1942 Dawson won election to Congress, where he served for 14 terms. He became one of the most influential Chicago politicians of his era and controlled a large block of political patronage, earning him the nickname, "The Man." He was highly regarded for returning to his home district as often as he could and meeting regularly with constituents to discuss their concerns and issues.

He made history on this date in 1949 when he became chairman of the House Committee on Government Operations (then called the Committee on Expenditures in Executive Departments), making him the first black to chair a regular House committee.

Dawson's other civil rights contributions include his leading role in defeating the Winstead Amendment, a measure that would have permitted military servicemen and women to choose whether they would serve in integrated units. He also spoke vigorously against and campaigned to defeat the poll tax, which was used especially in Southern states to keep blacks and poor whites from voting.

Dawson worked hard in 1960 to help elect Senator John F. Kennedy to the presidency, and as a reward Kennedy later offered him the office of U.S. Postmaster General. But Dawson said he believed he could do more good in Congress and he declined the appointment.

He retired in 1970 and died soon afterwards.

— JANUARY 4 —

1969

CONGRESSIONAL BLACK CAUCUS FORMED

On this day in civil rights history, 13 black members of the U.S. House of Representatives organized the "Democratic Select Committee," which in 1971 was renamed the Congressional Black Caucus with the goal of speaking with a united voice on issues of special interest to African Americans.

The Caucus first came to wide public attention in 1971 when its members presented then-President Richard Nixon with a list of about five dozen recommendations for domestic and foreign policy actions by the U.S. government.

Founding members included Representatives Shirley Chisholm, New York; William Clay, Missouri; George Collins, Illinois; John Conyers, Michigan; Ronald Dellums, California; Charles Diggs, Michigan; Augustus Hawkins, California; Ralph Metcalfe, Illinois; Parren Mitchell, Maryland; Robert Nix, Pennsylvania; Charles Rangel, New York; Louis Stokes, Ohio; and Delegate Walter Fauntroy, District of Columbia.

The CBC primarily sought to achieve greater equity for African American citizens, but the group has also been a leading voice in legislative campaigns for human and civil rights around the world. Over the years the Caucus has achieved significant successes toward the original goal "to promote the public welfare through legislation designed to meet the needs of millions of neglected citizens."

Its legislative initiatives range "from full employment to welfare reform, South African apartheid and international human rights, from minority business development to expanded educational opportunities. Most noteworthy is the CBC alternative budget, which the Caucus has produced continually for over 16 years," according to former Caucus director Amelia Parker. She said the alternative budget "seeks to preserve a national commitment to fair treatment for urban and rural America, the elderly, students, small businessmen and women, middle- and low-income wage earners, the economically disadvantaged, and a new world order."

— JANUARY 5 —

1804

NATION'S FIRST 'BLACK LAWS' ENACTED IN OHIO

On this day in civil rights history, the nation's first "Black Laws" were enacted in Ohio. These laws restricted the rights of free blacks and were the precursors of the later "Jim Crow" laws, which enforced legal segregation in the post-Civil War period.

The Ohio law made it illegal to hire any black or mixed-race individual who did not possess a "certificate of freedom," which had to be obtained from a court. In fact, free people of color could not even settle in Ohio without such a document, and they were required to register their names along with the names of their children and pay a registration fee of 12.5 cents per name.

In addition, the Ohio law made it a crime punishable by a $1,000 fine to harbor or give aid to fugitive slaves. The law was revised to make it even stronger in 1807, and similar laws were passed in other states. The push for the law in Ohio came primarily from business interests related to slavery in the Southern states, and from settlers newly arrived in Ohio from Virginia, Kentucky, and what is now West Virginia.

In 1855, on the eve of the Civil War, "Black laws" were similarly passed in the Kansas territorial legislature to encourage slavery in Kansas. These laws imposed stiff penalties, including the death penalty in some instances, for anyone interfering with the possession of slaves in the Kansas territory. Anyone opposed to slavery was barred from serving as a juror in a trial of a defendant under the Kansas "black laws."

After the Civil War and after the end of Reconstruction, white supremacists used "black laws" to impose rigid segregation throughout the Southern states. Often called "Jim Crow" laws, these statutes attempted to prevent blacks and whites from using the same schools, churches, restaurants, hotels, public transportation, restrooms, and water fountains. Blacks and whites were prohibited from giving each other nursing or medical care in clinics and hospitals. "Whites Only" and "Colored" signs were posted over waiting rooms, drinking fountains, toilets, and other facilities.

The laws were also widely used to restrict voting by African Americans. For example, in Louisiana in 1896, 130,334 blacks were registered to vote, but the number fell to only 1,342 by 1905.

These laws remained in effect until the courts began striking them down in the 1950s and 1960s.

— JANUARY 6 —
1987
JOHN LEWIS SEATED IN CONGRESS

On this day in civil rights history, John Lewis took his seat in the 100th U.S. Congress. He is presently serving his 10th term as a U.S. representative from Georgia.

It could be said that Lewis elected himself to Congress, for no one worked harder or had a more significant role than he did in winning passage of the 1965 Voting Rights Act which ultimately allowed himself and thousands of other blacks to win elective office in the Deep South.

Lewis, often described as one of the most courageous of all civil rights figures, was born into a sharecropping family in 1940. He attended segregated schools in rural Alabama and from an early age wanted to be a preacher. He worked his way through American Baptist Theological Seminary in Nashville, and then through Fisk University.

Photo courtesy of Library of Congress

Lewis, as a young activist

While at Fisk, he got involved in the student sit-in movement to desegregate Nashville lunch counters and was also an organizer of the Student Nonviolent Coordinating Committee. In 1961, he was one of the freedom riders and was brutally beaten. From 1963 to 1966, Lewis was the chairman of SNCC.

He was involved in almost every key civil rights action of the 1960s, and at age 23 was considered one of the "Big Six" leaders of the movement (with Whitney Young, A. Philip Randoph, Martin Luther King Jr., James Farmer, and Roy Wilkins).

In 1964, Lewis coordinated SNCC efforts to register voters and implement community action programs during the "Mississippi Freedom Summer." The following year, Lewis was, with Hosea Williams, at the head of the column of marchers who crossed the Edmund Pettus Bridge in Selma, Alabama, to be beaten and gassed by state troopers in what became known as "Bloody Sunday." He suffered a fractured skull in that incident, but it and a subsequent march between Selma and Montgomery led to the Voting Rights Act of 1965.

Lewis was arrested more than 40 times during his civil rights career. As the movement began to wind down, he became associate director of the Field Foundation and later the director of the Southern Regional Council-sponsored Voter Education Project, that registered nearly four million new black voters.

In 1977, he was appointed director of ACTION, the federal volunteer agency, and in 1981 he was elected to the Atlanta City Council. Finally, in 1986, he defeated his friend and fellow civil rights activist Julian Bond to win his seat in Congress.

— JANUARY 7 —
1919
SURGEON DOROTHY LAVINIA BROWN BORN

On this day in civil rights history, Dorothy Lavinia Brown was born in Philadelphia, Pennsylvania. She became the first black female surgeon in the South and was also the first African American woman to serve in the Tennessee legislature.

As an infant, she was placed by her unmarried mother in an orphanage. After high school, she won a scholarship to Bennett College, and after graduating there in 1941 she entered Meharry Medical College in Nashville, Tennessee, graduating in 1948.

Her medical internship was served at New York's Harlem Hospital but there she encountered gender resistance and was denied residency as a surgeon. She then returned to Meharry and completed a surgical residency in 1954, making her the first black female surgeon in the Southern states.

She later became chief of surgery and educational director of the Riverside-Meharry Clinic in Nashville, as well as an attending surgeon at George W. Hubbard Hospital and a professor of surgery at the Meharry Medical College.

Always a pioneer, she also became the first single woman in Tennessee to adopt a child, and in 1966 she became the first African American woman elected to the Tennessee state legislature. Two years later she sought election to the state senate but lost in a campaign during which she was criticized for her efforts to reform Tennessee abortion laws.

Brown was an active writer and essayist and was a frequent public speaker on medical, political, religious, and social subjects. In addition to many honorary degrees and other awards, she served on the boards of schools, colleges, and professional and civic organizations, including her sorority, Delta Sigma Theta. Professionally, she was a fellow of the American College of Surgery.

She died in Nashville on June 13, 2004.

— JANUARY 8 —

1912

AFRICAN NATIONAL CONGRESS ORGANIZED

On this day in civil rights history, the African National Congress was founded as a nonviolent civil rights organization to promote the interests of black Africans. Although the organization was later identified mostly with South Africa, W. E. B. Du Bois was one of its founders and leading philosophical voices, and the ANC had a wide following among middle-class and professional blacks in the U.S. and abroad.

The ANC stressed constitutional means of change through the use of delegations, petitions, and peaceful protest. By the 1940s, the organization began to change, partly as a result of the entry of more outspoken younger members such as Walter Sisulu, Nelson Mandela, and Oliver Tambo, and by the use of increasingly harsh policies by South Africa's white-minority government.

In the early 1950s, the ANC found itself in escalating political conflict with the South African government over the apartheid practices of segregation and discrimination against black and mixed-race South African citizens.

The ANC's 1955 Freedom Charter declared, "South Africa belongs to all who live in it, black and white." Then, in 1961, a military arm, Umkhonto we Sizwe ("Spear of the Nation"), was formed by the ANC to carry out guerilla activities against the South African military and police. Mandela and Sisulu were subsequently sentenced to life in prison, and Tambo fled South Africa to set up an ANC operation in exile.

Over the next three decades, the ANC did its work largely underground, as Mandela and other key leaders remained in jail. The 1976 Soweto uprising intensified attacks on apartheid and brought increasing worldwide attention to South Africa.

In 1990, bowing to world pressure, the South African government ended its ban on the ANC and released Mandela from prison. Under Mandela's leadership, the ANC turned to politics and over the next few years reached an agreement with the more moderate white leaders then in office for a transitional government to rule for five years after the country's first all-race elections in April 1994. The ANC won those elections and Mandela served as president until his retirement in 1999.

— JANUARY 9 —
1866
FISK UNIVERSITY FOUNDED

On this day in civil rights history, the first classes of what would become Fisk University were convened in Nashville, Tennessee. Today Fisk is among the most significant of some 120 historically black colleges and universities surviving in the U.S. The school's alumni list includes many distinguished names, such as sociologist W. E. B. Du Bois, poet Nikki Giovanni, former U.S. Secretary of Energy Hazel O'Leary, and historian David Levering Lewis, to name just a few, and its faculty over the years has included sociologist Charles Spurgeon Johnson, artist Aaron Douglas, chemist St. Elmo Brady, and writers Arna Bontemps, Sterling A. Brown, Robert Hayden, and James Weldon Johnson.

Fisk University

Fisk's libraries and halls house a collection of murals by Aaron Douglas, a special collection on black culture, the Stieglitz Art Collection, and a collection of the works of composer W. C. Handy. Other research facilities at the university include the Fisk Race Relations Institute, the Fisk National Aeronautics and Space Administration Center for Photonic Materials and Devices, and the Howard Hughes Science Learning Center.

In addition to its impact generally on African American culture and education, Fisk ranks high among the black colleges in influence on civil rights, primarily through the key roles of several of its students in what came to be known as the Nashville student movement.

Students at Fisk and several other Nashville black colleges came under the influence of the Rev. James Lawson, a black graduate student who had been accepted into the divinity school at Nashville's Vanderbilt University. There in 1959 and 1960 he began teaching workshops on the techniques of nonviolent protest. Among the participants were Diane Nash, James Bevel, John Lewis, C. T. Vivian, and Bernard Lafayette, several of whom were Fisk students. Remarkably, all went on to play prominent roles in the widening civil rights movement, especially in the sit-ins, freedom rides, street protests, and voting rights activities of the 1960s.

— JANUARY 10 —

1957

VIOLENCE ERUPTS IN AFTERMATH OF BUS BOYCOTT

On this day in civil rights history, unknown assailants detonated six explosives at four churches and two ministers' homes in Montgomery, Alabama. The very public, very successful Montgomery bus boycott of 1955–1956 inspired and unified African Americans in the South and revealed the power of nonviolent protest.

Some of the groups involved—the Montgomery Improvement Association, the NAACP, the African Methodist Episcopal Zionist ministers, the Women's Political Council, and the Baptist Ministers Conference—had planned for this date a two-day conference at Atlanta's Ebenezer Baptist Church to create an organization that would capitalize on the momentum wrought from the boycott. The idea was to pool the various organizations' talents behind a unified movement, continuing to pressure both the state and federal governments with civil disobedience, public protests, further boycotts, and precedent-setting legal cases.

Hardcore segregationists, however, had other plans. The newly desegregated city buses were shot at in the first few weeks after the end of the boycott. Threats from the KKK along with intimidation from the local police created an ominous atmosphere. Further violence seemed inevitable.

The bombs exploded in the early morning, damaging the four black churches and the home of MIA leader Ralph Abernathy and MIA board member Robert Graetz, the only white minister who had supported the boycott. No one was injured.

Now thought to be the work of the Ku Klux Klan, the bombings rattled the burgeoning movement but ultimately had a galvanizing effect.

Martin Luther King Jr. was in Atlanta at the time, but returned to Montgomery to inspect the damage. The designated meeting was postponed until February 14 and moved to New Orleans. Here, the various groups came up with their new name: the Southern Christian Leadership Conference, or SCLC. They elected King as their leader, and went on to become one of the most powerful and effective civil rights organizations.

— JANUARY 11 —
1957
SOUTHERN CHRISTIAN LEADERSHIP CONFERENCE ORGANIZED

On this day in civil rights history, a group of about 60 ministers and activists meeting in Atlanta announced the formation of a new organization to coordinate protests against segregation across the South. Their statement emphasized that civil rights were essential to democracy and called for a broad-based nonviolent rejection of discrimination.

Convening again on February 14 in New Orleans, the group elected the Rev. Dr. Martin Luther King Jr. as president, Dr. Ralph Abernathy as treasurer, the Rev. C. K. Steele as vice president, Rev. T. J. Jemison as secretary, and attorney I. M. Augustine as general counsel.

King and Abernathy were fresh off the success of the Montgomery bus boycott that had made them nationally known leaders of the emerging post–World War II push for civil rights, equal rights, and voting rights. Also participating in the strategy and organizing sessions was Bayard Rustin, the pacifist and intellectual who had counseled King during the bus boycott and had helped shaped King's views on nonviolent resistance.

In August 1957, the new organization held a convention in Montgomery and named itself the Southern Christian Leadership Conference. With its strategy of nonviolent direct action and passive resistance to violent segregationist tactics, the SCLC quickly became one of the leading civil rights organizations in the United States.

King subsequently left his pastorate in Montgomery to take a part-time position at his father's church in Atlanta, a move that freed him to become a full-time national leader and activist for civil rights.

Working from a large base of local chapters, often headed by activist ministers, the SCLC launched one protest after another. Many of those campaigns—in Albany, Birmingham, Selma, and Chattanooga, to name just a few—became the defining struggles of the movement, often resulting in court decisions, legislation, and significant shifts in public opinion that eventually ended Jim Crow segregation.

The SCLC did not fight these battles alone. Older organizations like the NAACP, CORE, and the Fellowship of Reconciliation and new groups like the Student Nonviolent Coordinating Committee were also key players. But King's dynamic personal leadership and the deliberate ecumenical and biracial philosophy of the SCLC enhanced its appeal and effectiveness.

Martin L. King Jr. served the SCLC from its founding in 1957 until his death in 1968. He was succeeded by Abernathy (1968–1977), then Joseph E. Lowery (1977–1997), Martin L. King, III (1997–2004), Rev. Fred Shuttlesworth (2004), and Charles Steele Jr. (2004–).

— JANUARY 12 —
1920
CORE FOUNDER JAMES FARMER BORN

On this day in civil rights history, James Farmer, future founder of CORE, was born. A native of Texas, Farmer showed an aptitude for schooling at an early age, entering college at age 14, and eventually earning a Howard University divinity degree. After working for the Fellowship of Reconciliation (FOR), a Quaker organization seeking to promote pacifism, propagate fairness, and eliminate poverty, Farmer founded his own organization that utilized direct action to instigate change. He called it CORE—the Congress of Racial Equality, a pacifist organization dedicated to the pursuit of racial equality and harmony through nonviolent protest with the stated purpose of creating a society where "race or creed will be neither asset or handicap."

In 1947, FOR and CORE engaged in the first freedom ride, where black and white students rode on desegregated buses into the South to pit the federal government against Jim Crow segregation.

The ride ended with the arrests of the participants, but in 1960, Farmer resurrected the idea when the U.S. Supreme Court, in *Boynton v. Virginia*, declared that interstate transportation facilities must be desegregated. Farmer's idea was simple: send an integrated busload of black and white students into the South, forcing the federal government to act when the Southern municipalities tried to separate the passengers by race. The journey was met with harsh, violent resistance that sparked the imagination and resolve of many young reformers, galvanizing the civil rights movement at the start of the 1960s.

James Farmer

Farmer later grew unhappy with the rise of militant black nationalism that crept into CORE and many of the other notable civil rights organizations in the mid-1960s, and he retired in 1966 from the group he started.

In 1968, he entered the political arena, running for Congress as a Republican. He lost to Shirley Chisholm. In a strange turn of events, that same year Farmer was selected by President Richard Nixon to the position of Assistant Secretary of Health, Education, and Welfare.

In 1985, he published his memoir, *Lay Bare My Heart*. And in 1998, President Bill Clinton awarded him the Presidential Medal of Freedom. He died one year later.

Other more outspoken civil rights leaders have overshadowed Farmer's contributions, but he is generally considered one of the top three or four figures in the movement in the 1950s and 1960s, framing policy and working behind the scenes.

— JANUARY 13 —

1913

DELTA SIGMA THETA FORMED

On this day in civil rights history, 22 African American women formed Delta Sigma Theta at Howard University. The organization began with women's suffrage and human welfare at its core, naming dozens of influential civil rights movers as members of this influential sorority.

With stated aims of bettering the community and affecting better public policy, the sorority women grew into a large, powerful organization. Today it claims more than 200,000 members in more than 900 chapters around the world. Operating as a large network of educated women, Delta Sigma Theta has continually offered service and forums for many issues facing African Americans, and the world.

Delta Sigma Theta's impressive former members warrant attention. Singers Roberta Flack and Aretha Franklin, poet Nikki Giovanni, and actress Lena Horne are just a few of the high-profile women that have at one time or another been sorors. Breaking the color line in many different fields of endeavor, influential actors, writers, singers, directors, musicians, and artists all made Delta Sigma Theta their home.

Social pioneers such as Jocelyn Elders, Mary McCloud Bethune, Shirley Chisholm, Fannie Lou Hamer, Mary Church Terrell, and Marion Wright Edelman—many of the women who served as the bedrock of the grass roots movement in the 1940s, 1950s, and 1960s—all were members.

With its emphasis on social activism, human welfare and equality, and service to the larger community, Delta Sigma Theta reared dozens of influential women who went on to lead in the civil rights movement, from the grassroots level to national strategy.

— JANUARY 14 —

1963

GEORGE WALLACE PLEDGES 'SEGREGATION FOREVER'

On this day in civil rights history, Governor George C. Wallace delivered his infamous inaugural address, pledging the state of Alabama to the segregationist cause and raising the stakes for the movement across the South. Wallace became one of the symbols of the Jim Crow era, but many historians believe he acted mostly for political advantage, simply to get elected.

Many today are surprised to learn that four years earlier Wallace had campaigned against the Ku Klux Klan and had the endorsement of the NAACP. But after losing in 1958 to the blatantly segregationist John Patterson, Wallace famously declared, "I'll never be out-niggered again." With a boisterous new platform, the charismatic chameleon was elected in 1962 and entered the history books as one of the toughest segregationist governors.

"Segregation now, segregation tomorrow, segregation forever!" were the words written for Wallace by speechwriter Asa Carter, a KKK leader.

The polarizing effect of Wallace gave civil rights leaders a personalized enemy, while providing segregationists a leader for a last stand. A fiery orator, Wallace whipped segregationists into a frenzy, and many of the worst atrocities of the era happened in his Deep South state.

Under Wallace, Alabama became a focal point for the movement. It was to Wallace that the Selma-to-Montgomery marchers planned to deliver the body of Jimmy Lee Jackson. It was at Wallace's feet that Martin Luther King Jr. laid the blame for the church bombing in Birmingham that claimed the life of four girls.

At the time, Wallace was happy to play the role, relishing the power his policies brought him. He later expressed regret and tried to make amends.

Energetic and witty, Wallace possessed an astute political acumen and ran for president a number of times. In 1972, he looked as though he had a real chance at the Democratic nomination before being shot and crippled by an assassin. Wallace survived but was partially paralyzed. In the late 1970s, Wallace embraced Christianity and publicly apologized to African American leaders for his past actions. In 1983 he was elected governor of Alabama for a fourth and final time, winning a high percentage of the black vote. He subsequently appointed a record number of African Americans to governmental offices in Alabama.

Wallace died in 1998.

— JANUARY 15 —
1929
MARTIN LUTHER KING JR. BORN

On this day in civil rights history, Martin Luther King Jr. was born in Atlanta, Georgia, where he grew up as the son of a prominent Baptist minister. The senior King, originally named Michael, had his and his son's names legally changed to Martin Luther as a tribute to the famous German church reformer.

Young Martin graduated from Morehouse College, then entered the post-graduate theological program at Boston University, studies which introduced him to the philosophy of nonviolent protest used by the Indian leader Mohandas Gandhi. While in Boston he also met and wooed Coretta Scott, a music student from Marion, Alabama.

After college, the couple returned to Atlanta while King interviewed for several jobs as a minister, accepting the pastorate of the Dexter Avenue Baptist Church in Montgomery, Alabama, in 1954. The next year, the arrest of Rosa Parks triggered the Montgomery bus boycott and King, only 26, was chosen as its spokesperson.

Martin Luther King Jr.

The yearlong boycott was the first sustained, successful protest of legalized segregation in the United States in the 20th century, and it thrust the young preacher into the world spotlight. His eloquence, intellect, and personality quickly earned him the respect of much older and more experienced black leaders and by the end of the boycott, he was perhaps the nation's best-known civil rights leader.

King and his allies subsequently organized the Southern Christian Leadership Conference, which he served as president. Inspired by King's unparalleled oratory and guided by his doctrine of nonviolent civil disobedience, the SCLC became the dominant civil rights group and was involved in almost every major campaign against segregation during the late 1950s and 1960s.

In addition to his powerful speeches, King was an author of influential books and tracts (including *Stride Toward Freedom* and *Letter from a Birmingham City Jail*) that helped move American opinion toward the cause of racial justice. In 1964 he was awarded the Nobel Peace Prize.

Harassed throughout his adult life by police, Klansmen, street thugs, and the FBI, King was stabbed, shot at, jailed, beaten, and his home was bombed. But he never relented and as the major barriers of segregation began to fall he was turning his attention to the larger issues of poverty and war. He was assassinated in 1968.

— JANUARY 16 —

1967

LURLEEN WALLACE BECOMES SURROGATE GOVERNOR

On this day in civil rights history, Lurleen Burns Wallace succeeded her husband as governor of Alabama (she is to date the only woman to hold the office).

After making himself a household name as a segregationist, the ambitious George C. Wallace was barred from running again by term limits set in the 1901 Alabama Constitution, so Wallace enacted a plan. His wife would run in his stead, with the tacit understanding that he would continue to govern from behind the scenes. This scheme would also allow him the time and flexibility to seek the presidency of the United States.

Few blacks were yet voting in Alabama, and Lurleen Wallace defeated several more moderate challengers. She was inaugurated in January 1967. Her husband's policies remained in effect and his cronies in control, including continued harassment of civil rights activists and defiance toward federal intrusion. But while George Wallace began his presidential campaign, Lurleen fell ill with cancer. She died in 1968 and was succeeded by Lieutenant Governor Albert Brewer, a racial moderate who sought his own full term in 1970.

By then, George Wallace's unsuccessful third-party presidential bid was over, but he had succeeded in overturning the one-term limit on Alabama governors. Brewer ran hard, but Wallace proved too strong in a campaign marked by his charisma and dirty tricks including racial appeals. He returned to the governor's chair in January 1971.

In retrospect, Lurleen Wallace's election shows how desperate the segregationists had become. They elected the first and only woman to Alabama's highest office to maintain her husband's policies. To many, George Wallace's appeal lay in his stubborn resolve. He refused compromise and thus played into the hands of the civil rights organizations, who used his public outbursts as evidence of the irrationality—and violent inhumanity—of the racist point of view. The civil rights movement needed outrageous foils to engage the rest of the country and facilitate change on a national policy level.

One wonders what George Wallace, with his political gifts and aggressive drive, could have achieved as a moderate leader rather than as a reactionary against progress. But then, he might not have been elected, and the civil rights movement would have missed out on one of its great antagonists.

Lurleen Wallace, meanwhile, is remembered in Alabama as a basically decent woman who was used by her husband for his own political ends.

— JANUARY 17 —
1966
CHICAGO CAMPAIGN BRINGS NEW MOVEMENT TACTIC

On this day in civil rights history, Chicago's Coordinating Council of Community Organizations invited Martin Luther King Jr. to the Windy City to begin the Chicago campaign, a massive community-oriented project designed to break the slums of America's second biggest city. The campaign would represent a drastic new direction in strategy for the Southern Christian Leadership Conference.

Chicago was chosen for two reasons—the well-organized CCCO and the potentially friendly political machine of Mayor Richard Daley. Chicago was and still is one of the most segregated cities in the U.S. Discriminatory housing practices had resulted in a large ghetto on the Southside, replete with slum housing and inferior, segregated schools.

On January 26, 1966, King and his family moved into a renovated apartment in one of Chicago's worst neighborhoods in a well-publicized move intended to bring attention to the destitute living conditions. "We need massive programs that will change the structure of American society so there will be a better distribution of wealth," he said. "There are few things more thoroughly sinful than economic injustice."

This new focus shifted the civil rights spotlight from Southern segregation to the national plight of African Americans, especially in America's urban ghettos. With most of the barriers of Jim Crow segregation already down, the new emphasis would be on economic parity.

The shift, then, was not just South to North, regional to national, but from the simple to the more complex. King understood that the movement was in peril; the more subtle issues of class and wealth were not as easily digested as the clear-cut conflicts between black activists and white supremacists.

King also began to focus on peace abroad, connecting racism at home to militarism around the world. The Vietnam War weighed heavily on his conscience. "Violence is as wrong in Hanoi as it is in Harlem," he proclaimed. He more and more spoke out against the war, losing mainstream credibility while inviting attacks from the media. Internal problems with SCLC, centering on funding, added to the stress. And King's stature had taken control of his life. Endless phone calls, meetings, rallies, lectures—King was mired in a bureaucratic labyrinth that seemed to have no end. He began the Chicago campaign worn out and weary.

— JANUARY 18 —

1993

MLK HOLIDAY OBSERVED IN ALL 50 STATES

On this day in civil rights history, all 50 states for the first time joined in the observance of the Martin Luther King Jr. holiday. King was born on January 15, but the holiday in his honor is observed on the first Monday following that date.

Efforts to memorialize King with a national holiday began with a bill introduced by U.S. Representative John Conyers four days after King was martyred in Memphis in 1968, but it took 15 years and an intense lobbying campaign to make the dream a reality. Petitions with more than six million signatures were delivered to Congress in 1970. Conyers and Representative Shirley Chisholm reintroduced the bill each session until Congress finally passed, and President Ronald Reagan signed legislation in 1983 creating the King Holiday. But it took another decade before every state joined in.

King holiday placard

In retrospect, the delay should not be surprising considering that King was a controversial figure, a member of a minority race, and never held a national office or commanded an army or established a religion. In fact, King is one of only a few social leaders so honored in any country. King's philosophical mentor Mahatma Gandhi, whose birthday is observed in India, may be the only other one. Christopher Columbus and Jesus have U.S. holidays, but George Washington is the only other American with a national holiday on his birthday (Lincoln's birthday was never an official national holiday, though he has been honored since 1968 with Washington on what is now called President's Day).

Some opponents of the King holiday cited the estimated $8 billion that would be "lost" by closing down public and private services for a day. Senator Bob Dole responded, "I suggest the critics hurry back to their pocket calculators and estimate the cost of 300 years of slavery, followed by a century or more of economic, political and social exclusion and discrimination." Others objected to singling out King over other deserving heroes. Senator Jesse Helms predictably objected that King was a "communist."

Given all the anti-arguments, the enactment of the holiday was a tribute to King's special role in American history, to his philosophy, and, enemies notwithstanding, to the universal admiration for King's personal charisma, vision, and sacrifice.

"As usual with great figures, Dr. King was well ahead of his time. Even those opposed to him during his life now see that segregation, injustice and militarism are concerns which had to be addressed," said former SCLC President Joseph Lowery.

— JANUARY 19 —

1961

PGA LIFTS COLOR BARRIER

On this day in civil rights history, the Professional Golfers Association (PGA) officially allowed blacks into its organization, lifting the whites-only clause that had kept African Americans off tournament golf courses since the rule's inception in 1943.

Allowed in the PGA when it was formed in 1913, African Americans found themselves by the mid-1940s limited to one day a week on public golf courses. In 1950, the NAACP sued the city of Miami Springs, protesting the restriction. The Supreme Court sided with the NAACP and black golfers everywhere rejoiced. The precedent had been set: public golf courses could not legally limit access to black players.

Bill Spiller became the first black player in a PGA tour when he competed in the 1948 Los Angeles Open, but he was an anomaly. The PGA, the largest golfer's association and the major professional outlet, refused black entrance until 1961.

Charlie Sifford, the first full-time black PGA tour member, really broke through the color barrier in golf, playing in the 1961 Greensboro Open. He eventually went on to win a number of big tournaments, including the Los Angeles Open. Following in Sifford's footsteps came Calvin Peete, a successful black golfer in the mid-1980s. And, in the late 1990s, wunderkind Tiger Woods blazed onto the scene, winning every major tournament before the age of 30.

Although just one of many important sports dates, the desegregation of professional golf represents yet another step in the civil rights movement. Baseball was always a game of the streets, but golf represented to many a certain level of class, money, and sophistication. The symbolic import of the PGA allowing blacks in provided hope of racial reconciliation.

— JANUARY 20 —

1981

CLIFFORD ALEXANDER SERVES AS
FIRST BLACK ARMY SECRETARY

On this day in civil rights history, Clifford L. Alexander Jr. completed his term as the first African American Secretary of the Army.

Alexander was born September 21, 1933, in New York City. After earning degrees from Harvard University and Yale Law School, he joined the National Guard and served briefly with the 369th Field Artillery Battalion at Fort Dix, New Jersey.

He was later an assistant district attorney, director of several community organizations, and practiced law in New York City.

Photo courtesy of EEOC

Alexander

He began a career in Washington during the Kennedy and Johnson administrations, serving as a foreign affairs officer on the National Security Council, deputy special assistant to the President, associate special counsel, and deputy special counsel on the White House staff. He was chairman of the U.S. Equal Employment Opportunity Commission from 1967 to 1969, and during this period also served as President Lyndon Johnson's special consultant on civil rights issues.

He returned to private law practice in 1969, was a television news commentator, a law professor, and a candidate for mayor of the District of Columbia.

In 1977, President Jimmy Carter named Alexander U.S. Secretary of the Army. In that role, Alexander helped usher in the all-volunteer force. When his term ended in 1981, he returned to the private sector and created a consulting firm that specializes in minority business interests.

— JANUARY 21 —
2001
ASSASSIN OF MEDGAR EVERS DIES IN A MISSISSIPPI PRISON

On this day in civil rights history, Byron de la Beckwith, the murderer of civil rights hero Medgar Evers, died from heart complications in prison.

The murder happened almost 40 years earlier. On June 12, 1963, Evers was shot in the back in the driveway of his home in Jackson, Mississippi. The police charged Beckwith with the crime less than two weeks later and began formal procedures.

But Beckwith, an avowed white supremacist and KKK member, avoided prison time in 1964 through two hung juries; it later became known that the Klan had tampered with both juries. In 1969, Mississippi dismissed all charges against him.

In 1994, state prosecutor Bobby Delaughter reopened the case. He had discovered new evidence that Beckwith had bragged about the crime at a Klan rally. The retrial of Beckwith was among the first of a series of high-profile "redemption" trials where unsolved murder cases were revisited by a new generation of Southern lawmen.

At the time, Beckwith was 70 years old. Some felt that DeLaughter should let sleeping dogs lie. Beckwith's attorneys claimed double jeopardy and that the span of years between crime and prosecution would prevent Beckwith from getting a fair trial. But the young prosecutor persevered, stating, "No man, regardless of age, is above the law."

Evers's body was exhumed from Arlington National Cemetery and given a new autopsy.

The trial lasted one week. The controversy of the violent era in Mississippi's history was dredged up during the proceedings. DeLaughter, in his opening statement, said that Evers was killed with a bullet "aimed by prejudice, propelled by hatred and fired by a coward, a back-shooting coward."

The third trial proved Beckwith's downfall. Sentenced to life in prison on February 5, 1994, the unrepentant Beckwith became a symbol for contemporary white supremacists.

After serving six years, Beckwith died in prison of heart complications. He was 80 years old. By contrast, Evers had been cut down at the young age of 38.

— JANUARY 22 —
1973
CIVIL RIGHTS ALLY LYNDON BAINES JOHNSON DIES

On this day in civil rights history, President Lyndon Baines Johnson died, leaving behind a controversial legacy. Although he pushed for and signed the most significant civil rights legislation of any president, his handling of the Vietnam War overshadowed his accomplishments.

He was born in Stonewall, Texas, in 1908. In 1937, Johnson won election to Congress. He served with distinction in World War II and returned to be elected to the Senate in 1948. After just five years, he was elected Senate Minority Leader.

President John F. Kennedy was elected in 1960 with Johnson as his vice president. On November 22, 1963, Johnson became president after Kennedy was assassinated. As president, Johnson wielded the power politics that he had perfected throughout his career, using remarkable personal influence and intimidation to accomplish his goals.

Fearing a political backlash, Johnson opposed civil rights leaders when the Mississippi Freedom Democratic Party tried to unseat the Mississippi Democratic regulars at the Democratic National Convention in 1964. He then won a full term by a landslide margin over Republican challenger Barry Goldwater, thanks in part to "Solid South" Democratic bloc voting by Southern whites. He subsequently angered many of those white voters by pushing for a package of social reforms intended to "end poverty and racial injustice." LBJ's "Great Society" programs included Medicare, urban renewal, environmental conservation, crime control, and the right to vote.

Johnson signed the Civil Rights Act of 1964, outlawing segregation in public places and discrimination on the basis of race, creed, or color. The next year, sickened along with the nation by anti-civil rights violence in Selma, Alabama, Johnson called for passage of and signed the Voting Rights Act of 1965, which outlawed literacy tests and required states to preclear changes in voting laws that might affect minorities.

Johnson's Achilles' heel was the Vietnam War. He had inherited the conflict from Kennedy but then greatly expanded U.S. involvement even as antiwar protests escalated at home. He saw that he could not win re-election and in March 1968 shocked the nation by announcing that he would not run.

He retired to his ranch in Texas, but years of chain-smoking had ruined his health, and he died on this day in 1973 after suffering a third heart attack.

— January 23 —
1964
24th Amendment Abolishes Poll Tax

On this day in civil rights history, the 24th Amendment was ratified, abolishing the poll taxes in the South used to disenfranchise generations of African American and some poor white voters.

The poll tax was just one of many devices used by the white power structure in the South to regulate voting. During the Reconstruction era, blacks in the South voted in high numbers. In fact, more African Americans were elected into offices between 1865 and 1880 than at any other time in history until the late 20th century. This scared the South, both politically (the African Americans elected proposed legislation that was at the time considered radical, including public education) and racially.

So the Southern states devised a number of ingenious methods to prevent blacks from voting en masse. The first was the poll tax, a fee new voters had to pay to register. Not only was it expensive, but also confusing. The tax had to be paid by a certain date or the person in question couldn't vote. But often the location where it could be paid wasn't known. The poll tax affected both blacks and whites, but many poor whites were protected by a grandfather clause, which exempted anyone whose father or grandfather had voted before 1867.

A second barrier was the Understanding Clause, a law that required literacy tests to qualify to vote. The tests were difficult, devised to prevent the taker from passing. And, once again, the white voters were grandfathered in.

The few African Americans who paid the poll tax, passed the literacy test, or bypassed the myriad obstacles in place, including physical harassment and intimidation, found his vote meant nothing anyway, as elections in the solidly Democratic South were decided in the primaries, which, by law, were for whites only.

This dismal state of affairs offered a rallying point to civil rights groups. The right to vote symbolized the first step in freedom from oppression. With the entrenched power structure fighting every step of the way, it was an arduous process.

But once passed, the 24th Amendment was the first in a series of legislation that legally destroyed the racist apparatus that maintained the status quo in the South. African Americans still encountered fierce resistance when registering to vote, but now had legal recourse when they did.

— JANUARY 24 —
1987
'MARCH AGAINST FEAR' IN FORSYTH COUNTY, GEORGIA

On this day in civil rights history, veteran activist Hosea Williams led 20,000 people on a march through Forsyth County, a suburban county near Atlanta and one of the last bastions of segregation in Georgia.

During the 1960s, Williams was famous for his fiery personality, his stubborn streak, and his absolute fearlessness. Martin Luther King Jr. called him "my wild man." After King's death, Williams entered Atlanta politics, while also founding Hosea Feed the Hungry and the Homeless, a nonprofit shelter that still operates today.

But the call to agitate, set forth by Frederick Douglass a century before, always weighed on Williams. Twenty years after most civil rights marches had ended, he proposed a new march into familiar territory: a racist, all-white country town.

In 1912, African American citizens were driven from Forsyth County in the wake of the murder of a white woman and the subsequent lynching of the black suspect. In 1987, the town remained 99 percent white.

Williams's plan was to march into Cumming, the county seat, to draw attention to racial exclusiveness. A first march by 75 people on January 17 was met by white supremacists and Klan members who pelted the marchers with stones and other projectiles.

The clash drew national attention and Williams and his allies quickly called for a larger demonstration the following weekend. Dubbed the "March against Fear and Intimidation," this one had more than 20,000 marchers, along with helicopters, police officers, high-profile politicians, and international media. It was the largest civil rights demonstration since the 1960s. Williams demanded the establishment of a biracial committee to oversee the integration of the city.

Meanwhile, the Forsyth County Defense League organized a large counter-demonstration of almost 1,000 people.

After the march, Southern Poverty Law Center chief counsel Morris Dees represented Williams in a lawsuit against the Forsyth County Defense League. Williams and Dees lost, and the Forsyth County Defense League, emboldened by the victory, joined the White Nationalist Organization—a racist, nativist group empowered by the anonymity of the internet—which still operates.

Forsyth County has since become an exurb of Atlanta. Migratory forces of time and economics are doing the work that Williams started.

— JANUARY 25 —
1890
NATIONAL AFRO-AMERICAN LEAGUE FORMED

On this day in civil rights history, journalist Timothy Thomas Fortune co-founded the National Afro-American League in Chicago, the first modern all-black organization with the stated goal of facilitating equality for people of color in America.

Born a slave and self-educated, Fortune moved to New York in 1881 and started what eventually became the *New York Age,* one of the leading black papers of the era. In his heyday, Fortune was the most prominent and powerful African American journalist, a trailblazing muckraker. A believer in self-reliance and economic solidarity, Fortune became friends with Booker T. Washington, even though he was far more aggressive and radical in his ambitions for the race. They would later have a falling out.

The Afro-American League challenged commonly held assumptions about race and equality in a dark time for the black cause. In 1890, 85 blacks were publicly lynched. Poll taxes and literacy tests were passed in the South to disenfranchise black voters. African Americans constituted 11 percent of the country's population, but existed on the fringe.

After the failure of Reconstruction, the AAL tried to re-invigorate the debate. In his newspaper and through the League, Fortune spoke out against lynching, mob violence, and discrimination of all forms.

The public at large was not quite ready to listen.

The League disbanded after only four years, due to lack of economic and popular support. In 1898, it was revived as the National Afro-American Council, with Fortune acting as president, but again didn't last long.

Neither organization accomplished much in their troubled few years of existence. But the concept was revolutionary, serving as a springboard for other national Negro organizations.

Militant, uncompromising, and incendiary, Fortune was ahead of his time. He felt that blacks in America were "African in origin and American by birth," and therefore offered up the label Afro-American as the most accurate. The Afro-American League paved the way for the NAACP, UNIA, and other black organizations.

— JANUARY 26 —
1944
ACTIVIST ANGELA DAVIS BORN

On this date in 1944, political activist and educator Angela Davis was born in a section of Birmingham nicknamed "Dynamite Hill." The nickname was due to the number of Klan-related bombings that took place on the edge of a white neighborhood where African Americans were moving. Davis's powerful social consciousness was forged in the crucible of racially motivated violence and inequality in Alabama at the time.

Davis left Birmingham to attend the Elizabeth Irwin School in New York City and later

Photo courtesy of Associated Press

Angela Davis

Brandeis University. She studied philosophy and became intrigued by Marxism, combining Marx's thinking with her own thoughts on race, class, and inequality. A promising academic, she attended a doctoral program in Germany but returned to the United States in 1967 to take part in the civil rights movement.

Moving to southern California in the late 1960s, she also connected with the Black Panthers. In 1969, she began teaching philosophy at UCLA, but was fired by the University of California for her affiliation with the American Communist Party.

In 1970, Davis was accused of providing handguns to participants in a failed prison escape. When the police issued a warrant for her arrest, Davis went into hiding and was placed on the FBI's most wanted list. Captured two months later, Davis became a rallying point for radicals in the early 1970s. She spent 18 months in jail, rallying fellow prisoners, demanding better conditions, and organizing an effective system of bail. In the public arena, a "Free Angela Movement" centered on her treatment and upcoming trial. Both John Lennon and the Rolling Stones released songs about her predicament. As boxer Hurricane Carter had, Davis became a symbol to many of a white American justice system that seemed all-too eager to imprison militant blacks.

She was eventually acquitted of all charges.

Since then, Davis has spent much of her time working on prison reform, while advocating democratic socialism. A staunch feminist and dedicated radical, she has regained a position with the University of California and has spent much of her time writing books, including: *They Come in the Morning; Women, Race, and Class; Violence Against Women and the Ongoing Challenge to Racism;* and *Angela Davis: An Autobiography.*

— January 27 —
1810
Abolitionist, Civil Rights Forerunner
David Ruggles Born

On this day in civil rights history, early abolitionist and writer David Ruggles was born. Raised in the free state of Connecticut, Ruggles entered the antislavery movement in 1833 when he began writing for *The Emancipator* and *Public Morals,* an abolitionist journal in New York. He later published a magazine, *Mirror of Liberty,* recognized by many as the first periodical owned by a person of color.

Ruggles also became the first African American bookseller when he opened a bookstore in New York; the store was later destroyed by a mob.

As he continued to write and press for the immediate end of slavery, Ruggles's reputation grew. Men who would be free, he said, "themselves must strike the first blow." The author of several antislavery pamphlets, Ruggles worked as a conductor of the Underground Railroad in 1835, reputedly helping to free more than 1,000 slaves. It was there that he met Frederick Douglass, whom he later helped get established in Massachusetts.

Scene from the Underground Railroad

A notable public agitator, Ruggles committed numerous acts of civil disobedience, including sitting in a whites-only car at a railway station in 1841, a century before Rosa Parks would refuse to give up her bus seat. When dragged out by the authorities, Ruggles filed a lawsuit. He engaged in numerous such acts and was jailed repeatedly. Eventually, the constant agitation took its toll and he went blind.

His blindness led him to hydrotherapy, where he found a temporary cure for his vision. He began a career as a hydrotherapist, a field in which he excelled until his death in 1849.

Ruggles lived a hard life as a muckraking journalist. An uncompromising firebrand, he saw the need for organized civil disobedience combined with legal action. He started his own magazine while helping found antislavery organizations. A committed activist, Ruggles, like many of the early abolitionists, was a man ahead of his time.

— JANUARY 28 —
1948
MISSISSIPPI CONGRESSMAN BENNIE THOMPSON BORN

On this day in civil rights history, Bennie Thompson—grassroots volunteer, labor organizer, student activist, community leader, and politician—was born in Bolton, Mississippi.

Thompson attended Mississippi public schools before earning degrees from Tougaloo College and Jackson State University. His personal knowledge of disparities in education in the state led him in 1975 to become one of the plaintiffs in *Ayers v. Musgrove,* a lawsuit to increase resources at Mississippi's historically black universities, which had been grossly underfunded over the years in comparison to the state's historically white universities. After years of legal wrangling and negotiations, the case was settled in 2004, with the black schools to receive some $500 million in compensatory funding.

Immersed in the civil rights movement since he was a teenager, Thompson is an example of the thousands of young black Southerners who were able to enter politics and win elective office after black citizens were added to the voting rolls following the passage of the 1965 Voting Rights Act.

In Thompson's case, he began as an alderman in his hometown, then was elected mayor, then county supervisor, and finally, in 1993, as the U.S. Representative for Mississippi's second congressional district. He is presently serving his seventh term and is the longest-serving African American elected official in the state.

He is a founding member and past president of both the Mississippi Association of Black Mayors and the Mississippi Association of Black Supervisors.

In Congress, Thompson serves on the House Budget and Agriculture committees and he is the ranking Democrat on the House's Homeland Security committee.

Long considered a leading voice on civil rights, equal education, and health care reform, he wrote the legislation in 2000 that created the National Center for Minority Health and Health Care Disparities.

— JANUARY 29 —
1820
HARRIET TUBMAN BORN

On this day in civil rights history, Harriet Ross Tubman was born as a slave in Maryland. At age 16, an angry overseer smashed her in the head with a rock, almost killing her. She suffered from blackouts for the rest of her life. During one of these seizures, she had an epiphany: she had to escape. Leaving behind her husband, who refused to accompany her, Harriet Tubman fled through the Quaker and abolitionist network designed to help slaves escape, and made her way to Philadelphia and freedom.

Fittingly, she became the most famous Underground Railroad "conductor"—so named because the conductor would plan and execute a slave's run for freedom. Known as "Moses," Tubman made many trips into the South, leading groups of slaves to freedom, often disguised as a slave herself. She was a cunning conductor, repeatedly outmaneuvering slavers and bounty hunters with guile and her quick mind. "I can't die but once," she was known to say, and she lived with a fearlessness that allowed her to accomplish much.

Harriet Tubman

Photo courtesy of Library of Congress

She had simple rules freed slaves had to follow: don't be late, don't tell anyone of the plan, do what you're told without complaint, and be prepared to die. She carried a loaded pistol, threatening to shoot any freed slave who tried to turn back. No one ever did. In her tenure as an Underground Railroad conductor, she never lost a single passenger.

With her continued success, Tubman became a notorious figure in the late 1840s, with a $40,000 reward offered for her capture. Traveling in abolitionist circles, she met many of the era's most famous antislavery figures, including John Brown, who called her "one of the bravest persons on the continent."

During the Civil War, she worked as a spy, nurse, and scout for the Union Army. She continued to lead slaves to the North, serving as a liaison between freedmen and the Union soldiers.

After the war, Tubman continued to work for equal rights for African Americans, while expanding into women's issues as well. She struggled with little income, despite her tenure as a Union spy and her lengthy career with the Underground Railroad.

In 1869 she published her autobiography, *Scenes in the Life of Harriet Tubman*. She retired to a home for destitute ex-slaves she had helped found.

She died in 1913 at age 92 and was buried with full military honors.

— JANUARY 30 —
1956
BOYCOTT LEADER'S HOME BOMBED IN MONTGOMERY

On this day in civil rights history, the parsonage of the Dexter Avenue Baptist Church—then the home of the Rev. Martin Luther King Jr.—was bombed with dynamite.

The attack was part of the violent reaction by white supremacists to the Montgomery bus boycott. Two months into the boycott, it was already achieving success and attention far beyond the expectations of its planners. And King, who before the boycott began was simply the 26-year-old minister of a local Baptist church, was already recognized locally and nationally as the leader and spokesperson of a well-organized challenge against legalized segregation.

He was naturally a key target of local Ku Klux Klansmen who were determined to stop the boycott. However, when the bundle of dynamite tossed onto the porch of the parsonage exploded, King was at one of the weekly "mass meetings" the black community had been holding to keep up support for the boycott. King's wife, Coretta, their infant daughter Yolanda, and a family friend, Mrs. Roscoe Williams, were at home when the bomb tore apart the front of the house. Luckily, all three were in the kitchen at the back of the house and were not injured.

By the time King got word of the attack and sped home, police and firemen were already there, along with a crowd of frightened, angry black citizens, some of them armed. The police were trying to disperse the crowd, but no one was leaving.

King went inside and made sure that his family was okay, then he went back outside. The mayor, the police commissioner, and several white reporters were there, nervously facing the angry throng, which was growing by the second.

King turned to the crowd and asked for silence. He said that his family was safe. Then he said, "We believe in law and order. Don't do anything panicky. Don't get your weapons. He who lives by the sword will perish by the sword. Remember that is what God said. We are not advocating violence. We want to love our enemies and let them know you love them.

"I did not start this boycott. I was asked by you to serve as your spokesman. If I am stopped this movement will not stop. For what we are doing is right. What we are doing is just. And God is with us."

The people went away peaceably, and King's calmness and strength impressed not only his followers but also more than a few city officials, police, and news reporters.

— JANUARY 31 —
1865
13TH AMENDMENT ABOLISHES SLAVERY

On this day in civil rights history, Congress passed the 13th Amendment, abolishing slavery in the United States forever.

This pivotal moment in U.S. history was a long time in the making. Slavery had been a reality of life in the U.S. since before it had become a sovereign nation. And from the beginning, there were those opposed to the inhumane practice. At the start of the 19th century, abolitionists gained footholds in many major American cities, eventually birthing a political party, the Republicans, using the unofficial slogan, "Free soil, free labor, free speech, free men." As the abolitionists actively worked to free slaves from the South via the Underground Railroad, tensions between the North and South grew. The Compromise of 1850, designed to ameliorate the conflict, had the opposite effect.

In 1859, hard-line abolitionist John Brown tried and failed in an armed revolt. This action, and its fallout, combined with the increasingly volatile viewpoints of the North and South, eventually led to the Civil War. And although many elements constituted the reasons for the war (States'

Drawing of Lincoln's
Emancipation Declaration

Photo courtesy of Library of Congress

rights and conflicting economic paradigms among others), slavery was an essential motivation, the South to save its precious economic institution, the North to eliminate the practice.

At the end of the war, the North occupied the South and began the long process of Reconstruction. And as part of an almost utopian outpouring of goodwill, to both the South and the recently freed slaves, the United States began to rebuild, trying to make amends to the race of people it had so ill treated. African Americans began to vote in droves. Black schools popped up overnight. The situation was poised for a new dawning of a prosperous and racially harmonious region.

The measure is surprisingly brief: "Neither slavery nor involuntary servitude, except as a punishment for crime whereof the party shall have been duly convicted, shall exist within the United States, or any place subject to their jurisdiction." And, "Congress shall have power to enforce this article with appropriate legislation."

Sadly, Reconstruction failed. And the angry, resentful Southern whites regained power. Jim Crow segregation and economic subjugation resulted in a system that was in some ways as vile as the slavery that spawned it. The 13th Amendment remained, but no one seemed ready to act on it. It would be almost another hundred years before the United States government would revisit these broken promises.

This day in February

— FEBRUARY 1 —

1960

STUDENT SIT-IN MOVEMENT BEGINS

On this day in civil rights history, four African American students from North Carolina A & T College in Greensboro entered the local Woolworth's department store, sat down at the lunch counter, and demanded to be served. Woolworth's, like most retail establishments in the segregated South, was happy to accept African Americans' money but denied them use of lunch counters, restrooms, and water fountains.

With their spontaneous "direct action," the four young men launched a movement that spread rapidly among college students throughout the region. The effect of the sit-ins changed the course of the civil rights movement, shifting much of the focus from litigation and negotiation to confrontation and personal challenges of discriminatory conditions. The change in tactics made the movement more volatile and probably sped up the process of desegregation but at the cost of greater violence and unrest. The Greensboro sit-ins led directly to the organization a few months later of the Student Nonviolent Coordinating Committee (SNCC) and indirectly to the black power movement by the end of the decade.

The four A & T students—Franklin McCain, Ezell Blair Jr. (now Jibreel Khazan), David Richmond, and Joseph McNeil—entered Woolworth's late in the afternoon, bought a few items, then sat at the lunch counter and attempted to order. Service was denied, and the four sat quietly until the store closed.

The next day, 25 men and four women returned to continue the protest. The third day, students filled 63 of the 65 lunch counter seats. On February 4, four white students from Woman's College joined the protest, which by then had also spread to the Kress department store across the street. Within a week, more than 300 students were "sitting-in" in Greensboro, and similar protests were beginning in Charlotte and other cities. Within two months, the sit-ins had spread to more than 50 cities in nine states.

By July, Woolworth's economic losses were so great that the store quietly desegregated its lunch counter. Today, the lunch counter where the sit-ins began can be seen in the Smithsonian Institution in Washington, D.C.

— FEBRUARY 2 —

1989

EVELYN J. FIELDS, MARITIME PIONEER, TAKES THE HELM

On this day in civil rights history, Evelyn J. Fields became the first African American woman to command a U.S. government oceangoing vessel. This was just one of many firsts in the distinguished career of the pioneering Fields, who rose to become a rear admiral, the director of the National Oceanic and Atmospheric Administration (NOAA) Marine and Aviation Operations, and director of the NOAA Commissioned Officer Corps. She was also the first woman and the first African American to serve in these positions.

Photo courtesy of National Oceanic and Atmospheric Association

Rear Admiral Evelyn Fields

Fields began her career with NOAA in 1972 as a cartographer, and then was commissioned as an ensign and served on board the *Mt. Mitchell* as junior officer. Later she was operations officer on the *Pierce*, then executive officer on the Rainier, and finally commanding officer on the *McArthur*.

After her sea tours, Fields participated in the U.S. Department of Commerce's Science and Technology Fellowship Program, then was administrative officer of NOAA's National Geodetic Survey, chief of Coast Survey's Hydrographic Surveys Division, director of the NOAA Corps' Commissioned Personnel Center, and deputy assistant administrator for NOAA's National Ocean Service.

Her list of honors and commendations stretches almost as far as the decks of the ships she sailed on. Among the highest are the Metcalfe Health, Education, and Science Award from the Congressional Black Caucus Foundation, the U.S. Department of Commerce Gold Medal, and the Lowell Thomas Explorer Award for outstanding achievement in ocean exploration from the Explorers Club in New York.

Rear Admiral Fields is a member of several professional societies and has served in various offices in those organizations.

— February 3 —
1870
15th Amendment Ratified

On this day in civil rights history, the 15th Amendment to the U.S. Constitution was ratified. The amendment states: "The right of citizens of the United States to vote shall not be denied or abridged by the United States or by any State on account of race, color, or previous condition of servitude."

The 13th Amendment had outlawed slavery, and the 14th had bestowed full U.S. citizenship upon former slaves. But Republicans feared that ex-Confederates would attempt to regain political control, so Congress passed the 15th hoping to secure forever the rights of the freed slaves.

The amendment empowered blacks across the South during Reconstruction. Thousands of African Americans were elected to political office. The Congress and the state legislatures began passing "radical" measures to eliminate all race-based laws, while also instituting reforms such as universal public education. Meanwhile the defeated South was rebuilding. A large number of African Americans were holding public office, and the federal government ws mandating policies intended to protect full citizenship for all. Good times seeemed ahead.

But what African Americans and their Republican allies saw as hopeful signs of progress, the defeated white power structure, mostly Democrats, saw as an intolerable threat. President U. S. Grant had to send federal troops to New Orleans to dispel a white mob angry about interracial government.

Then Grant's successor, Rutherford B. Hayes, made cautious by his bitterly contested election in 1877, withdrew federal troops occupying the South and ended many of the policies specifically enacted to help and protect African Americans. Reconstruction was essentially over. Violence and intimidation returned to Southern polling places. Black politicians were voted out, and the 15th Amendment signified little just 20 years after it was passed.

After Reconstruction failed, Southern legislatures passed poll taxes, literacy tests, and various measures establishing Jim Crow segregation. The result was further violence and disenfranchisement as white terrorist groups such as the KKK made sure blacks were frightened into submission. The dismal state of affairs would last until 100 years after the Civil War, when the 1965 Voting Rights Act signed by President Lyndon B. Johnson again returned African Americans to Southern political life.

— FEBRUARY 4 —

1913

CIVIL RIGHTS ICON ROSA PARKS BORN

On this day in civil rights history, Rosa Louise McCauley, who would become famous for sitting down so a people could stand up, was born in Tuskegee, Alabama. She grew up on a farm until moving to Montgomery for high school. When her family fell on hard times, she quit school and worked as a house servant. Later she married Raymond Parks, a barber, and finished high school.

In 1943, Parks joined the Montgomery branch of the NAACP. She became its secretary, working closely with the fearless local civil rights pioneer E. D. Nixon and later with the young attorney Fred Gray. She was a sponsor for the NAACP youth chapter and generally was a quiet but resolute activist a full ten years before the incident that made her famous.

Parks was employed as a seamstress in a local department store. On the evening of December 1, 1955, she boarded a segregated city bus to go home from work, and a few stops later was ordered to give up her seat so a white man—who was standing in the front of the bus because the white section was full — could be seated. She refused to move and was arrested.

The arrest triggered the Montgomery bus boycott and made her an immediate heroine of the nascent civil rights movement and, eventually, an international icon.

The boycott succeeded but Montgomery remained a racially divided city and segegationist whites retained control of most jobs and institutions. Partly because of her celebrity, Parks and her husband found it difficult to obtain employment and to live in Montgomery. They moved to Detroit, Michigan, where Mrs. Parks worked from 1965 to 1988 as a staff member for U.S. Representative John Conyers.

Over the years, recognition of and appreciation for her singular act of courage grew and she became more and more famous as the "Mother of the civil rights movement." Schools and streets have been named for her, she has received thousands of awards, in Montgomery a museum tells her story, and the Rosa and Raymond Parks Institute for Self-Development conducts educational work on her behalf.

In 1994, a black man assaulted Parks in her Detroit home. "Do you know who I am?" she asked. He said he knew but didn't care, savagely attacked her, and stole $53. She recovered from the attack and continued to speak out and give interviews until her health began to fail about 2002. She died October 24, 2005.

— FEBRUARY 5 —

1869
FIRST BLACK POSTMISTRESS BECOMES POLITICAL ISSUE

On this day in civil rights history, Minnie Cox, the first black postmistress in the United States, was born in Lexington, Mississippi. Cox later moved to Indianola, a small, Mississippi town, and began a career as an educator, teaching at the Indianola Colored Public School, where her husband Wayne was principal.

In 1891, President Harrison appointed Cox postmistress of Indianola. President McKinley renewed her position, while also elevating her status. Offered a full four-year term, she became the first black postmistress in the U.S.

The backlash to Reconstruction, however, took hold. The great strides black communities had made after the Civil War were being overturned. Angry whites began devising a variety of methods to regain total control. This included voting disenfranchisement along with a vast conspiracy to remove blacks from political positions to end, as was commonly said, "the nigger domination."

In 1902, Cox briefly gained the focus of this reactionary movement. Whites in Indianola delivered a petition demanding Cox's resignation. When she refused, she was threatened with physical harm. The harassment increased. Sensing an imminent attack or worse, Cox finally tendered her resignation to take effect in January 1903.

But new President Theodore Roosevelt would have none of it. Roosevelt worked to improve relations with the black communities, having Booker T. Washington to dinner (a move harshly criticized by many of the nation's papers). Refusing Cox's resignation, Roosevelt closed down the Indianola post office and rerouted the mail through Greenville, Mississippi, while Cox stayed out of harm's way. She continued receiving her salary, while the national media became involved. Cox's battle for her job became front-page news. Eventually the situation was debated on the Senate floor for four hours. Roosevelt stood resolute. Unless Cox's detractors could prove a reason for her dismissal other than the color of her skin, she would remain the Indianola postmistress.

In 1904, Cox's term ended and the Indianola post office reopened with a white postmaster.

Minnie Cox died in 1933.

On this day in civil rights history, the Peabody Fund was established. George Peabody, a wealthy industrialist with vast financial holdings and considered by many to be the first American philanthropist, saw in the South crushing poverty and a dearth of education. So he established the Peabody Fund "for the promotion and encouragement of intellectual, moral or industrial education among the more destitute portions of the south and southwestern states of our Union."

The "more destitute portions of the South" included hundreds of thousands of recently freed slaves.

Philanthropist George Peabody

The Fund was designed to help augment public education in the eleven former Confederate states. Also known as the Peabody Education Fund, it stabilized many struggling schools and provided money to build new ones, to create scholarships and endowments, and to educate future teachers.

Led by a commission of handpicked dignitaries, including Adm. David G. Farragut and Gen. U. S. Grant, the Fund searched for communities with enough students and tolerant public officials willing to cooperate. Many of the schools helped by the Peabody Fund were fledgling African American entities.

The Fund's money was delivered strategically to maximize its impact. Local communities had to raise funds, through taxes or otherwise, to match the grant. This was in keeping with Peabody's philosophy, similar to Booker T. Washington's, of self-reliance. Peabody believed that the poor, in this case, the poor whites and blacks in the South, needed just a little push to level the playing field.

The Peabody Education Fund was a great success. A large number of schools and universities were helped or created by the Fund. A whole generation of students—African American and white—benefited from Peabody's vision of equality through education.

Peabody did much in the way of philanthropy during his lifetime—funding libraries, museums, and housing projects—but it is the Peabody Fund, the first private philanthropic organization in the United States, for which he is remembered.

On this day in civil rights history, Carter G. Woodson—African American writer, scholar, and organizer—began Negro History Week.

Woodson was born in the South to former slaves and worked as a coal miner until he enrolled in high school at age 20. He eventually earned a PhD from Harvard. In his studies, Woodson realized that little about Negro accomplishments had been recorded in American history. What he did find in the history books was mostly a reinforcement of negative cultural stereotypes. Blacks in America, Africa, and Europe lacked a cultural presence in the Western world.

While some activists strived for equality in the present, Woodson looked to balance the record of the past in history, literature, and popular stories. In 1915 Woodson founded the Association for the Study of Negro Life and History (later called the Association for the Study of Afro-American Life and History). He began publishing a series of books on black history: *The Education of the Negro Prior to 1861, A Century of Negro Migration, The History of the Negro Church,* and most famously, *The Negro in Our History.* He also began *The Journal of Negro History,* which still exists.

Woodson's goal was to weave into the tapestry of American history the narrative of people of African descent. With his meticulous scholarship and uncompromising stance, Woodson eventually crossed paths with many famous African Americans of the day, including W. E. B. Du Bois and Archibald Grimke, as well as Pan-Africanist Marcus Garvey, whom Woodson wrote for as a regular columnist for Garvey's weekly newspaper, *Negro World.*

More than just an academic, Woodson was also an early civil rights thinker and campaigner. Affiliated with the NAACP, Woodson proposed early acts of civil disobedience, such as boycotting businesses that were prejudiced against black customers. "Let us banish fear," he said in a letter to the NAACP. "We have been in this mental state for three centuries. I am a radical. I am ready to act, if I can find brave men to help me."

Woodson's most famous accomplishment was his creation of Negro History Week, setting the celebration during the week in which both Frederick Douglass and Abraham Lincoln were born. Intended as a celebration of the African American experience, Negro History Week eventually grew into Black History Month.

— FEBRUARY 8 —

1968

ORANGEBURG MASSACRE IN SOUTH CAROLINA

On this day in civil rights history, in what become known as the Orangeburg Massacre, state troopers fired on a student protest at South Carolina State University.

Four years after the 1964 Civil Rights Act made segregation illegal, many public places across the South still openly practiced racial discrimination. In Orangeburg, black students from South Carolina State and Chaflin College, a Christian agricultural school, began a series of escalating protests around the All Star Bowling Lanes, which refused black patrons. As the picketers neared the bowling alley, local police rebuffed the students with nightsticks. With each confrontation, the tension built. The National Guard was called in, setting up roadblocks around the city and in front of the bowling alley.

Photo courtesy of Associated Press

Orangeburg, 1968

Three days after the initial protest, a few hundred students, isolated on the campus lawn by the guardsmen who surrounded them, built a bonfire and started chanting. Suddenly, the officers opened fire. After a few moments of gunfire, three students were dead: Samuel Hammond, Delano Middleton, and Henry Smith. Twenty-seven others were injured.

The white press reported that militant agitators had attacked the police who were only defending themselves. But other accounts suggested otherwise. All eyewitness accounts reveal an edgy police force that fired on an unarmed, fleeing crowd of underage students.

In the aftermath, Martin Luther King Jr., at work on his Poor People's Campaign in Tennessee, called for the trial and incarceration of the officers involved. But to many younger civil rights activists, the three dead innocents proved that King's nonviolent philosophy no longer worked.

Nine officers charged in the shooting were acquitted by a local jury. Meanwhile, Student Nonviolent Coordinating Committee (SNCC) staffer Cleveland Sellers, wounded in the shootings, was charged with rioting, was convicted, and served one year in prison.

Now largely eclipsed by the Kent State shootings two years later, the Orangeburg Massacre was the first incident of troops firing on protesting college students, and it is one of the darker moments in the civil rights movement history. Orangeburg was a devastating reminder of how much more the movement had to achieve. Nonetheless, later in February 1968, the All Star Bowling Lanes did begin admitting black patrons.

— FEBRUARY 9 —
1828
MINSTREL ACT LENDS NAME TO 'JIM CROW' SEGREGATION

On this day in civil rights history, approximately, Thomas Dartmouth "Daddy" Rice popularized a minstrel act in which he darkened his face with soot, donned a costume of ragged, floppy clothes, and generally acted the fool.

Rice's character, a crippled slave, danced a jig and sang:

> Weel about and turn about and do jus' so,
> Eb'ry time I weel about, I jump Jim Crow.

Mississippi historian Charles Wilson attributes Rice's inspiration to a Louisville, Kentucky, performance by a slave owned by a Mr. Crow. Whatever its origins, the act came to be called "Jim Crow," and the term then evolved into a derogatory term toward blacks in general, stereotyping them as foolish, childlike, and inferior to whites.

In the 1840s, segregated railway carriages were already being referred to as "Jim Crow cars." By the Civil War, the term was in common usage in the North and the South and the "Jim Crow" character adorned sheet music, illustrations, and novelty items.

With the exception of abolitionists, white audiences were comfortable being entertained by the stereotyped image of the happy, buffoonish, Negro slave. One actor who gave more along these lines than some audiences expected was Ira Aldridge, one of the few black actors on the stage in the years before the Civil War. In his performances, Aldridge sometimes sang a mournful version of "Jump Jim Crow," then closed with a plea for the abolition of slavery.

After the end of Reconstruction, as racial segregation based on white supremacy became institutionalized, "Jim Crow" came to mean any of the laws and customs that set the races apart. The term persisted until the civil rights movement brought the end of legalized segregation in the 1960s.

— FEBRUARY 10 —
1956
WHITE CITIZENS COUNCIL RALLIES AGAINST BUS BOYCOTT

On this day in civil rights history, 12,000 people attended a White Citizens Council rally in Montgomery, Alabama, to protest a boycott by blacks against segregated city buses.

Created two years earlier as a response to the *Brown v. Board of Education* ruling that de-segregated public schools, the White Citizens Council first formed in Indianola, Mississippi, and then spread across the South. Drawing its support from white local politicians, business-men, bankers, law enforcement, and other middle-class constituents, the WCC sought to defeat integration through public policy and opinion. Instead of advocating terrorism or violence, the WCC promoted economic and civic manipulation. "We intend to make it impossible for any Negro who advocates desegregation to find and hold a job, get credit, or renew a mortgage," described a founder of the Alabama chapter.

The WCC enacted boycotts against black businesses while also refusing supplies, credit, or other services. Early on, the WCC's various activities achieved much success.

At the time, the WCC was called the "Klan with a smiling face"; its members were often described as "Klansmen without hoods." The WCC perceived itself as a public service organiza-tion, an all-white racial interest group. Of course, many WCC members were covert members of the KKK as well. The Klan terrorized the night; the White Citizens Council antagonized during the day. While the Klan's activities perpetuated fear and intimidation, the WCC made inroads by making life difficult for civil rights supporters.

The WCC worked to create all-white "council" schools to combat desegregation. Some of these schools later transformed into private academies, technically integrated, but still closed off to poor students of color.

Like the KKK, the White Citizens Councils saw their influence fade as integration policies took hold and the mindsets of average white Southerners slowly changed.

— FEBRUARY 11 —
1920
GENERAL DANIEL 'CHAPPIE' JAMES BORN

On this day in civil rights history, Daniel "Chappie" James, the first black U.S. four-star general, was born in Pensacola, Florida. The youngest of 17 children, this future war hero entered Tuskegee Institute in 1937, studying for a degree in education while becoming a civilian pilot. He spent his free time dreaming of flying for the military.

After an altercation with another student, James was expelled from Tuskegee. In 1943, he entered the Army Air Corps program as a cadet. He transferred to Selfridge Field in Detroit, where he was assigned to the all-black 477th Bombardment Group. Over the next six years, he served on various fighter squadrons, including the 99th Pursuit Squadron.

At the time, blacks in the U.S. military were mostly cooks and laborers, and most facilities remained segregated. James and a hundred other black officers staged a non-violent sit-in at a segregated officer's club. The protesters included future Detroit Mayor Coleman Young and future U.S. Secretary of Transportation William T. Coleman. Arrested and charged with mutiny, the black officers faced courts martial until General George Marshall stepped in, ordering the charges dropped. On July 26, 1948, President Harry Truman issued Executive Order 9981, desegregating the armed forces.

Photo courtesy of Library of Congress

General Chappie James

Remaining in the military after the end of World War II, James distinguished himself in aerial combat, winning the Distinguished Flying Cross in the Korean war. His career included assignments in Africa, Asia, and the Middle East. Over the years he accumulated numerous accolades as an officer, leader, and public speaker, slowly rising up the ranks.

In 1975, James was named commander of the North American Air Defense Command, and was made a four-star general.

James spent much of his free time speaking to minority students. He advocated hard work and resilience, and offered up his own life as an example of what the U.S. military could offer young black men.

He died of a heart attack on February 25, 1978, not long after his retirement from the U.S. Air Force.

— FEBRUARY 12 —
1909
NAACP FOUNDED

On this day in civil rights history, the National Association for the Advancement of Colored People was founded in New York City.

Disturbed by a violent race riot in Atlanta in 1905, W. E. B. Du Bois headed the call for a meeting on the Canadian side of Niagara Falls to discuss the problems facing African Americans and other minorities in the U.S. The biracial group of writers, scholars, and philanthropists who joined Du Bois in this effort came to be known as the Niagara Movement.

The Niagara Movement struggled to develop support and funding. Leaders decided a new national organization was needed and chose February 12, 1909, Lincoln's birthday, to annouce the formation of one, though the name was not selected for another year.

In its charter, the NAACP stated its mission: "To promote equality of rights and to eradicate caste or race prejudice among the citizens of the United States." The new organization had as its mouthpiece a publication called *The Crisis*, edited by Du Bois. *The Crisis* had a readership of more than 30,000 in its early days and showcased many emerging African American writers and thinkers, including Jean Toomer and Langston Hughes.

The early NAACP organized protests and planned legal campaigns to overturn Jim Crow segregation in the South. It was in the legal arena that the NAACP would shape the civil rights movement and make its most effective contributions. Led by Thurgood Marshall and Charles Hamilton Houston, the NAACP orchestrated a decades-long campaign to destroy the separate but equal doctrine that permeated the first half of the twentieth century. By systematically attacking law after law in the courts, the NAACP did much to end segregation across the South.

When groups such as SNCC and the SCLC mounted civil disobedience and mass protests, the NAACP continued to challenge in the courts. Although the NAACP's insistence on legal maneuvering resulted in some loss of prestige in the mid-1960s when direct action was driving the movement, the NAACP remained essential to the lobbying and litigation that resulted in most of the key rulings and legislation that destroyed segregation.

The NAACP still exists as the preeminent African American social and political organization in the United States.

— FEBRUARY 13 —
1920
NEGRO NATIONAL LEAGUE FOUNDED

On this day in civil rights history, Rube Foster founded the National Association of Professional Baseball Clubs, also known as the Negro National League, the first stable, all-black professional baseball league in the United States. Foster is recognized as the father of the Negro leagues.

Foster was born in Texas in 1878. He was an enormous man and an outstanding athlete who excelled as a baseball pitcher, perhaps one of the greatest in the game. But with professional sports segregated, he could play only in exhibitions against white teams. He soon became manager-coach of the Chicago and later American Giants, and also played for the team. He was an innovative pitcher and baseball thinker. Managers of white teams would attend his games to observe his strategies.

He formed the National Negro League in 1920 in Kansas City. It operated in the South and in the Midwest, with eight member teams. As its president, Foster ran the league the same way he ran his team, with total authority. In 1923 an Eastern Negro league formed, and soon the two leagues played in an all-black World Series.

In 1926, Foster fell into poor health, becoming deranged after an accident involving a gas leak. He was committed to an asylum, where he died in 1930. Without Foster, the league fell apart in 1931. The apparatus of players, fields, managers, and fans was in place, however, and in 1933 a new league of the same name was formed. It would grow into one of the most profitable black-owned businesses in the country.

The Negro leagues produced some of the biggest names in baseball history, including Hank Aaron, Jackie Robinson, Willie Mays, and Satchel Paige. The leagues were profitable and full of talent, and the combination eventually broke the color barrier in professional baseball. In 1947, Jackie Robinson would join the Brooklyn Dodgers as the first black player in the segregated major leagues. His accomplishment was a major source of inspiration to African Americans across the nation, but as the color barrier fell in major-league baseball, so also fell the Negro leagues.

— FEBRUARY 14 —
1957
SOUTHERN CHRISTIAN LEADERSHIP CONFERENCE FOUNDED

On this day in civil rights history, the Southern Christian Leadership Conference was founded. The SCLC, SNCC, and the NAACP, along with CORE and the Urban League—sometimes working in tandem, often not—planned, financed, and executed the majority of civil rights events in the 1950s and 1960s.

Originally called the Southern Negro Leadership Conference, the SCLC was created to capitalize on the momentum gained through the success of the Montgomery bus boycott. Comprised primarily of ministers from various churches across the South, the SCLC planned to push beyond the NAACP's legal wrangling into the world of direct action. The president of this new organization was Martin Luther King Jr. Other founding members included firebrand Fred Shuttlesworth, Bayard Rustin, Andrew Young, and Ralph Abernathy.

The operating principles of the SCLC were simple. Combining Gandhian non-violent principles with the tenets of New Testament Christianity, the SCLC propagated a school of civil disobedience straight out of Thoreau.

The SCLC planned a vigorous assault on the white pro-segregation infrastructure of the South, executing carefully organized protests in select cities, including Albany, Selma, and Birmingham, among others. The attacks consisted of boycotts, sit-ins, and mass protests, in relatively brief hit-and-run events. The design was to tax a state to the breaking point by filling the prisons, exhausting the guards, and maintaining in full view of the nation the atrocities of Jim Crow segregation with a relentless vigil. When the municipal governments fought back with batons, nightsticks, and bullets, the SCLC hoped the federal government would step in. Once involved, the feds, it was believed, would do the right thing and abolish the segregation it found.

While the NAACP rolled back legislation with its trials and legal precedents, the SCLC paraded in the streets.

With King at its helm, the SCLC enacted many of the era's most famous events.

— FEBRUARY 15 —
1851
ABOLITIONISTS FREE FUGITIVE SLAVE IN BOSTON

On this day in civil rights history, a group of black abolitionists broke into a Boston courthouse and liberated Shadrach Minkins, a fugitive slave living as a free man in Massachusetts.

The story began in 1850, when Minkins escaped from Virginia to Boston and began his life anew. Unknown to him at the time, Congress had just passed legislation that greatly hindered his prospects. Under the 1850 Fugitive Slave Law, any federal agent not immediately arresting persons assumed to be escaped slaves was subject to a steep fine. Part of a larger compromise between the Northern and Southern states, the new law made life considerably more difficult for abolitionists and greatly enhanced the South's ability to recover runaway slaves. Some Northern states, such as Massachusetts, took measures that ensured at least a semblance of a trial for suspected escaped slaves, but a result of the law was that Canada became the main destination point for the Underground Railroad.

Minkus's newfound freedom did not last long. On February 15, 1851, he was the first man arrested in New England under the new law, and he was taken to a nearby courthouse for an immediate trial and most likely deportation. Attorney Robert Morris, hearing of the disturbance, appeared to provide legal counsel.

When the judge refused Minkins's writ of *habeas corpus*, several abolitionists, in a daring rescue, forced their way into the courtroom, overcame the armed guards, and wrested Minkins away.

Hidden in an attic in a nearby black neighborhood, Minkins waited patiently. Prominent black leaders Lewis Hayden and John J. Smith eventually transported Minkins to Canada, where he lived out the remainder of his life a free man.

Morris and eight others were charged with various infractions. All were acquitted. The much-publicized episode galvanized abolitionists across the country, emboldening antislavery activists to further action.

Minkins, by all accounts an unassuming man yearning for a simple life of freedom, became an icon of the antislavery movement as the nation moved closer to civil war.

— February 16 —
1944
U.S. Navy Begins African American Officer Training

On this day in civil rights history, the first African American naval officer training program began.

U.S. armed forces were still segregated and most black military personnel worked as cooks or laborers. At this point in World War II, there were more than 100,000 African American enlisted men in the navy, without a single officer.

The NAACP and other civil rights organizations applied pressure to the navy, and navy officials responded by commissioning 16 black officers and sending them for training to Camp Robert Smalls in Illinois. That first African American officer training program was a startling success: the class average was 3.89, a record still unbroken.

The Golden Thirteen

Two months later, 13 of the trainees became the U.S. Navy's first black active duty officers. They became known as the Golden Thirteen and the enterprising and talented young men seemed poised for greatness.

But the story doesn't end there. The Golden Thirteen encountered a military infrastructure unwilling to recognize their achievements. They were routinely disrespected by other officers and were often given menial assignments while their white counterparts were leading campaigns in the closing months of World War II.

Still, the officers collectively served in their various capacities with excellence. Their hardships paved the way for the armed services to be desegregated both in word and deed in 1947, when President Harry Truman issued Executive Order 9981, integrating the United States military.

Only one of the original Golden Thirteen made a career in the navy; the others achieved success through a variety of civilian pursuits.

— FEBRUARY 17 —
1942
BLACK PANTHERS CO-FOUNDER HUEY P. NEWTON BORN

On this day in civil rights history, Huey Newton, co-founder of the Black Panther Party, was born in Louisiana, the youngest of seven children. His family migrated to Oakland, California, a few years later, and Newton entered high school an illiterate petty thug, rebelling against his religious upbringing.

Newton quickly overcame his disabilities and entered college, where he became involved with black student activism. After the passage of the Voting and Civil Rights Acts of 1964 and 1965 did little to ameliorate the harsh conditions of poor urban blacks, Newton concluded that a a radical liberation movement was needed. He decided to create an organization that would bring about the long-awaited revolution.

In 1966, Newton joined Bobby Seale in forming the Black Panther Party for Self Defense.

Newton's philosophical influences included Che Guevara, Frantz Fanon, W. E. B. Du Bois, Karl Marx, and Robert Williams, author of *Negroes with Guns*. But his biggest influence was Malcolm X.

Newton laid the groundwork for the Panthers with his tracts, pamphlets, and articles in the newspaper, *The Black Panther*. As its "Minister of Defense," Newton wrote many of the party's mandates and directives, including Executive Mandate number 2 on June 29, 1967, calling for "revolutionary law, order, and justice" across the United States. This mandate drew SNCC's Stokely Carmichael to the BPP's ranks.

The Panthers advocated armed defense against police brutality and almost immediately began a system of armed neighborhood patrols in Oakland, resulting in open antagonism with the Oakland police.

The Panthers' top priority was community-building. To that end they provided free breakfasts to local children, a free clothing program, a busing program for relatives and friends of prisoners, and other health and education programs. They wrote petitions and staged protests like other rights groups. The Panthers, however, were armed.

The BPP's aggressive, radical stance scared both the federal government and the average American, who didn't see the progressive community programs. They instead saw a group of unrepentant Negroes dressed in all black, brandishing shotguns while loose in the streets.

This high profile and revolutionary rhetoric quickly drew trouble.

— FEBRUARY 18 —
1688
GERMANTOWN ANTISLAVERY RESOLUTION PASSED

On this day in civil rights history, almost a century before U.S. independence, a group of Quakers in Germantown passed the first formal antislavery resolution.

Also known as the Religious Society of Friends, the Quaker variant of Christianity formed from the chaos of English civil wars in the mid 1600s. The Quakers lived quiet lives of moral rectitude combined with a sharp sense of social justice. This small but devout group rejected slavery and warfare. Quaker colonies were egalitarian places: women had equal status. The Quaker view of God was egalitarian as well: anyone could experience God directly without any aid or guidance from a recognized priest or church.

For these reasons, Quakers were persecuted in England and in the new world. The Puritans often confiscated Quaker property. Quaker books were burned. When caught, Quakers were flogged, branded, and sometimes executed. Like many minority groups coming to the New World, the Quakers found a place not of religious tolerance but the exact opposite.

The colonies that allowed the Quakers to settle—Pennsylvania, New Jersey, Delaware, Rhode Island, and Maryland—discovered small pockets of Christian utopianism popping up overnight. In the 1700s, the Quakers mounted campaigns for better treatment of the mentally ill, women's suffrage, and various prison reforms, as well as a system of trade based not on profit but mutual benefit.

But the Quakers' strong stance against slavery proved the most prophetic. The Germantown resolution—written by Dutch-speaking Quakers who had recently escaped persecution—condemned the practice in no uncertain terms. "To bring men hither [to America]," it states, "or to rob and sell them against their will, we stand against . . . here there are those oppressed which are of a black colour . . . what thing in the world can be done worse toward us, than if men should rob or steal us away, and sell us for slaves to strange countries." The resolution did not want manumission, but rather a permanent, universal moratorium on slavery.

This official protest was ignored. But the Quakers would remain a strong protesting voice in the 200 years of slavery to follow, eventually becoming the bedrock of the abolitionist movement.

— FEBRUARY 19 —
1942
TUSKEGEE AIRMEN INITIATED

On this day in civil rights history, the 332nd Fighter Group known as the Tuskegee Airmen was initiated into the U.S. armed forces. Already the first black fighter group, the Tuskegee Airmen would go on to distinguish themselves for their skill and bravery, offering a high-profile example of equality of the races.

After Congress (pressured by the NAACP) passed legislation to allow African Americans more opportunity in the armed forces, the U.S. War Department grudgingly created a black squadron, setting high standards and high levels of experience as requisites for admittance. This policy, intended to strangle the program before it began, had the unintended consequence of training only the best and most capable pilots.

The new recruits trained at the Tuskegee Army Air Field in Tuskegee, Alabama. Opening in July 1941, the base graduated its first class in March of 1942. The pilots were immediately deployed.

Led by squadron commander Benjamin Davis, the Tuskegee Airmen, nicknamed "the Black Birdmen" by the German Luftwaffe, terrorized Axis air forces in the European theatre, ultimately claiming more than 400 enemy planes. The Tuskegee Airmen destroyed fuel dumps, supply trains, and naval units. Collectively, they were honored with more than 800 combat medals. Perhaps most noteworthy, not a single bomber escorted by the 332nd was shot down.

Tuskegee Airman receives award

Meanwhile, segregation in the armed forces continued throughout the war. Black officers were mistreated, harassed, and denied promotions. Black pilots and soldiers slept in segregated barracks, and on one occasion 100 were refused entrance into a white officer's mess, and then received official reprimands for trying to enter.

At war's end, many black servicemen returned home disillusioned by racism. After risking their lives for their country, they wanted equal rights and recognition of their contributions. They would have to wait years for both, although President Harry Truman did officially desegregate the U.S. military in 1948.

The men of the 332nd continued to distinguish themselves in the airways, winning the 1949 national gunnery competition. For their skill, bravura, and fearlessness, the 332nd—the Black Birdmen of the skies—became one of the most sought-after units in the newly formed U.S. Air Force.

— FEBRUARY 20 —
1956
WARRANTS ISSUED IN MONTGOMERY BUS BOYCOTT CASE

On this day in civil rights history, arrest warrants were issued for 89 persons in the Montgomery Bus "Protest," including Martin Luther King Jr. and Ralph Abernathy.

Racial tension in Montgomery was high. Two effigies had been hung in downtown, one labeled "NAACP" and the other, "I talked integration." At night, African Americans endured threatening phone calls and harassment, incuding a series of bombings that damaged many churches and private residences. During the day many black citizens were hassled by police for petty infractions.

The February arrests were based on a 34-year-old anti-boycott statute. The Montgomery Improvement Association knew of this statute and thus was careful to call the boycott a "protest." Meanwhile, local white officials were intent on stopping the boycott before the integrationists got out of hand.

As King's stature and influence increased, many blacks were worried that if he were jailed, the white power structure would try to isolate and injure or kill him while he was behind bars. This was no idle fear. All across the South the threat of torture or death loomed whenever a protester was arrested away from the eyes of the public.

King, Abernathy, and the others voluntarily went to jail. The arresting officers were unusually polite as they processed the boycotters. Some spectators volunteered to join the arrestees. Reporters and other media were on hand to witness the event.

Most of those arrested were released immediately and the charges were dropped. King, however, was indicted, along with a few others. Attorneys Fred Gray, Arthur Shores, Peter Hall, and Orzell Billingsley handled the protesters' legal defense. King was first to go to trial. Judge Eugene Carter presided over the case; there was no jury. In King's defense, Gray argued that the statute for which King was arrested was unconstitutional. The Supreme Court, he showed, had struck down a similar anti-picketing law. Gray also argued that there was "legal excuse and just cause" for the protest, as a response to the years of mistreatment Montgomery-area blacks had endured.

Judge Carter disregarded these arguments and fined King $500. A motion for a new trial fell through. But the charges against King were ultimately dismissed.

In the end, none of the protesters paid any fines or spent any time in jail for the charges. The issued warrants were one of the first salvos the jittery municipality would fire against the civil rights protesters and their leadership.

— February 21 —
1965
Malcolm X Assassinated in Harlem

On this day in civil rights history, Malcolm X was murdered. One of the most controversial and outspoken black leaders of the 1960s, he was a charismatic speaker and a strong thinker, a hero of the ghetto and one of the first black revolutionaries. He inspired the Black Panther Party and other militant black organizations.

After a childhood of petty larceny, Malcolm converted to the Nation of Islam while in jail in the late 1940s and soon met leader Elijah Muhammad, who saw great potential in young Malcolm and mentored him.

During the 1950s, Malcolm traveled the country speaking at Nation of Islam temples and gaining converts. His oratorical style matched Martin Luther King Jr.'s in power and effectiveness and he became a popular speaker on college campuses. His message focused on exploitation, disenfranchisement, and the economic oppression of American blacks. The media treated Malcolm X as a dangerous but influential leader and he was closely watched by the FBI.

Malcolm X

Photo courtesy of Library of Congress

As Malcolm became more famous, Elijah Muhammad apparently became jealous and resentful of his protégé. At the same time, Malcolm X's personal philosophy was evolving, and in 1964, he broke with the Nation of Islam, converting to mainstream Islam. He said he had begun to see the problems of African Americans as international. He traveled through Africa and to Mecca and saw white Muslims worshiping alongside black Muslims.

Returning to the States he founded the Organization for Afro-American Unity to cooperate with other civil rights groups. He toned down his militant speech, preaching instead a message of peaceful self-reliance.

On this date in 1965, Malcolm was speaking to a group of 400 at a ballroom in Harlem when his guards rushed toward a disturbance in the crowd, leaving him alone on the stage. A gunman charged through the melee and discharged two shotgun blasts into Malcolm's chest. Two other assailants ran forward and unloaded handguns into Malcolm's prostrate body. He died instantly.

Three Nation of Islam members ultimately were convicted of the murder.

Historians debate what Malcolm X—with his fiery energy and keen intellect—might have accomplished had he lived. Malcolm X was 39 when he was assassinated, the same age Martin Luther King would be when he was killed three years later.

On this day in civil rights history, the first all-female, all-black antislavery group formed in Salem, Massachusetts. An earlier manifestation of the group, dedicated to charity, had called themselves the Colored Female Religious and Moral Society of Salem. But in 1832 the group entered the political arena, changing its name to the Female Anti-Slavery Society. A separate organization, the Colored Female Produce Society, urged boycotts on any goods produced with slave labor.

Abolitionism was a powerful political trend early in America's history, especially in New England before the Civil War. By the 1830s there were over a thousand antislavery groups, many of them interracial and female. Women were considered unfit for regular employment or political life, but perfectly suited for charity work and anti-slavery causes. Early female abolitionists included Elizabeth Cady Stanton, Lucretia Mott, sisters Angelina and Sarah Grimké, and Susan B. Anthony, all of whom would become the forebears of the women's movement.

Photo courtesy of Library of Congress

Anthony and Stanton

Women also formed the bedrock of the American Anti-Slavery Society, serving as agents, writers, and organizers, even though that Society was male-dominated.

The era was full of fiery abolitionists, including William Lloyd Garrison, Maria Miller Stewart, Charles Remond, David Ruggles, Samuel Cornish, and former slaves William Wells Brown, Frederick Douglass, among many others. These men and women toured the country, giving lectures while agitating for the end of slavery.

Taken as a whole, the thousands of abolitionist organizations argued, wrote, petitioned, and dragged the public discourse to the question of slavery. They pursued their goals with zealous relentlessness. Although the antislavery movement was itself not immune to racism and prejudice, it was in many ways the first biracial political coalition in the U.S.

The goals of the Female Anti-Slavery Society and similar organizations of their period were exactly the goals of the later civil rights leaders: the right to vote, the end of oppressive racism, and fair treatment under the law.

— February 23 —
1868
W. E. B. Du Bois Born

On this day in civil rights history, William Edward Burghardt Du Bois, the intellectual backbone of the early civil rights movement, was born.

Arguably one of the most important figures in African American history, Du Bois's life spanned from Frederick Douglass to Martin Luther King Jr., from Reconstruction to the March on Washington. Although too intellectual and perhaps too arrogant to become a mainstream leader of people, Du Bois's influence still resonates. Scholar, sociologist, novelist, poet, journalist, educator, and activist, he has few peers.

Born in Great Barrington, Massachusetts, Du Bois distinguished himself at an early age. Graduating at the top of his class, he attended Fisk University in Tennessee, his first contact with Jim Crow segregation. The humiliating racial prejudice he found there permanently altered his view of life. "The problem of the 20th century," he would later prophesy, "is the problem of the color line."

Photo courtesy of Library of Congress

W. E. B. Du Bois

After earning a PhD from Harvard, Du Bois entered academe as a sociology professor. But it was the publication in 1903 of his first major book, *The Souls of Black Folk,* a collection of essays on race relations, that brought him fully into civil rights circles. In it, he demanded three basic rights for African Americans immediately: "the right to vote," "civic equality," and "education of the youth according to ability." Later in life, he would begin to ask for more. Du Bois also criticized Booker T. Washington for his accommodating stance to the white patriarchy.

Washington's paradigm hinged on a temporary cessation of civil rights agitation, arguing instead for a utilitarian approach. Blacks, Washington argued, should become so useful to their communities through their contributions that whites would have to accept them and grant them full citizenship. This was one vision of a solution to the problem. Du Bois offered quite another.

In 1905, Du Bois formed the Niagara Movement, an organization that eventually became the NAACP, which he co-founded.

In 1910 he left academia to work for the NAACP full-time. Under his tutelage, the NAACP started *The Crisis,* a publication that for many years served as the voice of the movement, garnering an eventual circulation of 100,000 readers. Du Bois operated as editor-in-chief and regular columnist. From this position, he shaped the public discourse of African American politics, art, and literature for more than 25 years.

— FEBRUARY 24 —
1968
MONTGOMERY SCHOOLS ORDERED TO END DUAL SYSTEM

On this day in civil rights history, Montgomery, Alabama, schools were ordered to end their dual education system, 14 years after a U.S. Supreme Court ruling officially ended segregation of public schools, and 11 years after the Arkansas school system was integrated.

The long delay is an indication of how little immediate change the NAACP's victory in the 1954 *Brown v. Board of Education* decision brought to the public school systems of the Deep South, where protracted legal battles over *Brown*'s meaning and application continued. *Brown* stated that "separate facilities are inherently unequal" and ordered that dual school systems be dismantled "with all deliberate speed," but it would take until 1969 for all Alabama schools to be desegregated. (By that time a system of segregated private schools had been established, and today in many parts of the rural South, classrooms are often as racially divided as before 1954.)

Widespread indignation, and in some places, apathy, to the 1954 ruling revealed a powerful mindset not easily changed. Local school boards ignored the ruling, citing states' rights and tradition as a trump card to the new federal ruling. It was clear that the issue would have to be forced, by mass action, by protest, by stricter federal mandate. Although a huge step forward for the civil rights of African Americans, *Brown* provided a bureaucratic loophole by not specifically defining ways in which public schools had to desegregate.

Subsequent Supreme Court decisions, however, made the states' obligations clear. In 1968's *Green v. County School Board of New Kent County*, six areas of desegregation were outlined: student enrollments, faculty and administration assignments, extracurricular activities, transportation to and from schools, and physical facilities. The message was clear: every facet of school operations had to be desegregated, from the students to the faculty.

In 1968, in a lawsuit filed by Rosa Parks's original lawyer, Fred Gray, schools were desegregated in Montgomery—the heart of Dixie and the former capitol of the Confederacy. It was one of the few good moments in what was an otherwise awful year for race relations in America, with the assassinations of Martin Luther King Jr. and Robert Kennedy, and riots all over the country.

— FEBRUARY 25 —

1987

ALABAMA RIGHTS PIONEER E. D. NIXON DIES

On this day in civil rights history, E. D. Nixon, early activist and instrumental figure of the Montgomery bus boycott, died. This strong, unsophisticated, and uncompromising man lived a life of service to the movement, but died bitter and angry over his obscurity.

Nixon spent most of his working life as a railroad Pullman car porter, and was a dedicated member of A. Philip Randolph's Brotherhood of Sleeping Car Porters union, eventually becoming the president of the Montgomery branch.

In the 1940s, Nixon organized the Alabama Voters League, leading a march to the Montgomery courthouse to register black voters. The effort failed, but Nixon remained an influential black leader, often acting as an intercessor for mistreated blacks. In 1947, he became president of the Alabama branch of the NAACP.

When Rosa Parks was arrested in Montgomery in 1955, it was Nixon who posted her bail, using his house as collateral. Nixon aggressively argued for using her as a test case against segregation laws. "This is the case," he said. When some local ministers were reticent to be involved, Nixon publicly admonished them. "Somebody in this thing has got to get faith. . . . If we're gonna be mens, now's the time to be mens." The rebuke worked.

The Montgomery Improvement Association was formed in response to Parks's arrest. Nixon and his long-time rival, former college coach Rufus Lewis, were among the MIA founders. Historians disagree on whose idea it was to elect Martin Luther King Jr., only 26 years old at the time, as head of the new organization, but Nixon played a large part and was subsequently elected treasurer.

As the boycott wore on and national attention was drawn to it, Nixon began to resent the attention received by King and Ralph D. Abernathy. Nixon eventually had a falling out with the MIA and King, and resigned with an angry letter.

The boycott worked. But Nixon no longer felt he had a role in the movement. He would later say, "I have organized over 15 organizations including the Montgomery Improvement Association, and it was I who found Rev. King. As a spokesman he is very good but no one man can do this job, but when people give all recognition to one because of academic training and forget others who do not have that kind of training but are making a worthwhile contribution to the comity that makes it hard. . . I just want to be left alone now."

— FEBRUARY 26 —
1925
BLACK NATIONALIST ROBERT WILLIAMS BORN

On this day in civil rights history, Robert Williams, controversial expatriate and civil rights leader was born. An advocate of armed defense and resistance to the Klan and the White Citizen's Council, Williams argued against King's nonviolence and was one of the primary influences on the Black Power movement of the late 1960s.

Like many African Americans in the South, Williams migrated northward for work in the 1940s. He landed in Detroit, where he witnessed the 1943 Detroit race riots. He also met with delegates from the American Communist Party, who treated him with respect he never received from other whites. Both events left an indelible impression on his mind.

He returned to his home in Monroe, North Carolina, where he became president of the Monroe branch of the NAACP in 1954, shortly after the *Brown v. Board* decision. Williams rebuilt the floundering chapter with a grassroots effort, drawing members from the lower classes. He quickly began mounting campaigns to desegregate Monroe's public places.

He rose to national prominence, however, during the "Kissing Case"—where two African American children, Simpson, 8, and Thompson, 10, played an innocent kissing game with three white girls. Newspapers exaggerated the details into a grotesque sexual violation of the sacred social taboo against miscegenation. A white mob began scouring the city for the two boys. Police found them first; the two youths were pulling a red wagon of empty drink bottles, oblivious to the storm. The police beat the two youths then imprisoned them; they were charged with assault and sentenced to ten years in reform school.

The case earned international attention. Williams became publicly involved. The Klan descended on Monroe, as did reporters. Williams began speaking around the country, stumping both for the end of segregation and the release of the two boys. Eventually a second hearing developed. The boys were eventually released.

Williams seemed poised to be a national civil rights leader. But his fiery stance of armed defense earned him expulsion from the NAACP. The FBI began to hound him for his connection to communism. The persecution forced Williams to flee the country. He went to Cuba, where he began calling for black revolt on his Radio Free Dixie broadcasts which could be heard throughout the Southern states. He later published *Negroes with Guns*, which Black Panther Party leaders called one of the most influential documents in the Black Power movement.

Williams lived in Cuba as a folk hero until the charges against him were dropped in 1976. He died in 1996, at age 71.

— FEBRUARY 27 —
1897
MARIAN ANDERSON BORN

On this day in civil rights history, Marian Anderson, one of the most celebrated contraltos of all time, was born into poverty in Philadelphia, Pennsylvania.

Anderson began her music career in children's choir at the age of six, displaying a rare vocal talent. Her family could not afford voice lessons, so her church paid for a tutor. After graduating high school, she was rejected by an all-white music school. This would be the first of many encounters with institutionalized racism that plagued her career.

But her fortunes changed when she placed first in a prestigious competition in New York City with the Philharmonic Orchestra in 1925. Launched by this success, she made a series of remarkably successful trips to Europe. Finnish composer Sibelius dedicated his piece, *Solitude*, to her. And Arturo Tuscanini, one of the greatest conductors of his era, heaped high praise on her abilities. Overnight, she became world famous.

Marian Anderson

Talent and fame, however, could not break the color line. Back in the U.S., Anderson played in Town Hall and Carnegie Hall, both previously closed to African Americans. Critical praise increased for her smooth, strong voice and Anderson began headlining sold-out venues. But in 1939 when her agent tried to book a show at the Constitution Hall, owned and managed by the Daughters of the Revolution (DAR), who also used it as their headquarters, she was rebuffed. A public outcry followed.

First lady Eleanor Roosevelt resigned her DAR membership and invited Anderson to perform in front of the Lincoln Memorial, on April 9, Easter Sunday. Seventy-five thousand people attended, and millions more heard a nationwide live radio broadcast.

The DAR later recanted, inviting Anderson to sing at Constitution Hall on numerous subsequent occasions. She later broke an even bigger barrier as the first African American to sign at the Metropolitan Opera in New York City, in 1955. Her performance was acclaimed, but at age 58 she was no longer at the height of her vocal powers. She still won accolades, but her best days were behind her, just as African Americans began to surface in opera due to her efforts.

After retiring from music, she went on to become a U.S. ambassador to the United Nations, and in 1972, she was awarded the UN Peace Prize. She received awards—a Grammy and a U.S. National Arts Medal, among others—until the end of her life, in 1993.

— FEBRUARY 28 —
1943
DETROIT RACE RIOT ERUPTS

On this day in civil rights history, the first in a series of race riots in Detroit city took place. The sad violent saga has its roots in the booming economy jumpstarted by America's entrance into World War II.

In an effort to gain workers to fill the new war factories, Detroit recruiters papered the South with promises of high wages. Blacks moved to Detroit in droves—part of the Great Migration. The city they found was not very friendly, however, and was just as segregated as the South they had just left. The Black Legion, a midwestern off-shoot of the KKK, greeted the new black populace with threats. The police practiced consistent racial profiling, harassment, and abuse of its new black citizens. Detroit's white residents resented the huge new black population. The only positive was the abundance of decent-paying jobs.

Detroit during rioting

But the city lacked the necessary infrastructure to deal with such a large influx of people. Grocery stores, gas stations, and public transportation all were strained by the massive amounts of people. There were lines everywhere, too many people, not enough services. Detroit's new citizens had money in their pockets but nothing to spend it on; wartime rationing limited the amount of food and products that people could buy.

Worst, however, was a housing shortage. At the time, blacks were excluded from public housing. White landlords charged three and four times fair market rates. Even then there wasn't enough living space. With over 200,000 African Americans migrating to Detroit by the beginning of 1943, something had to be done.

One temporary solution to the housing problem was to integrate the existing public housing at the Sojourner Truth housing project. This was met with widespread picketing from whites. On February 27, a few hundred picketers swelled into over a thousand people, some of whom were armed. A cross burned in an empty field nearby. Violence started when two blacks tried to drive through the picket line to move into their new homes. Police doused the crowd with tear gas. Black families moved into the housing project with police protection. There were no fatalities, but the violence was a shadow of the chaos to come. A few months later, in the raw heat of June, a massive riot broke out, lasting 36 hours and resulting in the deaths of 34 people.

Detroit's motto: We hope for better things.

— FEBRUARY 29 —

1940

HATTIE MCDANIEL WINS ACADEMY AWARD

On this day in civil rights history, Hattie McDaniel won an Academy Award for her supporting role of Mammy in *Gone With the Wind*. She thus became the first African American not only to win an Oscar but also to attend the ceremony as a guest instead of a servant.

African Americans had a precarious relationship with the movie industry. One of the first blockbusters, *Birth of a Nation*, portrayed Southern blacks as marauding, pillaging hordes that were fought off by brave Ku Klux Klansmen. Blackface was common in many high-profile films. Movies were immensely popular in the first half of the 20th century and played an important part in the popular consciousness of America. But black actors were consigned to play porters, servants, boxers, roustabouts, drunks, second-tier musicians, or simpletons; mostly they were part of the background scenery.

Born in Wichita, Kansas, in 1895, McDaniel moved to Hollywood in 1931. She made her screen debut the next year in *The Golden West*. She went on to act in more than 300 films, mostly reprising the same maternal Southern African American woman with an infectious laugh and a jovial demeanor. "I'd rather play a maid than be one," she was known to have said. In *Gone With the Wind*, McDaniel elevated her signature character, giving Mammy a humane dignity and resolute strength.

McDaniel enjoyed great success and was sometimes called "Hi-Hat Hattie." While the country at large was suffering during the Great Depression and its aftermath, she was making $1,000 a week as the best-known African American actress in the movie industry.

But her success got her into trouble. Black protesters harangued McDaniel for her consistent portrayals of black servitude. As the NAACP and Americans at large stepped up criticism of the "plantation" films that made McDaniel famous, her roles shrank. She shifted to radio, acting in *Amos and Andy*, and from 1947 to 1951 as the title character in her own radio show, *Beulah*.

She died of breast cancer in 1952. McDaniel willed her Oscar statuette to Howard University, but during riots on the campus in the 1960s, the statue disappeared and has never been recovered.

This day in
March

— March 1 —
1960
Alabama Students Join Sit-in Movement

On this day in civil rights history, six hundred Alabama State College* students attempted to march on the state capitol to protest the expulsion of sit-in participants; they didn't get far.

Four days earlier, on February 25, a group of Alabama State students (emulating the sit-ins that had begun a few weeks earlier in North Carolina and were now spreading rapidly across the South) entered the basement cafeteria at the state capitol, asked for service, were denied, and then walked out. This mild action led Governor John Patterson to label the students "race agitators" and demand their expulsion from the black college. Fearing a loss of state funding, the college president complied.

Civil rights activists vigorously responded. The SCLC's Fred Shuttlesworth, Ralph Abernathy, and Martin Luther King Jr. joined Bernard Lee (a student leader who later became King's primary aide) in a rally attended by 4,000 persons, the largest local rally since the Montgomery bus boycott. The students, it seemed, were now leading the teachers.

Bernard Lee and half the ASC student body held a prayer service on the steps of the capitol at the end of February. They sang "The Star Spangled Banner" and peacefully walked back to campus. Patterson was furious, and demanded more expulsions. Again, Alabama State complied: Lee and eight others were expelled. Alabama State students, enraged at the treatment, promised not to register for spring classes until their fellows were reinstated. In response, the school banned unregistered students from the cafeteria.

The subsequent student-led protest on March 1 was squelched almost before it got underway. The protesters carried placards and posters condemning Patterson and Jim Crow as they set out for the capitol. But the college, desperate to keep its funding and the jobs of its administrators and faculty, herded the students off campus, directly into the arms of the police. Thirty-five students were arrested and the student protest in Montgomery was temporarily over.

The Montgomery Improvement Association, the organization which had run the bus boycott five years earlier, refused to issue a statement of support, apparently believing the students were too brash, too wayward, and maneuvered themselves into situations that were too dangerous.

*Now Alabama State University

1955

ARREST OF CLAUDETTE COLVIN IN MONTGOMERY

On this day in civil rights history, 15-year-old Claudette Colvin was arrested for violating the segregation laws on a Montgomery, Alabama, city bus.

The dividing line between the white and black sections on Montgomery city buses was arbitrary, and drivers moved the line depending on the circumstances. Colvin was sitting in the first row of the "colored" section of a bus beside a pregnant woman, Ruth Hamilton. The other two seats on the row were empty, but all other seats on the bus were filled. When whites would have had to sit beside Colvin and Hamilton, driver Robert Cleere ordered the two blacks to stand so segregation could be maintained. Both first refused, and Cleere called police. Another black passenger subsequently gave the pregnant Hamilton his seat, leaving Colvin alone in defiance of the driver and the police.

When she continued to protest and became increasingly agitated, she was arrested and taken off to jail, kicking and screaming, where she was charged with disorderly conduct and assaulting an officer as well as violating the segregation ordinance.

Colvin was by no means the first African American charged with violating segregation on Montgomery buses. But unlike most, she pled not guilty and through her attorney, Fred D. Gray, challenged the segregation ordinances. Legal maneuvers followed between Gray and Montgomery prosecutors, and eventually all the charges against Colvin were dismissed except the one for disorderly conduct, for which she was convicted and, as a minor, placed on probation.

Gray appealed, but he no longer had any basis for challenging the constitutionality of the segregation laws, because that charge against Colvin had been dismissed. Over the following months, he and other Montgomery black leaders discussed boycotts and filing a federal lawsuit, but the unmarried Colvin subsequently became pregnant and her parents refused to let her be a plaintiff. She thus became a historical footnote.

A year later, when attorney Gray did file a federal lawsuit following the arrest of Rosa Parks, he named Colvin as one of the four plaintiffs in the case, *Browder v. Gayle*. It was the success of that lawsuit that ultimately ended segregation on Montgomery city buses—and by precedent across the nation—so Colvin did play an important role in the civil rights movement, even though her own arrest did not lead directly to immediate change. Interestingly, Colvin was a member of the NAACP youth group to which Parks was an adviser. And Parks's family had contributed to the bond to get Colvin out of jail after her arrest.

— MARCH 3 —
1965
MURDER OF JIMMIE LEE JACKSON TRIGGERS SELMA MARCH

On this day in civil rights history, the funeral of Jimmie Lee Jackson was held. His death roused activists and resulted in the Selma-to-Montgomery March.

Marion, Alabama, about 40 miles from Selma, had gained national media attention a month earlier when hundreds of black children were arrested in a voting rights march. Two weeks later, on the evening of February 18, a large group of Marion residents walked to the county jail to sing for the release of SCLC worker James Orange. The night march was risky, and the Marion police force, reinforced by cops from all over the state, attacked in force. Shooting out the streetlights, the police descended on the marchers in the anonymity of darkness. The marchers broke rank and fled. The police followed, beating stragglers.

The fleeing marchers included 80-year-old Cager Lee, whose grandson, Jimmie Lee Jackson, was inside Mack's Cafe with his mother and sister. Jackson saw troopers attacking his grandfather and ran outside to protect him, pulling him inside. Police followed them into the restaurant, swinging billy clubs indiscriminately. Jackson tried to protect his mother and was pinned down in the corner and then shot in the stomach. Jackson fled into the street, where policemen beat him viciously as he stumbled forward. He eventually fell in the street and ceased to move.

Eight days later, he died.

No one was charged with the murder, and state authorities defended the actions of the troopers on that night. On February 28, the first service for Jackson was held. A homemade banner proclaimed "Racism killed our brother." Some among the civil rights activists wanted to march with Jackson's body from Selma to Montgomery, to lay the body on the steps of the state capitol, symbolically at the feet of Governor George Wallace. Many civil rights dignitaries attended a second service for Jackson and Martin Luther King Jr. preached the memorial sermon. More than 700 people followed the hearse on a rainy, dreary day to the grave site.

Twenty-two days later, the Selma-to-Montgomery March did reach the steps of the state capitol. Jackson's senseless death had galvanized the movement, and the national outcry over violence and denial of the ballot to blacks in Alabama inspired Congress to pass the 1965 Voting Rights Act.

— MARCH 4 —

1861

HONEST ABE INAUGURATED

On this day in civil rights history, Abraham Lincoln was inaugurated the 16th President of the United States. He had retired from politics 13 years earlier after serving in the Illinois state senate with no particular distinction.

But Lincoln reentered politics in 1856, joining the new Republican Party, and two years later ran against Stephen A. Douglass for one of the U.S. Senate seats from Illinois. The seven Lincoln-Douglass debates, highlighting the increasing national divide over slavery and the Kansas-Nebraska Act, became part of the nation's political legend.

"A house divided against itself cannot stand," Lincoln said. He argued against slavery as an evil against humanity and vowed to fight against its expansion. He advocated a return to the egalitarian ideals of the Declaration of Independence, criticizing the compromises made to the slave-holding states. Lincoln lost the Senate race, but through his passionate oratory he became a leading political figure and in 1860 the Republicans nominated him for the presidency.

Republicans were the minority party and did not expect to win. But the Democrats split into factions and ran three separate candidates. The impossible happened: Lincoln was elected with a minority popular vote. His views were well known and his success was seen by North and South as heralding the eventual death of slavery. By his inauguration, seven Southern states had seceded. Lincoln condemned the action and promised to preserve the Union at all costs. On April 12, 1861, Confederates fired on Fort Sumter, South Carolina.

Lincoln acquitted himself during the Civil War with resilience, skill, and full use of his executive powers. He blockaded Southern ports and suspended the rights of Confederates and Southern agents on Northern soil. He replaced generals and bent and sometimes broke the laws to achieve victory. He wrote both the Emancipation Proclamation and the Gettysburg Address. And at war's end, he extended a peaceful hand to the conquered South, as characterized in his declaration, "With malice toward none; with charity toward all."

Lincoln's personal racial beliefs continue to be debated, and he has been criticized simultaneously for being too liberal and too conservative. But Lincoln was a powerful visionary, and his election did exactly what the South feared: ended slavery. Meanwhile, he preserved the Union.

On April 14, 1865, while attending a play, Lincoln was shot and killed by John Wilkes Booth, an actor with Confederate sympathies. Lincoln did not live to see his vision of a reconstructed South, nor did he live to see Reconstruction fail and a de facto form of slavery, Jim Crow segregation, settle in.

— MARCH 5 —

1897

AMERICAN NEGRO ACADEMY FORMED

On this day in civil rights history, the American Negro Academy was founded in Washington, D.C. It was the first scholarly enclave for black writers and thinkers and a prelude to later African American institutions.

ANA was created as a reaction to deteriorating conditions for blacks. Just one year earlier, the Supreme Court legalized the separate-but-equal doctrine of Jim Crow segregation with its ruling in *Plessy v. Ferguson*. The sharp curtailment of their political power and civil rights in the South, following the failure of Reconstruction, left blacks of all social classes in a crisis of belief. With lynchings on the rise and an apathetic federal government, African Americans and progressives across the country were deeply worried.

Alexander Crummel, 78, recognized the need for an organization attuned to the plight of African Americans—a body of black intellectuals to counter the dismal trends in American politics and letters by speaking the truth of the African American experience. "We have got to meet the minds of this country . . . It is only scientific truth, in every department, that is going to do anything for us."

Thus the American Negro Academy was formed to propagate "literature, science, and art," and for "the defense of the Negro against vicious assault." Focusing on higher education for blacks, ANA sought to create a new African American aesthetic by endorsing and supporting black writers, scientists, and artists in an international think tank that focused on both practical and academic issues.

Its all-male membership included Booker T. Washington, W. E. B. Du Bois, James Weldon Johnson, Alain Locke, and Archibald Grumke, among others.

Over the next two decades, ANA fostered many academic works including some of the first sociological studies of African Americans. Its members went on to become leaders in education, art, science, and other endeavors, including the civil rights movement.

In 1924, the ANA closed its doors. In 1969, the organization was revived as the Black Academy of Arts and Letters.

— MARCH 6 —
1820
MISSOURI COMPROMISE DEEPENS SLAVERY DIVIDE

On this day in civil rights history, the Missouri Compromise of 1820 was passed into law. The new nation rested precariously on a not so unified collection of states, separated into factions along economic, social, and moral lines.

Legal wrangling over slavery prevented new territories from becoming states, as pro- and antislavery factions refused to relinquish legislative power to the opposing side. The expansion of the country was inextricably tied to the issue.

Photo courtesy of Library of Congress

A slave auction

The agrarian South was dependent on the "free" labor of slaves and had built a corresponding social paradigm around this need. The capitalist North was flirting with a merchant economy and early forms of industrialism. These dueling political mindsets battled over their distinct visions of the future of the country. The abolitionists wanted slavery abolished completely, the slaves wanted to be free, the Whigs wanted slavery contained, and the Southern Democrats considered these state issues outside the realm of federal law (or universal morality, for that matter).

The result was a conflicted federal government unsure of what to do with its new western provinces acquired through the Louisiana Purchase. Multiple bills were proposed on how to deal with the Missouri territory, including complete prohibition of slavery. Alabama was admitted as a slave state in 1819, making the slave and free states equal in number. A proposal to admit Maine as a free state threatened to disrupt the political parity. The resulting compromise was that Missouri would be free to draft slavery into its constitution, but other territories, if and when they became states, would be free. A precedent was set: Congress could pass laws restricting the internal workings of U.S. states.

Neither side was happy with the result. The Democratic Party felt that an over-reaching Congress was violating the rights of new states. The Whigs eventually imploded over the issue of slavery and out of its rubble emerged the Republican Party.

These two sides and their corresponding arguments never fully went away. The same modes of thinking defending slavery were used to justify the segregation and oppression that led to the civil rights movement. Thus, the Missouri Compromise of 1820 was one of the first pieces of federal legislation grappling with the slavery issue that would haunt America well into the 20th century.

Meanwhile, the atrocities of slavery continued.

— MARCH 7 —
1965
BLOODY SUNDAY IN SELMA, ALABAMA

On this day in civil rights history, Alabama state troopers attacked peaceful protesters on the Edmund Pettus Bridge in Selma, Alabama. Reporters recorded the carnage, and the subsequent broadcasts of the violence shocked the country. The event would later be called "Bloody Sunday."

After the murder of Jimmie Lee Jackson in Marion, Alabama, at the hands of Alabama state troopers, civil rights leaders called for a march where Jackson's body would be carried from Selma to the steps of the capitol building in Montgomery. Jackson was buried, but the plans for the walk remained.

Hearing the news, Governor George C. Wallace dispatched state troopers to Selma to aid Dallas County Sheriff Jim Clark in dispersing the march for "public safety" reasons.

On Sunday, March 7, John Lewis of SNCC and Hosea Williams of SCLC gathered 500 marchers at Brown Chapel A.M.E. Church. The procession advanced in pairs across the bridge, where they were stopped on the other side by an army of blue-suited policemen, 50 uniformed troopers, and a deputized posse, including 15 on horseback. "This is an unlawful march," Major John Cloud pronounced. "It will not be allowed to continue. I give you two minutes to disperse and go back to your church."

Lewis and Williams decided to hold a prayer and contemplate their options. But as they knelt, the troopers charged forward, firing tear gas into the crowd and running through them on horseback, swinging nightsticks at the fleeing protesters. The marchers fled back over the bridge, pursued by mounted police who hollered obscenities and war yelps as they beat the marchers back across town to Brown Chapel. Sixty-five were treated in local hospitals for injuries.

The police victory, however, turned into defeat when the footage was aired on national news networks that evening. The footage of the savage attack on innocent protesters brought forth a flurry of outrage and support. Thousands of activists traveled to Selma to resume the march.

— MARCH 8 —

1972

JESSE JACKSON DEVELOPS PUSH

On this day in civil rights history, Jesse Jackson, after leaving the SCLC, was busily developing his organization PUSH (People United to Save Humanity).

Born October 8, 1941, in Greenville, South Carolina, Jackson was raised by his single mother, who was 18 years old when she gave birth to him. In high school he showed athletic and academic aptitude and in 1959, he attended the University of Illinois on an athletic scholarship. He transferred to North Carolina A&T before he finished his first year. In North Carolina, Jackson joined CORE and became a student leader of protests and marches. It was the beginning of a long civil rights career. After graduating, he enrolled at the Chicago Theological Seminary.

Photo courtesy of Library of Congress

Jackson and PUSH activists

In 1965, Jackson traveled to Alabama to take part in the Selma-to-Montgomery March, where he met Martin Luther King Jr. and joined the SCLC. One year later, the SCLC began the Chicago campaign, where Jackson's local contacts were put to good use. He headed Operation Breadbasket, the SCLC program that utilized boycotts and selective purchasing to leverage white business owners to hire more black workers.

He was in Memphis with King when King was assassinated, and in King's absence appeared to be one of the SCLC's prominent leaders. But others resented his ambition and publicity-seeking, and he feuded with Ralph Abernathy, who had succceeded King as SCLC president.

In 1971, Jackson resigned from the SCLC and formed PUSH. He traveled and lectured widely, often leading audiences of black youths in chanting "I Am Somebody," which became Jackson's catchphrase.

In 1984, he formed the Rainbow Coalition—an umbrella group representing poor whites, women, and minority groups—and mounted a major campaign for the Democratic presidential nomination. He did surprisingly well, coming in third after Gary Hart and the eventual nominee, Walter Mondale. Four years later, he almost won the Democratic nomination, finally losing to Michael Dukakis. Jackson had become perhaps the nation's most prominent black leader and a political power player.

Jackson remains controversial and contentious. He is scrappy and confrontational and never far from the limelight. His supporters say he remains a major civil rights figure. Critics argue that he is in love with his own celebrity and is self-serving and hypocritical, far removed from his activist days of old.

— MARCH 9 —

1965

'TURNAROUND TUESDAY' IN SELMA MARCH NEGOTIATIONS

On this day in civil rights history, a second Selma-to-Montgomery march began, this time ending without violence but being labeled "Turnaround Tuesday" as a condemnation of what many activists saw as a failure of civil rights leaders to respond to earlier events.

After "Bloody Sunday" took place March 7, Martin Luther King Jr. and many other civil rights leaders and activists returned to Selma, calling for the blocked march to be resumed. In Montgomery, U.S. District Judge Frank M. Johnson, well-known for his decisions favoring civil rights, issued an order blocking further marching pending a hearing.

King and the other leaders argued over the course of action. The march had already been announced and the protesters had momentum thanks to the March 7 attack by Sheriff Clark and his posse. But King had yet to defy a federal court order, as he and the movement generally saw the federal government as their greatest protector.

King addresses Selma marchers

A compromise was worked out. King led marchers to the same spot where Lewis and the others had been attacked, and then they all knelt in prayer. Meanwhile, the troopers who were waiting in the same spot opened their ranks, taunting the marchers with an open path. But King turned back and led the protesters back across the bridge to safety. Many activists felt betrayed by King's actions, including many within SNCC.

In response, a group of Tuskegee Institute students staged a sit-in on the capitol steps, protesting both segregation and King's inaction. The students stayed in the streets until rain forced them inside.

But the day's events were not over. That evening, James Reeb, a white minister from Boston who had responded to the March 7 news coverage and had traveled to Selma to take part in the march, was attacked after eating dinner at an integrated restaurant. Walking past the Silver Moon Café, Reeb was accosted by four white males who clubbed him in the head with a pipe. He was transported to a hospital but fell into a coma and died two days later. His death shocked the nation further and was one of the catalysts to President Lyndon B. Johnson shepherding the Voting Rights Act through Congress.

— MARCH 10 —
1969
JAMES EARL RAY SENTENCED TO PRISON

On this day in civil rights history, James Earl Ray was sentenced to 99 years in prison for the murder of Martin Luther King Jr.

Ray was captured in London's Heathrow Airport one month after King's death. Extradited back to Tennessee, Ray pleaded guilty to the shooting and murder on March 10, his birthday.

But three days later he recanted, claiming his brother and a mysterious Raoul were involved. Ray proceeded to spend the rest of his life declaring his innocence, trying to retract his guilty plea.

In 1977, Ray testified before the House Select Committee on Assassinations, once again denying any participation in King's murder. A short time later, he escaped from prison, only to be recaptured.

His protestations eventually drew the attention of King's family, who in the late 1990s mounted a campaign to free Ray from prison. The odd relationship between King's family and Ray culminated in the King family providing legal counsel. King's family believed his death was the result of a conspiracy and felt a new trial might reveal those responsible. But time was running out; Ray was dying of health complications brought on by a blood transfusion received almost a decade earlier. If he died before new evidence could exonerate him and begin a new trial, the case would in all likelihood remain closed.

Many conspiracy theories abound about the assassination. King's hard stance against the Vietnam War and his slide toward socialism had earned him many enemies in high places, including J. Edgar Hoover, who labeled King one of the most dangerous men in America. A complicated network of possible players—gangsters, covert government operatives, and street-level thugs—has been proposed. (Similar allegations exist in all of the 1960s assassinations: Malcolm X, King, and both Kennedys.) Some evidence of a conspiracy, however, emerged in the 1993 confession of a man named Loyd Jowers.

Ray died at age 70 in April 1998, and the chances of a new trial and new official inquiries died with him. Further details of Jowers, the FBI, and Raoul all remain a mystery.

Did James Earl Ray kill Martin Luther King Jr.? If yes, did he act alone? If no, why did he profess his guilt in the first place? How did he finance his travels? Many still wait for answers.

— March 11 —
1965
Unitarian Minister Clubbed to Death in Selma

On this day in civil rights history, white Unitarian minister James Reeb died after a beating by segregationists in Selma, Alabama.

After the aborted second Selma-to-Montgomery march on March 9, 1965, a great debate arose within the civil rights community. Some felt Martin Luther King Jr. had betrayed the cause by not going forward on March 9. Others felt that the march would never happen now that the federal court had intervened. Many activists left Selma that evening, and Reeb had his bags packed to leave.

But at the last minute he decided to stay to see what would happen. It proved a fatal decision. Reeb was attacked on the street near a Selma cafe, clubbed in the head with a pipe during an attack by four whites. The fatal blow fractured his skull, causing a blood clot and brain damage. A black doctor decided Reeb needed better medical attention then he could get in Selma and he was transported to Birmingham. He died in the early morning, shortly after his wife and father arrived.

Reeb's death provided further evidence to a watching nation that the South had lost its way, that there was no moral order below the Mason-Dixon Line. President Lyndon Johnson immediately called for passage of a Voting Rights Act to secure by federal law the rights that the Selma demonstrators had been seeking for years. "Bloody Sunday" and Reeb's death focused the attention of the nation on the plight of Southern blacks.

Of course, many African American activists had been killed in the movement— Sammy Younge, Medgar Evers, and a few weeks earlier, Jimmie Lee Jackson, to name just a few examples. It took the death of Reeb, a white minister, to intensify national support for the movement. The irony was not lost on the civil rights community, that it took a white man's death to usher in federal protection.

Four days later, Martin Luther King Jr. gave the eulogy at Reeb's funeral. "Who killed James Reeb?" he asked. "He was murdered by the irresponsibility of every politician who has moved down the path of demagoguery, who has fed his constituents the stale bread of hatred and the spoiled meat of racism."

Three men were indicted in mid-April for the murder of Reeb, but they were acquitted by all-white Alabama juries.

— MARCH 12 —
1956
'SOUTHERN MANIFESTO' PROTESTS BROWN DECISION

On this day in civil rights history, 19 U.S. senators and 77 representatives released the Southern Manifesto in response to the growing pressure for school integration. A short, eloquent declaration, the Manifesto laid out the South's reasons for adhering to segregation and the arguments why the federal government should leave well enough alone. It advocated states' rights, a literal reading of the Constitution, and separation of the races. Representatives from all the former Confederate states signed the document.

Strom Thurmond prepares draft

The right for a local community to govern the education of its young "is founded on elemental humanity and commonsense, for parents should not be deprived by Government of the right to direct the lives and education of their own children," the statement said, and the Supreme Court "undertook to exercise their naked judicial power and substituted their personal political and social ideas for the established law of the land."

The Brown decision, according to the Manifesto, was "destroying the amicable relations between the white and Negro races that have been created through 90 years of patient effort by the good people of both races. It has planted hatred and suspicion where there has been heretofore friendship and understanding.

"We pledge ourselves to use all lawful means to bring about a reversal of this decision which is contrary to the Constitution and to prevent the use of force in its implementation.

"In this trying period, as we all seek to right this wrong, we appeal to our people not to be provoked by the agitators and troublemakers invading our States and to scrupulously refrain from disorder and lawless acts."

The Manifesto, an artifact of civil rights history, shows the Southern mindset at work: rule of law based on tradition and a conservative interpretation of the Constitution, hypocrisy predicated on lies and self-deception, and a zealous adherence to self-determination. The document clearly meant: We will not give up.

The white establishment of the day was serving notice that it would defend institutionalized racism as a constitutional right at any cost, and would employ legal and illegal means to do so.

This entrenchment prolonged the inevitable collapse of segregation by a decade and allowed some angry white Southerners to justify violence and murder.

— MARCH 13 —
1920
DYER LOBBIES FOR ANTI-LYNCHING BILL

On this day in civil rights history, groups continued to rally for and against the proposed anti-lynching bill authored by Leonidas Dyer.

Dyer was born in Warren County, Missouri, in 1871. He practiced law in St. Louis and served in the Spanish-American War before being elected to Congress as a Republican.

The issue most important to Dyer was lynching. A 20th-century William Wilberforce, Dyer made several attempts to pass federal antilynching laws. Lynchings increased after World War I and Dyer redoubled his efforts.

In 1919, he proposed the Dyer antilynching bill. The bill would have made lynching a felony. It also would have sanctioned any state or local official who failed to try to prevent a lynching, or any official who failed to prosecute a lynching. A five-year minimum prison sentence would have been imposed on anyone who participated in a lynching. Finally, the bill would have allowed victims' families to receive reparations from the county that allowed a lynching to take place.

It was a strong bill that would have forced state officials to take action against mob violence, while providing victims with legal recourse.

The NAACP rallied behind the measure. Following in the footsteps of Ida Wells-Barnett, Mary Talbert formed the Anti-Lynching Crusaders and began touring the country in support of the bill. President Warren G. Harding publicly supported the bill, as did Republicans in both houses. Prominent black businesswoman Madame C. J. Walker gave a sizeable donation to the antilynching cause. The proposed bill unified many disparate black figures in support of it and was a focal point of black activism in 1920 and 1921.

The bill eventually passed the House of Representatives, 230-119, in January 1922. Only eight Democrats voted in favor of the measure.

But a filibuster by Southern Democrats in the Senate killed the bill after 21 days of debate. Dyer was crushed. In 1933, he was defeated when he tried to get re-elected. The NAACP pushed for anti-lynching bills as late as the 1950s, but the Dyer bill was as close as any measure ever came to success.

Dyer died in 1957, just as the slumbering conscience of the United States was beginning to awaken. In 2005, the U.S. Senate apologized for its past inaction against lynchings.

— MARCH 14 —

1794

COTTON GIN PATENT LEADS TO INCREASED SLAVERY

On this day in civil rights history, Eli Whitney patented the cotton gin.

The device automated the removal of seeds from cotton fiber, and thus made cotton production more profitable. As a consequence, the demand for slave labor significantly increased in the South, leading to the development of ever larger plantations and the spread of these plantations, along with slaves and slave trading, into new territories.

The fledgling federal government fought to contain slavery. Before the United States even became a country, its founding fathers argued bitterly over the issue, the antislavery faction only compromising when the future of the nation was at risk.

Photo courtesy of Library of Congress

Slave and cotton gin

The Northwest Ordinance of 1787 restricted slavery in new territories west of the Mississippi. And in 1808, importation of new slaves into the United States was declared illegal. The interior slave trade was by this point self-sustaining, however, and slave trading continued between the large plantations in the Carolinas, Virginia, and elsewhere across the South.

Whitney's cotton gin increased productivity of U.S. agriculture. But it had a terrible unintended consequence on Africans worldwide. Cotton output increased and profits went up. Plantations had more money to spend on new slaves and more land. As they expanded, the Southern economy became almost totally dependent on the plantation system, fueled by the blood and sweat of uprooted Africans. The Southern slave trade claimed millions of lives through back-breaking work, severe punishments, and dismal living conditions. The descendants of those poor, miserable souls, sacrificed to a backwards, agrarian mindset, would eventually rise up in a peaceful revolt now called the civil rights movement.

Whitney no doubt had none of this in mind when he patented his invention. He was an inventor prone to the manufacturing mindset; he simply wanted to mechanize menial tasks to make America more economical and earn some money along the way. Whitney proved to be a man of the future. Others would follow in his footsteps, including Henry Ford, resulting in mass manufacturing and hyper-capitalism on a global scale.

Interestingly, Whitney's design proved too easy to replicate, and his cotton gin business went bankrupt in 1797.

— MARCH 15 —
1965
DEPUTIES EVIDENTLY MISS PRESIDENT'S POINT

On this day in civil rights history, as behind the scenes negotiations continued over the pending Selma-to-Montgomery March, sheriff's deputies in Montgomery attacked a group of SNCC activists who were protesting at the state capitol. The assault was vicious, as the mounted officers clubbed the protesters with bullwhips and canes.

Just the night before, Lyndon Johnson had delivered to Congress a hopeful message that was nationally televised. Disturbed by "Bloody Sunday" in Selma, Johnson confronted the South. "It is wrong—deadly wrong," he said, "to deny any of your fellow Americans the right to vote." After praising the protesters, he ended with, "We shall overcome America's crippling legacy of bigotry and injustice." He then called on both houses to approve the Voting Rights Bill. It was the most powerful endorsement the civil rights movement had received. SCLC and NAACP staffers, the older administrators of the movement who had called for a temporary moratorium on demonstrations, were enthusiastic. But the young activists within SNCC were cynical about the president's promises; they felt that nothing had changed and, highlighting the tensions and philosophical differences within the movement, went ahead with a demonstration on the capitol steps to protest the Selma abuses and Alabama's segregationist stance.

The violent reality of the South reasserted itself, confirming SNCC's fears. As club-wielding mounted deputies and police dispersed the SNCC students, a white mob began to join in the attack. The protesters fled while reporters captured the whole thing on film. It was "Bloody Sunday" all over again. Outrage was again expressed in much of the country.

King, meanwhile, felt stretched; he was waiting on a sympathetic federal judge to allow the Selma march to proceed and to order protection. At the same time, he was fund-raising around the country.

The multiple pressures disrupted the unity that top-level civil rights leaders were trying to preserve. The more radical activists, including much of SNCC, advocated more protests, more direct action, the jamming of of the streets with righteous indignation, while more conservative activists within the NAACP and SCLC wanted to see how the new federal role would play out. And some, like King, may have simply wanted to rest. The movement seemed poised either for success or collapse.

Meanwhile, after the attack on the SNCC demonstrators, King returned to Montgomery to attend their rally planned for the next day at Beulah Baptist Church.

— MARCH 16 —

1965

FORMAN SPEECH PORTENDS SPLIT WITHIN THE MOVEMENT

On this day in civil rights history, SNCC leader James Forman addressed an angry crowd at Beulah Baptist Church, after the brutal beating of SNCC protesters in downtown Montgomery, Alabama, the day before. Forman's militant outrage revealed a deep-rooted disillusionment within the movement; it would lead to the further radicalization of SNCC and the eventual Black Power movement, which, arguably, split the civil rights movement into opposing camps and damaged the fragile coalition that had worked together for so long.

SNCC had reason to be angry. Besides being assaulted by law enforcement officers and a white mob the night before, they had also been assailed by SCLC's workers. The two groups were often at odds. The older SCLC staffers felt SNCC sometimes did more harm than good; the younger SNCC workers felt SCLC was elitist, conservative, bourgeois, and opportunist, sweeping in for a few days to steal the limelight, then leaving the community-building to others. SCLC was autocratic; SNCC was community-minded. SCLC operated in a cult of personality; SNCC worked behind the scenes to empower local people.

SCLC staffer James Bevel castigated Forman for leading a demonstration in Montgomery that took attention away from Selma. Then the Dexter Avenue Baptist Church, King's old pulpit, refused to let SNCC use the church as a headquarters. Worst of all, SCLC had taken over the action in Selma that was largely the result of two years of SNCC work. It was clear that the two organizations would not be able to work together much longer.

SNCC was tired of waiting and felt that baby steps toward peace and harmony were coming at too high a price. The segregationists seemed bolder than ever, as evidenced by the attacks in broad daylight of Bloody Sunday on March 7 and then the rout of the March 15 protest in Montgomery.

King attended the SNCC rally after failing to mediate the situation. Forman took to the podium. "If we can't sit at the table of democracy," he yelled, "we'll knock the fucking legs off." King spoke immediately afterwards, attempting to ameliorate Forman's incendiary speech.

Montgomery County Sheriff Mac Sim Butler later apologized for the actions of his deputies, but by that point the media had moved on to the events unfolding in Selma.

— MARCH 17 —
1912
ACTIVIST BAYARD RUSTIN BORN

On this day in civil rights history, Bayard Rustin was born to a Quaker household. One of the primary civil rights movers of the 20th century, Rustin is relatively unknown despite his enormous contributions.

Rustin was an extraordinary activist, organizer, and thinker. After a stint in the American Communist Party (which would haunt him for the rest of his life), he became a proponent of democratic socialism. In the 1940s, Rustin helped form the Congress for Racial Equality, and was one of the primary organizers of the Journey of Reconciliation, the first freedom rides. He also helped influence President Harry Truman to desegregate the armed forces.

He came to Montgomery in 1956 and coached Martin Luther King Jr. on the strategy of nonviolent resistance as the Montgomery Improvement Association planned the Montgomery bus boycott. Rustin also played an important role in the formation of the Southern Christian Leadership Conference.

Photo courtesy of Library of Congress

Bayard Rustin

He was not afraid to participate in the events he organized. In 1942, Tennessee police savagely beat him after he refused to give up his seat on a segregated bus. And he spent time on a chain gang for his participation in a freedom ride.

One of his most important contributions was in the 1963 March on Washington. Although technically led by A. Philip Randolph and made famous by King's "I have a dream" speech, the march's success was in large measure due to Rustin's work.

So why is he so neglected? The answer lies at the heart of intolerance that crossed color lines. Bayard Rustin was gay. The FBI used Rustin's former communist ties and sexual preferences to discredit him and the movement. Senator Strom Thurmond publicly attacked Rustin before the March on Washington, calling him a "communist and homosexual." Rustin was publicly shunted aside because civil rights leaders feared negative publicity. The success of the March on Washington was credited to Wilkins, Randolph, and King and their corresponding organizations.

Rustin never lost hope, however, and continued to work for the causes he believed in. He spent the 1970s and 1980s working for gay causes. He died in 1987, obscured by his lifestyle and politics, relatively unnoted in the history of the movement of which he played such an essential part.

On this day in civil rights history, firebrand activist Fred Shuttlesworth was born in Mugler, Alabama. He became a minister and NAACP member in Birmingham in the early 1950s and was the primary architect for the Birmingham campaign of the 1960s.

Although an essential leader, Shuttlesworth had a hard-edged confrontational fearlessness and unwillingness to compromise that made it easy for his enemies to hate him and sometimes hard for his friends to love him. He had no use for anyone not working full bore to end the evils of segregation; this sometimes included other civil rights leaders.

Fred Shuttlesworth

In 1956, the state of Alabama outlawed the NAACP. Shuttlesworth, the Alabama NAACP membership chairman, formed the Alabama Christian Movement for Human Rights as a response. He then began organizing campaigns to desegregate Birmingham, which at the time was in the grip of segregationist police commissioner Eugene "Bull" Connor.

In 1957, Shuttlesworth was one of the organizers of the Southern Christian Leadership Conference. That same year, he almost died after being savagely beaten with chains as he tried to enroll his daughter in an all-white school.

Following a less than successful SCLC campaign in Albany, Georgia, from 1962 to 1963, Shuttlesworth asked Martin Luther King Jr. to help desegregate Birmingham, arguably the most violently segregated city in the country. Nicknamed "Bombingham" due to the frequent Klan-related dynamite attacks on blacks, Birmingham had been the site of a mob attack during the 1961 freedom rides, the site of an attack on entertainer Nat King Cole, and the site of the castration of a black man, to name just a few examples.

The carefully arranged campaign to change Birmingham would be called "Project C." It began on April 3, 1963, with a series of marches, sit-ins, and direct actions involving thousands of protesters. During one of the marches, Shuttlesworth was hit by a blast of water and smashed into a building. Thanks to Connor's dogs and fire hoses, all captured on news cameras and broadcast across the country, Project C was a success.

Time and time again Shuttlesworth placed himself in harm's way, facing down angry white mobs and armed police with equal aplomb. This peerless personality at one point declared, "I will either kill segregation or be killed by it." As of 2005, Shuttlesworth still lived while segregation was, officially at least, dead.

— MARCH 19 —
1966
BLACK PLAYERS WIN NCAA BASKETBALL TITLE

On this day in civil rights history, in one of the most momentous events in sports, Texas Western College, playing with an almost all-black team, defeated the all-white Kentucky Wildcats to win the NCAA championship.

The game had immediate consequences. Blacks across the country cheered for the underdogs, and the game hastened the end of segregation in college sports. Similar to the Joe Louis–Max Schmeling fights decades earlier, the matchup was seen as symbolic of the prevailing social order.

The University of Kentucky was the favorite to win. The legendary Adolph Rupp, one of the most successful college basketball coaches of all time, coached Kentucky. The team boasted an all-white roster of highly touted players. Rupp, probably misrepresented as a racist, was nonetheless reluctant to recruit black players.

The 1966 champions

Texas Western (now the University of Texas at El Paso) had a strong team, and coach Don Haskins had recruited widely among African American athletes. Outside the South, most intercollegiate programs had integrated during the 1950s. But segregation was still the rule below the Mason-Dixon Line. Many traditionally white schools in the powerhouse Southeastern and Atlantic Coast athletic conferences even refused to play colleges that weren't racially segregated.

But by reaching the finals of the NCAA basketball tournament, Texas Western had forced the issue. The two teams faced off in the NCAA finals in College Park, Maryland. Texas Western went ahead early and never relinquished their lead. While the country watched on national television, Haskins won the title, playing only black players. Haskins later said he was not making a social statement but that he merely used the best players he had. Nonetheless, he received thousands of hate letters and dozens of death threats after the game.

Black success in sports has often produced mixed social effects. African Americans gained recognition through the victories of Jackie Robinson, Joe Louis, and the Texas Western basketball team. But integrating sports did not eliminate the social oppression of Jim Crow segregation.

A film, *Glory Road*, based on the 1966 events, was to be released in 2006.

— MARCH 20 —

1932

FREE SOUTHERN THEATER FOUNDER TOM DENT BORN

On this day in civil rights history, Tom Dent was born in New Orleans, Louisiana.

Dent's father was president of Dillard University and Dent was raised in an environment of black intelligentsia. In 1952, Dent graduated with a degree in Political Science from Morehouse University. He eventually earned a PhD, served two years in the military, and ended up in Harlem, working as a reporter. While in Harlem, he also worked with the NAACP Legal Defense Fund, where he met and worked with Thurgood Marshall. In 1962, Dent with a few other writers formed the Umbra Writer's Workshop, the major black writers' workshop of New York City.

Dent felt the call of the South, however, and returned to his hometown of New Orleans in 1965, where he established the Free Southern Theater (FST), along with John O'Neil and Gilbert Moss. FST was a community-based theater project, designed to inspire the black and working-class peoples of the South to overcome their surroundings. The FST portrayed the brutal oppression of the segregationists, the dignity of the oppressed, and the vitality of the civil rights movement. It was an activist theater, inspired by the plays of Bertold Brecht and the heroism of the civil rights workers risking their lives across the Deep South. FST's example inspired many African American community-based theater troupes across the country.

While in New Orleans, Dent also taught at a local college and edited *The Black River Journal* and *Callaloo*, which he also founded. Throughout, Dent wrote plays, including *Ritual Murder* and *Negro Study No. 34A,* and poems.

In 1978, Dent began compiling oral histories of the Mississippi civil rights movement. He returned to this information-gathering project in the 1990s, interviewing local participants in the movement from North Carolina to Mississippi, resulting in the publication of *Southern Journey* in 1996. This return to the movement's essential but mostly unknown activists revealed how much had been accomplished, and how much remained undone. After years as a playwright, poet, and activist, Dent's greatest contribution would be as one of the movement's biographers.

On June 6, 1998, Dent died of complications from a heart attack at Charity Hospital in New Orleans. He was 67.

— MARCH 21 —
1965
FINAL SELMA-TO-MONTGOMERY MARCH BEGINS

On this day in civil rights history, the final Selma-to-Montgomery march began. Unlike "Bloody Sunday" and "Turnaround Tuesday," the marchers would walk all the way to the state capitol.

Legal wrangling had delayed the march. A federal injunction against the protest stayed in effect while U.S. District Judge Frank Johnson listened to arguments for and against the right to march. Sensitive to the movement's precarious relationship with the federal government and not wanting to alienate one of the few Southern judges who had been sympathetic to civil rights, King agreed to wait on the court's opinion. Johnson ruled in the protesters' favor: "The law is clear that the right to petition one's government for the redress of grievances may be exercised in large groups . . . the extent of the right to assemble . . . should be commensurate with the enormity of the wrongs . . . In this case, the wrongs are enormous."

Marchers on their way to Montgomery

The march was back on, this time with the legal support of the federal government. While the march planners worked on logistics, Alabama national guardsmen were federalized to protect the event.

Two weeks after Bloody Sunday and 10 days after the death of James Reeb, roughly 3,000 marchers, led by King, John Lewis, and other SCLC and SNCC activists, left Selma on their 50-mile walk through the heart of Dixie. They walked 12 miles a day, sleeping in bedrolls and makeshift tents at campsites along the highway at night. Despite early rain and cool temperatures, the mood was festive. Campfires, singing, and dancing marked the evenings.

The cavalcade reached Montgomery on March 24, stopping just short of downtown at a Catholic church-school-hospital complex serving Montgomery's black community. That evening, dozens of stars, including Sammy Davis Jr.; Peter, Paul, and Mary; Tony Bennett; and Harry Belafonte gave a concert for the marchers.

The next day, the protesters' numbers swelled to 25,000 people for the five-mile final leg of the trip. A rally was held at the capitol steps, with King delivering his powerful "How long, not long" speech: "We are still on the move to the land of freedom. How long will it take? However difficult the moment, however frustrating the hour, it will not be long." It was a pivotal event in the civil rights movement.

That evening, white marcher Viola Liuzzo was murdered.

— MARCH 22 —
1988
CIVIL RIGHTS RESTORATION ACT PASSED

On this day in civil rights history, over President Ronald Reagan's veto, Congress passed the Civil Rights Restoration Act, which expanded the reach of nondiscrimination laws within private educational institutions receiving federal funds. The Act essentially made illegal any discriminatory behavior in any entity receiving any federal money.

The 1980s were disappointing years for civil rights. With Ronald Reagan in the White House, and an emphasis on free-market principles combined with Cold War military spending, efforts toward a more progressive economic system were put aside. The American public was said to be weary of civil rights. Dozens of federal "Great Society" programs were cut, and a "me first" attitude prevailed.

The resulting shift in social values proved disastrous for the movement. The community-minded, egalitarian, and progressive spirit of the 1960s seemed to be gone with the wind. Many of the leading civil rights organizations had either gone radical or mainstream, and from either place were unwilling or unable to change the status quo.

The middle class expanded as more African Americans became doctors, lawyers, executives, and politicians, but poor blacks remained in dire straits, suffering from disproportionate illiteracy, dropout, and imprisonment rates. The "war on drugs" ravaged black communities, swelling U.S. prisons with new black inmates. Unfair tax policies left highly unequal schools; many of the nation's cities fell into disrepair.

Reagan also cut welfare programs and attacked affirmative action. Cutbacks in both taxes and services on the one hand, with increasing military spending on the other, left many Americans disillusioned. The federal government, it seemed, had turned its back on minority rights. At the beginning of the decade, the Klan even had a resurgence in membership.

The 1984 case of *Grove City v. Bell* centered on gender rather than racial rights, as the U.S. Supreme Court ruled in a Title IX case that an education institution could discriminate against female athletes if the specific program at issue did not receive federal funds. While crippling Title IX enforcement for girls' programs, the ruling had serious implications for the rights of all minorities.

Thus, Congress determined to override the ruling, which it did with the 1988 Civil Rights Restoration Act. The Act states that "... an institution which receives federal financial assistance is prohibited from discriminating on the basis of race, color, national origin, religion, sex, disability or age in a program or activity which does not directly benefit from such assistance."

Despite efforts to dismantle them, affirmative action and welfare survived the Reagan, George H. W. Bush, and Clinton administrations.

— MARCH 23 —

1916

MARCUS GARVEY COMES TO AMERICA

On this day in civil rights history, controversial Renaissance man Marcus Garvey first visited America, as part of a lecture tour encouraged by Booker T. Washington.

Born in 1887 in Jamaica, Garvey was raised to love books; one of his favorites was Booker T. Washington's *Up from Slavery*. In 1910, Garvey traveled across the Caribbean and Central America. In each country he visited, he was struck by the harsh conditions for blacks and the widespread discrimination.

He returned to Jamaica in 1914, convinced that salvation for black people lay in an international organization, and formed the Universal Negro Improvement Association and African Communities League (UNIA). In just a few years it would become the largest black organization up to that point.

By 1920, Garvey had moved his UNIA base of operations to Harlem and had 20,000 members. Garvey and the UNIA opened black grocery stores, restaurants, and other businesses. He took to wearing elaborate uniforms and developed a messiah complex. He grew to despise W. E. B. Du Bois, who reciprocated the feeling.

In 1919, UNIA launched the Black Star Line, which was intended to use steamships to transport African Americans to Liberia, where Garvey planned to purchase land and start a new country. The Black Star Line bought a ship and dubbed it the *Frederick Douglass*. But the shipping operation was beset with internal problems, including corruption, inefficiency, and government infiltration (led by a young J. Edgar Hoover). Within three years, the quixotic "back to Africa" movement was over and the Black Star Line had closed.

Garvey was charged by the U.S. government with mail fraud and convicted. In 1925, he was imcarcerated in an Atlanta federal prison. Two years later he was paroled and deported to Jamaica, where huge crowds welcomed him. Persecution by the United States had made him an international hero.

Garvey turned toward a philosophy of racial purity in the mid-1920s, leading to collusion with the KKK to organize a black separatist state.

In 1928, Garvey released a "Petition of the Negro Race" to the League of Nations; it was ignored. In 1935, Garvey left Jamaica for London, never to return.

He died June 10, 1940.

— MARCH 24 —
1912
DOROTHY HEIGHT BORN

On this day in civil rights history, Dorothy Height was born.

Raised by parents who moved north during the Great Migration, Height was raised in a relatively stable environment, aware of the racial inequalities but safe from the harshness of the violently segregated South. She moved to New York for college and met many influential artists, poets, and musicians during the Harlem Renaissance. These friendships would blossom over the years.

Height graduated with a master's degree in psychology in the early 1930s and became a caseworker for the New York welfare department. But she became a civil rights advocate when she joined the National Council of Negro Women in 1937, where she met both Eleanor Roosevelt and Mary McLeod Bethune, who told her, "The freedom gates are half ajar. We must pry them fully open." Under the tutelage of these two strong, enterprising women, Height became indispensable to the Council, of which she later served as president for more than four decades, and to the larger civil rights movement, where she worked as an advocate, organizer, and adviser.

During the 1940s, 1950s, and 1960s, Height worked behind the scenes, meeting with such civil rights luminaries as W. E. B. Du Bois, Roy Wilkins, James Farmer, Martin Luther King Jr. and Malcolm X. Her friends and acquaintances were a who's who of the movement.

Highlighting her prominence in the various civil rights organizations, Height was one of the few women on stage during the 1963 March on Washington. She was an adviser to Presidents Eisenhower and Kennedy, who appointed her to the women's commission chaired by her mentor, Eleanor Roosevelt.

Like many African American women who were essential to the movement, Height has been somewhat neglected by popular history. The quiet, refined, resolved, and effective Height, however, does not seem to care.

In 2003, Height published *Open Wide the Freedom Gates*, her memoir of more than 60 years in the movement.

— MARCH 25 —

1965

VIOLA LIUZZO MURDERED BY KKK IN ALABAMA

On this day in civil rights history, the Selma-to-Montgomery March ended at the capitol steps in Montgomery, Alabama. But as the protesters departed in cheerful hopefulness, four KKK members ran white activist Viola Liuzzo off the road and killed her.

At the end of the historic march, the thousands of marchers in Montgomery needed to be transported back to Selma and elsewhere. A string of private vehicles began to carpool people back and forth. Liuzzo volunteered her car and joined the effort.

A Detroit resident, Liuzzo had been outraged by the "Bloody Sunday" television images and by the death of James Reeb and decided to drive to Selma to take part. After a harried three-day trip, she reached Alabama just in time to march from Selma to Montgomery and, with thousands of others, celebrated when the proceedings went off without a hitch.

National guardsmen had protected the marchers on the walk to Montgomery, but with the march over, the troops disappeared. Liuzzo and an activist named Leroy Moton took a final carload to Selma in the late evening. Liuzzo offered to give Moton a ride to the Montgomery airport and he accepted. On the way, a car pulled alongside and one of the four men inside shot her through the window of her vehicle, killing her instantly. Her car rolled harmlessly into a ditch. Moton was not injured.

Four members of the United Klans of America were quickly arrested. One, Gary Thomas Rowe, it turned out, was an FBI informant. He testified against Collie Wilkins, William Eaton, and Eugene Thomas, but all were acquitted by an all-white jury in Lowndes County. The U.S. Justice Department then prosecuted the men for violating Liuzzo's civil rights and they were convicted and sentenced to ten years in federal prison.

A memorial service was held for Liuzzo in Selma. And speaking in San Francisco a few days later, Martin Luther King Jr. said: "If physical death is the price some must pay to save us and our white brothers from eternal death of the spirit, then no sacrifice could be more redemptive."

Liuzzo's death revealed the moral vacuity of the segregationists. Along with the deaths of James Reeb and Jimmie Lee Jackson, whites and blacks across the country were faced with a terrible truth: despite all the gains made, the segregationists—the Klan, the White Citizen's Council, and their ilk—would not quickly disappear. But the martyrs deaths did spur President Lyndon Johnson to pass the Voting Rights Act.

On this day in civil rights history, Martin Luther King Jr. and Malcolm X met for the first and only time, in a brief, chance encounter in Washington, D.C.

During the early 1960s, each had criticized the other's point of view. King held Malcolm's overall strategy to be dangerous and counterproductive, while Malcolm thought King was naïve and misguided. But each held the other in high esteem. Malcolm repeatedly invited King to speak and debate with him. King always declined.

Photo courtesy of Library of Congress

Martin Luther King Jr. and Malcolm X

Despite his criticism of King, Malcolm recognized that they were part of the same vast struggle against exploitation and racism. In fact, when King opened a campaign in St. Augustine, Florida, Malcolm offered assistance in forming self-defense groups that would fight back against the Klan; King refused. When King was jailed in Selma in 1965, Malcolm traveled to Selma to give speeches in support of King. When he met with Coretta Scott King, he once again offered help. "I want Dr. King to know," he told her, "that I didn't come to Selma to make his job difficult. I really did come thinking I could make it easier. If the white people realize what the alternative is, perhaps they will be more willing to hear Dr. King."

Popular history has presented these two men as representative of the two major factions of the movement, a view which simplifies two complex men. For as time passed, King proved to be more radical than it first appeared, while Malcolm was softening when he was shot down in February 1965.

Yet the two seem inextricably linked in the popular consciousness. Malcolm was from the North, King was from the South. Malcolm represented the city, while King fought for the rights of the rural poor. Both men were dynamic speakers and intellectuals.

And both, sadly, were assassinated at the age of 39.

No one knows exactly what words were exchanged between the two men, but the exchange was amiable, if brief.

— MARCH 27 —
1960
UNITA BLACKWELL ROSE FROM SHARECROPPER TO MAYOR

On this day in civil rights history, Unita Blackwell worked as a sharecropper, snared in the oppressive cycle of Southern rural poverty. She would soon escape the hard farm life through her involvement in the civil rights movement.

Born in Lula, Mississippi, on March 18, 1933, to sharecropping parents, Blackwell grew up picking cotton. "The day I was born, I was born black," she later said. To attend school, she had to cross state lines into Arkansas. She worked as a sharecropper until she was an adult.

In 1964, a SNCC worker spoke at Blackwell's church. Invigorated by SNCC's Freedom Summer organizing, Blackwell became a field worker for the group. "I knew nothing. I didn't know anything, absolutely nothing till 1964," she said. She began working to register blacks across the state to vote. She met and worked with Stokely Carmichael, John Lewis, Bob Moses, Lawrence Guyot, and knew U.S. Justice Department official John Doar. As Mississippi's grassroots movement heated up and drew in other civil rights organizations and leaders, she met Andrew Young and Martin Luther King Jr., among other SCLC activists.

Near the end of Freedom Summer, Blackwell was chosen to serve as a delegate to the Mississippi Freedom Democratic Party, alongside Fannie Lou Hamer and Aaron Henry, among others.

She was threatened numerous times. In 1965, she was arrested with hundreds of other marchers in Jackson, Mississippi. She and the other prisoners were corralled into a stadium. "Through that period of time," she later said in an interview, "I saw the most worst torture that could be done to women. They brought in doctors, looking in our vaginas and sticking things in them. It was just terrible. And classifying us that we was diseased and just a lot of filth went on, you know. Police would come up and pull up, you know, the women's dresses."

In the late 1960s, Blackwell left SNCC to work as a community specialist for the National Council of Negro Women. She became a well-known lecturer and expert on rural housing development.

In 1977, Blackwell was elected mayor of Mayersville—the first black woman to be mayor of a Mississippi town. Two years later, she attended President Jimmy Carter's Energy Summit. In 1984, she was a speaker at the Democratic National Convention. In 1992, Blackwell received a MacArthur Foundation Fellowship.

— MARCH 28 —
1968
SANITATION WORKER STRIKE DRAWS CIVIL RIGHTS LEADERS

On this day in civil rights history, Martin Luther King Jr., James Lawson, and Ralph Abernathy led a march of sanitation workers down Beale Street in Memphis, Tennessee.

A month and a half earlier, over one thousand sanitation workers went on strike mainly over the refusal of the city of Memphis to recognize the sanitation workers' union, Local 1733, which also happened to be all black. Instead of listening to demands, the city of Memphis hired strikebreakers, ignoring the demands until the strikers could no longer afford to refuse to work.

King's final speech, Memphis, 1968

But the sanitation workers' strike grew into a city-wide demand for better wages and nicer living conditions. Memphis had a large African American population, over 200,000. As the city's intransigence on even discussing the issues at stake became clear, the large African American population of Memphis grew angrier.

At the beginning of 1968, King was spending most of his time working on the Poor People's Campaign. He saw in the Memphis struggle—where organized labor, the poor, and African American causes all overlapped—part of the new direction in his thinking. He agreed to lead a procession of sanitation workers through downtown Memphis to city hall. Many of the SCLC heads would join him.

But King's flight was delayed, and the march started an hour late. Many of the marchers were young and impetuous. As the march moved down Beale Street, some of the marchers began breaking store windows and looting followed. The police closed in, using the looting as a pretext to bash innocent and guilty marchers alike. The march broke. Full of panic, King fled the scene with Bernard Lee and Abernathy. The papers pounced on the marchers' behavior and King's fear. Suddenly, King's reputation as a non-violent leader was at stake.

Now involved, the SCLC planned a new march for April 5. On April 3, King addressed more than 2,000 people at a rally:

"We've got some difficult days ahead. But it really doesn't matter with me now. Because I've been to the mountaintop, I won't mind. Like anybody, I would like to live a long life. Longevity has its place. But I'm not concerned about that now. I just want to do God's Will. And He's allowed me to go up to the mountain. And I've looked over, and I've seen the Promised Land. I may not get there with you, but I want you to know tonight that we as a people will get to the Promised Land."

He would not live through the next day.

— MARCH 29 —
1964
SCLC CAMPAIGN BEGINS IN ST. AUGUSTINE

On this day in civil rights history, nine protesters were arrested at a sit-in in St. Augustine, Florida, the precursor to what would become a major Southern Christian Leadership Conference campaign. The oldest U.S. city, St. Augustine was a segregated town with a large Klan presence and a history of racially motivated violence. A number of strong NAACP members fought against the conditions there, sometimes with guns. Robert Hayling, Goldie Eubanks, and Henry Twine were the main leaders who struggled for years against harassment and intimidation. Unhappy with the NAACP, the three quit the organization and affiliated with the SCLC.

As a new SCLC member, Hayling seized momentum by inviting outside clergy to St. Augustine for a series of protests. In mid-March people began arriving, including SCLC lieutenants Bernard Lee and Hosea Williams. On March 28, 26 protesters were arrested in the first sit-in. The next day, nine more were jailed. With the ever-growing number of visiting activists, the local community became more involved and a weeklong city-wide assault on segregation began, as sit-ins, marches, and protests took place in hotels, restaurants, and businesses.

Meanwhile, SCLC, now the nation's leading civil rights group, found itself awash with potential projects. James Bevel wanted full attention on his Alabama project, and Williams and Lee wanted St. Augustine to be the next major SCLC target while Congress was debating the Civil Rights Act. Heading into a quadricentennial celebration, with an economy largely dependent on tourism, St. Augustine was chosen; the Alabama project was postponed until later in the year.

Building on the earlier activity, SCLC President Martin Luther King Jr. arrived in St. Augustine on May 18, a precursor to the "nonviolent army" that would soon abolish segregation in America's hottest city. May 26 was announced as the beginning of the new campaign. SCLC organizer Wyatt T. Walker laid out a plan of escalating marches, designed for maximum exposure. They would hit St. Augustine where it hurt the most: in the pocketbook.

Florida Klan members flocked to the northeast corner of the state to disrupt the planned protests with death threats and physical violence.

— MARCH 30 —
1870
15TH AMENDMENT GUARANTEES RIGHT TO VOTE

On this day in civil rights history, the 15th Amendment to the U.S. Constitution was officially ratified, guaranteeing African Americans the right to vote. The amendment states: "The right of citizens of the United States to vote shall not be denied or abridged by the United States or by any State on account of race, color, or previous condition of servitude."

This did not, of course, include women.

During Reconstruction, Republicans in Congress passed three amendments to address the conditions of African Americans. The first was the 13th, which abolished slavery. The 14th granted former slaves full U.S. citizenship. And the 15th was passed to prevent voter tampering or black disenfranchisement in the South.

Photo courtesy of Library of Congress

Editorial illustration of the first vote

The Republicans had an admittedly political reason for the legislation. By empowering the legions of former slaves, the Republicans hoped to gain a foothold in the solidly Democratic South.

These three amendments resulted in an enormous surge in Southern black voters. African Americans were elected to many state legislatures, and many progressive, localized statutes and measures were passed. For the next 20 years, African Americans in the South participated in their state governments in numbers that rival or even exceed today's. U.S. troops were deployed to prevent racial violence, and to protect black voters at the polls.

But things fell apart when a backlash to black political participation erupted in the 1870s. After an election scare, President Hayes and the federal government withdrew from the occupation, leaving the South to its own devices. Southern Democrats used poll taxes, literacy tests, and, when these failed, physical intimidation and lynching to prevent black voting. The 15th Amendment was effectively mooted, as was the 13th, as institutionalized sharecropping resulted in a life for many not that different from slavery.

The strides African Americans made—in government, education, and society—were quickly rolled back. A clever white power structure, cemented into place through exploitative economic policy and racist social traditions, fearful over the potential power of an educated black voting population, emerged from Reconstruction intent on never allowing a single black vote again.

Still, the 15th Amendment created the legal precedent for the civil rights legislation of the 1960s.

— MARCH 31 —

1971

LAWSUITS BY MORRIS DEES SCORE CIVIL RIGHTS VICTORIES

On this day in civil rights history, approximately, Morris Dees worked as the co-founder and lead trial lawyer of the Southern Poverty Law Center.

Dees was born in Shorter, Alabama, in 1936, into a farming family. In 1955, he was named Star Farmer by the Alabama chapter of the Future Farmers of America.

But after high school, Dees enrolled at the University of Alabama, where in addition to his studies as an undergraduate and later a law student, he was a successful entrepreneur. With another student, Millard Fuller, he began a direct-mail publishing venture that was so profitable they were able to sell it in the late 1960s, leaving both millionaires before they were 30 years old.

Fuller became a missionary and went on to found Habitat for Humanity. Dees became a volunteer lawyer for the ACLU on civil and voting rights cases and also began experimenting with structures for his own nonprofit legal foundation. In 1971, with another Montgomery lawyer, he established the Southern Poverty Law Center, and hired civil rights icon Julian Bond to be its president and spokesperson.

Over the years, the SPLC won significant legal victories in areas including voting, employment, sex discrimination, criminal defense, and occupational safety. Few if any progressive groups in the post-civil rights movement era had as much success using the law to effect social change.

Dees financed the SPLC through direct mail fundraising campaigns, at which he is widely considered a master. He also used those skills to raise funds for other liberal causes and for the presidential campaigns of Geoge McGovern, Jimmy Carter, and Edward Kennedy.

In 1979, Dees and the SPLC became involved in litigation and later in educational campaigns against the then-resurgent Ku Klux Klan and other white supremacist groups. The Klanwatch Project, established in 1980, was one result. [Disclosure: the lead author of this book was the founding director of Klanwatch and an SPLC employee from 1976 to 1986.] Lawsuits bankrupting three KKK and/or neo-Nazi organizations during the 1980s was another.

Its anti-Klan work brought the SPLC even greater public attention and fundraising success. Begun with two lawyers and a 16-year-old secretary in 1971, the SPLC today has a multi-million dollar endowment and houses some 100 staffers in a modern, heavily fortified 10-story building in downtown Montgomery.

Dees remains the SPLC's chief trial counsel. His successes against the KKK and the like have made him a hero to many and a target to white supremacist extremists.

— APRIL 1 —

1962

VOTER EDUCATION PROJECT BEGINS

On this day in civil rights history, the Voter Education Project (VEP) began in Atlanta, Georgia, led by lawyer Joseph Haas and the Southern Regional Council.

On June 16, 1961, President John F. Kennedy had held a conference with skeptical civil rights leaders, promising federal funding for voter registration. He and his brother, Attorney General Robert Kennedy, encouraged philanthropic organizations to channel money into grassroots registration campaigns in the South.

The VEP was formed to foster cooperation and efficiency among the various civil rights groups working to register black voters. The VEP doled out funds to participating organizations— including SNCC, CORE, SCLC, the Urban League, the Southern Regional Council, and the NAACP, among others. The VEP's focus was on literacy and education, and its desired outcome was to create a swell of new black voters who would elect moderate or progressive officials committed to abolishing segregationist practices.

Voting rights pamphlet

If successful, the VEP theoretically over time would have "fixed" the South. Civil rights leaders such as Roy Wilkins, Whitney Young, Charles McDew, and Martin Luther King Jr. all approved the idea.

Wiley Branton was selected as the VEP's first executive director. Vernon Jordan and John Lewis would serve as heads of the organization in later years.

The formation of the VEP marked the shift of civil rights goals from the desegregation of public accommodations to voting and thus to long-term political and economic power. This strategy united the conservatives and the radicals within the myriad civil rights organizations behind a common, recognizable cause.

One of the projects to receive VEP funds was COFO, the Council of Federated Organizations, the umbrella organization that ran Freedom Vote and later Freedom Summer in Mississippi.

In 1965, the Summer Community Organization and Political Education (SCOPE) Project began a massive registration campaign that involved more than 1,200 workers and spanned six Southern states. SCOPE was also funded by VEP money.

In its first few years, VEP-affiliated projects registered some 600,000 voters across the South and helped influence passage of the 1965 Voting Rights Act. By 1974, 2 million voters had registered through VEP projects.

— APRIL 2 —

1963

COMEDIAN DICK GREGORY LEADS VOTER DRIVE

On this day in civil rights history, comedian Dick Gregory led a registration drive in Greenwood, Mississippi.

Gregory worked at a post office before getting his big break in 1961 when Hugh Hefner invited him to perform at the Chicago Playboy Club. One year later he was one of the most famous men in stand-up comedy.

Gregory used satire and race in his act, to great comedic effect: "I never believed in Santa Claus because I knew no white dude would come into my neighborhood after dark." His jokes centered on prejudice and segregation: "I never learned hate at home, or shame. I had to go to school for that." His act was fiery and controversial, but also very funny: "Last time I was down South I walked into this restaurant and this white waitress came up to me and said, 'We don't serve colored people here.' I said, 'That's all right. I don't eat colored people. Bring me a whole fried chicken.'"

Gregory campaign button

Photo courtesy of Stephen Cresswell

Civil rights leaders such as Medgar Evers and Martin Luther King soon discovered Gregory through his high profile and effective satire and invited him to join the movement. Gregory began speaking at CORE and NAACP events, but also entered the fray as a front-line field worker.

In 1963, SNCC was actively registering voters in Mississippi for a project funded by the Voter Education Project that would eventually turn into Freedom Summer. But local resistance was extreme. National media attention spotlighted the small Mississippi town of Greenwood when Jimmy Travis, a young SNCC worker, was shot in the neck.

SNCC stepped up the activity. Bob Moses, James Forman, Gregory, and others went to Greenwood and led three marches to the courthouse, each forcibly rebuffed by police. A photograph of Gregory being manhandled by a policeman was on the front page of the *New York Times*.

Gregory later became friends with Martin Luther King Jr., and took part in the Chicago campaign and the March Against Fear, among other actions. He was jailed many times. In 1964, Gregory published the book *Nigger*. "Whenever you hear the word nigger," he said to his mother, "you'll know they're advertising my book."

In 1968, Gregory ran for president as a write-in candidate for the Freedom and Peace Party. In the late 1970s, Gregory became a fitness guru, while continuing to speak out for African American rights.

— APRIL 3 —

1944

SUPREME COURT STRIKES DOWN ALL-WHITE PRIMARIES

On this day in civil rights history, the U.S. Supreme Court decided the case *Smith v. Allwright*, which eliminated whites-only political primaries in the South. Thurgood Marshall would later call this decision more important than the landmark *Brown v. Board* school desegregation case a decade later.

Lonnie Smith, a black voter in Texas, sued for the right to vote in the Democratic primary after a local county official, S. S. Allwright, denied him access. It's hard to believe today, but in the first half of the 20th century, the South was solidly Democratic. This was because the Republican Party was identified with Abraham Lincoln, abolition, Reconstruction, and support for black rights, while the Democrats were identified with slavery, the Confederacy, white redemption, and segregation. This pattern began to change with FDR's New Deal, then with Harry Truman's desegregation of the armed forces, and finally reversed itself completely in the 1960s after the Democratic administrations of John F. Kennedy and Lyndon Johnson supported civil rights. Conservative Southern whites then switched to the Republican Party, which was by then opposing civil rights and other black issues.

Prior to the 1960s, in many voting districts in the region, the Republican Party was so weak it never had viable candidates, so all state and local elections were effectively decided during the Democratic primary. And the law of the day allowed these primary elections to be restricted to whites on the ground that the political parties were private organizations.

Smith v. Allwright sliced through this racial subterfuge and declared that elections were a matter of state policy and were operated by the states, and thus were covered by constitutional guarantees of equal rights: "Since the right to organize and maintain a political party is one guaranteed by the Bill of Rights of this state, it necessarily follows that every privilege essential or reasonably appropriate to the exercise of that right is likewise guaranteed. . . . Without the privilege of determining the policy of a political association and its membership, the right to organize such an association would be a mere mockery."

It was a small step, but the ramifications were enormous. The South continued to discourage black voter registration, often through intimidation, but the Supreme Court had declared that registered black voters could not be excluded. The decision encouraged voter registration drives, and urged on the NAACP's legal strategy of carrying segregation cases to the U.S. Supreme Court to have them overturned. *Smith v. Allwright* thus helped pave the way for the modern civil rights era.

— APRIL 4 —
1968
DR. KING ASSASSINATED IN MEMPHIS, TENNESSEE

On this day in civil rights history, Martin Luther King Jr. was shot and killed in Memphis, Tennessee.

Having returned to Memphis to regain momentum in the sanitation workers' strike, King was staying in a room on the second floor of the Lorraine Hotel. In the early evening, King readied himself for dinner. Outside, Hosea Williams, James Bevel, Andrew Young, and Jesse Jackson waited for him. Ralph Abernathy was inside with King, going over the day's events.

King tombstone, Atlanta

King stepped onto the balcony to greet his friends and aides, and, turning to go back inside, was shot through the jaw and crumpled to the ground. The shot seemed to come from across the hotel courtyard. As others called for help, Abernathy held King's head in his hands.

King died within the hour. The country went into shock. King was the ultimate hope to so many that his death in a very real sense marked the symbolic end of the 20th century civil rights movement. The philosophy of nonviolence he valued so highly was temporarily cast aside: riots broke out in more than 100 cities. "Martin Luther King was a saint and a martyr," one black radical said. "But we ain't saints, and we don't intend to let the white man make us martyrs!" President Lyndon Johnson declared a national day of mourning, then promptly deployed the National Guard to quell the violence. There were more than 20,000 arrests, and almost 50 dead.

On April 8, more than 300,000 people lined the streets of Atlanta as King's funeral procession passed, with his casket borne on a simple wagon pulled by a mule.

Abernathy stepped into King's shoes at the Southern Christian Leadership Conference and continued the Poor People's Campaign that King had worked so hard for. King's widow, Coretta, maintained his legacy with the creation of the Martin Luther King Jr. Center for Nonviolent Social Change and with the ultimately successful effort to have his birthday made a national holiday.

But with King's death the movement lost its most powerful voice and its moral center. Leading up to his death, King had been formulating a new, holistic approach to the ills of modern society. Where this would have led him, the black community, and the nation, no one can say.

James Earl Ray was arrested two months later and charged with King's murder.

— APRIL 5 —

1856

EDUCATOR BOOKER T. WASHINGTON BORN IN VIRGINIA

On this day in civil rights history, Booker T. Washington was born into slavery in Virginia.

After the Civil War, Washington worked as a destitute laborer in West Virginia. At age 16, he enrolled at the Hampton Normal and Agricultural Institute, a Quaker-run school that trained black teachers.

In 1881, Washington became the first principal of the Normal School for Colored Teachers in Tuskegee, Alabama. The college was built from scratch, with the students providing much of the labor and know-how. The Normal School, which later became internationally famous as Tuskegee Institute (now University), was founded on principles of self-reliance and community-building. The school taught practical trades—shoemaking, farming, and carpentry, among other subjects.

Booker T. Washington

As Tuskegee grew into a premiere black institution under his care, Washington became a powerful man and a major black figure. But his famous 1895 "Atlanta Compromise" speech, which accepted segregation while calling for Negroes to work hard to be useful to larger society, put him in opposition to other prominent black leaders. Washington argued that blacks might as well accept segregation and work to better themselves individually and within their own communities. In reaction, W. E. B. Du Bois called him "the Great Accomodator." Washington further incensed his critics when he argued that the descendants of African slaves were better off in America than if their parents had remained free in Africa. Washington and Du Bois, once friends, became bitter rivals.

In 1900, Washington founded the National Negro Business League to foster black business and agricultural leaders. One year later, to instant acclaim, he published his best-selling autobiography, *Up From Slavery*. That same year he dined with President Theodore Roosevelt. He began to invest in black businesses, such as Thomas Fortune's *New York Age*, while also donating generously to integrationist organizations.

A man dedicated to education and the black community, Washington believed that the future of African Americans was hard work, entrepreneurship, and commercial viability; to Washington, looking to the federal government for help would only hinder the progress of African Americans.

He died November 14, 1915, in Tuskegee, after suffering a collapse from overwork. More than 8,000 people attended his funeral.

— APRIL 6 —

1968

POLICE KILL BLACK PANTHER BOBBY HUTTON IN SHOOTOUT

On this day in civil rights history, police gunned down an unarmed Bobby Hutton, after a 90-minute gun battle between the police and the Black Panthers.

An early recruit to the Black Panther Party, Hutton was a well-dressed youth who distributed pamphlets around Oakland and Berkeley, California, while working as an unofficial treasurer for the organization.

Two days after the assassination of Martin Luther King, Oakland, along with dozens of U.S. cities, broke down into anarchy, as angry African Americans began rioting. Earlier that evening, two carloads of Black Panthers, including Eldridge Cleaver, David Hilliard, and Bobby Hutton, began driving around the city. As was the BPP practice, they were armed with shotguns and rifles.

The events that followed are disputed and unclear. Around 9 o'clock that night, two policemen were shot and wounded. Police cordoned off the area, claiming that Black Panthers were the shooters. While chaos continued in Oakland, police ambushed the two BPP cars. The Black Panthers split up and fled. Cleaver and Hutton ended up trapped in the basement of a Panther office. Oakland police surrounded the building and a protracted gun battle began.

After more than an hour, police set fire to the building and tossed tear gas canisters into the basement. Declaring defeat, Bobby Hutton, stripped to the waist, emerged from the basement with his hands up. Shortly after he stumbled into the police spotlight, he was cut down by a volley of bullets and instantly killed. Cleaver emerged seconds later, undressed so as to refute any confusion about his being armed and crawling due to a wound in his leg.

The police admitted that Hutton was unarmed, but refused to comment further on the matter. They seized weapons and ammunition. Cleaver and others were charged with assault with a deadly weapon and jailed.

Hutton, 17, became a folk hero. More than 2,000 people attended his funeral, including Marlon Brando, who later denounced Hutton's murder on live television.

Along with the high-profile murders of Fred Hampton and Mark Clark one year later, the death of Bobby Hutton was the most publicized example of police harassment and brutality aimed at the BPP. In beleaguered communities across America, African Americans started to wonder if the Black Panthers were not in fact right, that freedom lay in the way of the gun, not in non-violence.

— APRIL 7 —

1934

ACTIVIST, WRITER WILLIAM MONROE TROTTER DIES

On this day in civil rights history, William Monroe Trotter, crusading protest leader and firebrand reporter, died. He accomplished much in his life, but it is generally agreed that he was born 50 years too early; it would take that long for the country to catch up with this remarkable man.

Ohio-born Trotter worked in real estate after graduating with honors from Harvard University in 1895. In 1901, he and George Forbes founded the *Boston Guardian*, to issue "propaganda against discrimination based on color and denial of citizenship rights because of color." Trotter wrote with clear outrage at the state of affairs in the country, and often organized protests. He attacked racists, segregationists, and accomodationists. Like W. E. B. Du Bois, Trotter became a vocal critic of Booker T. Washington.

Trotter's eloquent indignation and leadership abilities soon brought him into Du Bois's sphere of influence. In 1905, Trotter, Du Bois, and 30 others formed the Niagara Movement. Its declaration of principles, which Trotter helped draft, stated: "We refuse to allow the impression to remain that the Negro-American assents to inferiority, is submissive under oppression and apologetic before insults." Black pride, self-determination, and equal rights—the Niagara Movement encapsulated the themes of the civil rights to come over the next half-century.

In 1909, the Niagara Movement evolved into the NAACP. But in Trotter's eyes, the NAACP was too moderate. Dispirited by white influence and financing of the fledgling organization, he left and started the National Equal Rights League.

For the rest of his life, Trotter criticized politicians, businesses, and the country at large, pushing for immediate reform. No one was above his abuse, not even presidents.

In 1914, Trotter confronted President Woodrow Wilson in the White House, accusing him of hypocrisy, among other things. After lambasting Wilson with vitriolic invective for nearly 45 minutes, Trotter was forcibly removed. The following year, he organized a movement to ban the film *Birth of a Nation* in Boston; Wilson, meanwhile, held a screening in the White House.

Inflammatory and uncompromising, Trotter dedicated his life to the cause of equality. In his enthusiasm, he often offended potential allies. His indignant activism made him the first militant black leader of repute and an antecedent to the black rebels of the 1960s.

Trotter did not live to see any of the major positive changes take place for his race. He died in 1934 with segregation still in place and lynching still a common practice.

— APRIL 8 —

1933

JURY DELIBERATIONS BEGIN IN SCOTTSBORO BOYS TRIAL

On this day in civil rights history, an all-white jury began deliberating the fate of Haywood Patterson, one of nine black men and youths accused of raping two white women on a freight train in 1931.

The case of the "Scottsboro Boys," as they were known, is one of the most shameful episodes in U.S. legal history. It highlighted the extreme racial prejudices of the era.

On March 25, 1931, a fight had broken out between a group of blacks and a separate group of whites "hoboing" in a boxcar in north Alabama. The whites included two women, unemployed cotton mill workers, dressed as men in work overalls. Some of the white men were thrown from the train and then told authorities of an "assault" by blacks. The stationmaster telegraphed the next station and a posse assembled to intercept the train. Every black male on the train was arrested and taken to jail in Scottsboro, Alabama.

The two white women then reported that they had been raped on the train by a gang of blacks and identified as their assailants six of the nine. That night, a white mob gathered and lynchings were avoided only because the governor quickly called out the National Guard.

Within two weeks, trials were held and eight of the "boys" were convicted and sentenced to death; the ninth received a mistrial. One defense lawyer was drunk during part of the trial; the other was 70 years old and had not tried a case in many years.

The story might have ended there and the defendants might have been electrocuted except that the Communist Party's International Labor Defense arm took note of the case and sent lawyers to file an appeal. Then the NAACP also tried to get involved.

On appeal, the U.S. Supreme Court reversed the conviction in a landmark ruling, *Powell v. Alabama*, that established the due process right to competent counsel in criminal trials. The cases were sent back for retrials, which began with Haywood Patterson's on March 30, 1933, before a new judge, James Horton.

Patterson was now represented by celebrated New York criminal defense attorney Samuel Liebowitz and the ILD's Joseph Brodsky. They put on a spirited defense before an all-white jury, dismantling the testimony of one of the alleged victims and then, in a surprise move, producing the other "victim" to testify for the defense that the rapes had never happened in the first place.

None of it mattered to the white male jurors. The very concept of sexual contact between black men and white women was enough offense for them. They found Patterson guilty anyway and he was again sentenced to the electric chair.

The verdict was immediately appealed.

— APRIL 9 —

1866

RECONSTRUCTION CIVIL RIGHTS ACT PASSED

On this day in civil rights history, Congress passed the Reconstruction Civil Rights Act over the veto of President Andrew Johnson.

Formerly Lincoln's vice president, Johnson, a Tennessean, had been against the act from the start. "White men alone must govern the South," he said. He worked to exclude blacks from life in the post-war South. In his estimation, the bill would "operate in favor of the colored and against the white race," and he promptly vetoed it.

The act declared that all persons born in the United States were now citizens, regardless of race, creed, or previous condition, and guarantee, on paper, full rights to all the formerly enslaved blacks. It reads: ". . . and such citizens, of every race and color, without regard to any previous condition of slavery or involuntary servitude, except as a punishment for crime whereof the party shall have been duly convicted, shall have the same right, in every State and Territory in the United States, to make and enforce contracts, to sue, be parties, and give evidence, to inherit, purchase, lease, sell, hold, and convey real and personal property, and to full and equal benefit of all laws and proceedings for the security of person and property, as is enjoyed by white citizens..."

A person found guilty of denying another these rights would be fined or imprisoned.

The bill was in response to the "black codes" forming all over the South, the precursor to Jim Crow segregation. Republicans in the senate began impeachment proceedings against Johnson and passed the 14th and 15th amendments, which granted blacks full citizenship and the right to vote. They also divided the South into five military districts under Northern rule, enforcing the antisegregation laws.

Under these conditions, blacks voted in enormous numbers, electing blacks to all levels of public office.

Johnson's impeachment trial lasted 11 weeks, but he retained his office on the strength of one vote. He continued to veto pro-African American legislation, but Congress continued to override him.

Reconstruction eventually failed, however, and the Reconstruction-era civil rights acts were ignored. Southern whites regained control, literacy tests, poll taxes, and other impediments were put in place. A brutal era of oppressive exploitation took hold, a dehumanizing system that would remain in place for almost 100 years.

— APRIL 10 —
1967
NAACP VOTES AGAINST PEACE MOVEMENT MERGER

On this day in civil rights history, the NAACP voted against merging the peace movement with the civil rights movement.

Four days earlier, Martin Luther King had delivered his first antiwar speech in public in New York City. King had privately voiced concern over the issue for some time, but after viewing an article on Vietnam that showed a photograph of a wounded child, he declared, "Never again will I be silent on an issue that is destroying the soul of our nation and destroying thousands and thousands of little children in Vietnam."

King saw a convergence of interests amongst blacks, poor whites, labor, and antiwar activists, among others. Militarism siphoned off government money that could be spent at home, while also focusing attention on faraway problems.

With his powerful oratory, he delivered the fiery antiwar speech he called "Beyond Vietnam": "A few years ago . . . it seemed as if there was a real promise of hope for the poor—both black and white—through the poverty program. . . . Then came the buildup in Vietnam, and I watched this program broken and eviscerated as if it were some idle political plaything of a society gone mad on war. And I knew that America would never invest the necessary funds or energies in rehabilitation of its poor so long as adventures like Vietnam continued to draw men and skills and money like some demonic, destructive suction tube."

This and subsequent speeches brought mainstream media attention against King and against the SCLC. As King was the movement to many in America, they saw this direction as troubling, evidence of communist sympathies. Some leaders in the movement felt that the negativity over the unpopularity of the position (before large numbers of Americans began to turn against Vietnam) could result in a removal of popular support for black causes.

The negative attention moved some civil rights leaders to distance themselves from King. Six days after the speech, the NAACP released a statement declaring itself against combining with the antiwar movement. Undaunted, King led an antiwar rally two weeks later. King remained involved in the war until his death, hoping to combine the progressive movements of labor, antiwar, and civil rights into a cohesive rehabilitating movement.

The NAACP's public admonition of King further illustrated its conservatism that would result in decades of irrelevance, as black youths flocked to the more radical groups, leaving the NAACP behind.

— APRIL 11 —
1968
CIVIL RIGHTS ACT OF 1968 BECOMES LAW

On this day in civil rights history, President Lyndon Baines Johnson signed into law the Civil Rights Act of 1968, also known as the Fair Housing Act.

When proposing the legislation to Congress, Johnson said very clearly: "I am proposing fair housing legislation again this year because it is decent and right. Injustice must be opposed, however difficult or unpopular the issue."

The law prohibited discrimination in the sale, financing, or rental of housing property and created protections for civil rights workers. Devised as a follow-up to the 1965 Civil Rights Act, the bill had been watered down and compromised through its debate in Congress. But the death of Martin Luther King Jr. helped propel a stronger bill through both houses of Congress.

LBJ signs Fair Housing Act

Photo courtesy of Library of Congress

Fair housing had long been an essential platform for the civil rights movement. Desegregating public schools would be ineffective if neighborhoods remained segregated due to prejudicial real estate policy. "Housing is central to the whole field of civil rights," A. Philip Randolph said in 1964, "and no amount of success in any single phase of the civil rights movement can be sustained as long as racial discrimination in housing persists."

The bill was designed to remove the last major obstacle to desegregation by making all housing open to all races. Victims of housing discrimination were given legal recourse.

Part of Johnson's "Great Society," the Fair Housing Act attacked one piece in a large web of interconnected problems. Johnson himself recognized it: "It is self-evident that the problems we are struggling with form a complicated chain of discrimination . . . All the links—poverty, lack of education, underemployment and now discrimination in housing—must be attacked together." But Johnson's credibility was undermined by the U.S. involvement in Vietnam and the budgetary crisis the escalating war was creating. The U.S. did not have the available funds to implement Johnson's wide-reaching series of reforms, and he eventually gave up.

The Fair Housing Act was the last major civil rights legislation of the 1960s. Meanwhile the country became increasingly polarized. Even as the "New Left" movements of students, women, and blacks seemed to coalesce around the war in Vietnam, a new generation of conservatives was entering politics. The level of government spending on social programs was shrinking.

— APRIL 12 —
1963
MARTIN LUTHER KING JR. JAILED IN BIRMINGHAM

On this day in civil rights history, Martin Luther King Jr. was arrested, as planned on Good Friday, while taking part in the Birmingham campaign. His arrest proved instrumental in the movement, as he wrote the very influential "Letter from a Birmingham Jail" while incarcerated.

Fred Shuttlesworth, a charter member of the SCLC, orchestrated the Birmingham campaign. The civil rights organization realized that intense, focused campaigns in select cities with entrenched white municipalities, such as Birmingham, would yield more success. It would allow the organization to utilize its entire resources. So as a shift in strategy, the SCLC, in cooperation with the NAACP, SNCC, and other organizations, began mass protests in select cities, working in tandem with local organizations.

Shuttlesworth, Abernathy, and King

But the 1962 Albany campaign had proved lackluster when police chief Laurie Pritchett did not use violence against demonstrators. The SCLC, at Shuttlesworth's request, chose Birmingham as its next target. They would call the campaign Project C.

Birmingham public safety commissioner Eugene "Bull" Connor was a temperamental and avowed segregationist. His city was a scary place, with a history of mob and racial violence Eighteen recent unsolved bombings were believed to be the work of the Ku Klux Klan.

But Birmingham also had a large black middle class, anchored by insurance magnate A. G. Gaston, one of the country's wealthiest black businessmen. On April 3, Project C began with boycotts, marches, sit-ins, and direct action; thousands of determined activists took part. Unlike Albany's Pritchett, Connor did not disappoint. The police began making mass arrests. Over the next few days, hundreds of protesters were incarcerated. A Birmingham judge issued an order prohibiting King, Shuttlesworth, Abernathy, and the SCLC from organizing protests.

Project C leaders decided that King, already the public face of civil rights nationally, would defy Birmingham authorities so that he would be arrested. "I don't know whether I can raise money to get people out of jail," he said. "I do know that I can go into jail with them." He was arrested and placed in solitary confinement. He passed the time reading the *Birmingham News*, where he learned he was being called a troublemaker by some white clergymen. He decided to respond to them in a letter.

— APRIL 13 —
1964
SIDNEY POITIER WINS BEST ACTOR AWARD

On this day in civil rights history, Sidney Poitier became the first African American to win the best actor Academy Award, for his role in "Lilies of the Field." Poitier became one of the most heralded U.S. actors and a paragon of personal and artistic integrity.

Raised in the Bahamas in abject poverty, Poitier at age 15 moved to Miami to live with his brother, and discovered the abhorrent racial conditions in America at the time. Poitier moved north, ending up as a menial laborer in Harlem. He eventually joined the American Negro Theater. After good reviews on the stage, Poitier faced the decision to continue with the theater or go west to Hollywood. In 1950 he starred in *No Way Out* as a black doctor treating a white bigot. Although there were few substantive roles offered to African Americans in the 1950s and 1960s, Poitier became a star anyway. He was a leading man when other black actors were still relegated to playing servants.

With his newfound fame, Poitier chose roles that challenged American assumptions about race and poverty. *To Sir with Love, The Defiant Ones, The Blackboard Jungle*, and *In the Heat of the Night* all deal with race issues. Poitier imbued his characters with a quiet but stern dignity, and he played strong, sympathetic, unabashedly black men. As the wider civil rights movement fought for equal rights, Poitier, along with Harry Belafonte, Sammy Davis Jr., Paul Robeson, and James Earl Jones won fans that spanned the spectrum of color.

With a few notable exceptions, Hollywood avoided the race issue. Individual actors (such as Marlon Brando and Charleston Heston) and directors (Stanley Kramer and Sidney Lumet) were sympathetic and did what they could, but Hollywood, then and now, mostly delivered what audiences wanted. And mainstream America did not want to be lectured about race.

Poitier's most controversial and groundbreaking role was in *Guess Who's Coming to Dinner*, where he plays the male lead in an interracial romance. Co-starring Spencer Tracy and Katharine Hepburn, the film is funny, tender, and way ahead of its time, dealing with the very issue white America was so afraid of.

Martin Luther King Jr. said of Poitier: "He is a man of great depth, a man of great social concern, a man who is dedicated to human rights and freedom. Here is a man who, in the words we so often hear now, is a soul brother."

On this day in civil rights history, the first abolition society in the United States—named the Society for the Relief of Free Negroes Unlawfully Held in Bondage—was organized in Pennsylvania, a full year before the United States declared itself a sovereign country. Abolitionist Anthony Benezet formed the largely Quaker group to help a local African American woman faced with being resold into slavery. John Baldwin was the Society's first president. The group's constitution stated its goals:

> Whereas, there are . . . a number of negroes and others kept in a state of slavery, who, we apprehend, from different causes and circumstances, are justly entitled to their freedom by the laws and Constitution under which we live . . . but as in their situation they being tied by the strong cords of oppression, are rendered incapable of asserting their freedom, and many through this inability remain unjustly in bondage during life; it therefore has appeared necessary that some aid should be extended toward such poor unhappy sufferers, wherever they may be discovered . . . and as loosing the bonds of wickedness, and setting the oppressed free, is evidently a duty incumbent on all the professors of Christianity.

Photo courtesy of Library of Congress

Benjamin Franklin

In 1787, this same group was incorporated as the Pennsylvania Society for Promoting the Abolition of Slavery and for the Relief of Free Negroes Unlawfully Held in Bondage and for Improving the Condition of the African Race (PSPAS). Besides calling for the end of slavery, this organization also called for educational and employment opportunities for blacks. The group then elected former slave owner Benjamin Franklin as its president. Benjamin Rush and Thomas Paine were also members. The PSPAS became a lobbying group for African American and abolitionist causes, pushing for antislavery legislation. It also helped freed blacks adjust to Northern society, and funded schools and other organizations.

As time passed, PSPAS membership began to slide and the organization's usefulness declined. In 1833, the American Anti-Slavery Society and the Pennsylvania Abolition Society were formed in Philadelphia from the remnants of the PSPAS. Together these two organizations would claim many famous members, including James Forten, Robert Purvis, James McCrummel, and Lucretia Mott.

— APRIL 15 —

1889

LABOR LEADER A. PHILIP RANDOLPH BORN

On this day in civil rights history, stalwart activist A. Philip Randolph was born in Crescent City, Florida. He moved to New York as a young man and studied economics and philosophy at City College of New York. He became a socialist and, with Chandler Owen, founded *The Messenger*, a leftist magazine.

In 1925, Randolph formed the Brotherhood of Sleeping Car Porters, an all-black union affiliated with the American Federation of Labor. The BSCP members' jobs as railroad porters regularly took them across the country, and they often became ambassadors for both labor and civil rights causes.

Randolph's skill as an organizer and his advocacy of direct action made him a model of the civil rights leaders to come. "Freedom is never granted," he said. "It is won. Justice is never given; it is exacted."

In 1936, Randolph was named president of the National Negro Congress. And in 1937, he negotiated an agreement between the Pullman Company and the BSCP, the first labor agreement between a black union and a major corporation.

In 1941, Randolph envisioned a daring march on Washington at which thousands of African Americans would rally to protest segregation in the defense industries. But after President Franklin Roosevelt signed the Fair Employment Act, the march was cancelled. In 1948, Randolph played a key role in the desegregation of the armed forces.

When the American Federation of Labor merged with the Congress of Industrial Organizations to form the AFL-CIO, Randolph became vice president. In his mind, racial equality and economic justice were inextricably linked.

Entering the 1960s, Randolph revisited his earlier idea of a march on Washington. He included Bayard Rustin in the planning of the event. Other leaders and organizations became involved, and eventually the 1963 March on Washington for Jobs and Freedom was the result. On August 28, 1963, Randolph saw his vision realized and, being the elder statesman, was chosen as the first speaker. "We are not a mob," he proclaimed. "We are the advance guard of a massive moral revolution for jobs and freedom."

In 1964, Randolph received the Medal of Freedom from President Lyndon Johnson. One year later, in his 70s, Randolph participated in the Selma-to-Montgomery March.

He died in New York City on May 16, 1979.

— APRIL 16 —
1963
MLK ISSUES 'LETTER FROM A BIRMINGHAM JAIL'

On this day in civil rights history, Martin Luther King Jr. released his now famous "Letter from a Birmingham Jail" while placed in solitary confinement.

Just a few weeks into the Birmingham campaign, things were not looking good for Project C. Fewer arrests than expected took place, and the press, from both liberal and conservative media, was critical of King and the protests. King, Abernathy, and 50 other protesters were in jail, King in solitary confinement.

Pamphlet with King's letter

But perhaps worse than jail was a "Call to Unity," released by a group of white Birmingham ministers who acknowledged that segregation was wrong but asked the protesters to stop the demonstrations. The white ministers urged the civil rights protesters to be patient and wait for the federal government, the state and local officials, and white Southerners to come around.

King began drafting a response to the white preachers. He wrote in the margins of old newspapers and on scraps of toilet paper. Aides smuggled the lengthy notes out of jail; the document exceeded 20 pages when dictated to an SCLC secretary.

On April 16, King's "Letter from a Birmingham Jail" was released to the public. King offered a harsh response to the moderate, white ministers: "This 'Wait,'" he says, "has almost always meant 'Never'... I have heard numerous religious leaders of the South call upon their worshippers to comply with a desegregation decision because it is the law, but I have longed to hear white ministers say, 'follow this decree because integration is morally right and the Negro is your brother.'.... the Negro's great stumbling block is not the White Citizen's Council or the Ku Klux Klanner, but the white moderate who is more devoted to 'order' than to justice, who prefers a negative peace which is the absence of tension to a positive peace which is the presence of justice. . ."

Over time, King's letter has become an acclaimed example of protest literature and civil disobedience, and a fine insight into King's superior elocutionary powers—behind the pulpit or on paper. "Injustice anywhere is a threat to justice everywhere," he wrote in one of its many memorable passages. "We will win our freedom because the sacred heritage of our nation and the eternal will of God are embodied in our echoing demands."

The Birmingham campaign, in large part thanks to the intransigence of police commissioner Eugene "Bull" Connor, was beginning to succeed. The marchers grew in number. The national media took notice. The stage for a great civil rights victory was set.

— APRIL 17 —

1960

SNCC ORGANIZED AT SHAW UNIVERSITY CONFERENCE

On this day in civil rights history, the Student Nonviolent Coordinating Committee—SNCC, as it was commonly known—was formed at a youth conference at Shaw University in Raleigh, North Carolina. The group emerged from the student sit-in movement that had begun in Greensboro and Nashville earlier that year, and had as its goal the coordination of student protests across the country.

The SCLC's Ella Baker oversaw the conference, and SCLC gave the students an $8,000 grant to get SNCC off the ground. SNCC invigorated the movement in the early and mid 1960s, only to fall apart as the decade ended.

Despite SNCC's early support from SCLC and the fact that the two groups both worked in many campaigns, theirs was often an uneasy alliance. SNCC saw SCLC as too conservative, and the NAACP as a dinosaur. SNCC's members were radical, impulsive, brave, and impatient. When the first freedom ride stalled in 1961, SNCC immediately organized a new ride. SNCC field workers disseminated across the South into segregated communities, large and small. They opened voter registration drives, educational initiatives, and mounted desegregation campaigns.

The leadership of SNCC included Charles McDew, Julian Bond, John Lewis, James Lawson, Diane Nash, Marion Barry, James Forman, and Robert Moses. SNCC became the foremost civil rights group in the nation during Freedom Summer, the massive Mississippi voter registration campaign that resulted in a new political party almost unseating the entrenched Democrats. SNCC was involved in almost every major civil rights event of the 1960s, from the 1963 Birmingham campaign and March on Washington to the 1964 Mississippi campaign to the 1965 Selma-to-Montgomery March, and many more.

After Charles McDew, John Lewis led the group from 1963 until Stokely Carmichael replaced him in 1966. Carmichael's ascendancy reflected the organization's growing disillusionment with mainstream America toward a more militant and nationalist stance. When Carmichael gave his famous "Black Power" speech in 1966, many of SNCC's members left the organization; shortly afterwards, SNCC expelled all of its white members.

Under Carmichael's leadership, SNCC became increasingly radical, changing its name to the Student National Coordinating Committee. Many in SNCC had lost faith in nonviolence. In 1967, Carmichael left SNCC to join the Black Panther Party. Bankrupt and irrelevant, SNCC—once the very heart of the movement—disbanded in 1970.

— APRIL 18 —

1959

SECOND MARCH FOR SCHOOL INTEGRATION IN WASHINGTON

On this day in civil rights history, the second Youth March for Integrated Schools took place in Washington, D.C.

In the wake of the success of the first Youth March on October 25, 1958, a second, larger march was planned. The first ended on a high note but organizers felt that the demand for immediate school desegregation needed even more emphasis. The NAACP and SCLC played greater roles in the second march.

Although many civil rights luminaries took part in the march, the idea began with A. Philip Randolph; Bayard Rustin made it happen. Rustin organized the event, and planned the logistics of organizing students for an orderly march within the nation's capital.

This time, more than 25,000 high school and college students participated. They marched down the streets of Washington with signs and posters. Civil rights leaders Roy Wilkins, Daisy Bates, Jackie Robinson, Harry Belafonte, Ralph Bunche, Kenyan leader Tom Mboya, and A. Philip Randolph were all present. But Martin Luther King Jr. delivered the main speech.

"This is really a noble cause. As June approaches, with its graduation ceremonies and speeches, a thought suggests itself. You will hear much about careers, security, and prosperity. I will leave the discussion of such matters to your deans, your principals, and your valedictorians. But I do have a graduation thought to pass along to you. Whatever career you may choose for yourself—doctor, lawyer, teacher—let me propose an avocation to be pursued along with it. Become a dedicated fighter for civil rights. Make it a central part of your life," King told the students.

"It will make you a better doctor, a better lawyer, a better teacher. It will enrich your spirit as nothing else possibly can. It will give you that rare sense of nobility that can only spring from love and selfessly helping your fellow man. Make a career of humanity. Commit yourself to the noble struggle for equal rights. You will make a greater person of yourself, a greater nation of your country, and a finer world to live in."

The speech foreshadowed John F. Kennedy's inaugural exhortation of two years later: "Ask not what your country can do for you. Ask what you can do for your country." Both speeches motivated thousands of youth to become activists.

In many respects, the second youth march was a trial run for the 1963 March on Washington. The 1958 and 1959 successes persuaded Randolph that a widespread adult march was needed, while Rustin had once again proven he was the man for the job.

— APRIL 19 —
1969
ARMED BLACK STUDENTS TAKE OVER BUILDING AT CORNELL

On this day in civil rights history, 80 armed African American students brandished arms and took over the student union during parents' weekend at Cornell University in Ithaca, New York. "If we die, you are going to die," was the warning from the students, members of the Afro-American Society. The organization, led by Ed Whitfield, had a list of demands, including the institution of a degree-granting black studies program. Police forces and television, radio, and newsprint reporters converged on the scene. A tense standoff ensued.

At the time, the revolutionary fervor of the late 1960s fermented among college students. Gains made in the civil rights movement had whetted the appetite of young radicals across the country, and outrage over American inequality, American colonialism, and mostly about American involvement in the Vietnam War led many students to action. Protests for more female professors, more black professors, more liberal professors, protests against Vietnam, capitalism, Democrats and Republicans, Nixon and Humphrey—protests were an everyday occurrence across the country as emboldened students sought to revamp and reshape the educational institutions in which

The 1969 protest at Cornell

Photo courtesy of Associated Press

they were enrolled. Increasing frustration with the lack of progress led some to cast aside non-violent philosophy. A "by any means necessary" approach began to develop, exemplified by the Weathermen, former students that began a guerilla campaign to overthrow the government.

Students began to call for independent black studies programs taught and administered by African Americans. The lack of black-centered programs became a hot-button issue within the Black Power and Black Pride trends in radical thought. Education about black history and black contributions were essential to black liberation.

The armed students made the Cornell protest one of the most sensational of the era, and after 36 hours, Cornell officials announced they would establish an African Studies and Research Center. The Afro-American Society members emerged from the student union with rifles, shotguns, and black fists held high in victory. Some saw the university's response as wise, fair, and progressive, while others viewed it as a capitulation to the young and the furious. Other universities soon established black studies programs and hired black academics.

— APRIL 20 —

1971

SUPREME COURT APPROVES BUSING FOR SCHOOL INTEGRATION

On this day in civil rights history, the U.S. Supreme Court ruled unanimously in the *Swann v. Charlotte-Mecklenburg* decision that busing students to achieve school integration was constitutional.

Two decades after *Brown v. Board*, many local school districts remained segregated due to white flight to the suburbs, increased enrollment in private schools, and racially imbalanced zoning. In 1968, the Supreme Court in *Green v. County School Board* declared that desegregation had to take place immediately. One method school boards used in an effort to achieve balance was forced busing, where students would be transported to sometimes-faraway schools. Busing was often an unpopular solution. In Boston, for example, it led to rioting.

In Charlotte, North Carolina, a segregated school system was being run despite both the *Brown* and *Green* rulings. A case eventually made its way to the Supreme Court. The justices' decision was lengthy and complicated. Chief Justice Warren Burger delivered the opinion of the court: "This Court, in *Brown* I, appropriately dealt with the large constitutional principles; other federal courts had to grapple with the flinty, intractable realities of day-to-day implementation of those constitutional commands. Their efforts, of necessity, embraced a process of 'trial and error,' and our effort to formulate guidelines must take into account their experience."

He went on, "School authorities are traditionally charged with broad power to formulate and implement educational policy and might well conclude, for example, that in order to prepare students to live in a pluralistic society each school should have a prescribed ratio of Negro to white students reflecting the proportion for the district as a whole.

"All things being equal, with no history of discrimination, it might well be desirable to assign pupils to schools nearest their homes. But all things are not equal in a system that has been deliberately constructed and maintained to enforce racial segregation. The remedy for such segregation may be administratively awkward, inconvenient, and even bizarre in some situations and may impose burdens on some; but all awkwardness and inconvenience cannot be avoided in the interim period when remedial adjustments are being made to eliminate the dual school systems."

The ruling upheld mandatory busing in pursuance of integration as constitutional, and was thus a victory for civil rights campaigners hoping to provide blacks with equal education. The problem of integrated public schools, however, was not fully solved.

— APRIL 21 —
1960
EISENHOWER SIGNS 1960 CIVIL RIGHTS ACT

On this day in civil rights history, President Dwight D. Eisenhower signed the Civil Rights Act of 1960 into law.

Although not known as friendly to civil rights causes, President Eisenhower passed two civil rights bills during his tenure. Eisenhower was a moderate and perhaps even a progressive when it came to race. He eliminated the last vestiges of segregation in the armed forces and in the federal government and appointed the first African American to a high position on the White House staff. But politically he was not sure that federal intervention would erase the stains of racism that marred much of the country. In this regard, he was a gradualist who believed that change of this sort must happen over a period of time. He was also more concerned with foreign policy, distracted by the growing conflict with the Soviet Union and the spread of communism in foreign lands.

At the polls in 1960

The Civil Rights Act of 1957, the first civil rights bill since Reconstruction, established a civil rights commission. The 1960 Act, the second, followed a spate of bombing violence in the South. The bill allowed the U.S. attorney and federal judges to assign local inspectors to investigate local voter registration, empowering the federal government to levy fines for those who obstructed the right to vote. Southerners accused the federal government of overstepping its powers, and Southern Democrats, led by Mississippi Senator James Eastland, through a strategic filibuster, watered down the bill to almost complete uselessness. The Republican and liberal Democratic minority that supported the bill was outmaneuvered.

The bill's weakness centered around the fact that African Americans had to legally prove they were being obstructed in a court of law to have inspectors sent in the first place. This was expensive, time-consuming, and in the Deep South, dangerous.

Civil rights leaders were disappointed in the bill, although they all found hope in the government's admittance of a problem. A. Philip Randolph organized a march on both the Republican and Democratic Conventions, stumping for stronger legislation, calling it the "March on the Conventions Movement for Freedom Now."

This piece of legislation was unimportant in its immediate effects, as less than 3 percent of black voters registered beneath its protections, but it led the way to the more sweeping civil rights legislation of the 1960s.

— APRIL 22 —
1969
HARVARD CREATES AFRICAN STUDIES PROGRAM

On this day in civil rights history, amid social pressures and rampant student protests, Harvard University created a Committee on African Studies, that would lead ultimately to creation of a department for Afro-American studies.

Many African American writers and scholars are associated with Harvard: W. E. B. Du Bois, Cornel West, Countee Cullen, Henry Louis Gates, Charles Hamilton Houston, and Carter G. Woodson, among others.

But even at Harvard there was no academic home for African American historians and theorists writing about African American subjects. As the 1960s came to an end, this became an important issue for many progressive, black nationalist, and radical organizations, especially among students. Student organizations began making demands to the administration in the late 1960s for the school to create a degree-granting black studies program, arguing that minority groups needed their own academic institutions within the boundaries of the best schools. The all-white administrations of the day were viewed as conservative, reactionary, and complicit in the systematic exclusion of blacks from positions of power.

In response, Harvard created a student-faculty committee, chaired by Henry Rosovsky. The Rosovsky Committee delivered its report in January 1969, recommending the formation of an Afro-American studies program, increased graduate fellowships to African American students, and more attention to black student life on campus. The administration studied the report and finally approved it. The situation appeared to be mollified.

In early April, however, Students for a Democratic Society occupied University Hall to protest of the presence of U.S. military recruiters on campus. The police arrived and forcibly removed the protesters. A campus-wide student strike was called. Harvard University, like Berkeley, Cornell, and others, was facing a student uprising that could shut down operations indefinitely.

The Association of African and Afro-American Students seized the opportunity to utilize the crisis for their own benefit and demanded a new, separate Afro-American Studies program, staffed by black professors about whom the students would have a say. Scared by the armed occupation of Cornell a few days earlier, and facing a campus-wide shutdown, Harvard acquiesced to most of the students' demands, despite protests from many of the faculty, including Rosovsky who favored instead a black studies program.

Black studies programs soon began popping up at every major university.

— April 23 —
1965
King Leads March in Boston

On this day in civil rights history, a major Boston civil rights march took place. Thousands of local residents paraded through the streets asking for better economic conditions and an end to *de facto* segregation. Martin Luther King Jr. led the march.

Boston has a unique but troubled history with African Americans. In 1683, one of the first slave ships to America arrived in Boston. Many of the pre–Civil War abolitionists were located there, including William Lloyd Garrison and Charles Sumner. And many prominent black historians received degrees from Harvard, including W. E. B. Du Bois, who went on to establish the oldest NAACP branch there. Booker T. Washington founded the National Business League in Boston and fiery journalist William Monroe Trotter called Boston his home.

White abolitionists, however, bumped heads with rising black leaders who resented what they sometimes felt was a paternalistic attitude on the part of the white abolitionists.

Despite its longstanding liberal tradition, widespread employment discrimination maintained an obvious class structure in Boston. Irish unions preserved a patronage system that favored their own ethnic group. The Irish fought to keep jobs within their community. Boston accrued a reputation of being unfriendly to black laborers, and thus during the Great Migration was passed over by Southern blacks looking for work. By the 1960s, Boston was a segregated city.

Both CORE and the NAACP worked in Boston to eliminate segregation and to end job discrimination. Local activist Phyllis Ryan helped organize the 1965 march, and upwards of 20,000 people participated. Led by King and carrying signs and placards, marchers paraded through slum neighborhoods in the Roxbury area. The event culminated in a rally on Boston Common, where King spoke, emphasizing that the North needed a civil rights movement as much as the South.

Two months later, the Boston state legislature passed the Racial Imbalance Act, requiring an immediate end to segregation. One solution legislators decided upon was forced busing, which then led to riots in the 1970s.

— APRIL 24 —
1877
LAST FEDERAL TROOPS LEAVE SOUTH

On this day in civil rights history, the last federal troops were withdrawn from the South, ending the Reconstruction era.

During Reconstruction, the South was divided into five military-controlled districts, each run by a U.S. Army general. Thousands of troops occupied the war-ravaged South, enforcing the reforms passed by the Republican Congress, while also rebuilding the decimated infrastructure of the gutted Southern cities.

Three constitutional amendments were passed during Reconstruction: the 13th, which abolished slavery, the 14th, which granted citizenship to African Americans, and the 15th, which insured the right to vote to all males over age 21. African Americans voted and were elected in large numbers. Previously enslaved individuals became citizens overnight. The South responded with riots and an invisible empire of the Ku Klux Klan that dominated black citizens with violence and intimidation. In response, President U. S. Grant made the KKK illegal in 1870.

The military occupation was expensive and unpopular. The U.S. had accumulated a huge debt through the course of the war. Businessmen wanted a return to normality, while America at large wanted to heal. As America was expanding into the West, military forces were needed to commit to the American Indian campaigns. Whites in the South wanted autonomy, and complete control over what it considered its own affairs. African Americans in the South were precariously balanced at the center of these controversies. Despite the advances they were making, they were almost universally considered inferior. White Southerners considered it an affront to their traditions and way of life to share the power of governance with their former property. Meanwhile, Northerners were growing tired of the financial drain.

In 1877, President Rutherford B. Hayes won a close election, winning favor with the Southern states by agreeing to withdraw federal troops. This decision is now called the Compromise of 1877. As the troops left and the federal authority dissolved, the civil, economic, and political rights of African Americans disappeared with them.

— APRIL 25 —

1944

UNITED NEGRO COLLEGE FUND ORGANIZED

On this day in civil rights history, Frederick Patterson and Mary McCloud Bethune, among others, founded the United Negro College Fund. The program offered aid to aspiring low-income students and worked to keep down the costs of tuition at historically black colleges and universities (HBCUs). Many of America's future civil rights leaders would benefit from the program.

HBCUs were higher education institutions created to serve African American communities, usually incorporated before 1964. Many early African American leaders attended HBCUs.

In 1943, Patterson, then president of Tuskegee Institute, wrote an open letter to the *Pittsburgh Courier,* asking private black colleges in the U.S. to pool their money and "make a united appeal to the national conscience." Twenty-seven colleges joined in, polled their resources, and began fundraising to offer financial support to students and to increase each school's services. Many of the HBCUs became centers of student activism in the 1960s, funneling new generations of activists into SNCC, CORE, SDS, and other civil rights organizations.

Early supporters of UNCF were President Franklin Delano Roosevelt and John D. Rockefeller Jr.

In the 1970s, the UNCF adopted the slogan, "A mind is a terrible thing to waste"—one of the most effective and well-known advertising campaigns in U.S. history.

The program has grown to include 39 HBCUs and since its inception has raised more than $2 billion in aid for minority students. The UNCF is still a thriving organization, partly due to the tremendous fundraising efforts of many African American entertainers who donate time to UNCF events, and ranks in the top ten of charitable organizations operating in the U.S. every year.

— APRIL 26 —
1964
MISSISSIPPI FREEDOM DEMOCRATIC PARTY ORGANIZED

On this day in civil rights history, the Mississippi Freedom Democratic Party was officially created. The organization was an outgrowth of the Council of Federated Organization's Freedom Vote held in Mississippi the year before. The idea for a "Freedom Summer" grew out of that 1963 mock election. Hundreds of volunteers registered voters throughout Mississippi during the summer of 1964, while also educating them in "Freedom Schools" that offered an alternative to the mainstream segregated facilities. The Freedom Schools taught black history, math, reading, and American politics, among other subjects.

The vote this time would be for real.

Photo courtesy of Library of Congress

Fannie Lou Hamer addresses MFDP

Although the NAACP, CORE, and the SCLC were involved, the project was in reality almost completely a SNCC operation. Hundreds of white students from non-Southern middle-class families answered the SNCC call to work in the project. Bob Moses and other SNCC leaders reasoned that the presence of rich white college kids would bring national attention and federal protection.

The volunteers canvassed neighborhoods, explaining civic rights and responsibilities to illiterate sharecroppers who had never voted. The second step was driving people to courthouses to register, which resulted in delays and harassment.

In fact, Mississippi whites terrorized both the registration of black voters and the Freedom Schools for the whole summer. By summer's end, there had been more than 1,000 arrests of civil rights workers, 80 reported beatings, and more than 60 black churches and houses bombed, along with countless threats and harassing letters and phone calls.

At the time, Mississippi was a one-party state. Democrats dominated, and African Americans were prevented from voting by a complex series of controls. Hence, the formation of the MFDP. The MFDP was the most audacious part of the summer-long event, a new political entity. SNCC leaders decided a bold move was needed in the struggle in the South. Their plan was to harness the black voting potential in the state through a grassroots registration campaign, and then appear at the Democratic National Convention to be held in Atlantic City. Once there, the MFDP would bid to become the Democratic Party in Mississippi, eclipsing the segregated state delegation. It was a grand, risky plan, an all-or-nothing venture hinging on the sympathy of white Democrats from outside Mississippi.

— APRIL 27 —

1927

CORETTA SCOTT (KING) BORN IN ALABAMA

On this day in civil rights history, Coretta Scott was born in Marion, Alabama. From humble beginnings she would become one of the most important and recognizable African Americans of the 20th century, a great woman behind a great man.

After high school, she attended Antioch College in Ohio. From there Scott moved to Boston to study voice and violin at Boston's New England Conservatory of Music. She met a young theological student while living in Boston, and soon she was engaged to a future Nobel Prize winner and leader of the civil rights movement.

In 1953, she married Martin Luther King Jr. One year later, Coretta moved with King to Montgomery, assuming the pastor's wife's duties at Dexter Avenue Baptist Church. From this position King would become the unofficial leader of a widespread movement. Mrs. King encouraged her husband's civil rights efforts from the start, joining him on marches and protests. She faced daily death threats and harassment with undaunted courage. On one occasion she was almost killed by explosives meant for King.

She and King had four children. As King spent much of his time touring or participating in campaigns away from home, Mrs. King spent much of her time raising her children. But she always took an active role in the movement, speaking at churches, rallies, and other civic events.

After King was murdered, Mrs. King became a national civil rights leader. She worked on building the Martin Luther King Jr. Center for Nonviolent Social Change in Atlanta. As its acting president for more than two decades, Mrs. King worked in a variety of roles. She helped implement training programs in King's methodologies, as well as oversaw the accumulation of the largest collection of civil rights material.

In 1983, Mrs. King chaired the Martin Luther King Jr. Holiday Commission, which eventually established a Martin Luther King Jr. national holiday.

During her lifetime she has traveled around the world in pursuit of equality, including Ghana, Mexico, Switzerland, India, and Norway. She has campaigned for full employment, complete nuclear disarmament, and religious freedom.

In August 2005, Coretta Scott King suffered a stroke, but she seemed on the road to recovery.

— APRIL 28 —

1951

RUBY HURLEY OPENS SOUTHERN NAACP OFFICE

On this day in civil rights history, Ruby Hurley worked on setting up her office in Birmingham, Alabama. Hurley, like Daisy Bates and Rosa Parks, played a significant role in the movement, but unlike Bates and Parks, Hurley is mostly unknown today. This is a shame, for Hurley had a hand in many seminal events on the civil rights timeline and is an NAACP legend. She helped Marian Anderson find another venue, for example, when Constitution Hall was closed to the black singer by the Daughters of the Revolution.

In 1939, Hurley organized a youth council, and she became the national youth secretary of the NAACP in 1943. She proved adept at her job, enlarging youth membership to 25,000. But she entered the history books when she moved south.

She opened the first permanent NAACP office in the Deep South in 1951, in Birmingham, giving her the distinction of being the first full-time professional civil rights worker in the South, male or female. Hurley later became regional secretary—in charge of the NAACP activities in all the Deep South states. As a field worker, Hurley investigated lynchings of African Americans across the South. Her work in the South at that time was dangerous. During her tenure in Alabama, she received threatening letters, harassing phone calls, and was accosted on the street. At least one bombing attempt was made on her house.

Hurley's role as regional secretary placed her at the center of many important events. In 1955, Hurley helped Autherine Lucy desegregate the University of Alabama. Later that year, with Medgar Evers and Amzie Moore, Hurley investigated the Emmett Till case in Mississippi, seeking witnesses to Till's murder.

On June 1, 1956, the state of Alabama barred the NAACP from operating in the state. The action was eventually overturned in the courts, but in the meantime Hurley closed shop in Birmingham and moved to Atlanta to continue her work. She remained the regional secretary and was later involved in the Albany campaign.

Hurley spent most of her life working in the movement. She retired just two years before she died in 1980.

— APRIL 29 —
1992
RIOTERS PROTEST RODNEY KING VERDICTS IN L.A.

On this day in civil rights history, rioting broke out across black neighborhoods in Los Angeles. The riots signified how little conditions had changed for urban African Americans and offered a chilling look at black rage and the gaps that still remained between white and black America.

Conditions in south central L.A in 1992 were similar to those identified by the Kerner Commission as having sparked the Watts riots in 1965—poor living conditions, high unemployment, and little chance of economic betterment, leading to widespread disillusionment with the United States.

Also, large numbers of Latinos and Koreans had moved into the area, opening businesses and attending mostly black schools, straining cultural and racial tensions in new ways. Finally, the Los Angeles police department's reputation of racial profiling and excessive force had stripped it of credibility in the black community.

These factors helped make the Rodney King affair so incendiary. On March 3, 1991, four LAPD officers pulled King over for erratic driving. King resisted arrest and the four knocked him to the ground and tasered him senseless, then beat him mercilessly with nightsticks. That no doubt would have been the end of the incident, except that a bystander videotaped the attack. The video was released to the media and became a national sensation. The four officers were eventually indicted on charges of using excessive force.

Police arresting rioters in L.A.

When an all-white jury found the officers not guilty, African Americans in south central L.A. tore the city apart with widespread looting and vandalism. Korean businesses were attacked. Carjackers prowled the streets. Homemade firebombs were tossed into display windows. Flights to and from L.A. were canceled. Roving gangs fought each other in the streets while bystanders were trapped in the anarchy. The city shut down.

The National Guard was called in. The same steps that ended the Watts riot were taken: a curfew was put in place, and armed roadblocks and checkpoints were established. Intermittent looting lasted for weeks.

The resulting devastation was enormous. More than 50 people died, 2,000 were injured, and almost $1 billion of property damage was done.

A short-lived Rebuild L.A. program began, but with lack of corporate investors it quickly folded. The dream of racial harmony and equality envisioned by the civil rights movement had never seemed so far away.

On this day in civil rights history, President Woodrow Wilson denied his initial praise of the film, *Birth of a Nation.*, which he had screened in the White House. The film was, he said, "Like writing history with lightning." Wilson's subsequent recants meant little, however. Sections from his writings are quoted throughout the film.

Directed by D. W. Griffith, *Birth of a Nation* is considered U.S. cinema's first masterpiece and was immediately and hugely successful. Unfortunately, the film—based on the 1905 Thomas Dixon novel, *The Clansman*—is also a masterpiece of racist propaganda and historical revisionism. The film depicts a Reconstruction-era South overrun by vile carpetbaggers and devious scalawags. Blacks are shown as indolent, drunken, simple, and lascivious. The white knights of the Ku Klux Klan ride gloriously to the rescue of the South's traditions, and especially its white women. The film glorifies the KKK and lynching, while demonizing African Americans and sympathetic whites.

Photo courtesy of Library of Congress

President Wilson

The NAACP picketed, protested, and tried to have the film banned and then censored, all to no avail. "My only regret is that it is all so terribly true," President Wilson had also said after his private screening. The quote was used to promote the film.

White moviegoers loved the movie, firing pistols at screenings, and attending in Klan apparel. Later that year, an entrepreneur revived the dormant KKK in a dramatic ceremony—using imagery adapted from the film—at Stone Mountain, Georgia. Over the next decade, in an era of nativism and white supremacy, the resurrected KKK spread across the enrolled. Millions of white Protestants joined, more in the North than in the South.

Wilson's withdrawal of his endorsement of the film was too little and too late. Despite being in many ways a progressive visionary, Wilson's record in racial matters was abysmal, both at home and abroad. Under Wilson, the U.S. government became more rigidly segregated. And through military force, Wilson installed pro-American regimes which then proceeded to oppress indigenous peoples in Nicaragua, Haiti, and Panama.

Today, *Birth of a Nation* is a historical oddity, seen mostly in film classes. However, its potent imagery continued to fuel the imaginations of Klansmen and other white sympathizers throughout the civil rights years of the 1950s and 1960s and even during the KKK resurgence of the late 1970s and early 1980s.

This day in

May

— MAY 1 —

1933

MYLES HORTON OPERATES HIGHLANDER SCHOOL

On this day in civil rights history, Myles Horton continued his second year of operating the Highlander School.

Born on July 5, 1905, in Savannah, Tennessee, Horton enrolled at Cumberland College in 1924. In the summer of 1927, Horton's experiences teaching Bible classes to the mountain people of Ozone, Tennessee, exposed him to the social problems of Appalachian poverty and profoundly influenced him. He determined to continue his studies so he could return to the region and start a school.

In 1928, Horton organized interracial meetings of the YMCA and later attended seminary in New York. He then transferred to the University of Chicago, where he met Jane Addams, famous for her Hull House that provided free healthcare to immigrants. Horton admired Addams and took her lessons back to his home state.

Horton and Don West founded the Highlander School in Monteagle, Tennessee. The school's mission statement was: "To provide an educational center in the South for the training of rural and industrial leaders, and for the conservation and enrichment of the indigenous cultural values of the mountains."

The Highlander School taught blacks and whites together, in defiance of segregation laws. The Highlander School taught literacy classes as well as leadership skills. Early on, Horton taught coal miners, helping organize unions to help fight the dismal conditions that claimed so many lives in mine explosions or through the ravages of black lung disease. Horton's labor affiliations brought him enemies, who labeled him a communist. He denied the charge but kept on teaching and organizing.

By the 1950s, Highlander had became a training ground for civil rights activists. Many influential figures attended or taught classes there, including Rosa Parks, Septima Clark, Martin Luther King Jr., Andrew Young, Eleanor Roosevelt, Fannie Lou Hamer, Pete Seeger, and Stokely Carmichael, to list a few.

As the modern civil rights movement gained steam, Horton's little school was increasingly vilified by segregationists. U.S. Senator James Eastland of Mississippi accused the school of being a communist haven. In 1960, Tennessee officials closed the school down for violating segregation laws and confiscated the school's property. Horton moved the school to Knoxville, renaming it the Highlander Research and Education Center.

As the civil rights movement wound down, Highlander moved into environmentalism and economic justice, maintaining a close connection to the still dirt-poor mountain people of Tennessee.

In 1990, Myles Horton died. He was 84.

— MAY 2 —

1963

CHILDREN'S CRUSADE REVITALIZES BIRMINGHAM CAMPAIGN

On this day in civil rights history, large groups of black teens began a series of marches through downtown Birmingham. The local police, under the command of notoriously segregationist public safety commissioner Eugene "Bull" Connor, responded with a savage attack, using dogs and fire hoses against the protesters. The resulting public backlash ultimately led to the integration of most Birmingham businesses.

The youths had answered a call from SCLC leaders, who needed more bodies to fill Birmingham jails to dramatize the simple demands of Project C: desegregation of all public facilities; better employment opportunities; dismissal of charges against jailed protesters; and the establishment of a biracial committee to implement the above.

But Project C ran out of momentum. Lackluster support from adults produced too few protesters. In-fighting among the various civil rights personalities strained their fragile unity. And Connor, who had been expected to attack demonstrators, had yet to fully tip his hand.

Enter the children. SCLC staffer James Bevel came up with the idea of using the enthusiastic local high schoolers as protesters. Others argued that the students were too young and were untrained in the methods of nonviolence. But with Project C in danger of faltering—the media had grown bored and the city thus far had no trouble absorbing the pressure—the teenagers were unleashed.

Using Sixteenth Street Baptist Church as headquarters, waves of teenagers began to march toward city hall, led by Bevel. The first throngs were arrested on sight. But as the jail began to fill up, Connor decided against further arrests. The next day, more protests took place. A few marchers allegedly tossed bottles, which provided Connor with the pretense he needed. He ordered the attack dogs, police, and firehoses into action. Reporters on the scene captured the savage attack on celluloid. The resulting carnage shocked the nation. President John Kennedy said the photos made him sick.

The children continued to march. Over the next few days, more than 1,000 were arrested, overflowing the jails. The city's coffers were taxed by the movement's efforts. And the boycott was beginning to hurt many businesses.

Acting without Birmingham officials' approval, a committee of white businessmen said they would meet the movement's demands. Thanks to the participation of young people in what came to be called "the children's crusade," the SCLC's Birmingham campaign was saved; white lunch counters and fitting rooms were desegregated.

— MAY 3 —

1898

SEPTIMA CLARK BORN IN SOUTH CAROLINA

On this day in civil rights history, Septima Poinsette Clark, a powerful leader for civil rights and voter education, was born in Charleston, South Carolina. She was the second of eight children of a Haitian-born mother and an an ex-slave father.

After high school, she taught at a segregated school and married World War I vet Nerie Clark in 1919. He died in 1925, leaving Clark with two children to raise.

After a series of teaching positions, she ended up in Columbia, where she became involved with community organizations and the NAACP, which was then engaged in a court case demanding equal pay for black teachers. Thurgood Marshall was the lead attorney, and Clark helped him with preparation and during the proceedings. When she returned to Charleston in 1947, she carried a master's degree and the NAACP with her.

After the *Brown v. Board* decision, states began requiring teachers, black or white, to list organizations they were a part of. As had other Southern states, South Carolina passed a law forbidding any public employee from belonging to any civil rights organization. Clark declared her NAACP membership; she lost her job and her pension as a result.

She then accepted a job offer from Myles Horton to become director of the Highlander Folk School in Tennessee. Highlander held workshops on desegregation, among other topics, and it was here that many future civil rights heroes—including Rosa Parks and Martin Luther King Jr.—cultivated civil rights philosophies. In 1957, with Esau Jenkins and Bernice Robinson, Clark began a series of evening citizenship schools, teaching adults to read and how to register to vote.

After the state of Tennessee forced Highlander to close, Clark moved her work to the SCLC. She became an influential recruiter for the organization and its director of education. In 1962, the SCLC joined with other civil rights groups to launch the Voter Education Project, built on Clark's citizenship school model.

Andrew Young called the citizenship schools the foundation of the civil rights movement, "as responsible for transforming the South as anything anybody did."

When Martin Luther King Jr. was awarded the Nobel Prize in 1964, he insisted that Clark join him on his trip to Sweden. He later declared that she deserved the award as much as he did.

After a long, full life in the movement, Septima Clark died in 1987.

— MAY 4 —
1961
FREEDOM RIDES BEGIN

On this day in civil rights history, 13 passengers—seven black, six white—left Washington, D.C., to challenge the illegal segregation taking place across the South in interstate facilities. The action was called a freedom ride. The plan was to travel through the South to New Orleans, to arrive on May 17, the seventh anniversary of the *Brown* decision.

The U.S. Supreme Court, in its 1960 *Boynton v. Virginia* decision, had mandated the desegregation of all interstate transportation facilities including restrooms, bus stations, and coffee counters. But in the South, the ruling was ignored.

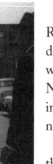

Freedom Rider Bus

The notion to test the situation arose with the Congress of Racial Equality. In 1947, CORE had sponsored an earlier freedom ride, the 1947 Journey for Reconciliation, which had ended with its participants jailed and sentenced to county work gangs. Now, with the John F. Kennedy administration newly installed in the White House, and with the federal government taking a new interest in civil rights, CORE decided to act once again.

"We plan to challenge every form of segregation met by the bus passenger," James Farmer, president of CORE, said in a letter to President Kennedy and his brother, Robert, the U.S. attorney general.

As the bus left Washington, the whites freedom riders sat in the back while the blacks sat in the front. At rest stops and bus stations, the white passengers would go into the "colored" areas, and vice versa. "We planned the freedom ride with the specific intention of creating a crisis," Farmer said later. "We were counting on the bigots in the South to do our work for us. We figured that the government would have to respond if we created a situation that was headline news all over the world, and affected the nation's image abroad. An international crisis, that was our strategy."

By crisis, Farmer meant a crisis of America's international image. Kennedy became president at the height of the Cold War; all around the globe the United States portrayed itself as the champion of democracy against the iron fist of Soviet communism. But at home, the U.S. image was undercut by the spotlight the civil rights movement was shining on violence, intimidation, repression, and discrimination against the nation's own black citizens.

In this context, the freedom riders set out to determine whether the new administration was committed to equality under the law. Others were not hopeful. "You will never make it through Alabama," Martin Luther King Jr. said to one of the participants.

— MAY 5 —
1905
INFLUENTIAL "CHICAGO DEFENDER" BEGINS PUBLICATION

On this day in civil rights history, Robert S. Abbott founded the *Chicago Defender*. It grew into the most influential black newspaper of its day, attacking lynching and other racial injustices. Pullman porters carried the paper south of the Mason-Dixon Line, distributing it one railroad stop at a time. During its heyday, the *Defender* had a readership of almost half a million.

In the 1920s, the *Defender* campaigned for Southern blacks to move north where there were more jobs and less oppression. The movement of African Americans lasted until the 1960s and became known as the Great Migration. Its causes were many. The Great Depression sent many families northward looking for work. Lagging prices for cotton forced many sharecroppers off the land and into factories. The World Wars suppressed immigration, and thus industry needed cheap labor from home. Finally, lynchings and other racial violence in the South scared many families away.

African Americans moved in droves to Detroit, Pittsburgh, Chicago, New York, Milwaukee, and Cleveland—cities with thriving industry. The cities welcomed their new citizens by herding them into dilapidated neighborhoods through discriminatory real estate practices. Low wages and harsh working conditions wrecked men's health and drove many into further destitution. The resulting segregation was in some ways more profound than in the South. As blacks continued to move northward, white populations reacted violently, sometimes resulting in race riots. Blacks could vote, but gerrymandering rendered their nascent political power almost useless in local elections.

The Southern farming industry did not want African Americans to leave, as they were the primary source of labor. Some planters promised better working conditions and wages, while others used harassment and intimidation. Everyone wanted blacks for cheap labor, but no one wanted them on an equal political footing.

Eventually more than a million African American families moved north. The result was a shift in lifestyles for many African Americans from a rural to an urban setting. The *Defender's* campaign to draw Southern blacks to Chicago worked. By 1918, the city's black population had tripled.

— MAY 6 —

1961

'WE SHALL OVERCOME' BECAME ANTHEM OF THE MOVEMENT

On this day in civil rights history, protesters across the South sang the song that became the anthem of the movement, "We Shall Overcome."

In 1965, in his speech for the passage of the Voting Rights Act, President Lyndon Johnson said: "It is the effort of American Negroes to secure for themselves the full blessings of American life. Their cause must be our cause too. Because it's not just Negroes, but really it's all of us, who must overcome the crippling legacy of bigotry and injustice. And we shall overcome."

He chose his words carefully. "We shall overcome" was the chorus and title of the key protest song of the modern civil rights movement. Protesters sang the song, arms interlaced, as police kicked, shoved, and beat them with clubs and unleashed attack dogs on them. The song drifted on the currents of the movement from Montgomery, Alabama, to Washington, D.C. Soon it was the major anthem of the Southern labor and civil rights movements.

People of all ages belted out the song as they marched, boycotted, or waited in jail, taking solace and courage in the simple, rhythmic declaration of the inevitability of love, peace, and justice. Joan Baez sang the song at civil rights rallies and concerts; Martin Luther King Jr. referred to it in many of his sermons.

The song itself has a strange history. Zilphia Horton, the wife of Highlander Folk School founder Myles Horton, overheard a black woman singing a slow, old spiritual on a picket line in 1946. The song's radiating hope tinged with sadness affected Horton. She returned to the Highlander School in Tennessee and taught the song to Pete Seeger, the folk singer and activist. Seeger altered the song then taught it to Frank Hamilton, another folk singer.

Hamilton changed it some more, and then taught the song to folk singers Guy and Candie Carawan. The Carawans, later folk-singers-in-residence at the Highlander Center, taught it to the young people who were organizing the Student Nonviolent Coordinating Committee.

The chorus is simple: "Oh, deep in my heart / I do believe / We shall overcome some day."

— MAY 7 —
2000
BLACK JOCKEY BREAKS BARRIER AT KENTUCKY DERBY

On this day in civil rights history, Marlon St. Julien rode in the Kentucky Derby, the first African American since 1921 to do so.

Horseracing was the first spectator sport to gain widespread fans in America. Before the Civil War, before America was even a country, hundreds of thousands of Americans cheered the first professional athletes as they raced horses. At the beginning, most of the riders were black and many of the best were slaves. Horseracing was popular across the Atlantic, too, and blacks rode in races in Europe.

In the first Kentucky Derby in 1875, 13 of the 15 riders were black; African American Oliver Lewis won the first race.

Race day at Churchill Downs

Photo courtesy of Library of Congress

In fact, black riders won 12 out of the first 16 derbies. African Americans worked as horse trainers and jockeys and dominated the sport. The first racing star was black. Abe Hawkins, a former slave, won national prominence for his performances, gaining praise in white newspapers across the country.

Another African American, Isaac Murphy, was the most successful jockey of all time, winning over 40 percent of all the races he competed in. When he died, he was buried next to the most famous horse of all time, Man O' War.

But as the sport gained popularity, African Americans were pushed to the background, as stable boys and hired help. African Americans migrated in large numbers to the North, while the South began to focus mythic attention on horseracing, claiming it as a tradition and sacred institution. The Kentucky Derby is an especial oddity. Dozens of traditions, including high hats, mint juleps, fancy umbrellas, and ritualized songs, now exist as part of the ceremony. In the popular consciousness, the race has become synonymous with well-heeled Southern gentry. There are other important races, but the Kentucky Derby is the most prestigious.

The last black rider to win the Kentucky Derby was James Winkfield in 1902. After 1921, no black jockeys could be found. Eight decades would go by without a single black rider in the race.

In 2000, an African American returned to the sport his people helped perfect. Marlon St. Julien, 28 years old, became the first to enter the Kentucky Derby since 1921. "I just want to be considered as a jockey," he said, "not a black jockey or a white jockey."

— MAY 8 —
1915
JOHN HOPE FRANKLIN BORN

On this day in civil rights history, distinguished historian John Hope Franklin was born in Rentiesville, Oklahoma. His childhood was marred by the secondhand status of African Americans, and in nearby Tulsa in 1921, horrible race riots caught the young Franklin's fear and imagination.

After graduating from Fisk University, Franklin earned his PhD from Harvard University. He moved to New York City to chair the history department of Brooklyn College. Franklin found treatment of African Americans in the North to be only marginally better than their treatment in the South.

Franklin served on the editorial board of the *Journal of Negro History*. He has received honorary degrees from more than 100 universities.

Despite his impressive academic career, however, it is Franklin's histories that have earned him the highest esteem. From the outset he sought to apply a scrutinizing black eye to history. "It was necessary," he said, "as a black historian, to have a personal agenda." He began publishing in the early 1940s. *From Slavery to Freedom*, released in 1947, was an enormous success, eventually selling millions of copies. Through the book's critical and popular success, Franklin established the legitimacy of African American history in a time when it scarcely existed. Franklin was declared the successor of W. E. B. Du Bois as the preeminent black scholar in the United States.

Franklin also took part in the civil rights movement. He helped Thurgood Marshall research the *Brown v. Board* case that served as a catalyst to the modern civil rights movement. He later took part in the 1963 March on Washington for Jobs and Freedom and the 1965 Selma-to-Montgomery March.

He has published many books, including *The Emancipation Proclamation; The Militant South; The Free Negro in North Carolina; Reconstruction after the Civil War; A Southern Odyssey: Travelers in the Ante-bellum North; Race and History: Selected Essays, 1938-1988*; and in 1993, *The Color Line: Legacy for the Twenty-first Century*.

Looking at history, he said, "When we also learn that this country and the Western world have no monopoly of goodness and truth or of skills and scholarship, we begin to appreciate the ingredients that are indispensable to making a better world. In a life of learning that is, perhaps, the greatest lesson of all."

In 1995, Franklin was awarded the Presidential Medal of Freedom. Two years later, President Bill Clinton appointed Franklin as chairman of a committee intended to create a national dialogue on race and reconciliation.

— MAY 9 —

1994

NELSON MANDELA ELECTED PRESIDENT OF SOUTH AFRICA

On this day in civil rights history, South Africa elected Nelson Mandela president in a historic move for international race relations.

Government-sanctioned segregation became the official policy of the Republic of South Africa in 1948 with the ascendancy of the Nationalist Party. The systematic oppression, economic exploitation, and segregation, based on the colonial and neo-colonial policies of the Afrikaner government, became known as apartheid. As in the Southern U.S. variety, black South Africans were denied the right to vote. Living conditions on the whole may have been even worse for South African blacks. Resettlement campaigns forcibly removed blacks from their lands. White police acted with impunity against black protests. Blacks in South Africa were kept in almost complete servitude, and were denied education or knowledge of the outside world.

South African apartheid was in many respects a darker cousin to U.S. racism. The movement to end apartheid, like the U.S. civil rights movement, was met with harsh resistance. In the U.S., there was a white supremacist-Klan conspiracy perpetuated by federal complicity and apathy; in South Africa, segregation was maintained by a harsh military regime.

The African National Congress, the leading South African protest organization, was outlawed and went underground after a series of government-sponsored massacres. The ANC eventually adopted guerilla tactics, including terrorist bombings of civilian targets. Nelson Mandela, a lawyer and leader of the ANC, was arrested in 1962. He remained in prison for almost 30 years, and as the years passed, he became an international symbol of the fight against apartheid.

Entering the late 1970s and early 1980s, South African apartheid became a hot-button issue. Pop songs, books, articles, and rallies cried "Free Nelson Mandela" in countries around the world. South Africa became externally isolated and internally fragmented. The white government felt its power slipping and in the late 1980s embarked on a series of brutal repressions.

But change was on the wind. In 1990, Mandela was released, a hero to black and oppressed peoples everywhere. The Nationalist Government finally agreed to open elections and in 1994, Mandela was elected president by an overwhelming majority. As president, he then began a series of reforms designed to heal the racial divisions within his country. The experiment of post-apartheid South Africa is still underway.

Mandela, meanwhile, is an international statesman and one of the most admired figures in the world.

— MAY 10 —
2004
JUSTICE DEPARTMENT REOPENS 1955 TILL MURDER CASE

On this day in civil rights history, the case of the 1955 murder of Emmett Till was reopened. Although the self-confessed but acquitted killers of young Till had long since died, new evidence suggested that others, probably still living, were involved in the murder. The changed racial climate in the state of Mississippi made a new investigation possible.

The new evidence was revealed by documentary filmmaker Keith Beauchamp, who found new witnesses who claimed at least ten other participants were involved in the murder. Beauchamp used these new witnesses to good effect in his film, *The Untold Story of Emmett Louis Till.*

The reopening of the Till case is part of a contemporary movement by states, localities, and even the federal government to atone for the failure to adequately prosecute and punish atrocities during the civil rights era. Many civil rights-related murders have been revisited in the past couple of decades, including the 1963 deaths of the four girls in the Birmingham church bombing, the 1963 assassination of Medgar Evers, and the 1964 murders of the three SNCC workers in Philadelphia, Mississippi. More than 25 cases have been reopened, and several high-profile convictions have resulted. The "atonement trials" are a part of the United States trying to come to terms with its past failings in regard to its African American citizens.

The renewed Till investigation began with the exhuming of Till's body for an autopsy, since no autopsy was originally performed—a lack of forensic evidence that gave the all-white 1955 jury its rationale for the not guilty verdicts.

Emmett Till's remains

The autopsy was performed, and Till was reburied on June 4. The slow investigation continues, with at least five suspects facing potential criminal prosecution. All maintain their innocence.

Till's murder had a significant impact: Langston Hughes, Toni Morrison, James Baldwin and Bob Dylan all used the Till case as inspiration for stories, plays, and songs. Till's senseless death offered a stark example of the perils and violence of institutionalized racism that existed prior to the gains won in the civil rights movement.

Despite his murderers going free, Till's death was not in vain. He became a martyr for the civil rights cause, inspiring his country to change.

— MAY 11 —
1956
'BROWDER V. GAYLE' HEARING BEGINS

On this day in civil rights history, a panel of three judges began listening to arguments in the *Browder v. Gayle* case. Although the famous bus boycott gets the glory, it was this lawsuit in federal court in Montgomery, Alabama, that ultimately desegregated the city buses, established legal precedent, and handed the modern civil rights movement one of its first and greatest victories.

After Rosa Parks was arrested and the boycott was begun by the Montgomery Improvement Association in 1955, a series of mishandled negotiations stalled, mostly due to the intransigence of white city politicians; the privately owned bus company wanted to negotiate and settle. African Americans held fast to the boycott, while white resistance grew.

On February 1, 1956, attorney Fred Gray filed a class action lawsuit in U.S. District Court on behalf of four women—Aurelia Browder, Susie McDonald, Claudette Colvin and Mary Louise Smith—who had either been mistreated or arrested on the buses in circumstances similar to Rosa Parks's case, but before her arrest.

Gray was Rosa Parks's and Martin Luther King Jr.'s attorney, as well as the lead attorney on the Montgomery bus boycott-related cases. He would go on to represent the NAACP when Alabama expelled the organization from the state; the Selma-to-Montgomery marchers; and the plaintiffs in numerous school desegregation cases. Through his legal work, Gray played a pivotal role in the movement during a crucial period.

The federal courts had upheld segregation in the 1896 *Plessy v. Ferguson* case, but the "separate but equal" doctrine of *Plessy* was overturned by the 1954 *Brown* decision. Gray was hopeful that a new legal day was dawning.

Because of the issues involved, the *Browder* case was assigned to a three-judge panel, and, by custom, the least senior judge was responsible for researching and presenting the opinion to be rejected or approved by his colleagues. That judge was Frank M. Johnson Jr., who was appointed by President Dwight Eisenhower just a few months before Rosa Parks was arrested.

Johnson believed in the Constitution, and he believed that the same legal principles that guided the Supreme Court in *Brown* also applied to this case. His opinion declared that Montgomery's segregated bus seating was unlawful. Circuit Judge Richard T. Rives agreed, so Johnson's opinion prevailed (the third judge dissented). The city of Montgomery appealed the ruling, but the U.S. Supreme Court refused to hear the case, thus affirming the district court.

The black citizens of Montgomery had defeated segregated city buses.

1862

SLAVES SEIZE CONFEDERATE STEAMSHIP

On this day in civil rights history, Southern slaves seized control of the Confederate steamship, the *Planter*. The leader of the raid was Robert Smalls, a crafty, courageous man who would become a major African American figure.

Born in 1839, the same year the Amistad slaves revolted against their slavers, Smalls worked as a quartermaster aboard the *Planter*, a cotton steamer that General Roswell Ripley used as his base of operations in Charleston, South Carolina. The *Planter* was a huge transport ship, converted to carry troops if necessary and outfitted with cannons.

Photo courtesy of Library of Congress

The 'Planter'

Smalls was trusted by the Confederates, and on the evening of May 12, he was left alone on board. Familiar with the Confederate gun positions, Smalls dressed himself up like a Confederate captain and navigated the huge converted war ship out of the harbor, sailing past the guns of Fort Sumter, carrying his wife and 12 other slaves to freedom.

The *Planter* hoisted its white flag as it sailed into the Union blockade. Smalls and the others were freed, the ship taken as contraband. The daring escape was an unequivocal success; Smalls and his crew were given a reward for their efforts.

Smalls was not unique. After the Emancipation Proclamation freed slaves in the Confederate states, more and more African Americans began to enlist. Over 175,000 blacks fought for the Union during the war, with more than 70 percent of eligible free, black males enlisting, many fighting in the famed all-black 54th Infantry Regiment of Massachusetts. They served in segregated units underneath white commanders. They fought with inferior equipment and less pay, with the hope that the war would end their collective suffering.

Smalls worked as a Union recruiter and navy captain during the remainder of the war, eventually earning the rank of captain. Due to his exploits, he became a minor celebrity, and met with President Lincoln. During Reconstruction, Smalls was elected to the U.S. House of Representatives as a congressman from South Carolina, propelled by the huge influx of new black voters. He served five terms until 1885, and was one of the last African Americans to be voted out of office as Reconstruction came to an end.

Smalls died in 1915 as a Civil War hero and trailblazing African American politician.

— MAY 13 —
1888
BRAZIL ABOLISHES SLAVERY

On this day in civil rights history, Brazil formally abolished slavery, the last country in the Western hemisphere to do so, 23 years after the practice was formally abolished in the United States by the 13th Amendment.

Founded as a Portuguese colony, in the 1700s Brazil became an enormous slave plantation used mostly for growing and processing sugar cane. The indigenous peoples were exterminated or forcibly removed and were replaced with African slaves. In 1822, Brazil declared itself in-dependent from Portugal and operated as a constitutional monarchy, but slavery and the plantation economy remained, however. Much of the country's history, finance, and culture were tied to the practice of slavery.

The empire of Brazil had two kings. The second, Pedro II, recognizing the immorality of slavery, abolished the prac-tice in his kingdom in 1888. But one year later, a coalition of planters, farmers, and military men rose up against the royal family. The United States of Brazil was born.

Slavery, and the racial prejudice that sustained it, was a worldwide problem. Many European countries imported slaves, including Holland, England, and France, while also profiting from the slave trade to the Americas. European countries, including Germany and Belgium, began to occupy African lands, enslaving the native peoples and conscripting them into military and other types of service, while exploit-

Don Pedro II

Photo courtesy of Library of Congress

ing the continent's resources to fill the coffers of their royal families back home. Slavery was always first and foremost an economic venture; it was highly profitable for all involved, except, of course, the slaves.

Although the slave trade was mostly practiced by Europeans, sizeable portion of Africa and the Middle East also participated in large slaving operations.

Slavery in Brazil, as in the United States and elsewhere, resulted in a disparity between the different shades of colored peoples. Gradations of color served as a stratifying mechanism: in general, the darker the skin, the lower on the socio-economic ladder a person will fall. In fact, Brazil today suffers from some of the harshest economic disparities in the world. And forced labor, similar to the indentured servant practice of the 1700s, still exists in Brazil.

— MAY 14 —

1961

FREEDOM RIDERS ASSAULTED IN ALABAMA

On this day in civil rights history, the CORE-sponsored freedom ride from Washington, D.C., to New Orleans was disrupted by brutal mob attacks in two Alabama cities.

Since leaving Washington on May 4, the ride was mostly uneventful. In Atlanta, the 13 riders—seven black, six white—split into two groups heading toward Birmingham by different bus lines. When the group on the Greyhound line reached Anniston, Alabama, a waiting white mob attacked, smashing the bus windows and slashing the tires. The driver managed to pull away from the station but made it only a few miles before the tires blew out. The mob had pursued in cars, and resumed its attack. The bus was firebombed, and as the passengers fled the burning bus, they were beaten. Miraculously, no one was killed. The second group on a Trailways bus made it to Birmingham, where they were met at the terminal by another white mob. The freedom riders were brutally beaten.

The Anniston attack

In both attacks, the mobs, led by the KKK, were able to do their vicious work because police were absent. Investigations later revealed that Birmingham police had agreed to wait 15 minutes before responding to the mob attack. Police Commissioner Eugene "Bull" Connor later said his officers were absent because they were all visiting their mothers—the attacks occurred on Mother's Day.

The savage violence brought national attention, and state and federal officials debated what to do. The freedom riders, CORE, and other civil rights groups were also divided on the options. Some called for more freedom riders, while others advocated a cooling-off period before someone got killed. Also, the bus companies could not find willing drivers to take the freedom riders on the next leg of their journey.

Meanwhile, students from the Nashville movement—John Lewis, Henry Thomas, Diane Nash, and others—resolved that the rides had to continue; they were simply too important to the movement to abandon. A new group of riders came to Birmingham and attempted to board buses to go on to Montgomery, the next stop. They were arrested by Birmingham police and taken to the Tennessee state line and dumped off in the middle of the night. They made their way back to Birmingham and again attempted to board a bus.

Federal and state officials had been negotiating behind the scenes with the freedom riders, the bus companies, and civil rights leaders. A bus driver was found, and, on May 20, the reinforced freedom riders pulled out of Birmingham under state police escort and headed toward Montgomery.

— MAY 15 —

1938

NASHVILLE/SNCC LEADER DIANE NASH BORN

On this day in civil rights history, Diane Nash was born in Chicago, Illinois.

Nash enrolled at Fisk University in Nashville, Tennessee, in the late 1950s. Here she met Reverend James Lawson and took part in his nonviolent civil disobedience workshops for the Nashville Christian Leadership Conference in 1959. Elected chair of the Student Central Committee, Nash helped plan and was one of participants in the sit-ins at Nashville lunch counters. She was promptly arrested. After three months of sit-ins, Nashville became the first Southern city to desegregate its dining facilities.

Attending the Southwide Youth Leadership Conference at Shaw University in 1960, Nash became one of the founding members of the Student Nonviolent Coordinating Committee and was an influential leader of the group. In 1961, when the sponsors of the freedom rides wanted to call off the rides due to the danger, Nash helped regain momentum by coordinating new rides with new riders.

Nash worked for multiple civil rights organizations, including a stint as an organizer for SCLC. Throughout her career with SNCC and the SCLC, Nash helped mold important campaigns— in Birmingham, Selma, and Mississippi.

Nash married fellow Nashville activist James Bevel. In 1962 they moved to Mississippi and began teaching workshops on nonviolence and voter registration. She was promptly arrested. During the course of the legal proceedings, it became known that Nash was pregnant. In a public statement, she then determined to have her baby in jail. "This will be a black baby born in Mississippi, and thus wherever he is born, he will be in prison." Her sentence was immediately commuted.

President John F. Kennedy later appointed Nash to a committee that helped draft the Civil Rights Act of 1964. In 1965 she and Bevel received the SCLC's Rosa Parks Award. Although instrumental in many of the great civil rights actions of the 1960s, Nash turned away from the SCLC due to its male dominance. In 1966, Nash broke ties with SNCC as well, over Stokely Carmichael's leadership; she felt the organization was heading in the wrong direction.

She and Bevel had two children before they divorced. Nash moved to Chicago, where she still lives, and began a career as an educator and fair-housing advocate. In 2004 she received the Distinguished American Award from the John F. Kennedy Library and Foundation.

On this day in civil rights history, sides in the *Briggs v. Elliot* case began aruging their respective cases.

For years the NAACP and other organizations had looked for legal challenges to Southern segregation. In South Carolina, the Rev. Joseph DeLaine, local activist and principal of an all-black school in Clarendon County, led the early drive for desegregation. Underfunded black schools, often lacking basic amenities and up-to-date textbooks, were not providing a decent education.

Photo courtesy of Library of Congress

Thurgood Marshall

DeLaine and other black citizens of Clarendon County had repeatedly requested school buses for their children and even filed a lawsuit when county officials failed to respond. The case was thrown out over a technicality. A group of African American parents then purchased their own buses, asking the school system simply to pay for maintenance and gasoline. The county again refused.

Then the NAACP asked 20 parents to to become plaintiffs on behalf of their children in a general lawsuit against segregated schools. Harry and Eliza Briggs were the first to sign and *Briggs v. Eliot* was filed in 1949.

Thurgood Marshall handled the case, leading a team of lawyers and assistants that included Modjeska Simpkins. Marshall utilized the testimony of sociologist Kenneth Clark, whose research had revealed the psychological damage segregation caused African American children.

Despite Clark's and other compelling testimony, a three-judge panel voted two to one against the plaintiffs. U.S. District Judge Waites Waring wrote a dissenting opinion, declaring that segregation was "per se inequality."

Briggs was appealed to the U.S. Supreme Court, which sent the case back to the lower court for retrial. The lower court again sided against the plaintiffs, and the case was appealed again. Marshall argued that no matter how close facilities came to being equally funded, enforced separation was inherently biased and unfair.

The Briggs case and four others were consolidated into one large case called *Brown v. Board of Education*. The Supreme Court would decide the issue of school desegregation in one fell swoop.

South Carolina schools were still more than a decade away from desegregation.

— MAY 17 —

1954

SUPREME COURT ANNOUNCES SCHOOL DESEGREGATION RULING

On this day in civil rights history, the U.S. Supreme Court announced its landmark *Brown v. Board of Education* decision, legally abolishing segregation of public education.

For years, the NAACP had dedicated much of its lawyers' time and its resources to an all-out effort to eliminate segregation in the public schools. Finally, NAACP cases pending in the courts in five states—Delaware, Kansas, Virginia, and South Carolina—and the District of Columbia were consolidated into one case for argument before the Supreme Court.

In Topeka, Kansas, the NAACP represented 13 parents in a class action suit against the Topeka Board of Education. The U.S. District Court, citing as precedent the "separate but equal" doctrine of the 1896 *Plessy v. Ferguson* decision, had ruled against the parents. The NAACP attorneys appealed to the Supreme Court, and the Kansas case was selected by the Court to be the title case among the consolidated cases it would hear. Thus the case was officially named *Oliver Brown, et al. v. Board of Education of Topeka*. but is usually referred to as *Brown v. Board* or simply *Brown*.

Newly integrated school

The NAACP attorneys arguing the case included George E. C. Hayes, Thurgood Marshall, and James Nabrit. They that African Americans, despite being promised the full rights of U.S. citizenship, were being denied the fundamental right to education.

The court delivered a unanimous verdict in favor of the plaintiffs. Chief Justice Earl Warren read the opinion of the court: "We come then to the question presented: Does segregation of children in public schools solely on the basis of race, even though the physical facilities and other 'tangible' factors may be equal, deprive the children of the minority group of equal educational opportunities? We believe that it does. . . .We conclude that, in the field of public education, the doctrine of 'separate but equal' has no place. Separate educational facilities are inherently unequal."

It would take more legal battles, individual heroism, and systematic civil disobedience to put the new ruling into practice, but the precedent was set: segregation was unconstitutional. The NAACP had achieved a great victory. The decision was the major catalyst to the modern civil rights movement.

— MAY 18 —

1896

SUPREME COURT UPHOLDS 'SEPARATE BUT EQUAL' DOCTRINE

On this day in civil rights history, the U.S. Supreme Court established the "separate but equal" doctrine of Jim Crow segregation in its ruling in the case of *Plessy v. Ferguson.*

During Reconstruction, Congress passed a series of protections for African Americans, including full citizenship. But the protections extended to the actions of the states and not the actions of individuals or private organizations. Whites in the South used this loophole to enact a series of strict social controls. In 1890, Louisiana passed a law prohibiting blacks and whites from riding in the same cars on railroad lines. A biracial group of concerned citizens called The Citizens' Committee to Test the Constitutionality of the Separate Car Law formed to combat the law. Attorney Albion Tourgee provided legal counsel. Homer Plessy, a light-skinned African American who could pass as white, was chosen as the test case. On June 7, 1892, Plessy bought a ticket and sat in the "white's only" section of a rail car. When he refused to move, he was promptly arrested.

"Colored" water fountain

The state trial court ruled against Plessy, arguing that the state had power to regulate transit within its own borders. The case was appealed to the Supreme Court, where Tourgee argued that Plessy's rights guaranteed him by the 14th Amendment were being abridged. Eight of the nine justices ruled against Plessy. Chief Justice Henry Billings Brown delivered the majority opinion: "Legislation is powerless . . . to abolish distinctions based on physical differences . . . If the civil and political rights of both races be equal, one cannot be inferior to the other civilly or politically. If one race be inferior to the other socially, the Constitution of the United States cannot put them on the same plane."

Justice John Harlan was the lone dissenter. "Our Constitution is color-blind . . . In respect of civil rights, all citizens are equal before the law . . . The present decision, it may well be apprehended, will not only stimulate aggressions, more or less brutal and irritating, upon the admitted rights of colored citizens, but will encourage the belief that it is possible, by means of state enactments, to defeat the beneficent purposes which the people of the United States had in view when they adopted the recent amendments of the Constitution."

Harlan's dissenting opinion proved prophetic. Emboldened by federal apathy, Southern states enacted Jim Crow laws that resulted in decades of oppression, intimidation, and outright murder. It would be 58 years before the Supreme Court returned to the issue and reversed the "separate but equal" doctrine.

— MAY 19 —

1997

MISSISSIPPI LEADER AARON HENRY DIES

On this day in civil rights history, Aaron Henry, Mississippi activist and lifelong civil rights advocate, died of heart failure in his hometown of Clarksdale. He was 74. Along with Fannie Lou Hamer and Medgar Evers, Henry was among the most important figures in the movement in Mississippi, which was the most violently segregated state.

Born to sharecropper parents in 1922, Henry served in the U.S. military and used the GI bill to get an education from Xavier University in New Orleans. Henry returned to Clarksdale and opened a pharmacy that served as his business and as a community center for civil rights groups in the 1950s and 1960s.

In 1959, Henry became the state president of the Mississippi branch of the NAACP, and from this position helped mediate conflicts between the NAACP and the more radical organizations, such as SNCC that arrived a year later. Henry was an early leader in the Council of Federated Organizations, the umbrella group that housed the NAACP, SCLC, SNCC, CORE, and other local organizations in Mississippi, and that launched Freedom Vote and Freedom Summer.

Aaron Henry at Democratic National Convention

Photo courtesy of Library of Congress

During the mock election of Freedom Vote in 1963, Henry was the name on the ballot and the candidate who won. One year later, Henry was elected the head of the Mississippi Freedom Democratic Party. When later asked about the MFDP, he insisted that it was first and foremost a local grassroots organization. "Of course, Ella and Bayard were all in and out of here during that time and probably there were discussions about what we were doing, but they did not bring the idea. . . . let nobody ever feel that the Freedom Democratic Party movement in the long hot summer of 1964 was an idea imposed upon us—it was us!"

Henry was jailed more than 30 times during his career. He maintained a stoic attitude about the constant harassment. "Whenever there is a bomb thrown in the house or the window is shot out . . . or a bomb thrown in the drugstore, sugar put in the gas tank of the car . . . I just know it's all in the game."

He left the MFDP in the late 1960s over philosophical conflict, but remained a presence in the movement. In 1982, Henry was elected to the Mississippi House of Representatives.

— MAY 20 —
1961
FREEDOM RIDERS BRUTALLY BEATEN IN MONTGOMERY

On this day in civil rights history, freedom riders were attacked at a bus station in Montgomery. The ride had originated May 4 in Washington, D.C., and was headed for New Orleans. White mobs attacked the riders in Anniston, Alabama, and in Birmingham. Continuation of the ride was delayed, and some civil rights leaders advised calling it off.

But in Nashville, youthful members of SNCC knew better. They saw the momentum the freedom rides had gained for civil rights, and they knew it would be a mistake to let violent racists stop them. A group of 10 reinforcements went to Birmingham to resume the freedom ride.

In Birmingham, Police Commissioner Eugene "Bull" Connor immediately had the 10 jailed, and on the night of May 19, he personally escorted seven of them to the Alabama-Tennessee border, where he put them out on the side of the road. After some difficulty, they found a black resident who helped them get word to SNCC's Diane Nash in Nashville, who sent a car to take them back to Birmingham.

In Birmingham, the bus lines reported that none of their drivers were willing to drive a bus with the freedom riders on it. While officials of the U.S. Justice Department negotiated with Alabama and bus-line officials to solve the problem, the riders spent the night at the Birmingham bus terminal.

The next morning, May 20, the riders left Birmingham for Montgomery on a Greyhound bus protected by state troopers. When they arrived in Montgomery, by prearrangement, the state troopers pulled away and local police were to take over protection. But when the vehicle pulled into the Montgomery station, no police were to be found. Instead, a large white mob was waiting with sticks, chains, whips, and other weapons. The riders exited the bus and were brutally beaten. Several, including James Zwerg and John Lewis, had to be hospitalized. John Siegenthaler, the representative of U.S. Attorney General Robert Kennedy, tried to rescue some of the women riders and was himself knocked unconscious. The beatings stopped only when State Trooper Commander Floyd Mann, having heard that Montgomery police were not doing their job, rushed to the scene and waded into the attack with his pistol drawn. It is a miracle that no one was killed.

That evening, the riders were cared for and protected by the black community, led by the Montgomery Improvement Association. While state and federal officials debated what to do, a rally in support of the freedom riders was called at Ralph Abernathy's church. Martin Luther King Jr. flew in to speak. Learning of this, the white mob that had attacked at the bus station began reassembling outside the First Baptist Church.

— MAY 21 —

1961

WHITE MOB SURROUNDS CHURCH IN ALABAMA

On this day in civil rights history, a rally at Montgomery's First Baptist Church was surrounded by an angry white mob. The rally inside was in support of the freedom riders who were beaten the day before at the Greyhound bus station. The mob outside was led by the some of the same people who instigated the riot at the bus station.

Stranded after being attacked at the bus station, the freedom riders were given medical attention and protection under the auspices of the Montgomery Improvement Association, while Martin Luther King Jr.—who had rushed to Montgomery from Chicago—Ralph Abernathy, and other civil rights leaders appealed to the federal government for help. The rally was in Abernathy's church, and he and King got on the phone to U.S. Attorney General Robert Kennedy.

Some 1,000 blacks and a few supportive whites attended the rally. While King took to the pulpit, the white mob swelled outside the church. King laid the blame for the violence on then-governor John Patterson: "Among the many sobering lessons that we can learn from the events of the past week is that the Deep South will not impose limits on itself. The limits must be imposed from without." If the federal government did not supply help, King said, then the region "will be plunged into a dark abyss of chaos."

Outside, the mob turned into a riot. Federal marshals fired tear gas into the crowd, to little effect. The frenzied whites set fire to a few vehicles and surged forward to attack the church. The marshals held their ground, but the situation looked desperate. If the church were set on fire, many inside would be killed.

King described the situation to Kennedy in Washington, and Kennedy called Governor Patterson. After a heated argument, National Guardsmen were dispatched to the scene. The African Americans inside passed the time by singing hymns, trying to ignore the riot outside. Around 5 a.m., the mob had dispersed enough for the crowd to leave. The church and everyone in it escaped unharmed except for some broken windows.

The civil rights leaders pondered their next move. Most had been against continuing the freedom ride after the earlier violence in Anniston and Birmingham, but now the stakes were raised and the national attention it was getting was undeniable. The Rides would continue. SNCC wanted King to join them on the ride, but he was facing legal problems in Georgia and trying to keep Kennedy's trust and help, so he declined, a decision that incensed many younger activists.

Three days later, on May 24, two buses of freedom riders left Montgomery for Jackson, Mississippi, under police escort. The trip was uneventful, but in Jackson, the riders were arrested when they tried to use the restroom facilities. Another crisis loomed.

— MAY 22 —
2002
KLANSMAN BOBBY FRANK CHERRY CONVICTED IN 1963 CASE

On this day in civil rights history, Bobby Frank Cherry was convicted for his part in the Sixteenth Street Baptist Church bombing in Birmingham, Alabama. Nearly 40 years after the crime, justice was finally served.

On September 15, 1963, four Klansmen in the Eastview Ku Klux Klan Klavern 13—Robert Chambliss, Bobby Frank Cherry, Thomas Blanton, and Herman Cash—carried out a deadly terrorist attack on the black Baptist church while Sunday school was in session. "Dynamite Bob" Chambliss was identified at the scene of the crime and convicted in 1977. He refused to cooperate with investigators, however, and died in prison without naming any of his accomplices. Herman Cash died in 1994 to little fanfare.

Photo courtesy of Associated Press

Bobby Frank Cherry and his attorneys

The case appeared to be closed. However, two of the four suspects were still alive.

In 1997, the FBI and Alabama police reopened the case due to new evidence. A task force began interviewing witnesses and compiling their case. The new evidence, it turned out, was firsthand testimony from undercover FBI agents who had infiltrated the KKK at the time.

In 2001, Thomas Blanton Jr. was arrested for his involvement in the bombing. Blanton declared his innocence, despite his membership in the KKK and his connection to Chambliss. The circumstantial evidence against him was mostly recorded conversations alluding to the bombing and little else. Despite the lack of evidence, Blanton—still protesting his innocence—was indicted and sent to prison.

Questions over Cherry's mental competence had delayed his trial. Finally deemed competent, Cherry went to trial in 2002. The evidence against him, including testimony from his own granddaughter, painted a picture of an unrepentant former Klansman who was a close associate of Chambliss and Blanton and was linked to the bombing. After seven hours the jury found Cherry guilty and sentenced him to life in prison. Like Blanton, Cherry maintained that he was innocent. Cherry died in prison in 2004.

On this day in civil rights history, the first all-black Broadway show, *Shuffle Along*, hit the big stage.

As in later eras, black artists and musicians were confined to second-tier roles. As blackface minstrel shows were still popular, some light-complexioned black musicians had to apply more burnt cork to their faces to fit with the theme. Negro theater had been around for more than two decades by this time, with black producers James Weldon Johnson and Bob Cole putting on shows in the first years of the 20th century. But worsening race relations in northern cities, brought on partly due to population pressures from the Great Migration, derailed black theater companies.

Written, produced, directed, and performed by African Americans, *Shuffle Along* played for both white and black audiences in New York City for over a year before beginning a tour. Featuring a chorus line of jazz dancers and a sweet, romantic love story, the show was an immediate hit. President Harry Truman later picked one of his campaign slogans from "I'm Just Wild About Harry," one of the show's songs.

Vaudeville veterans Eubie Blake and Noble Sissle wrote the music, while Flournoy Miller and Aubrey L. Lyles wrote the play. The cast featured many future superstars, including a young Paul Robeson, Florence Mills, and in the chorus, a young Josephine Baker. The ragtime musical comedy opened to almost instant acclaim. New York theatergoers loved it. Langston Hughes was a regular attendee. The show would eventually be the first live radio broadcast of a Broadway musical.

The show laid the groundwork for future black-oriented plays, providing jobs for black actors and a forum for black writers. Nine African American musicals would open in the following three years. The cavalcade of black stars to descend on Harlem would result in a flourishing community of artists. *Shuffle Along* and its subsequent success were large contributing factors to the flourishing of an era that has since become known as the Harlem Renaissance.

— MAY 24 —

1941

PROTEST SINGER BOB DYLAN BORN

On this day in civil rights history, Bob Dylan was born in Duluth, Minnesota. The multitalented folk rocker would become an uncomfortable figurehead of the counterculture movement during the 1960s, with songs like "Blowin' in the Wind," and "The Times They Are a Changin'," becoming anthems of the civil rights movement.

Dylan did not just write songs. He donated many performances to the movement, including a live performance at the 1963 March on Washington when he was just 22 years old. His protest songs mix personal philosophy, observation, indignation, and poetry into chilling high art. He later distanced himself from the movement, but his album *The Times They Are a Changin'* remains an artistic highlight of the era.

Dylan was not alone in his support of the movement. Other white celebrities rallied to the cause, including Marlon Brando, Charlton Heston, Paul Newman, Burt Lancaster, Joan Baez, Peter, Paul, and Mary, Shelly Winters, Tony Bennett, Pete Seeger, and Frank Sinatra, among others, who all devoted money and time.

Although the Hollywood rank and file was mostly on the side of the civil rights movement, producers mostly avoided controversial material. They were concerned with money first, and the majority of white America did not want its hypocrisy jammed down its throat. The white entertainer risked much by associating with the civil rights movement, as their income was predicated on their popularity. And in large parts of the country the civil rights movement was very unpopular.

The commitment of these white actors and entertainers was in some cases absolute. Baez offered to take a solid year from her career to help teach nonviolent techniques, and Brando offered the SCLC his services indefinitely and without reservation, including frontline civil disobedience. Celebrities wanted to do more in the movement, but they were usually asked to help with fundraising, which they did. During the 1950s and 1960s, white and black entertainers raised millions of dollars for the movement, through benefit concerts and the like. Their contributions helped keep the movement going financially.

— MAY 25 —
1889
BALTIMORE NAACP STALWART LILLIE M. JACKSON BORN

On this day in civil rights history, Lillie M. Carroll Jackson was born. She was the president of the Baltimore NAACP branch for many years and is an example of the thousands of local leaders who never became famous on the national stage but were instrumental in destroying Jim Crow segregation in their own communities.

Born into a black middle-class family, she graduated in 1908 from Baltimore's Colored High School and then taught in Baltimore's segregated school system. She married an evangelist and traveled the country with him until the two returned to Baltimore to begin their family.

In 1935, Jackson took over Baltimore's moribund NAACP chapter and rebuilt it from the ground up, to as many as 17,600 members. She served as its president until 1970 and became known locally as "that NAACP lady" and "Dr. Lillie" and eventually as "Mother of Freedom."

Baltimore was as segregated in many respects as the Deep South states, so she had plenty of opportunities to advocate for civil rights, which she did at the legal, legislative, and grassroots levels. She led the picketing of a segregated Baltimore theater for six years before its doors were opened to blacks on an equal basis.

In 1931, she and her 18-year-old daughter organized a boycott of Baltimore businesses that practiced discriminatory hiring. In 1938 she led the legal campaign that equalized pay for black and white school teachers. In 1942 she organized a massive voter registration campaign. In 1953 she saw the success of an NAACP campaign to desegregate the University of Maryland Law School. And in 1958 she oversaw the passage of Baltimore's Fair Employment Practices Law.

She was, by all accounts, persuasive and persistent. Maryland Governor Theodore McKeldrin once said, "I'd rather have the devil after me than Mrs. Jackson. Give her what she wants."

Her local successes led to her presidency of the Maryland State Conference of NAACP branches, and in 1948 she won a seat on the NAACP's national board.

And that 18-year-old picketing daughter—Juanita Jackson Mitchell grew up to became the legal counsel for the Baltimore NAACP and herself led campaigns, under her mother's guidance, of course, that desegregated city golf courses, swimming pools, state parks, and public schools.

Dr. Lillie M. Carroll Jackson died in 1975. Her descendants remain active in Baltimore politics and civic affairs.

On this day in civil rights history, Althea Gibson won the women's singles in the French Open, the first major tennis award won by an African American.

Born in South Carolina but raised in Harlem, Gibson developed an interest in tennis at an early age. But like golf, tennis clubs were off-limits to all African Americans, and Gibson had to locate all-black tennis clubs, which were rare. Barred from public tennis courts, Gibson began practicing on the private court of Dr. Walter Johnson, who would later help Arthur Ashe. She embarked on an amateur career, winning more than 50 titles before becoming a full-time professional.

Althea Gibson

In 1957, Gibson won a U.S. national championship. That same year she was the first African American to be named Female Athlete of the Year by the Associated Press. She would win many major tournaments over the years and become an international super star. In 1968 she was the first African American inducted into the Tennis Hall of Fame.

Following in Gibson's footsteps was Arthur Ashe. Like Gibson, Ashe excelled on the court. He became the number-one ranked player in the world in the mid-1970s when he won Wimbledon. But Ashe was also a committed activist. He campaigned to end apartheid in South Africa, among other civil rights causes. In 1988, he wrote *A Hard Road to Glory: A History of the African American Athlete.*

Sadly, Ashe contracted the HIV virus during a blood transfusion in 1983. In 1992, he announced his condition to the world and founded the Arthur Ashe Institute for Urban Health. He spent the last few months of his life trying to raise AIDS awareness across the globe, while wasting away from the effects of the disease. On February 6, 1993, he died.

Gibson spent the 1980s and 1990s as an advocate for physical fitness. In 2003, she died from respiratory failure. Together, she and Ashe did much to inspire their fellow African Americans, breaking the color line in one of white America's most beloved and most segregated sports.

— MAY 27 —
1956
TALLAHASSEE BUS BOYCOTT BEGINS

On this day in civil rights history, the Tallahassee bus boycott began. The day before, two Florida A & M students—Wilhelmina Jakes and Carrie Paterson—like Rosa Parks before them, refused to give up their seats on a bus and were promptly arrested.

While local NAACP leaders Robert Saunders and C. K. Steele, one of the founding members of the Southern Christian Leadership Conference, reviewed the case, Florida A & M students decided to boycott the city's buses for the rest of the semester. Sensing the potential, Steele called for all Tallahassee blacks to participate in the boycott, modeling it after the Montgomery bus boycott that was then in progress. The Inter Civic Council—composed of ministers, CORE members, students, and businessmen—was formed to operate the boycott; Steele was elected president. The group demanded an end to segregation on the city's bus lines and the opening of bus-driving jobs to African American applicants.

The boycott had an immediate economic impact. The city tried to mediate the issue by offering a compromise while maintaining the system of segregation. The ICC denied the city's offer. The city then outlawed carpools, and later Steele was arrested for violating the ordinance.

On June 17, the NAACP filed suit against the state's segregation laws.

When a state judge found the ICC guilty of operating an illegal transportation operation, the ICC removed its sponsorship of the boycott. Steele remained in place as the leader, and the boycott continued. Months passed.

By December, the city was in a state of lockdown. The local chapter of the White Citizens' Council and the Ku Klux Klan stepped up intimidation tactics—burning crosses, beating boycotters, and calling on Governor Leroy Collins to step in. The Klan held a rally outside city limits and more than 1,000 people attended.

By January, a federal judge ruled Florida segregation unconstitutional. The Tallahassee bus boycott was given a public victory. But the system of segregation continued, under the guise of reserved seating. Steele and other activists did not back down, growing the movement to include sit-ins, marches, and other protests to integrate Tallahassee's schools, theaters, restaurants, and playgrounds. Two years after the boycott began, the city's buses were finally integrated. It was a major civil rights victory.

1964

GUNFIRE AIMED AT MARCH IN ST. AUGUSTINE

On this day in civil rights history, a night march in St. Augustine was disrupted by violence, culminating in a rain of gunfire on residential houses, including a cottage rented to Martin Luther King. Alarmingly, the local police appeared to be in collusion with the attackers.

Despite the attacks, the St. Augustine campaign was going well. A coalition of white and black activists and preachers had arrived to participate and Wyatt Walker of the SCLC was coordinating things nicely. Part of Walker's plan was a series of night marches. Hoping to goad the local toughs into violence, the SCLC would then be able to appeal to the federal government for help. And once involved, the federal government would remain until order was restored, which they hoped meant the desegregation of St. Augustine.

The plan worked. Federal agents arrived and night marches were temporarily suspended while Simpson, a federal judge, deliberated on the many issues. King put forth a series of suggestions: desegregation, new jobs for blacks, and a biracial city committee, among others. If the city refused, massive demonstrations would begin anew.

On June 9, Judge Simpson sided in the marchers' favor. A new series of marches took place, each broken by white attackers. Calling attention to the violence, King called for President Johnson to intervene. Two days later, King submitted to arrest after trying to desegregate the Monson Motor Lodge and spent the evening in solitary confinement.

Sporadic talks continued between the city and the SCLC officials. The presence of the government did not remove St. Augustine's intransigence.

On June 18, seven protesters both white and black staged a swim-in at the Monson Motor Lodge. James Brock, manager of the lodge, yelled at the swimming youths and finally tossed hydrochloric acid in the pool. Police had to forcibly remove the swimmers who were promptly arrested.

With minor violence occurring during each march, and the threat of more night marches, a crisis loomed. The city did little to ameliorate the situation, waiting for the protests to run out of momentum. "I must come out of St. Augustine with honor," King told state attorney Dan Warren. "I must come out of here with a victory."

— MAY 29 —
1961
ICC ORDERED TO ENFORCE BUS TERMINAL DESEGREGATION

On this day in civil rights history, U.S. Attorney General Robert Kennedy, responding to pressure from civil rights groups and worried over America's reputation abroad, announced that the U.S. Interstate Commerce Commission had banned segregation from all interstate travel facilities and that the ban would be enforced. The decision was a victory for the freedom rides, but also a temporary setback.

A few days earlier, Kennedy had called for a halt to the freedom rides. The riders, jailed in Jackson, Mississippi, waited out the debate over their situation. Martin Luther King Jr. chastised Kennedy for his decisions up to that point; protecting freedom riders from attacks did no good if the government wouldn't protect everyday black riders.

Kennedy wanted a cooling-off period. King refused. "It's difficult to understand the position of the oppressed people," he said to Kennedy in a phone call. "Ours is a way out—creative, moral, and nonviolent. It is not tied to black supremacy or communism, but to the plight of the oppressed. It can save the soul of America. You must understand that we've made no gains without pressure and I hope that pressure will always be moral, legal and peaceful."

Although the freedom rides had begun as a CORE venture and were then continued by SNCC, King once again became the spokesman for the movement. SCLC, CORE, and SNCC decided to continue the freedom rides. More rides were planned for May 28, while the SNCC riders stayed in Jackson jail. The various civil rights groups decided that the rides would continue until desegregation was achieved.

On May 29, Kennedy announced that the ICC had banned segregation from all interstate travel facilities. The riders had won a huge, public victory. But the desegregation of interstate facilities was only one step in the long march toward equality. Kennedy's pronouncement killed the momentum of the freedom rides.

King and the other leaders of the movement turned their attention elsewhere, leaving the freedom riders feeling a little betrayed. Yes, they had won, but SCLC had taken much of the credit, and then removed its support once the government gave in.

The freedom rides were a monumental event in the movement, revealing yet again how far the South would go to defend institutionalized racism, while also bringing many of the disparate civil rights organizations into a more unified whole. But the rides also revealed a new generation of activists unwilling to wait or compromise while the lumbering federal government mulled over the fate of blacks in the South.

— MAY 30 —

1854

KANSAS-NEBRASKA ACT PASSED; FORESHADOWS CIVIL WAR

On this day in civil rights history, Congress passed the Kansas-Nebraska Act, foreshadowing the coming Civil War.

The Northern states and the Southern states had achieved a precarious truce, as they possessed roughly the same amount of political power. But the huge tracts of territory acquired in the Louisiana Purchase threatened this careful balance, as settlers were beginning to ask for statehood. The Missouri Compromise of 1820 had resulted in a temporary cessation of hostilities between the two camps, allowing Missouri to be admitted as a slave state but forbidding slavery in the rest of the Louisiana Purchase territory above a certain latitude.

But new territories lobbying to become states once again forced the issue. Two dueling ways of life each saw the other as an immediate threat. Would the U.S. remain a loose confederation of states or evolve into a more unified country under a monolithic federal government? The control of the presidency and both houses of Congress was at stake, as well as the moral future of the country.

The proposed act abolished the existing law passed by the Missouri Compromise. Senator Stephen Douglass of Illinois proposed the measure, which would allow each of the two new states, Kansas and Nebraska, to formulate its own constitution upon admittance; the slavery question under the new act would be decided by popular sovereignty, not federal oversight. It was the states' rights paradigm once again trumping deeper moral concerns.

Kansas became the battle state over the issue. Pro- and antislavery factions fought on the ballot and in the streets. Four different constitutions, drawn up by four different factions, were sent to Congress for approval. President James Buchanan selected the Lecompton Constitution, a proslavery document that stated in no uncertain terms: "The right of property is before and higher than any constitutional sanction, and the right of the owner of a slave to such slave and its increase is the same and as inviolable as the right of the owner of any property whatever."

Congress refused to ratify the document. Southern politicians were horrified as a new antislavery constitution was drawn up for Kansas and then promptly approved. South Carolina Senator James Hammond responded: "If Kansas is driven out of the Union for being a slave state, can any Southern state remain within it with honor?"

In January 1861, Kansas was admitted into the Union as a free state. The rift between North and South over the issue of slavery and sovereignty would only be solved by war.

— MAY 31 —

1955

IN FOLLOW-UP TO 'BROWN,'
COURT ORDERS 'DELIBERATE SPEED'

On this day in civil rights history, the U.S. Supreme Court issued what is now known as the "*Brown* II" decision, commanding communities to desegregate "with all deliberate speed."

After the landmark *Brown v. Board of Education* decision in 1954, the Supreme Court chose to wait one year before deciding on how to implement the new mandate. The justices recognized that the racial barriers enforcing segregation were deep-rooted.

In the intervening year, the *Brown* decision proved to be extremely unpopular in the South. Southern governors held a meeting vowing to defy the ruling. Southern congressmen, headed by Strom Thurmond, released the Southern Manifesto, which harangued the ruling as biased, illegal, and immoral. Riots, protests, and violence followed.

Others had problems with the ruling's legality. Critics felt that previous precedents, such as *Plessy v. Ferguson,* were cast aside, mainly on the basis of the research of social scientists, and charged that the court had made a decision based on emotional appeal rather than the rule of law.

The early days of school integration

Chief Justice Warren delivered the majority opinion of the court. "All provisions of federal, state, or local law requiring or permitting such discrimination must yield to this principle. There remains for consideration the manner in which relief is to be accorded."

And the manner in which relief was to be accorded was the sole reason for Brown II. Despite appearances to the contrary, however, Brown II was in many ways an ambivalent ruling, open to interpretation. The court did not require a specific timetable to accomplish desegregation, nor did it threaten consequences for failing to do so: "While giving weight to these public and private considerations, the courts will require that the defendants make a prompt and reasonable start toward full compliance with our May 17, 1954, ruling."

This seemed a reasonable step, but the South responded with delaying tactics, hiding behind the enormity of the task. Of course, phasing two school systems, two races, and two separate communities into one was a complex and difficult process. But the South was never going to integrate without federal intervention, which is what happened when President Eisenhower sent federal troops to Arkansas to oversee the integration of Little Rock schools in 1957.

— JUNE 1 —

1921

RACE RIOT BREAKS OUT IN TULSA

On this day in civil rights history, the worst-ever U.S. race riot broke out in Tulsa, Oklahoma. In its aftermath hundreds would be dead and an entire community would lie in smoking ruins. Despite the viciousness of the attack, the story of the Tulsa riot is today mostly unknown.

At the time, Oklahoma claimed the largest Ku Klux Klan membership in the country. At the same time, Tulsa's small but vibrant black community thrived, partially due to the Greenwood District, a financial center known as the "Black Wall Street."

On May 31, black shoeshiner Dick Rowland was accused of assaulting white elevator operator Sarah Page. Rowland was arrested and a sensationalized if not fabricated story was reported in the local press. On June 1, a white mob went to the jail to lynch Rowland, where a crowd of blacks gathered to protect him. The standoff did not last long. A white man tried to disarm one of the African Americans and the gun went off. A minor war followed as sporadic fighting broke out all over the city.

Black veterans of World War I formed an impromptu battalion and dug trenches around their community. White mobs and local police attacked, dropping makeshift bombs from airplanes onto the black defenders, who were outnumbered and soon overrun.

Elsewhere, more angry whites invaded the black part of Tulsa and began beating any African Americans they encountered, while setting fire to the Greenwood District. Black churches, hospitals, businesses, and homes were destroyed. Machine-gun fire swept indiscriminately through the black neighborhoods. Hundreds were killed and more than 35 blocks were reduced to ashes. The city's two black newspapers were destroyed. Survivors were rounded up by the Oklahoma National Guard and herded into the local baseball stadium.

The victims were buried in mass graves. Greenwood would never recover. White, official Tulsa began a campaign to suppress the deadly riot and their complicity in it; the riot became an anecdote, blamed by many on unruly blacks. In 1997, Tulsa formed a commission to investigate and in 2001 delivered to the governor a report that revealed some of the truth about the terrible incident.

— June 2 —
1962
Walter Fauntroy Leads SCLC's D.C. Division

On this day in civil rights history, Walter Fauntroy was the Southern Christian Leadership Conference point man in the U.S. capital.

Born February 6, 1933, in Washington, D.C., Fauntroy attended Virginia Union University before enrolling at Yale University Divinity School. After graduating, he became minister of Washington's New Bethel Baptist Church. His pastorship plugged him into the network of activist-preachers, and he soon joined the SCLC.

Comfortable inside the beltway, in 1961 Fauntroy was appointed by Martin Luther King Jr. as the Washington director of the SCLC. He would go on to become a trusted King lieutenant. From his base in the capital, he worked as the local coordinator for the 1963 March on Washington. He would later work as an organizer for the 1965 Selma-to-Montgomery March and the 1966 March Against Fear.

In 1966, President Lyndon Johnson appointed Fauntroy as vice president of the "To fulfill these rights" conference. In 1969, Fauntroy became the national director of the Poor People's Campaign.

Two years later, he was elected as the D.C. delegate to the U.S. House of Representatives, where he served for 20 years. A founding member of the Congressional Black Caucus and one of its early chairmen, Fauntroy became a powerful and influential black politician.

In the late 1970s, Congress formed the House Select Committee on Assassinations to investigate the deaths of King, the Kennedys, and Malcolm X. Fauntroy was named chairman of the subcommittee on King's assassination. During the investigation, the extent of the FBI's subversion of King and other civil rights leaders was uncovered, revealing a vast covert surveillance operation called COINTELPRO.

In 1984, Fauntroy was arrested for protesting at the South African embassy against apartheid as part of the Free Nelson Mandela movement.

Fauntroy left Congress in 1991. When former SNCC member Marion Barry was forced to resign the office of mayor of Washington, D.C., after a drug scandal, Fauntroy ran unsuccessfully for the office.

Fauntroy remains in Washington and is a regular commentator on news and interview programs while again pastoring New Bethel Baptist Church. He works with Project We Care, which encourages churches to take an active role in rebuilding their communities, and is a prominent member of the Center for Economic and Social Justice.

— JUNE 3 —

1946

SEGREGATED INTERSTATE BUS TRAVEL RULED ILLEGAL

On this day in civil rights history, in *Morgan v. Commonwealth of Virginia,* the U.S. Supreme Court declared segregation on interstate bus travel unconstitutional.

Jim Crow laws had existed since Reconstruction, but in 1930 the state of Virginia passed a law explicitly dealing with segregated bus seating. Eleven years before Rosa Parks refused to give up her seat on a city bus in Montgomery, a young black woman named Irene Morgan did the same thing on an interstate bus. In July 1944, Morgan boarded a Greyhound bus in Virginia, headed to Baltimore. Soon afterwards, the white bus driver ordered her from her seat to make room for boarding white passengers. She refused and was arrested.

Freedom Riders under guard

The NAACP had been waiting for just such a case and promptly filed a lawsuit on Morgan's behalf. Two years later the case was argued before the U.S. Supreme Court by NAACP attorney Thurgood Marshall. In a clever shift in strategy, rather than relying on the 14th Amendment, Marshall argued that segregation across state lines violated the Interstate Commerce Clause. One state, Marshall argued, could not dictate seating policy to another.

The Supreme Court agreed, declaring: "As no state law can reach beyond its own border nor bar transportation of passengers across its boundaries, diverse seating requirements for the races in interstate journeys result. . . . It seems clear to us that seating arrangements for the different races in interstate motor travel require a single, uniform rule to promote and protect national travel. Consequently, we hold the Virginia statute in controversy invalid."

Although the court did not bar segregation within a state's borders, the ruling was still a big victory for the NAACP.

In 1947, in an effort to test enforcement of the *Morgan* decision, the CORE and the Fellowship of Reconciliation conducted the first freedom rides, sending integrated busloads of people into the Deep South. The test failed, and it would be another 14 years before a new round of freedom rides finally resulted in the end of segregated bus seating on the nation's highways.

— JUNE 4 —

1899

NATIONAL DAY OF FASTING PROTESTS LYNCHINGS

On this day in civil rights history, the Afro-American Council declared a national day of fasting to protest lynching and violence against African Americans.

Lynchings, a symbol of white oppression and a mechanism for rigid social control, were a major issue of the late 1800s and early 1900s. Countless African Americans were murdered by lynching after being merely accused of social transgressions: a passing glance at a white woman, forgetting to show proper deference to a white man, and so on.

It is hard to comprehend today that lynchings at the turn of the century were often social events in white communities. Lynchings had evolved into more than just simple hangings; ritualistic torture, sexual mutilation, and burning were also employed, to the apparent glee of white onlookers. Photographs of lynched blacks appeared on promotional postcards for some towns and cities. Body parts of the victims were sold as souvenirs. For the period 1882 to 1968, some 5,000 lynchings have been documented, and countless more went unrecorded.

In this context, in 1890 Thomas Fortune founded the National Afro-American League, a black anti-lynching organization. The league fell into financial troubles and disbanded in 1894. The Afro American Council reconstituted the league in 1898 in Rochester, New York, in response to a lynching of two black postal workers. Bishop Alexander Walters was its first president. The AAC struggled due to infighting, as liberal and conservative elements in the organization fought over its direction.

The AAC sent an official request to President McKinley to deal with racially motivated violence in the South. McKinley ignored the request. Subsequent presidents would offer little help in this regard, with President Wilson actually praising the film *Birth of a Nation* that glorifies the KKK and Klan-inspired lynching.

The Afro-American Council, unsure of how to proceed, created a day of fasting in protest. The event apparently had little impact on U.S. popular consciousness or government policy.

The short-lived Afro-American Council was a precursor to the Niagara Movement and later the NAACP, which adopted the AAC's tactics of protests, fasts, and letter-writing campaigns in pursuit of racial justice. Lynching diminished after the 1930s, but instances still occurred as late as the 1990s.

— JUNE 5 —

1944

BIRTHDATE OF TOMMIE SMITH, BLACK POWER OLYMPIAN

On this day in civil rights history, future Olympian Tommie Smith was born.

In 1968, Smith made the U.S. Olympic track team. Some civil rights leaders suggested that black athletes and fans should boycott the Olympics (in Mexico City) as a protest against the conditions blacks were living under. The boycott did not materialize, but Smith and other black athletes kept the idea in mind. In the 200-meter dash, Smith won the gold medal and set a world record of 19.83 seconds. His teammate at San Jose State University, John Wayne Carlos, won the bronze.

During the presentation ceremony, the world watched as Smith and Carlos, standing on the dais while the U.S. national anthem played, lowered their heads and raised their gloved black fists in a black-power salute. They stood barefooted with civil rights pins on their jerseys in silent salute while the anthem played. Smith raised his right hand to signify black power; Carlos raised his left to represent black unity. Photographers and television cameras snapped away. The resulting image was powerful, angry, and beautiful, and still one of the most famous photographs in sports history.

The crowd booed Smith and Carlos as they left the podium. Smith said afterwards in a press conference, "If I win I am an American, not a black American. But if I did something bad then they would say 'a Negro.' We are black and we are proud of being black. . . . Black America will understand what we did tonight."

White America, however, was enraged. In their eyes, the purity of the Olympic games had been tarnished. Of course, black Americans did not see it that way. The U.S. had hidden its racism from the world as best it could for a long time. Two proud black men had unveiled it for all to see.

Despite being a new world-record holder, Smith and Carlos, the bronze medalist, were expelled from the games, stripped of their medals, and banned for life from the Olympics.

Both Smith and Carlos went on to have successful careers as coaches and educators. Today both are in the National Track and Field Hall of Fame and San Jose State has erected a statue commemorating their Olympic moment.

On this day in civil rights history, presidential candidate Robert Kennedy died after being shot by an assassin the day before. His death was the last major assassination of the 1960s and ushered in a cynical era. He was considered by many to be the last, great white hope for African Americans.

As U.S. Attorney General in the John F. Kennedy administration, Bobby Kennedy had been antagonistic to the civil rights movement, authorizing wiretaps against some leaders and using delaying tactics to keep the NAACP, SCLC, CORE, and SNCC at bay. But as the movement continued, Kennedy's moral sense evolved. By 1964, he was a wholehearted supporter of civil rights.

Photo courtesy of Library of Congress

Robert Kennedy at playground

After President Kennedy was assassinated in 1963, Robert stayed on as attorney general until 1964, when he won a U.S. Senate seat from New York. As a senator, Kennedy laid the groundwork for his future thinking, visiting the Mississippi Delta, calling for an end to apartheid, and taking a stand against the Vietnam War.

In 1968, Kennedy decided to run for president. While campaigning, he visited small towns and urban ghettos in the South and the North. He began to emerge as a progressive, enlightened thinker, a prominent supporter of civil rights causes, and an ardent champion of the poor and the downtrodden.

Kennedy won Democratic primaries in Indiana, Nebraska, South Dakota, and California. With his good looks, passionate speeches, and celebrity, he seemed a good bet to win the nomination and then the presidency.

On June 5, at the Ambassador Hotel in downtown Los Angeles, he left the ballroom to greet the workers in the kitchen. While he was shaking hands, a 22-year-old student, Sirhan Sirhan, rushed forward, yelling, "Kennedy, you son of a bitch!" and fired a .22 pistol into Kennedy's head. Kennedy slumped to the ground, never to regain consciousness. He died the next day and the movement lost its last and best national defender. He is buried next to his brother in Arlington National Cemetery.

As with JFK's assassination, many conspiracy theories surround Robert Kennedy's death. Sirhan Sirhan is serving a life sentence for the murder, still claiming his innocence; he says he does not remember doing the shooting.

— JUNE 7 —

1963

DANVILLE PROTESTERS INDICTED UNDER 'JOHN BROWN' LAW

On this day in civil rights history, protesters in Danville, Virginia, were indicted under a pre-Civil War "John Brown" statute.

The NAACP had an early, strong presence in Virginia. In the 1930s, the NAACP mounted a campaign to use financial pressure until state and local governments saw the futility of separate educational facilities. The first step was equal pay for teachers. The NAACP led protests and parades, while pursuing the matter in the federal courts.

In fact, the majority of the NAACP lawsuits of the 1940s, 1950s, and 1960s, were filed in Virginia, including *Morgan v. Virginia* in 1944, which desegregated interstate buses, and *Davis v. Prince Edward County*, one of the five cases consolidated into *Brown v. Board of Education*.

But Virginia politics in the 1950s were firmly under the control of U.S. Senator Harry F. Byrd Sr., a fire-breathing segregationist and outspoken advocate of the "Southern Manifesto." When the *Brown* decision was announced, Byrd urged massive resistance, including the closing of schools, re-allocating of students, and so on. The Byrd machine inflamed resistance to integration.

In 1959, the public schools in Virginia officially integrated. Businesses, however remained segregated. Local CORE, SNCC, and SCLC groups began to fight back. Leaders like Lawrence Campbell, Alexander Dunlop, Curtis Harris, Oliver Hill Sr., and Calvin Miller worked in the various organizations to end American apartheid.

One year later, the student sit-in movement spread to Richmond and Arlington. Civil rights groups called for boycotts, protests, and picket lines. The white power structure responded with stiff resistance.

The worst violence occurred in Danville, a medium-sized mill town. A high school honor student, Thurman Echols, led a group of students on June 5 in civil disobedience against local discrimination. Police responded by buffeting the students with high-powered fire hoses and nightsticks. The protesters were arrested and charged with violating a statute almost 100 years old.

In response, SNCC and CORE showed up in force, as did William Kunstler and other National Lawyers Guild attorneys to defend the students. More protests ensued and more people were arrested as Danville officials refused to listen to African American demands. By July, more than 250 people were in jail.

Soon the March on Washington for Jobs and Freedom eclipsed the showdown in Danville. The cases involving the arrested students lasted until 1973, when they were finally acquitted.

— JUNE 8 —
2001
CIVIL RIGHTS COMMISSION CRITICIZES FLORIDA ELECTIONS

On this day in civil rights history, the U.S. Civil Rights Commission criticized Florida voting procedures as prejudicial.

The historic November 7, 2000, election between Democrat Al Gore and Republican George W. Bush resulted in an unlikely impasse as Florida ballots were announced first for Gore, then for Bush, then as too close to count. Eventually the U.S. Supreme Court gave the state's votes to Bush and he became president.

After this election, more than 3,000 voter complaints were registered by the Florida attorney general's office, with thousands of other voters complaining to federal officials or their party representatives. In all, some 180,000 ballots were contested and eventually thrown out. The controversy over alleged voting irregularities led to an investigation by the Civil Rights Commission.

The CRC, by federal law, must investigate any incident of voter discrimination, disenfranchisement, or lack of equal protection under the law. The 2000 investigation included public hearings in Tallahassee and Miami, hundreds of hours of testimony, and thousands of pages of data.

The CRC concluded that the situation, upon close scrutiny, was a mess. Absentee votes were mishandled, misplaced, or counted despite irregularities. Some polling precincts were moved without notice while others closed early. In one precinct, local police conducted an unauthorized vehicle checkpoint within blocks of the polling precinct. Voters showed up to vote and were told they were not registered, when they in fact were. In some counties, antiquated voting methods resulted in batches of votes being thrown out.

The most egregious issue was that the majority of the spoiled ballots or rejected voters were from predominantly black areas. The discrimination was not necessarily intentional, but the data was staggering; in some precincts more than 19 percent of African American votes were discarded, compared with less than 2 percent in the worst cases in non-black areas.

Purge lists of convicted felons—with the onus on the would-be voter to prove he or she was not the person on the list—turned many voters away; hundreds were illegally prevented from voting. Ex-convicts who had completed probation or parole were still refused their right to vote.

Widespread voter fraud, missing ballot boxes, excessive delays—the voting situation in Florida during the 2000 election was a catastrophe.

The Commission recommended uniform, statewide reform, and litigation against the state of Florida.

— JUNE 9 —

1950

LAST 'SCOTTSBORO BOY' RELEASED FROM ALABAMA PRISON

On this day in civil rights history, Andy Wright was released from prison in Alabama. He was the last of the famous "Scottsboro Boys" to regain freedom after being convicted of rapes that had never happened but which became an international cause celebre in the 1930s.

Nine black men and youths (one was 12 years old, another 13) were accused in 1931 of raping two female women "hoboes" on a freight train in north Alabama. The cases excited racial tensions and dragged out over six years of trials, reversals, and retrials in an atmosphere of judicial theater that brought into sharp focus the worst aspects of Jim Crow segregation and discrimination.

Under "normal" circumstances of the period, the nine blacks accused of raping white women would have been tried, convicted, electrocuted, and forgotten. But the charges against them were so egregious and their trials so obviously unjust, that they caught the attention of first the Communist Party (at the time, simply another political party, albeit a radical one) and then the NAACP.

High-powered attorneys were brought in to defend the nine, and the cases resulted in two precedent-setting U.S. Supreme Court decisions. Eventually prosecutors wearied of the expense of the trials and of the worldwide attention on Alabama's all-white juries. Charges against four of the nine defendants were dropped.

On retrial in 1936, defendant Haywood Patterson was again convicted (despite overwhelming evidence of his innocence), but this time he was sentenced to 75 years. Though undoubtedly a small consolation to Patterson, it was the first time in Alabama history that a black convicted of raping a white was not sentenced to death.

Fellow defendants Clarence Norris, Andy Wright, Charlie Weem, and Ozie Powell were also convicted and sent to prison. All were paroled in the 1940s, though Wright violated parole, returned to prison, and then was finally released for good in 1950. Patterson escaped in 1948 and was caught in Michigan, but the Michigan governor refused to extradite him back to Alabama.

Norris, the last surviving Scottsboro Boy, received a full pardon in 1976 from then-Alabama Governor George Wallace. Norris died in 1989, bringing to a close a shameful episode in which the worst of racial prejudices and the unfairness of Southern judicial systems were put on display for the world to see.

Scores of songs, books, and movies have memorialized the Scottsboro Boys.

— JUNE 10 —

1954

SOUTHERN GOVERNORS VOW RESISTANCE TO 'BROWN' DECISION

On this day in civil rights history, a group of Southern governors met in Richmond, Virginia, and vowed to defy the *Brown v. Board* ruling.

The Supreme Court had enraged the white South, which saw the long arm of federal control taking away their self-determination, saw an attack on their cherished traditions, and saw an imminent threat in their black populace. In response, Southern congressional Democrats issued the Southern Manifesto. Southern governors, meanwhile, initiated a systematic strategy of evasion, delay, and open defiance.

With few registered black voters, the South was a powerful political bloc. As such, the civil rights movement was a powder keg for presidents, who had to deal with the segregationists just to stay in office.

Southern politicians preyed on fear and misunderstanding. Ross Barnett of Mississippi, George Wallace of Alabama, Lester Maddox of Georgia, and Orval Faubus of Arkansas all advocated violence against African Americans in the fight to maintain segregation. There were others: Theodore Bilbo, James Byrnes, Thomas Bahson Stanley, John Patterson, William Umstead, Fielding Wright, and Herman Talmadge all hung their political careers on the controversial issue. To some it was a matter of states' rights; to others, it was unadulterated racism; yet to others it was politically savvy.

Those who refused to support segregation, such as populist Alabama governor Big Jim Folsom, were voted out of office. Moderate Florida governor Leroy Collins helped mediate the issue, minimizing violence and social unrest in the sunshine state. But Collins and Folsom were the exceptions.

Of course, the movement needed the fiery segregationists to garner national media attention and international sympathy. Without Birmingham's Bull Connor, Faubus, Barnett, or Wallace, there might not have been a movement; the civil rights movement needed its antagonists almost as much as its heroes.

Still, it can't be denied that the stance the Southern governors took contributed to the suffering of thousands of African Americans who lived under the dehumanizing tyranny of Jim Crow.

— JUNE 11 —
1963
GEORGE WALLACE STANDS IN SCHOOLHOUSE DOOR

On this day in civil rights history, Alabama Governor George Wallace, in an act of political grandstanding, stood in the doorway of the University of Alabama, barring two black students from entering. It was a momentous and theatrical occasion, rife with symbolic meaning and potential violence.

On the gubernatorial campaign trail in 1962, Wallace had promised to do whatever was necessary to uphold segregation. "I draw the line in the dust and toss the gauntlet before the feet of tyranny," he said in his January 1963 inaugural address, "and I say segregation now, segregation tomorrow, segregation forever." A few months later, he was given his chance.

A federal judge had already ordered that James Hood and Vivian Malone be admitted to the university. Wallace did not want a real confrontation with the U.S. government, but he had to make a symbolic gesture. The National Guard had surrounded the building and cordoned off a path for the two black students. By prearrangement with federal officials, Wallace stood behind a podium in front of Foster Auditorium, blocked the path of Hood and Malone, and gave an incendiary speech.

Wallace makes his gesture

"The unwelcomed, unwanted, unwarranted, and force-induced intrusion upon the campus of the University of Alabama today of the might of the central government offers frightful example of the oppression of the rights, privileges and sovereignty of this state by officers of the federal government," Wallace said. ". . . I stand here today as governor of this sovereign state . . . being mindful of my duties and responsibilities under the Constitution of the United States, the Constitution of the State of Alabama, and seeking to preserve and maintain the peace and dignity of this State, and the individual freedoms of the citizens thereof, do hereby denounce and forbid this illegal and unwarranted action by the Central Government."

He then stepped nimbly aside and Malone and Hood entered to register for classes. The crisis was averted. In the end, the Kennedy administration had faced down one of segregation's most ferocious bulldogs. Wallace and Kennedy emerged as heroes—Wallace to conservatives as a fire-eating, race-baiting man of the people, Kennedy to progressives as the president finally willing to bend the will of the unyielding segregationists.

— JUNE 12 —

1963

MEDGAR EVERS ASSASSINATED IN MISSISSIPPI

On this day in civil rights history, NAACP activist Medgar Evers was assassinated.

The first NAACP field secretary for the state of Mississippi, Evers spent most of his time investigating the deaths of African Americans across the state, including the killing of Emmett Till. Mississippi was the worst of the Deep South states, the most illiterate and the most backward. It had the fewest libraries and the most lynchings. One of the largest, and most uneducated, Black populations lived as wage laborers and tenant farmers, work that in most of the other states had been taken over by machinery. In five counties, there were no registered black voters.

Photo courtesy of Library of Congress

Evers

Evers received death threats daily. He continued about his business unfazed, keeping loaded weapons in his house.

In 1960, Bob Moses of SNCC met Amzie Moore, one of Evers's contemporaries, and was invited to bring SNCC to the state to see if their direct-action programs could help facilitate change. Moses agreed. SNCC began sending field workers to help with the NAACP voter-registration efforts. Classes were held to teach black Mississippians how to vote.

The white power structure—the White Citizens' Council during the day and the Klan during the night—took steps to squelch the burgeoning black vote. A variety of means were used: beatings, arrests, and eventually murder.

Evers helped organize boycotts for the three years after 1960, and he helped James Meredith in his legal case to desegregate the University of Mississippi in 1961. Entering 1963, Evers was the main civil rights leader in the darkest U.S. state. He began to use this clout to organize a mass movement to desegregate the entire state. In Jackson, a series of sit-ins and boycotts began after Evers gave an impassioned speech on live television. The Jackson police responded in kind. At a rally five days before his death, Evers said, "I would die, and die gladly, if that would make a better life for them [my children]."

The night of June 12, Evers arrived at his home. As he got out of his car, a gunshot broke the night's stillness; Evers had been shot in the back. He died shortly afterwards.

— JUNE 13 —
1967
THURGOOD MARSHALL APPOINTED TO U.S. SUPREME COURT

On this day in civil rights history, Thurgood Marshall became the first African American appointed to the U.S. Supreme Court.

Born in Baltimore, Maryland, Marshall graduated high school a mediocre student. In 1930, he graduated from Lincoln University and applied to Howard University Law School. There he fell under the sway of its new dean, Charles Hamilton Houston, one of the most famous civil rights lawyers and Marshall's mentor. Houston and Marshall would try many cases together as co-counselors.

After graduating in 1933, Marshall began handling the NAACP's legal cases. By 1939 he was the director of the NAACP Legal Defense Fund and a year later was named chief counsel. The NAACP's strategy involved setting legal precedents in the federal courts, reasoning that once the federal government was involved, they would stay involved. Houston and Marshall were instrumental in the application of this strategy.

Marshall was lead attorney for the NAACP on many historic cases, including *Murray v. Maryland*, *Morgan v. Commonwealth*, *Smith v. Allwright*, and most famous of all in 1954, *Brown v. Board of Education*. With other NAACP lawyers, Marshall crafted the major legal strategies that led to the dismantling of Jim Crow segregation.

Thurgood Marshall

Photo courtesy of Library of Congress

Marshall helped forge the legal path to integration, opening public schools, universities, and public transportation to black citizens. Because of these cases, Marshall is one of the most important civil rights figures ever.

On June 12, Supreme Court Justice Tom Clark retired from the court. President Johnson nominated Thurgood Marshall the next day, saying that it was "the right thing to do, the right time to do it, the right man and the right place."

Marshall was confirmed and served 24 years, applying his keen legal mind and acute moral sense to the cases he heard. He consistently voted against discrimination of any kind, promoted affirmative action, and was an outspoken critic of the death penalty. As the Court became more conservative in the 1980s, Marshall found himself in the minority and when he retired in 1991, was openly critical of the direction the court was taking.

He died two years later. Law libraries, colleges, and an airport have all been named in honor of this legal giant.

— JUNE 14 —
2005
CONGRESS APOLOGIZES FOR INACTION ON LYNCHING

On this day in civil rights history, Congress officially apologized for its failure in the first half of the 20th century to make lynching a federal crime. Presidents and politicians have apologized publicly to African Americans—for slavery and for Jim Crow segregation—but this marked the first time Congress acknowledged a failure toward the African American population.

There is a lot to apologize for.

Between 1882 and 1968, roughly 5,000 African Americans were lynched by white mobs, often helped by local authorities. Whites beat and killed blacks with impunity. Leaving the prosecution of lynching to the states resulted in lackluster prosecution and acquittal after acquittal, when the perpetrators were often captured on film.

Lynching has been with the country since its inception, often used to rid border towns of unwanted undesirables. But after the Civil War, lynching became synonymous with white terror. The South, occupied by the North during the period of Reconstruction, resented and feared both burgeoning black political power and what they saw as Northern interference in their way of life. During this period, ex-Confederates intent on maintaining the South's traditions founded the Ku Klux Klan. The Klan was a strong presence across the country, claiming over half a million members. Its existence spurred on—as either direct catalyst or indirect inspiration—thousands of lynch mobs, who used violence—by hanging or burning or both—to punish black breaches of Jim Crow etiquette. As the Klan was ensconced in local government, little was done to prevent mob violence. Lynching remained an immediate threat to all African Americans living in the South. Tiny infractions of Jim Crow mores—not showing enough deference in public, whistling at a white woman—could mean hanging or mutilation, oftentimes both.

The federal government began Reconstruction with President U. S. Grant's tough stance on racial violence. But after President Hayes effectively ended Reconstruction to get elected, the federal government turned its back on its African American citizens. With systematic prosecution by the U.S. government, perhaps lynching would have disappeared. Because of political expediency, however, the federal government decided to stay quiet on the issue.

The apology is a major step forward in race relations, but comes 100 years too late. The truth about lynching and government complicity remains. As a telling example of how far we have to go, 20 senators abstained from voting for the apology. When criticism began to mount, the number of abstaining senators dwindled to eight.

— JUNE 15 —
1966
MARCH AGAINST FEAR CONTINUES IN MISSISSIPPI

On this day in civil rights history, the March Against Fear begun by Mississippi independent activist James Meredith continued. Although begun as a solitary act of protest, it would become a major turning point in the movement.

Ten days earlier, James Meredith began walking, by himself, from Memphis, Tennessee, to Jackson, Mississippi. The march was supposed to inspire local African Americans to take risks—physical and economic—to register to vote and end segregation. He left Memphis amidst major publicity. The unarmed 32-year-old Meredith only made it 30 miles, however, before he was shot three times. Meredith was taken to a nearby hospital for treatment. Ironically, Meredith had made a very clear point: the South was still a dangerous place for a black man.

While Meredith was recuperating, civil rights leaders—including Martin Luther King, Floyd McKissick, James Lawson, Cleveland Sellers, Stokely Carmichael, and Dick Gregory—flew into Memphis from all across the country. CORE, SCLC, and SNCC announced, with Meredith's blessing, that the march would continue without him. A "March Against Fear" manifesto was released, demanding federal help from President Lyndon Johnson. On June 7, the march began anew.

The march quickly grew in size and scope. Hundreds of marchers slept in rented circus tents and were fed by local residents who donated warm meals. The protesters walked along Highway 51, escorted by highway patrolmen and dozens of reporters. Angry white protesters lined the streets, waving Confederate flags from their cars and trucks. As the march descended deeper into Mississippi, the armed guard reduced to four men. In the evenings, marchers would hold rallies and voter registrations in nearby cities. Nearly 3,000 black Mississippians registered to vote during the three-week event. And in Greenwood, on June 17, an incident would take place that would split the movement into two, as Stokely Carmichael, after being arrested, delivered his infamous "Black Power" speech. The fallout from the speech reverberated throughout the movement and in the national media.

On June 25, Meredith rejoined the march he had begun. The next day the march ended in Jackson, Mississippi, with a large rally of over 15,000 people in attendance.

— JUNE 16 —
1961
ATTORNEY GENERAL MEETS WITH CIVIL RIGHTS LEADERS

On this day in civil rights history, U.S. Attorney General Robert Kennedy met at the Justice Department with civil rights leaders to discuss black-voter disfranchisement in the South.

The meeting was productive but uncomfortable, as Kennedy made it clear that he and his brother, President John F. Kennedy, would encourage voter-registration drives, but wanted an end to mass demonstrations, freedom rides, sit-ins, and other confrontational activities. The meeting revealed the Kennedy brothers' tentative position on the race issue, but it also produced the kernel of an idea that would later become the Voter Education Project.

President Kennedy was in a hard position. His slim Democratic majority in Congress was threatened by Southern Democrats. Kennedy would need the white Southern vote to win in 1964, and he thus wanted to minimize the role of the federal government in the civil rights movement, to which he was otherwise sympathetic. His internal compromise resulted in a policy of strict adherence to existing laws, not new ones. Under Kennedy, federal authority was used to desegregate the universities of Alabama and Mississippi; he appointed Thurgood Marshall to a federal judgeship; and with Robert Kennedy, he helped form the Voter Education Project, coordinating with the Southern Regional Council and private philanthropic organizations. CORE, SCLC, the NAACP, the Urban League, and SNCC all took part.

Inconsistency, however, hurt the Kennedys and the civil rights movement. The Kennedy administration appeared at times to turn a deaf ear to the protests of black Americans, and at other times seemed a staunch ally. President Kennedy was mostly noncommittal on civil rights issues. As attorney general, Robert Kennedy followed the same path.

Over the next two years, however, the Kennedys became more decisive on civil rights as well-publicized incidents of violence repeatedly shocked the nation, particularly the brutal use of attack dogs, water hoses, and baton-swinging police by local authorities in Birmingham in May 1963. In a nationally televised speech on June 11, 1963, President Kennedy promised to send substantial civil rights legislation to Congress. Five months later he was assassinated. Robert Kennedy, however, continued to strengthen his support for civil rights up to the time of his own assassination in 1968.

— JUNE 17 —
1966
'BLACK POWER' SLOGAN MARKS TURN IN MOVEMENT

On this day in civil rights history, Stokely Carmichael, in a speech in Greenwood, Mississippi, popularized the phrase "Black Power."

Carmichael had recently replaced John Lewis as the head of SNCC, and the organization was quickly absorbing the charismatic Carmichael's more leftist politics.

After James Meredith was shot in north Mississippi during his "March Against Fear," many civil rights leaders, including Carmichael, Martin Luther King Jr., Floyd McKissick, James Lawson, Cleveland Sellers, and Dick Gregory, went to Memphis in support of the hospitalized Meredith. Meredith gave his approval for the march to continue without him, so 20 or so of the movement leaders set out for Mississippi, where they resumed the protest march—this time with an escort of hostile white Mississippi highway patrolmen.

After the first day, the leaders released a "March against Fear" manifesto that demanded President Lyndon Johnson firm up his proposed Civil Rights Bill and commit more money to antipoverty programs. Behind the scenes, the leaders clashed over the wording of the manifesto.

Black power poster

Photo courtesy of Associated Press

Meanwhile, the march continued, now numbering 400 marchers. As King left temporarily to work in Chicago, the state of Mississippi began making life difficult for the marchers. Their guard was reduced to just four men. Public campgrounds were declared off-limits. When Carmichael began setting up camp anyway, he was arrested in Greenwood, but released a few hours later.

At Broad Street Park, Carmichael gave a speech to hundreds of supporters and news reporters in which he attacked the philosophy and consequences of integration: "This reinforces . . . the idea that 'white' is automatically better and 'black' is by definition inferior. This is why integration is a subterfuge for the maintenance of white supremacy."

He urged blacks to defend themselves, form black communities, and stump for their special interests and self-determination. Until blacks had pride in being black, he said, any coalition with whites would result in disparity. As he warmed to his topic, his tone became more harsh. He declared, "Every courthouse in Mississippi should be burnt down tomorrow so we can get rid of the dirt. . . . We want black power!"

The slogan quickly began to supplant—especially among youth—the milder "Freedom Now!" that had been the main rallying cry of the movement. Carmichael's Greenwood speech was the beginning of the end of public unity among the various civil rights groups.

— JUNE 18 —
1961
WYATT T. WALKER SERVES SCLC AS CHIEF OF STAFF

On this day in civil rights history, Wyatt Walker worked as the chief of staff of the Southern Christian Leadership Conference.

Walker was a headstrong man. After hearing a speech by Paul Robeson as a New Jersey high school student, Walker joined the Young Communist League. He later changed his mind.

After graduating from college, Walker became a preacher in Petersburg, Virginia. During his first pastorship, he met fiery preacher and former Dexter Avenue Baptist pastor Vernon Johns. Under Johns's tutelage, Walker became an uncompromising preacher and a dedicated activist. When Virginia public schools closed instead of integrating in 1959, Walker led an Emancipation Day March, inviting Martin Luther King Jr. to speak. The march was a success, and King eyed Walker as a potential member of his team.

In 1960, Walker was named executive director of the SCLC, replacing Ella Baker, who had resigned. Walker proved to be an inspired choice—strong, tireless, and committed. Critics said he was also contentious, argumentative, and at times immature.

Walker became a close friend and confidant of King as well as a major SCLC planner and organizer. As the group's chief of staff, Walker was involved with the Albany and Birmingham campaigns. In Birmingham, Walker smuggled out the pieces of toilet paper and newsprint on which King had written his historic "Letter from a Birmingham Jail."

Walker worked hard at maintaining a well-oiled, financially solvent SCLC. He also operated by fiat and was prone to confrontation. He and fellow member James Bevel shared a particularly strong animosity.

The SCLC was a high-pressure organization staffed by people of large talent and equally large egos, all of whom were usually under severe stress. Despite his considerable contributions, Walker's autocratic style upset some within the organization. In 1964, he resigned and moved to New York. He worked in the private sector for a while, including a stint on the board of directors at Freedom National Bank.

Today, Walker is the pastor of the Canaan Baptist Church of Christ in Harlem, New York. He has become an expert on African American religious music and is a prolific writer. A dynamic speaker, he remains active in human rights issues.

— JUNE 19 —

1865

JUNETEENTH CELEBRATION

On this day in civil right history, two and a half years after the Emancipation Proclamation, Union General Gordan Granger arrived in Galveston, Texas, informing its black residents that the Civil War was over and slavery was no more.

His statement read: "The people of Texas are informed that in accordance with a Proclamation from the Executive of the United States, all slaves are free. This involves an absolute equality of rights and rights of property between former masters and slaves, and the connection heretofore existing between them becomes that between employer and free laborer."

The Texas ex-slaves reacted first in shock, then in jubilation. While some African Americans waited to see what the new relationship between former slave and former owner would be, others gathered their belongings and left their plantations behind. Many traveled to Arkansas, Louisiana, and Oklahoma, carrying their day of freedom with them. Some went north looking for jobs, while others traveled east in hopes of reuniting with long-separated family members.

June 19, or Juneteenth, as it was called, became a major holiday for African Americans, especially in Texas. In Galveston, an annual festival celebrated emancipation with food, music, dancing, and prayer—Juneteenth was holy day, party, and thanksgiving feast all in one.

During Reconstruction, similar festivals were widely held across the South. But by the end of the 19th century, Juneteenth celebrations declined as the tightening grip of Jim Crow segregation all but destroyed the spirit of the holiday.

But a half-century later, during the civil rights years of the 1960s, Juneteenth celebrations were revived. In 1980, Juneteenth became a state holiday in Texas. Many cities and states now have a variety of Juneteenth celebrations, a look back at the jubilation the Texas freedmen felt when their deliverance finally came. Juneteenth is a day of exuberance, pride, and remembrance.

The author Ralph Ellison was working on a book with the title *Juneteenth* when he died; the novel was published posthumously in 1999.

— JUNE 20 —
1967
MUHAMMAD ALI CONVICTED OF DRAFT EVASION

On this day in civil rights history, heavyweight boxing champion Muhammad Ali was convicted of evading the draft, stripped of his heavyweight title, forbidden to box professionally, and sentenced to five years in prison.

Ali (formerly Cassius Clay) was controversial from the start of his professional career, when he defeated Sonny Liston in 1965. He was disrespectful, arrogant, and most shocking of all, he had become a very public member of the Nation of Islam. He spoke out at every opportunity against racism, but not in the conciliatory tones of the SCLC or the NAACP. Ali was brash and full of invective, advocating black separatism.

Muhammad Ali being escorted by station commander

He was everywhere in the mid-1960s, in films, television specials, and dozens of high-profile boxing matches. Middle America hated him; young people loved him. "I am America," he said. "I am the part you won't recognize. But get used to me. Black, confident, cocky. My name, not yours. My religion, not yours. My goals, my own. Get used to me."

He also spoke out against the Vietnam War, famously saying, "Ain't no Vietcong ever called me a nigger." But his high profile earned him enemies and in 1967, the U.S. Army drafted Ali to fight in Vietnam. He claimed conscientious-objector status and refused to serve. The government pressed charges. By trial's end, he was no longer world champion, but instead faced five years in prison. It was hard not to read the verdict as white America punishing him for his successes.

"You want to send me to jail?" he asked. "Fine, you go right ahead. I've been in jail for 400 years. . . . I ain't going no 10,000 miles to help murder and kill other poor people. . . . You my enemy, not no Chinese, no Vietcong, no Japanese. You my opposer when I want freedom. You my opposer when I want justice. You my opposer when I want equality. Want me to go somewhere and fight for you? . . . You won't even stand up for my right here at home."

Ali did not go to jail. Instead, his conviction was appealed and overturned by the U.S. Supreme Court in 1970. He lost three years in the prime of his athletic ability, but his legend had only grown, and he fought and regained the heavyweight title. He is acknowledged by many experts as the greatest heavyweight fighter ever.

— JUNE 21 —

1964

CIVIL RIGHTS WORKERS MURDERED IN MISSISSIPPI

On this day in civil rights history, civil rights workers Andrew Goodman, James Chaney, and Michael Shwerner disappeared on the back roads near Philadelphia, Mississippi. Their bodies were found six weeks later.

Shwerner and Goodman had only arrived in Mississippi the day before, among the scores of young college students answering the SNCC call for volunteers in the Freedom Summer campaign. The two were promptly sent off with local volunteer Chaney to investigate the bombing of a black church, where the three SNCC staffers were themselves arrested on suspicion of arson. They were taken off to jail in the custody of Sheriff Lawrence Rainey and Deputy Cecil Price, both KKK members.

Evidence later revealed that while Goodman, Chaney, and Scwerner sat in jail, a KKK conspiracy to murder them was forming. Released after dark, the three young men headed toward Meridian in their blue station wagon. Along the way they were run off the road by several cars full of Klan members, including Deputy Price. The three men were kidnapped, then shot at point-blank range. Their bodies were buried in a dirt dam at a fish pond.

Photo courtesy of FBI

FBI Poster

Meanwhile, when the young men did not return to SNCC headquarters, fellow staffers immediately began placing worried phone calls. They eventually called John Doar, the U.S. Justice Department representative in Mississippi. Assuming the worst, Doar called for the FBI.

Local law enforcement downplayed the incident, arguing that the civil rights workers had simply left Mississippi. But when the burned-out blue station wagon turned up, outside pressure intensified. For 40 days the U.S. government searched Mississippi with hundreds of agents, including 400 navy personnel called in to help. The bodies were eventually found on August 4.

The disappearance of the three workers had a profound impact. The nation got a lesson about the violent conditions facing Mississippi blacks who tried to challenge segregation. And blacks were reminded that it took the murders of two white Northern college students to get official America to pay attention to their cause.

In 2005, Klansman Edgar Ray Killen was finally prosecuted and convicted in the murders of the three men.

— JUNE 22 —

2005

KLANSMAN SENTENCED IN 1964 MISSISSIPPI MURDERS

On this day in civil rights history, Edgar Ray Killen was sentenced for his part in the 1964 murders of Andrew Goodman, James Chaney, and Michael Schwerner.

Another of the recent "Redemption Trials" in the South, the Killen case shows the beginning stages of a region coming to terms with its dark history.

Despite strong evidence against them, Killen and seven other defendants were acquitted during the original state-court trial in 1967 (some defendants were convicted on lesser federal charges). In 2000, in a changed political climate and amid rising calls to prosecute old crimes, Mississippi Attorney General Michael Moore reopened the case. Five years later, Moore's successor, Jim Hood, charged Killen with his involvement in the 1964 murders.

In 1964, Killen was the top Ku Klux Klan organizer and recruiter in his county. He was also a Baptist preacher.

Attending the 2005 trial in a wheelchair, the 80-year-old Killen sat quietly throughout the proceedings as the state once again delivered a case against him. On June 21, 2005, on the 41st anniversary of the deaths of Goodman, Chaney, and Schwerner, a jury of nine whites and three blacks convicted Killen of manslaughter.

On June 22, Mississippi Judge Marcus Gordan sentenced Killen to three consecutive 20-year terms. He will be eligible for parole shortly after his 100th birthday.

Some saw Killen's trial as a needless resurrection of long-buried issues and questioned the justice in sending an old man to die in jail. But as Judge Gordon noted, Killen was directly responsible for the deaths of three young men: " . . . there are three lives in this case. . . the three lives should be absolutely respected."

Like Byron de la Beckwith, prosecuted in Mississippi many years later for the 1963 murder of Medgar Evers, the jailed Killen is viewed as a martyr and hero to the white nationalists still operating in the United States.

— JUNE 23 —
1963
MURDERER OF MEDGAR EVERS ARRESTED IN MISSISSIPPI

On this day in civil rights history, Byron de la Beckwith was charged with the murder of activist Medgar Evers.

The cowardly killing of Evers—he was shot in the back late at night in his driveway in the presence of his small children—reverberated throughout the world, and excepting Martin Luther King Jr., he was probably the most famous civil rights martyr.

Bob Dylan and Nina Simone both wrote songs about Evers's death, while President John F. Kennedy met with Evers's wife, Myrlie, to offer his condolences. One night after Evers's death, Myrlie spoke at a movement rally: "We cannot let his death be in vain." A military veteran, Evers was buried in Arlington National Cemetery; Myrlie later wrote *We the Living* about Medgar's place in the movement. Charles Evers, Medgar's brother, took over his job as NAACP field secretary and continued his work.

The police found the murder weapon, a hunting rifle, where the killer had lay in wait across the street. The rifle was traced to Byron De La Beckwith, a White Citizens' Council member from Greenwood, Mississippi. Beckwith was a virulent, outspoken racist with affiliations with the KKK. The evidence against him was strong: ballistics testing matched the bullet to the weapon, the weapon belonged to Beckwith, it had his fingerprints on it, and he was placed near the scene of the crime asking for directions to Evers's house.

The state brought Beckwith to trial in February 1964. Despite the abundance of evidence, the all-white jury was unable to reach a verdict, which surprised few in the climate of the times in Mississippi. Governor Ross Barnett, one of the most outrageous, shameless racist demagogues of the era, shook Beckwith's hand as a mistrial was announced.

A second trial took place two months later; Beckwith received a second hung jury on April 17. Later, documents unsealed by the Mississippi Department of Archives revealed that the Beckwith juries were in all likelihood tampered with by the Klan. Beckwith would later brag about having shot Evers and having beaten the justice system.

Thirty years after the two hung juries, in a different climate in Mississippi, Beckwith was reindicted and retried.

— JUNE 24 —
1968
POOR PEOPLE'S CAMPAIGN PROVOKES RIOT

On this day in civil rights history, Martin Luther King Jr.'s Poor People's Campaign sputtered to an end amid sparks and riots.

After King's assassination in April, Ralph Abernathy, King's best friend, most trusted confidante, and most loyal supporter, took over as head of the SCLC, including King's vision of a Poor People's Campaign that would dramatize the problems of the nation's urban poor through a massive squatter's camp on the National Mall in Washington, D.C.

The campaign began May 13, with thousands of people in a makeshift "Resurrection City" of tents, sleeping bags, canvas, and plywood on the Mall adjacent to the Lincoln Memorial. Jesse Jackson was in charge of logistics. Andrew Young, Bayard Rustin, and other SCLC members, reluctant about the idea at the beginning, wholeheartedly joined in.

Although Abernathy is often viewed only as King's sidekick, he was a charismatic speaker and leader in his own right. The Poor People's Campaign was Abernathy's chance to shine.

Each day, the population of Resurrection City grew. Poor people—whites and blacks—traveled from across the country to join in. But heavy rains in late May and early June slicked the ground beneath Resurrection City and covered everything in mud. The rain fell for weeks, drenching the beleaguered inhabitants and miring everyone and everything in foul-smelling muck.

On June 19, leaders scheduled a "Solidarity Day" rally. Coretta Scott King and Ralph Abernathy were the main speakers. The message of the day was economic justice—end the war in Vietnam, end U.S. militarism abroad, and focus the resulting monies on poverty at home. It was the articulation of King's evolving vision for a biracial coalition of the nation's hungry, downtrodden, and poor. But despite the often eloquent, often poignant speeches, the Poor People's Campaign failed to deliver concrete demands or a list of acceptable compromises.

Five days later, more than 1,000 police descended on the Mall, shooting canisters of tear gas and unleashing attack dogs. Hundreds were arrested, including Abernathy, and the meager little Resurrection City was torn down. The Poor People's Campaign was over.

— JUNE 25 —
1964
BLACK SWIMMERS ATTACKED IN ST. AUGUSTINE, FLORIDA

On this day in civil rights history, near the end of the St. Augustine campaign, white mobs attacked black swimmers trying to desegregate a beach. The attack was one incident in a campaign that highlighted the tensions between local and national civil rights interests.

After the earlier success of a "swim-in" at the Monson Motor Lodge, groups of black protesters began challenging the segregated beachfronts, which by law had already been desegregated. The idea of a "wade-in" took shape, and on June 17, 35 African Americans went swimming. Police protected the black swimmers and after two hours, they left.

St. Augustine attack

A few days later they were back, but this time a mob of angry whites descended on the swimmers and chaos erupted on the hard sandy beaches. Fistfights broke out in the breaking surf. Police quickly waded into the shallow water with nightsticks and began beating those in the melee, including the blacks they were there to protect. Dozens were injured. It seemed that even the most beautiful of America's places was subject to racial violence.

That evening, a Klan-inspired riot broke through police lines. Hundreds of whites roamed through the city, searching for blacks to attack. Twenty more African Americans had to be treated for injuries. The situation in St. Augustine seemed to be getting worse, not better. On June 30, the Florida governor asked civil rights leaders to suspend activities; in return, a biracial committee would be established and the protesters' demands would be reviewed. SCLC president Martin Luther King Jr. recognized the delaying tactic but accepted the conditions. King probably knew that the biracial committee did not really exist, but the governor's response gave the St. Augustine civil rights movement a public victory and he took it.

Demands on his time prevented King and the SCLC from staying in St. Augustine any longer. The Civil Rights Act was going to pass any day, and Jim Bevel's Alabama project was demanding more resources. And internal problems loomed, such as finding a suitable replacement for recently resigned SCLC executive director Wyatt Walker. The SCLC, unfortunately, had bigger fish to fry.

Like Albany before it, the St. Augustine campaign achieved mixed results. The city remained unchanged by the two months of civil rights activity. "Outside agitators" were blamed for the disruption of day-to-day local life, and St. Augustine's segregationists felt they had succeeded in keeping their traditions in place.

— JUNE 26 —
1938
JAMES WELDON JOHNSON DIES

On this day in civil rights history, poet, lawyer, songwriter, novelist, diplomat, early activist, and all-around Renaissance man James Weldon Johnson died.

Born in 1871 in Jacksonville, Florida, Johnson graduated from Atlanta University. He returned to Jacksonville and became one of the first African Americans to pass the bar and practice law. He formed the first black daily newspaper in Florida, *The Daily American,* but it did not last. He moved to Harlem to produce a number of black plays with his brother, John Rosamond, and producer Bob Cole. In addition to producing, Johnson also wrote the lyrics to the songs. In 1904, Johnson left the theater to become a mid-level player in Republican Party politics, leading to his appointment by President Theodore Roosevelt as the U.S. consul to Venezuela and later Nicaragua. When Democrat Woodrow Wilson became president, however, Johnson resigned and returned to the United States to take up writing novels.

In 1912, he anonymously published *The Autobiography of an Ex-Colored Man,* the story of a light-skinned African American who passes for a white man and finds success but at the expense of his own identity. The masterful, philosophical, and intriguing novel consists of the unnamed narrator's confession of this "crime." As the novel garnered attention, Johnson admitted to its authorship, but he never wrote another novel, instead turning to poetry, then activism, then nonfiction.

In 1916, Johnson became a field organizer for the NAACP, where he distinguished himself immediately. He eventually became its executive secretary, and through the 1920s was one of the main civil rights leaders in the country, working closely with Walter White and W. E. B. Du Bois. The NAACP grew during those years from 70 branches to more than 300.

In 1932, Johnson began teaching creative writing at Fisk University. While at Fisk, he also wrote and published his autobiographical *Along This Way,* which said that black advancement was essential because "if the Negro is made to fail, America fails with him."

Johnson is now best known for his role in the Harlem Renaissance, that great artistic and cultural flowering of black thought in the decades between the two World Wars. He was a sort of father figure to Langston Hughes, Claude McKay, and Jean Toomer, among others.

In 1938 while vacationing in Maine, this remarkable man was killed when a train hit his car. He was 67.

— JUNE 27 —
1919
CARL HOLMAN BORN

On this day in civil rights history, future poet, journalist, and playwright M. Carl Holman was born in Minter City, Mississippi.

After graduating with honors from Lincoln University, Holman attended the University of Chicago, later earning a Master of Fine Arts degree from Yale University, which he attended on a creative-writing scholarship. Holman went on to teach English at Hampton University, Lincoln University, and Clark College. During his tenure at Clark College, Holman helped start the *Atlanta Inquirer*, a weekly civil rights publication that still operates. He served as the journal's first editor.

In 1962, Holman moved to Washington, D.C., where he became involved in politics. He served as information officer for the U.S. Civil Rights Commission and in 1966 became its deputy director. In 1971, he became director of the National Urban Coalition, which was organized after the 1967 riots to facilitate partnerships among businesses, government, and communities so as to strengthen poor urban areas. The NUC has grown into an advocacy group for underprivileged and minority children.

Holman worked as director of the NUC for 17 years as an influential advocate for better housing and urban development. He met with President Jimmy Carter during the late 1970s to address the race issue in the United States, and was considered one of the 100 most influential African Americans by *Ebony* magazine.

Holman was also a writer. He published articles, poems, plays, and books, including an overview of the civil rights movement from 1965 to 1975. He was honored with numerous fellowships and awards, including first prize at the National Community Theatre Festival for his play, *The Baptizin*.

Holman dedicated his life to the movement, filling the much-needed role of advocate for urban communities and mediator between them and corporations and government. He died at age 69 on August 9, 1988, in Washington.

— JUNE 28 —
1967
CHARLES MORGAN JR. HEADS
THE ACLU SOUTHEASTERN OFFICE

On this day in civil rights history, ACLU attorney Chuck Morgan worked on civil rights cases from his office in Atlanta.

Morgan had been an up-and-coming lawyer in Birmingham. But after the Sixteenth Street Baptist Church bombing in 1963, he spoke at a civic club meeting and laid the blame for the four girls' deaths on the indifference of white Birminghamians to the festering sore of police overreaction and even collusion with violent racists. This was a message Birmingham whites were not ready to hear, and in one short speech Morgan ruined his legal career. He had to leave the state.

Morgan joined the ACLU was named director of its southern regional office in Atlanta. From that base of operations, Morgan, a brilliant lawyer and a colorful character, began working for civil rights through numerous high-profile legal cases. He worked on issues involving jury selection, voting rights, voting districts, free speech, racial violence, and more. Morgan represented Julian Bond, who won election to the Georgia legislature, which then refused to seat him because he had spoken out against the Vietnam War. Another famous client was Muhammad Ali, who was convicted of draft evasion and subsequently barred from boxing. Morgan won both cases.

Roger Baldwin and Crystal Eastman formed the National Civil Liberties Bureau, which later became the American Civil Liberties Union, in the 1920s. It was the first public-interest law firm of its kind, designed to protect any individual or agency against governmental tyranny. The ACLU took on cases in which the civil rights of individuals had been violated.

Fierce proponents of free speech and strict adherents to the principle of separation of church and state, the ACLU has taken on many famous cases, including the Scopes Monkey Trial in 1925 and the internment of Japanese Americans during World War II. During the 1950s and 1960s, the ACLU worked in tandem with the NAACP and other groups and played a role in the landmark *Brown v. Board of Education* case in 1954. In 1962, the ACLU organized the Lawyers Constitutional Defense Committee—a legal coalition of NAACP, CORE, the American Jewish Congress, and other groups—which provided legal counsel in civil rights cases.

In 1967, Morgan won an important case regarding jury selection and discrimination in *Whitus v. Georgia*. Morgan left the ACLU in 1974 and became a successful and wealthy attorney in private practice in Washington, D.C. As of 2005, he was retired in Destin, Florida.

— JUNE 29 —
1965
VIETNAM ESCALATION DRAWS IN CIVIL RIGHTS PROTESTS

On this day in civil rights history, the United States carried out day two of its first major offensive in Vietnam. Three thousand U.S. soldiers engaged the Vietcong in a dense jungle area. The battle lasted three days. There would be many more to follow.

Many in the civil rights movement were dedicated pacifists, refusing to resort to violence even in self-defense. However, most civil rights leaders were cautious in talking about the war. Some felt their focus should stay on political, economic, and social gains for African Americans.

Others, recognizing that the majority of the U.S. population supported the war, believed they would alienate Middle America and thus jeopardize civil rights gains if they attacked the war.

Meanwhile, still others jumped on the issue, calling the war racist and accusing the United States of using young black men as cannon fodder. This allegation was partially true. At the time, blacks were 11 percent of the U.S. population, but 12 percent of the military. Also, most black GIs were enlisted infantrymen, the category most likely to be on the front lines. From 1965 to 1967, 20 percent of the

Wounded servicemen arriving from Vietnam

Photo courtesy of Library of Congress

U.S. dead in Vietnam were African American. By war's end, black soldier deaths had fallen back to a rate proportionate to the black population, but for those crucial years, African Americans fought and died in disproportionate numbers.

But it was not black participation in the Vietnam War that gradually led mainstream civil rights leaders like Martin Luther King Jr. to denounce it. Rather, King saw a link between U.S. militarism abroad and social unrest at home. Every dollar spent fighting in a foreign land was a dollar taken out of the coffers for public programs. And King, as he developed into an international leader, increasingly felt a responsibility to speak out against what he saw as an unjust flexing of U.S. military might.

The war complicated politics for other black figures as well. Muhammad Ali was drafted but refused to serve. The Black Panthers condemned the war as imperialist. Eventually the Vietnam War overshadowed the civil rights movement as the cause celebre amongst students and radicals.

— JUNE 30 —
1958
SUPREME COURT UPHOLDS NAACP MEMBERSHIP PRIVACY

On this day in civil rights history, the U.S. Supreme Court sided with the NAACP in a dispute with the state of Alabama over privacy rights.

After the success of the 1955–1956 Montgomery bus boycott, white Alabama officials wanted to punish black organizations, and the NAACP was the biggest target. In 1956, Alabama barred the NAACP from operating within its borders, claiming that the organization was causing irreparable damage to the residents of Alabama.

Alabama demanded that the NAACP release its membership lists, in accordance with a state law that required foreign corporations to qualify to operate within its borders. Fearing for the safety of its members, the NAACP refused.

A state court then held the NAACP in contempt, and while the case was on appeal, the NAACP was effectively banned from operating in Alabama. The organization, whose civil rights strategy was based on its faith in the ultimate authority of the law, had no choice but to wait on the appeals process.

Meanwhile in Alabama, the White Citizen's Council enacted boycotts and hiring restrictions against blacks, especially against activists. The KKK terrorized with violence and intimidation. The police harassed with petty arrests, fines, and jailing. And the state courts systematically worked to suppress or destroy any challenge to white control. The result was an almost impenetrable lattice of bureaucratic bigotry held in place by strong-arm tactics.

Eventually, the U.S. Supreme Court ruled that the NAACP had the right to keep its membership rolls private, and the contempt charge was dropped. But the case did not end there, as the actual legality of the NAACP in Alabama had not been addressed. Then the Alabama Supreme Court reinstated the contempt charge, the U.S. Supreme Court again overruled the contempt charge, again the Alabama court reinstated it, and so on for the next six years. Finally, the NAACP prevailed after the U.S. Supreme Court ruled on both the contempt charge and the original case.

By then, the NAACP was no longer the leading civil rights organization, having been supplanted by the SCLC and SNCC.

Ironically, the Supreme Court ruling upholding the NAACP's privacy on membership would be used in the 1980s and 1990s by Ku Klux Klan groups that sought to shield their members from civil lawsuits. The KKK claims were denied, however, as judges correctly ruled that the KKK groups had a history of violence and criminality, while the NAACP was a law-abiding, political organization.

This day in July

— JULY 1 —

2027

MISSISSIPPI SOVEREIGNTY COMMISSION FILES TO BE OPENED

On this date, the remaining files of the Mississippi Sovereignty Commission were to be opened to the public after being sealed by state lawmakers in 1977.

The MSC was founded in 1956, to "do and perform any and all acts and things deemed necessary and proper to protect the sovereignty of the State of Mississippi and her sister states" from federal interference—in other words, to maintain segregation.

Mississippi's new state agency was similar to commissions created in other Southern states around this time in response to *Brown v. Board,* the Montgomery bus boycott, and other alarming challenges to Jim Crow. The sovereignty commissions were both propaganda machines and spying operations. All of them colluded with the White Citizens' Councils, other white supremacists, and local law enforcement to keep tabs on, frustrate, and punish civil rights groups and individuals. Mississippi's commission had an annual budget of $250,000, a respectable sum in the 1950s.

Gradually, as times changed, the agencies were mostly shut down. In Mississippi, Governor William Waller cut funding to the MSC in 1973, and in 1977 it was officially closed.

But intense debate arose over what to do with the resulting files and paperwork. Should the MSC's records be destroyed or saved? The Mississippi legislature decided to duck the issue by locking the files away for 50 years. Sealed file cabinets were transported to the Mississippi Department of Archives and History and secured in a vault.

But the Mississippi ACLU sued and in 1998, some 100,000 documents were released, following a $600,000 effort by the Department of Archives and History to index the files into a large online database.

The files reveal the paranoid delusions of a white supremacist bureaucracy controlled in the 1950s by people like former Governor Ross Barnett. At its best, the MSC compiled trivial and mundane information on the lives of its African American and white moderate citizens. Often the "intelligence" was simply a collection of lies and smears in articles, letters, memos, rumors, and bizarre minutia concerning prominent and minor civil rights figures. The MSC is a frightful reminder of past government complicity with racist organizations, and recent government attempts to cover it up.

— JULY 2 —
1964
CIVIL RIGHTS ACT OF 1964 SIGNED

On this day in civil rights history, President Lyndon Johnson signed into law the Civil Rights Act of 1964. After almost half a century of legal agitation from the NAACP, a decade of nonviolent civil disobedience by the SCLC, and four years of voter campaigns and community-building by SNCC, to name just a few, the federal government passed the most important civil rights legislation since slavery was abolished in 1865.

Republican Senate Minority Leader Everett Dirksen pushed hard for the bill. But opposition from Southern Democrats resulted in an 80-day filibuster. At the end, both parties voted in favor of the act, though Albert Gore Sr. and Barry Goldwater were among notable opponents.

The bill's preamble states its purposes well: "To enforce the constitutional right to vote, to confer jurisdiction upon the district courts of the United States to provide injunctive relief against discrimination in public accommodations, to authorize the Attorney General to institute suits to protect constitutional rights in public facilities and public education, to extend the Commission on Civil Rights, to prevent discrimination in federally assisted programs, to establish a Commission on Equal Employment Opportunity, and for other purposes."

Photo courtesy of Lyndon B. Johnson Library

President Johnson signs Civil Rights Act of 1964

Businesses were now required to provide equal services to customers of all races and creeds. The Act made discriminatory hiring practices illegal. The attorney general was given the power to use the court to enforce the Act. Literacy tests were dismissed, and an agency was formed to help African Americans face discrimination problems in their communities.

Though it took time to achieve compliance in the backwaters of the South, the Act meant the end of Jim Crow segregation in public life. From this point on, African Americans had federal protection to demand and get equal service in all businesses. Bowling alleys, movie theaters, restaurants—all became integrated. The change in the United States was profound.

Some Southern white business owners flouted the bill, but slowly, with the threat of lawsuits, jail time, and fines, the country accepted integration. The major battle over segregation had been fought and won. The civil rights groups now refocused their attention on voting and economic empowerment.

— JULY 3 —
1963
DOCTORS AND NAACP PROTEST AMA SEGREGATION

On this day in civil rights history, black doctors and the NAACP protested the American Medical Association in Chicago, Illinois.

The first black doctors' association was the National Medical Association, founded in 1895. It fought to integrate medical schools and hospitals from the 1930s to the 1960s.

Despite increasing numbers of black medical professionals, the practice of medicine remained as segregated as everything else—black pharmacists, doctors, and nurses had a hard time finding work. Underfunded black hospitals in the South were often too scarce and had too few resources to provide adequate health care.

Black doctors in the South were not allowed to join the American Medical Association and even outside the South, black medical professionals could not fully participate in the AMA, though the organization accepted its first black delegates in 1950.

A group of black doctors, led by Aaron Otis Wells, formed the Medical Committee for Human Rights as a response. MCHR provided doctors for the civil rights movement in the South, while highlighting inequalities in the medical profession. During Mississippi Freedom Summer, for example, MCHR set up medical stations in Mississippi to educate and assist with medical problems. MCHR had representatives at most of the major civil rights events in the 1960s, providing health care to the sick and the wounded. Generally speaking, the NAACP provided lawyers, the SCLC ministers, SNCC protesters, and MCHR doctors. MCHR doctors also performed autopsies of slain civil rights workers, such as Andrew Goodman, James Chaney, and Michael Shwerner.

MCHR decided to protest the American Medical Association's policies. On June 12, 1963, MCHR members marched in Atlantic City, New Jersey. Then the organization decided to picket the AMA's headquarters in Chicago. This time, the NAACP supported the protest. Doctors and other professionals carried placards protesting their exclusion.

The MCHR stayed in the South after Mississippi Freedom Summer, continuing its educational work in poor black communities, some of which had never seen a doctor. MCHR set up clinics, held classes, lectured on nutrition, and provided indispensable prenatal care. With their dedication and activism, the MCHR members played a necessary but unsung supporting role in the movement.

— JULY 4 —
1776
INDEPENDENCE DAY CREATES A CONUNDRUM
FOR AFRICAN AMERICANS

On this day in civil rights history, the founding fathers adopted Thomas Jefferson's declaration that "all men are created equal." Sort of.

That Independence Day has historically been bittersweet for African Americans is illustrated by the words of John Beecher in his poem "To Live and Die in Dixie," which includes this passage:

Marchers close ranks for safety

Photo courtesy of Library of Congress

The Fourth of July
was a holiday for everybody but people's cooks
Corinne was fixing us hot biscuits
when I marched into the kitchen
waving the Stars and Stripes
And ordered her to
"Salute this flag! It made you free!"
I just couldn't understand why Corinne
plumb wouldn't*

If nothing else, Independence Day was always a day off, often with frivolity and frolic. Ex-slave Douglas Parish described in a 1937 interview how his Florida master put on July Fourth celebrations for his slaves. It was a custom in those days, Parish said, for one plantation owner to match his "nigger" against that of his neighbor. Parish's master trained his runners by having them race to the boundary of his plantation and back again. The fastest runner represented his master in the Fourth of July races, in which runners from all over the county competed for top honors and the winner earned a bag of silver for his master. Prizes in less important races, Parish said, ranged from a pair of fighting cocks to a slave, depending upon the seriousness of the betting.

After Emancipation, some black communities combined July Fourth with "Juneteenth" celebrations of the date when they got news that they were free.

Black soldiers in World Wars I and II complained bitterly about fighting and dying for freedom overseas when it was still denied to them at home. Their acute sense of the hypocrisy of segregation motivated many to become involved in civil rights activities.

World War II veteran Rufus Lewis, for example, operated a nightclub to which he would admit no black men who were not registered voters. Lewis backed up his sentiments with action as one of the leaders of the Montgomery bus boycott; later he served in the Alabama legislature and was the first black U.S. marshal in his judicial district.

*Used with permission from *One More River to Cross,* NewSouth Books, 2003.

— JULY 5 —

1817

BUSINESSMAN-ABOLITIONIST JOHN JONES BORN FREE IN NORTH CAROLINA

On this day in civil rights history, future businessman and entrepreneur John Jones was born a free man in North Carolina.

Interestingly, two African Americans named John Jones were born in 1817, within two weeks of each other, and both contributed to the antislavery cause. John W. Jones was born a slave on a Virginia plantation. When his owner died, he and a few other slaves fled north to freedom, settling in New York. John W. Jones became involved in the Underground Railroad, offering his house as a refuge. Over 800 slaves passed through his doors, not a single one caught. He became a preacher and as sexton of the nearby cemetery during the Civil War was responsible for the burials of Confederate soldiers who died in the Elmira prison camp. He kept meticulous, perfect records, seeing to the proper burials of almost 3,000 men. The cemetery he watched over with such fastidious care became Woodlawn National Cemetery. After years of community service, he died in 1900.

The other John Jones started out as an apprentice tailor in North Carolina. He was a rare free Negro in the South at the time, and he worked hard to make a living. In his free time, he taught himself to read and write. In 1845, Jones left North Carolina with his wife and started his own tailoring business. Plying savvy business acumen to the trade, Jones expanded his business, eventually becoming one of the wealthiest black men in America.

Jones put his wealth to good use. His home also became an Underground Railroad station. He wrote, published, and distributed pamphlets against the Illinois Black Laws, which prohibited blacks from voting or serving on a jury. He was eventually elected Cook County Commissioner, perhaps the first African American to hold such an office in America. As commissioner, Jones abolished segregation in the Cook County school system. After a life of hard work, success, and antislavery service, he died in 1879.

The two John Jones were unheralded but significant figures in the Underground Railroad–abolitionist movement—one a community activist, the other a wealthy, self-made politician who fought for change.

— JULY 6 —
1962
BIRACIAL LEADERSHIP OF THE SOUTHERN REGIONAL COUNCIL

On this day in civil rights history, the Southern Regional Council worked as a biracial research and advocacy group, and as an important coordinator for the NAACP, the SCLC, SNCC, CORE, and the Urban League.

In the early 20th century, the Atlanta Christian Council and other civic organizations saw the need for an entity to foster race relations between blacks and whites. In 1919, the Commission on Interracial Cooperation was founded, with Will Alexander as its first director. Prominent black leaders such as Morehouse College President John Hope were invited to join, making the CIC a biracial organization from the beginning.

Funded by Northern liberals and operated by Southerners, the CIC was cautious in its early programs as it worked to improve educational conditions for Southern blacks but did not actively fight for integration.

During the Great Depression, the CIC concentrated on education and research, which often involved antilynching efforts. The organization also worked to make sure African Americans were included in New Deal programs.

The CIC floundered in the late 1930s. In 1944, the CIC disbanded, and the Southern Regional Council was formed during a conference in Durham, North Carolina, to replace it. The SRC's fundamental economic tenet was: if the South's economy improved, so would race relations. Thus the SRC began to advocate economic fairness and justice along with integration. Its mission was stated as: To fight "racist propaganda and prepare Southern opinion for gradual amelioration of black social conditions."

The SRC continued its civil rights work in the 1940s, seeking to rid the South of the all-white political primaries that effectively barred even registered black voters from the political process. In the 1950s, the SRC worked to desegregate public schools. Local affiliates, such as the Alabama Council on Human Relations, worked to solve racial problems in their communities.

In the 1960s, the SRC was the administering body of the Voter Education Project, which it also helped found. Headquartered in the SRC's Atlanta offices, the VEP's registration efforts brought more than two million new black voters to the polls in the turbulent 1960s, while funneling operating cash into the registration campaigns of Freedom Summer and Selma.

From the 1970s to the end of the century, the SRC shifted its emphasis toward equitable election districts, fair education and labor practices, and general advocacy and research to promote progress in the region. The SRC remained a leading progressive organization in the South to the end of the century.

— JULY 7 —
1969
CHARLES EVERS BECOMES MAYOR IN MISSISSIPPI

On this day in civil rights history, Charles Evers, the brother of civil rights martyr Medgar Evers, became mayor of Fayette, Mississippi. Born in Decatur, Mississippi, in 1922, Charles Evers was the first African American mayor in this Deep South state since Reconstruction.

He and Medgar both served in the U.S. Army during World War II. As kids, they made a pact: if one died, the other would carry on whatever the other was doing. Charlie and Medgar returned to Mississippi determined to change the miserable conditions segregation had forced on its black citizens.

They both graduated college and settled in Philadelphia, Mississippi, which was called by Martin Luther King Jr. "a terrible town, the worst I've seen. There is a complete reign of terror here." Here, where civil rights workers Andrew Goodman, James Chaney, and Michael Schwerner later disappeared, Medgar and Charles Evers were entrepreneurs and became active with the NAACP.

Medgar soon became the NAACP's Mississippi field secretary, but Charles fled to Illinois after some questionable business dealings. There he worked as a short-order cook, dishwasher, cotton picker, bootlegger, and numbers runner.

Medgar's 1963 assassination brought his unlikely brother into the forefront of the civil rights movement. Like Medgar, Charles was a courageous and committed man. He put aside his shady dealings and returned to Mississippi to take up his brother's work as NAACP field secretary.

He was outspoken and uncompromising, making him at times unpopular, but he nonetheless won election in 1969 as mayor of Fayette, a small town with a large black population but little industry. The NAACP named him Man of the Year, while novelist John Updike mentioned Evers in his seminal novel, *Rabbit Redux*.

Evers later ran unsuccessfully for governor with the slogan: "Evers for Everybody." He continued in the movement, carrying on his brother's work, just as he promised. Over the course of his life he advised presidents and millionaires—not bad for a poor black kid from Decatur. Ever controversial, he became a Republican and a broadcaster.

In 1996, he published his movement memoir, *Have No Fear*.

— JULY 8 —

1958

BALTIMORE SCHOOLS DESEGREGATE

On this day in civil rights history, Baltimore public schools continued the desegregation process while the city remained divided along racial lines.

From its inception in 1729, Baltimore was a thriving port city—a key entry point from the Caribbean sugar plantations. Frederick Douglass lived there for a time, and Thurgood Marshall and Billie Holiday were born there. Like Atlanta, Baltimore had a thriving black middle class, with many black-owned businesses along Pennsylvania Avenue. In 1912, the second permanent branch of the NAACP opened there. (In 1986, the NAACP moved its national headquarters to Baltimore.)

Although lacking the big events and the drama of the Deep South civil rights movement, Baltimore had its own civil rights leaders, including an aging but still feisty Vernon Johns, who had set the stage for civil rights as pastor of the Dexter Avenue Baptist Church in Montgomery before the arrival of Martin Luther King Jr.

In 1954, after the *Brown* decision, Baltimore and Washington, D.C., were the only cities to desegregate their public schools immediately. Whites picketed and protested, but the city avoided the violence of the Deep South.

Baltimore remained otherwise segregated, however. Students from Maryland colleges began sit-ins in 1960, while local black civic leaders, journalists, and activists negotiated for the end of segregation.

An unusual tactic by three reporters broke the city's racial barrier. Many African diplomats traveled through Maryland going to and from Washington, D.C. As the United States did not want an international incident due to segregation, the governor of Maryland made sure that African diplomats were treated with the utmost respect.

Three Baltimore reporters saw a story. Dressing up as African dignitaries, they visited a white-owned restaurant, mimicking African accents and customs. They were seated in the whites-only areas and ate their meal in comfort. A photographer took photos as evidence. When the story broke, the state of Maryland and the city of Baltimore were embarrassed, as was the United States. Less than a year later, the Baltimore Community Relations Commission outlawed segregation in Baltimore's public places.

But the victory for civil rights did not save Baltimore from industrial decline. The city lost more than 100,000 jobs in the second half of the 20th century, and white flight from the inner city left behind a crumbling infrastructure and a weakened tax base.

— JULY 9 —
1868
CONGRESS RATIFIES 14TH AMENDMENT

On this day in civil rights history, the 14th Amendment to the Constitution was ratified.

The second of three major amendments ratified by Radical Republicans during Reconstruction, the 14th Amendment effectively reversed the 1856 Dred Scott decision, declaring African Americans citizens of the United States.

The amendment states: "All persons born or naturalized in the United States, and subject to the jurisdiction thereof, are citizens of the United States and of the State wherein they reside. No State shall make or enforce any law which shall abridge the privileges or immunities of citizens of the United States; nor shall any State deprive any person of life, liberty, or property, without due process of law; nor deny to any person within its jurisdiction the equal protection of the laws."

Poster protesting the amendment

Equal protection for all citizens was a significant guarantee. The second section of this amendment detailed a right-to-vote provision for males over the age of 21. The third section prohibited insurrectionists or rebels against the federal government from serving in public office. Finally, the bill announced that the U.S. would not pay damages against lost slaves, forestalling suits from formerly wealthy planters over the loss due to war of their human property. The bill also refused to pay Confederate war debt.

The fifth section provided the U.S. government the power to enforce the new law.

Republicans in Congress were reacting to the Black Codes Southern states had installed immediately after the Civil War. These Black Codes attempted to return race relations to their slave-owner state. The 14th Amendment, backed by the U.S. military and bolstered by the 13th and 15th Amendments, worked. Blacks voted, started schools, and were elected to public office.

The Supreme Court, however, in *Plessy v. Ferguson*, undercut the three Reconstruction amendments by holding that separate-but-equal treatment was constitutionally permissible. New legislation in the next century would be necessary to break the hold of Jim Crow.

— JULY 10 —
1875
EDUCATOR-ACTIVIST MARY MCLEOD BETHUNE BORN

On this day in civil rights history, Mary McLeod Bethune was born in South Carolina, a daughter of former slaves. From this humble beginning she rose to national prominence as one of the most influential African American women ever.

Bethune received a formal education and became a dedicated teacher. She taught across the South in Georgia, Florida, and South Carolina, as well as in Chicago, Illinois. She also worked in a variety of volunteer and charity organizations.

Photo courtesy of Library of Congress

Mary McLeod Bethune

In 1904, Bethune formed the Daytona Normal and Industrial Institute for Negro Girls, charging 50 cents a week for tuition. She would remain president of the Institute for 40 years. In 1923, she oversaw her school's merger with the Cookman Institute into Bethune-Cookman College.

Bethune never allowed her second-citizen status—first as an African American, and second as a woman—to discourage her. She was more than an educator, however. With Bethune-Cookman College settled, she turned her attention to politics.

Bethune's political involvement led to the integration of the Red Cross in 1917, before women even had the right to vote. In 1935, she formed the National Council of Negro Women to work against segregation, inequality, and political disenfranchisement. And in 1936, she served as director of the Division of Negro Affairs within the Depression-era National Youth Administration, thus becoming the first African American woman to head a federal agency.

Bethune was friends with First Lady Eleanor Roosevelt and was a member of President Franklin D. Roosevelt's so-called "Black Cabinet." Bethune worked vigorously for a federal antilynching law. In 1940, she served as vice president of the NAACP. Throughout her life she worked with the National Urban League, the Association of American Colleges, the National Youth Administration, and the League of Women Voters, to name a few.

A tireless campaigner, Bethune worked for welfare reforms, fair housing, equal opportunity, and equal education under four presidents—Theodore Roosevelt, Calvin Coolidge, Herbert Hoover, and FDR.

Bethune died May 18, 1955, in Florida. Her epitaph reads: "I leave you faith, I leave you hope, I leave you love."

— JULY 11 —
1905
NIAGARA MOVEMENT FOUNDED

On this day in civil rights history, the Niagara Movement, taking its name from its meeting location on the Canadian side of the famous falls, was founded.

The all-black organization was the brainchild of Atlanta professor W. E. B. Du Bois who sought to counter his former friend Booker T. Washington's conciliatory stance toward segregation. Du Bois was convinced that accommodation was a terrible strategy for African Americans and would lead only to greater exploitation. He felt a more militant antisegregation platform was needed, and thus conceived of the Niagara Movement as a counterpoint to Washington and his policies.

The organizational meeting was originally to take place in the United States. But when the 29 conferees were refused rooms by American hotels, they crossed over into Canada where they were received without objection.

Their meeting lasted three days. The attendees included businessmen, newspapermen, professors, and writers, including J. Max Barber, Alonzo Herndon, Frederick McGhee, William Monroe Trotter, and C. E. Bentley, among others.

The meeting produced a manifesto, which read, "We claim for ourselves every single right that belongs to a freeborn American, political, civil and social; and until we get these rights we will never cease to protest and assail the ears of America. The battle we wage is not for ourselves alone but for all true Americans. It is a fight for ideals, lest this, our common fatherland, false to its founding, become in truth the land of the thief and the home of the slave—a byword and a hissing among the nations for its sounding pretensions and pitiful accomplishment. . . . We want full manhood suffrage and we want it now. . . . We are men! We want to be treated as men. And we shall win."

Du Bois was named general secretary of the organization, which quickly began lobbying for antilynching legislation and desegregation. In 1906, the Niagara Movement held its second meeting at Harper's Ferry, West Virginia. Though at its peak the Niagara Movement had hundreds of members and 30 local chapters, it had insufficient funding and never gained significant organizational momentum.

In 1909, white liberals joined with the core of the Niagara Movement to form the NAACP, which quickly became the most important civil rights group in the nation.

— JULY 12 —
1966
CHICAGO RALLY MARKS TRANSITION IN MOVEMENT

On this day in civil rights history, a rally was held at Soldier Field as part of the Chicago campaign, the SCLC's attempt to expand the movement beyond the South. The rally, attended by thousands of people, laid the framework for an even more radical set of demands, most of which would later surface in the Poor People's Campaign.

The issues targeted by rally speakers included discriminatory lending and housing practices, the desegregation of Chicago public schools, the establishment of a civilian police review committee, more low-cost housing, and, perhaps most radical, a federally "guaranteed income for every man."

These issues coalesced into a unifying call for elimination of urban ghettos. The ghetto, campaign organizers declared, was sustained through four problems that had to be rectified: lack of economic power, political disenfranchisement, lack of knowledge and information, and lack of self-respect and self-dignity by impoverished ghetto dwellers. The new movement in the North had to deal with all four problems.

In the days leading up to the rally, Martin Luther King Jr. toured many of the decrepit buildings on Chicago's Southside. In one dynamic action, King and SCLC staffers descended on the South Homan apartment building and collected the inhabitants' rent money, pledging to use the funds for desperately needed electrical and heating-system repairs. The overall campaign involved marches, protests, and rallies at local churches and parks. This went on during the early months of 1966. Local support was wavering as little seemed to be happening.

After the Soldier Field rally, some 5,000 marchers followed King to Chicago City Hall, where King symbolically tacked the demands to Mayor Richard Daley's door. But Mayor Daley in many ways proved as intransigent as had Southern mayors in the early 1960s. He made many promises but offered no timeline. On most issues he was noncommittal, and on some he refused to budge. In fact, Daley secured an injunction limiting the number of marchers through Chicago neighborhoods, effectively dampening the next string of marches planned by the SCLC and local organizers.

In echoes of Birmingham, Chicago seemed on the brink of chaos. Small-scale violence broke out between the Chicago police and black youths on the Southside and King and Daley both feared that a Watts-type situation was brewing. The two men called a meeting to quell the potential for violence and to discuss the city's racial problems.

— JULY 13 —
1964
BODIES OF HENRY DEE AND CHARLES MOORE FOUND

On this day in civil rights history, the bodies of Henry Dee and Charles Moore were found in the Mississippi River. The discovery was a chilling reminder of the danger facing blacks in general and civil rights workers in particular in Mississippi, the most violent of all the Deep South states.

After the disappearance of SNCC staffers Andrew Goodman, James Chaney, and Michael Schwerner, dozens of FBI agents and hundreds of navy recruits dredged rivers, combed forests and fields, and searched with police dogs. Some two weeks into the hunt, the investigation uncovered two badly decomposed bodies. The fact that these two victims were not even reported as missing underscored the cheapness of black life to Mississippi officials.

The FBI began investigating and soon learned that teenagers Dee and Moore were hitchhiking to attend a party. According to the FBI, a white truck driver and Klansman pulled over and told the boys he was a federal agent. He drove the two youths into the woods and then, at gunpoint, tied them to a magnolia tree. The FBI said the kidnapper believed the two youths were activists intending to cause trouble; he did not realize they were local teenagers looking for a good time.

Other Klansmen appeared. They cut branches off trees and began to whip the two boys, urging them to confess, but Dee and Moore had nothing to confess. Unconscious and barely breathing, Dee and Moore were put inside a plastic tarp and placed in the back of a truck. The kidnapper then drove about 100 miles before taking the two young men—badly beaten but still alive—from the back of his truck. He attached weights to their feet and pushed them into the Mississippi River, where they drowned.

In November 1964, James Ford Seale and Charles Marcus Edwards were arrested and reportedly confessed to the murders. But the State of Mississippi subsequently dropped the charges and Seale and Edwards went free.

As of 2005, the FBI has reopened the case.

— JULY 14 —
1822
DENMARK VESEY SLAVE REVOLT

On this day in civil rights history, Denmark Vesey's slave revolt was to begin. It would have been the largest slave revolt in U.S. history, but it was crushed before it could get started.

In the 1760s, Vesey was taken from the Virgin Islands and sold into slavery in Charleston, South Carolina. Vesey taught himself how to read. Later, in an amazing stroke of luck, he won $1,500 in a street lottery and used $600 of his winnings to buy his own freedom. Vesey then went into business as a carpenter as a rare free black man in South Carolina.

But he did not forget the terrible yoke of slavery, nor could he ignore the casual day-to-day violence he witnessed against slaves. He began to read abolitionist literature and soon conceived a plan to emulate the famous 1804 slave revolt in Haiti. Vesey organized a cabal of slaves and former slaves through surreptitious meetings throughout the city. A plan took shape: Vesey and his cohorts would attack Charleston's arsenals, arm themselves, kill every slave-owner they could find, and raze the city.

At least this is the official version. It isn't clear what Vesey's intentions were, as the only written records are the trial transcripts and white reactions to the event. One historian recently made the claim that Vesey was framed.

Regardless, Vesey's plan did not materialize. As 9,000 slaves waited on various plantations for Vesey to call them into action, a house servant, on May 30, revealed the plans to the authorities. The subsesequent investigation resulted in the arrest of more than 100 African Americans who were accused of a slave insurrection that never took place. On June 23, Vesey and 34 others were hanged.

Like Nat Turner and John Brown, Vesey is a controversial figure in American history. Over the years, he attained legendary status amongst African Americans and his name was used as a rallying cry for black regiments in the Civil War, while Southern whites considered him at best a murderous rogue. Today he is seen as a heroic figure who gave up his own life in an effort to free his brethren.

— JULY 15 —

1968

HUEY NEWTON GOES ON TRIAL FOR MURDER

On this day in civil rights history, Black Panther Party cofounder Huey Newton went on trial for the murder of an Oakland policeman.

From their beginning, the Panthers scared everyone. Their guns scared the local police. Their attitude scared the white citizens of Oakland. And their political messages of black power, armed resistance, and redistribution of wealth scared the U.S. government.

FBI Director J. Edgar Hoover called the BPP a national menace and began a program called COINTELPRO as a covert war against radical organizations, with the Panthers as one of the top targets. Wiretaps, burglaries, planted evidence, misinformation, and provocations were used by the FBI to undermine the BPP. Much of this law enforcement activity was questionable; the BPP, for all its controversy, was a legal organization that claimed the same constitutional gun rights as the NRA.

Huey Newton

Nonetheless, the Panthers' aggressive stance inevitably led to antagonism with the Oakland police department, who regularly harassed BBP members. This led to a series of escalating gunfights between police and Panthers.

One late evening in October 1967, two policemen pulled Huey Newton over. Newton complied with the officers and got out of his car. As he was following their instructions, one of the officers shot Newton in the stomach. Newton fell to the ground unconscious, missing the hail of bullets from unseen guns that killed one officer and injured the other. When the smoke cleared, Newton, though he had been unconscious at the time, was charged with murder.

Eventually there were three media-circus trials. Newton was seen in radical circles as a political prisoner and a much-publicized "Free Huey" movement began. Due to a lack of evidence and a strong defense by BPP lawyer Charles Garry, Newton was acquitted. He was released from prison a hero.

Entering the 1970s, the BPP emerged as the major voice of the black underclass, dominating the public discourse on race. The general mood of the nation had shifted. Jim Crow segregation had been defeated and the right to vote secured, but little progress had been made toward economic justice. Martin Luther King Jr. was dead, and the civil rights movement in the South was effectively over. America's urban ghettos seethed with untapped anger. With the women's liberation movement, the war in Vietnam, and the emerging drug and youth culture, issues grew increasingly complex. The revolution seemed nigh.

— JULY 16 —

1862

JOURNALIST IDA WELLS-BARNETT BORN IN MISSISSIPPI

On this day in civil rights history, Ida Wells-Barnett was born in Holly Springs, Mississippi. Orphaned at age 14, she spent her adolescence taking care of her siblings while eventually landing a job as a teacher.

One of the earliest civil rights campaigners, Wells-Barnett refused to move out of a segregated railroad car in Tennessee in 1884, 12 years before *Plessy v. Ferguson* made segregation legal. "I refused," she said in her autobiography, ". . . [The conductor] tried to drag me out of the seat, but the moment he caught hold of my arm I fastened my teeth in the back of his hand. I had braced my feet against the seat in front and was holding to the back, and as he had already been badly bitten he didn't try it again by himself."

She sued the rail company afterwards, winning in the lower courts but finally losing on appeal. The lawsuit made her a minor celebrity and sparked a career in journalism. In 1889, Wells-Barnett left teaching and became a full-time partner and writer for the *Free Speech and Headlight*, an antilynching paper in Memphis. Three years later three of her friends were lynched for competing with a white grocer in town. She wrote scathing articles about the murders, concluding, "There is therefore only one thing left to do; save our money and leave a town which will neither protect our lives and property, nor give us a fair trial in the courts, but takes us out and murders us in cold blood when accused by white persons."

Her office was destroyed by arson as a result. She moved to Chicago, but continued her fiery antilynching campaign, publishing *Southern Horrors: Lynch Law in All Its Phases* and later *Mob Rule in New Orleans*. Through her powerful words, she became one of the most important antilynching figures in post-Reconstruction America.

In 1906, she joined W. E. B. Du Bois and others in the Niagara Movement. And in 1909, Ida Wells-Barnett was one of the founders of the NAACP.

In 1930, she ran unsuccessfully for the Illinois state legislature, the first African American woman ever to run for major office in the United States.

She died one year later.

— July 17 —
1967
Riots Explode in Newark, New Jersey

On this day in civil rights history, five days of bloody riots in Newark, New Jersey, finally came to an end.

In the summer of 1967, race riots broke out in more than 120 cities across the country, including Milwaukee, Detroit, Boston, Cincinnati, Cleveland, Washington, D.C., and San Francisco. Of these, Newark and Detroit were the worst. The catalysts varied, but the reasons behind the social disorder were fairly uniform. Disintegrating urban neighborhoods, high poverty and unemployment levels, police brutality, widespread disillusionment, and federal inaction led to the summer of urban unrest (ironically also known as the "summer of love" for the burgeoning hippie peace movement). Systematic police brutality, often involving Irish and Italian cops harassing black youths, had resulted in deep antagonism between police forces and many black communities.

By the end of the long hot summer, thousands would be arrested, hundreds killed, and miles of city landscape burned to rubble. African American patience, it seemed, was at an end.

In Newark, the riot began when a cab driver named John Smith was arrested after passing a double-parked police car. The arresting officers took Smith back to the precinct and beat him senseless. Outside, a crowd of 200 formed. Rumors circulated that Smith had been killed, when in reality he had been taken to a hospital. The enraged blacks began pelting the police building with rocks, bricks, and glass bottles.

The mob eventually broke into smaller groups and began smashing out the storefronts along nearby streets. Soon looters were breaking into commercial buildings, setting fires in their wake. The rioting spread into downtown Newark. New Jersey state police tried to contain the outbreak, but were severely outnumbered. Two days into the looting, the National Guard was called in. Violence escalated as the guardsmen swept block by block through the city. Five days after Smith was arrested, the riots ended. The results were horrific: more than 25 dead, including a ten-year-old child, almost 800 wounded, and nearly 1,500 in jail. The estimated property damage was more than $10 million.

The riot that broke out in Detroit a few days later proved to be even worse.

— JULY 18 —
1968
MELVIN VAN PEEBLES DIRECTS 'LA PERMISSION'

On this day in civil rights history, the French film *La Permission* was drawing audiences in U.S. theaters, making director Melvin Van Peebles the first African American to break into mainstream feature film distribution in the United States.

Van Peebles stands as an iconoclast and oddity in the world of cinema. Military veteran, novelist, musician, poet, and filmmaker, Van Peebles is a trail-blazing Renaissance man, the first African American director to work in Hollywood.

Melvin Van Peebles

Photo courtesy of Associated Press

Actor Sidney Poitier dominated Hollywood in the 1960s with his strong, resolute performances, but he still operated in a mostly white world. There were no black directors, few writers, and only one or two stars.

During this time period, Van Peebles could not find work. But in 1967, he was funded by three French producers to shoot *La Permission* (retitled as *The Story of a Three Day Pass*). He leveraged the film into a Hollywood contract with Columbia Pictures. In 1970 he released the modestly successful *Watermelon Man*, the story of a well-intentioned white racist who one morning wakes up to find he's turned into a black man. The lead was a black actor in whiteface, a reversal of the historical minstrel stereotype.

In 1971, he wrote, directed, produced, and starred in *Sweet Sweetback's Baddasssss Song*, the story of a black man on the run after killing two policemen. The film cost $500,000 to make, was partially produced by Bill Cosby, and became a short-lived box office hit, mainly due to enthusiastic black audiences clamoring for black-oriented movies.

Along with *Shaft, Superfly, Dolemite,* and *Cleopatra Jones, Sweetback* is a classic example of the "Blaxploitation" genre, a series of 1970s low-budget, ultraviolent movies that satirized negative black stereotypes while their self-empowered African American heroes achieved comeuppance over white foils. To urban black audiences, these films were wish-fulfillment on a grand scale. Although largely unsophisticated and at times amateurish, these early films laid the groundwork for more probing meditations on race and America and the eventual recapture of the African American image from Hollywood stereotypes.

Melvin Van Peebles and Gordon Parks, among others, paved the way for the likes of John Singleton and Spike Lee, who would both deliver to the silver screen scathing indictments of U.S. racism in the late 1980s and early 1990s.

— JULY 19 —
1949
HARRY BELAFONTE BEGINS RECORDING CAREER

On this day in civil rights history, Harry Belafonte, singer, actor, and outspoken activist, began recording for Jubilee Records.

Born in New York City, at eight years old Belafonte was sent to Jamaica where he attended grade school and part of high school. Belafonte then enlisted in the Navy and served during World War II. In the late 1940s, Belafonte returned to New York and began working as a stagehand at the American Negro Theater. His remarkably beautiful singing voice was discovered, and soon he was singing in jazz clubs.

He did not sing pop songs for long, however. Belafonte began studying folk music and folk traditions. In 1956, he signed with RCA Records and his album *Calypso* was released. Featuring catchy, traditional Jamaican songs, *Calypso* was an instant hit and the first record to sell more than a million copies.

Harry Belafonte

Belafonte parlayed this success into a Hollywood acting career, starring in such films as *Carmen Jones, Odds against Tomorrow,* and *Buck and the Preacher.* Numerous records, films, and television specials followed. He was suddenly an international star.

But Belafonte was also deeply interested in the burgeoning civil rights movement. In the early 1950s he met and became friends with Martin Luther King Jr. Belafonte became an SCLC board member and was not just a figurehead for the organization. He helped shape its strategy, lent his presence to its events, including the 1965 Selma-to-Montgomery March, and worked all over the globe to raise funds.

In the 1980s, Belafonte remained a tireless voice for black and anticolonial causes. He lobbied for antiapartheid measures, helped create the USA for Africa organization, was appointed a UNICEF Goodwill Ambassador, and was a principal organizer for the "We Are the World" concert. In the 1990s, he began HIV/AIDS awareness work. In 2000, he formed the Julie and Harry Belafonte Fund for HIV/AIDS care and prevention in sub-Saharan Africa.

As he approached 80 years of age, Belafonte continued his various humanitarian endeavors, proving himself to be an entertainer with a mission.

— JULY 20 —
1955
REVEREND WILL CAMPBELL RAISES HELL AT OLE MISS

On this day in civil rights history, in his unique way, the Reverend Will Campbell agitated on the University of Mississippi campus.

Born July 18, 1924, Campbell grew up in the small town of Liberty, Mississippi. He attended Louisiana State University from 1941 to 1943, then enlisted in the Army, and afterwards enrolled at Yale University Divinity School. With his education complete, Campbell moved back to the South to serve as director of religious life at the University of Mississippi from 1954 to 1956. His participation in civil rights demonstrations got him fired from the job.

To Campbell, racism was a heresy, segregation an abomination. He believed in a populist Christianity, a radical reimagining of the Christian faith.

A pastor without a congregation or a church, Campbell became a minor but important figure in the civil rights movement, and has the distinction of being the only white minister present at the formation of the Southern Christian Leadership Conference. He became a friend and adviser to Martin Luther King Jr.

As a progressive preacher in the South, Campbell was supported by the National Council of Churches. He traveled across the South as an NCC agent for racial reconciliation.

The NCC began in 1950, the successor to the Federal Council of Churches, which formed in 1908. Headquartered in New York City, the NCC was a coalition of Protestant, Anglican, and Orthodox churches dedicated to environmental, peace, and justice issues. The NCC offered support to liberal Methodists and Baptists in the South who could not find a church to pastor, funneling them into the civil rights and labor movements.

Campbell was present during many big civil rights events, including the integration of Little Rock's Central High School, where alongside other activists he helped protect the black students from white mobs. Campbell was also involved with the Committee of Southern Churchmen, which was organized in 1964 to work for race and labor causes. Once again, Campbell was the only white member.

In the 1980s, Campbell became controversial again as he opened a ministry to poor whites—some of them in the Klan—and tried to help lead them away from prejudice and hate. He became a cult figure, a whiskey-drinking, guitar-playing minister hanging out with farmers, country musicians, and so-called rednecks. The preacher character in Doug Marlette's comic strip, *Kudzu*, is based on Campbell.

Campbell has told his stories of the South in several books, and he continues to be a successful writer and speaker, still a pastor without a church.

— JULY 21 —

1943

CLARENCE JORDAN OVERSEES CHRISTIAN COMMUNE IN GEORGIA

On this day in civil rights history, Clarence Jordan, a utopian dreamer in the Deep South, continued to develop an experimental society in rural Georgia based on Christ's teachings. Born in 1912 in Talbotten, Georgia, Jordan earned a degree in agriculture from the University of Georgia in 1933. At a young age, he wanted to work on food-supply issues and economics, hoping to better the lot of his fellow humans.

He witnessed firsthand the damage done by poverty and racism and how the two were often linked. Adding to his foundation in agriculture, he earned a PhD in Greek from the Southern Baptist Theological Seminary and merged the two disciplines into a unique ministry. In 1942, Jordan founded the Koininia Farm near Americus, Georgia, with his wife and one other couple. *Koininia* is the Greek word for fellowship.

The Koininia community was founded on principles taken from Jesus's Sermon on the Mount. An interracial commune, Koininia's people lived off the land, with shared meals, possessions, and Bible classes. The Koininians were also dedicated pacifists. Under Jordan's leadership, Koininia worked to develop Christ's community of equal brotherhood on earth, eschewing racism, militarism, and sexism.

Not surprisingly, many in Georgia wanted the biracial utopia to fail. The KKK made repeated threats and destroyed Koininia property in a series of bombings. Churches, politicians, and newspaper editors condemned the little farming community, excommunicating and denouncing its members, and calling for boycotts of its products. Jordan requested help from the government, but his pleas were ignored.

Jordan wrote the Cotton Patch Bibles, in which the New Testament was "translated" into terms and stories that poor Southerners could understand, using Southern locales and colloquialisms.

By the end of the 1960s, Koininia was no longer novel. Changing its name to Koininia Partners, the community, under Jordan's leadership, launched "partnership" programs, including one in which the community would come together to build affordable homes for poor families. Chosen families would purchase the houses with no-interest mortgages.

Jordan died of a heart attack on October 29, 1969.

In 1976, two of Jordan's friends modeled Habitat for Humanity after Jordan's Partnership Housing. To date, Habitat has built more than 100,000 houses for poor people around the world.

— JULY 22 —

1945

'AN AMERICAN DILEMMA' ENGAGES AMERICAN READERS

On this day in civil rights history, people read the best-selling *An American Dilemma.*

A few years earlier, the Carnegie Commission invited prominent Swedish economist Gunnar Myrdal to come to the United States to conduct a thorough research project on segregation. Myrdal employed some 50 writers and researchers to help with his task, including Ralph Bunche and Kenneth B. Clark. Bunche was especially involved with the book, collecting data throughout the South and delivering almost 3,000 research pages himself.

In 1944, the book was published as *An American Dilemma: The Negro Problem and Modern Democracy,* sold in two volumes topping 1,500 pages.

The book detailed the myriad obstacles and underlying causes that held African Americans in subservience. Myrdal saw racism as the major cause of the second-class status accorded blacks, but he argued that it was the court's failure to enforce the Constitution that kept segregation in place. By placing the onus on the state, Myrdal targeted the government's complicity in the maintenance of segregation. The problem was a moral one, the solution a legal matter.

Myrdal's bleak data led to a hopeful conclusion: Through legal intervention and a return to the principles of the Constitution, racism and its accompanying evils would disappear.

Myrdal was too much the optimist. He predicted that the courts would eradicate segregation while the consequent educational advances would eliminate economic disparity. Myrdal underestimated the opposition to integration, and he seriously misunderstood the racial situation in the Northern cities, where almost every major race riot of the 1960s would occur. Still, Myrdal showed that the "Negro problem" was in reality a white problem.

Novelist Ralph Ellison reviewed the book, saying: "Myrdal's stylistic method is admirable. In presenting his findings he uses the American ethos brilliantly to disarm all American social groupings by appealing to their stake in the American Creed, and to locate the psychological barriers between them. But he also uses it to deny the existence of an American class struggle, and with facile economy it allows him to avoid admitting that actually there exist two American moralities, kept in balance by social science."

The book sold more than 100,000 copies. In the 1954 *Brown v. Board of Education* case, *An American Dilemma* had a large influence on the Supreme Court's ruling.

— JULY 23 —

1962

JACKIE ROBINSON ENTERS BASEBALL HALL OF FAME

On this day in civil rights history, Jackie Robinson was admitted to the Baseball Hall of Fame.

Born in Cairo, Georgia, Robinson excelled in sports at an early age. But he dropped out of college in 1942 to enlist in the army. He graduated from officer training school as a second lieutenant but then was court-martialed when he refused to sit at the back of a segregated bus. In 1944 he was honorably discharged and the court-martial was dropped.

That same year he joined the Kansas City Monarchs in the Negro Leagues. He was an immediate success and soon caught the attention of Brooklyn Dodgers' manager Branch Rickey who deliberately signed him to break the color barrier in baseball.

On April 15, 1947, 28-year-old Jackie Robinson made his debut for the Dodgers as the first African American major league baseball player of the modern era. Although he went zero for three at bat that day, his appearance was a milestone for African Americans.

Many, however, did not want Robinson to succeed. Some fans taunted him with racial epithets and some players threatened to strike rather than play against him. Even some of his own teammates were against him at the beginning. The resistance did not matter. Robinson was an excellent baseball player, and he steeled himself to follow the Rickey's advice not to show his anger. Robinson led the National League in stolen bases and was named rookie of the year. Two years later, he was named league MVP.

His professional career lasted less than ten years. On January 5, 1957, Robinson retired, a well-respected superstar. He immediately became an active participant in the civil rights movement, serving as a board member of the NAACP and campaigning for and raising funds for many organizations.

When he was voted into the hall of fame, he was the first black player so honored.

Diabetes eventually left him mostly blind. In the 1972 World Series, he threw out the celebrated first pitch. Nine days later, on October 24, 1972, Robinson died.

But his legacy lives on. In 1997, Major League Baseball retired his number 42 from every team. His birthday is now a baseball holiday, and in 2003 he was posthumously awarded the Congressional Gold Medal.

— JULY 24 —
1967
RACE RIOTS ERUPT IN DETROIT

On this day in civil rights history, the worst race riot in a summer full of them continued in Detroit.

As in the earlier unrest in Newark, New Jersey, police brutality in the Motor City had eroded black confidence. Four-man police units called "Big Four" roamed the streets of Detroit, manhandling suspicious pedestrians and belittling black youths with racial slurs and insults. The strong-arm approach led to widespread distrust and animosity.

Poverty and inequality were also factors. Blacks paid higher rents than whites but still often had to live in decaying urban neighborhoods that were segregated through real estate practices. Worse, urban-renewal projects had bulldozed black neighborhoods—including Paradise Valley, the black cultural center—to create freeways. Finally, automation in the car industry had resulted in widespread unemployment in the black community, whose citizens felt disenfranchised and forgotten.

The riot began in the early morning of Sunday, July 23, when vice squad officers raided a "blind pig"—an illegal after-hours drinking operation—in a predominantly black neighborhood on 12th Avenue. Police burst in on 80 people having a party for two recently returned Vietnam War veterans and in a hasty decision arrested everyone present, not just the owners. As the patrons were carted away, an angry crowd formed. When the police left, the mob began breaking windows of nearby stores. The black community had had enough. By Monday a full-scale riot was under way. Violence, looting, and arson broke out across the city as rampaging African Americans released pent-up frustration. Black and white homes and businesses were broken into, robbed, and in many cases burned to ash.

President Lyndon B. Johnson sent in 8,000 federal troops. On July 28, the riot was over. More than 40 lay dead, with 1,000 injured and a staggering 7,000 arrested. More than 1,000 buildings were burned at an estimated loss of $22 million.

The riots of 1967 accelerated white flight that had begun in the 1950s, sapping America's urban centers of tax revenues and jobs while the suburbs had a huge explosion in the following years. Today, 81 percent of Detroit's population is black.

— JULY 25 —

1949

KENNETH AND MAMIE CLARK
RESEARCH PSYCHOLOGY OF RACISM

On this day in civil rights history, Kenneth and Mamie Clark continued their study of discrimination that would result in powerful psychological evidence against segregation.

Born July 14, 1914, in the Panama Canal Zone, Kenneth Clark moved at age five to Harlem, New York, where he attended public school. His mother encouraged him in his academics, and he found great success. He attended Howard University after graduating high school. At Howard he came under the tutelage of Ralph Bunche, who helped shaped the young student's goals. He also met his future wife and major creative partner, Mamie Clark.

In 1940, Clark became the first African American to earn a PhD from Columbia University. His wife was the second.

The Clarks then embarked on a series of sociological studies with school-age children. They would show black and white children white and black dolls and ask them a series of questions, such as which doll is pretty, which is ugly, which is good, and so on. Children of both races overwhelmingly preferred the white dolls. Even the black children associated the black dolls with inferior qualities. The Clarks concluded that segregation had a profoundly negative impact on black children's feelings of self-worth. "A racist system inevitably destroys and damages human beings," Kenneth Clark would later say. "It brutalizes and dehumanizes them, blacks and whites alike." He published their findings in a 1950 report.

NAACP attorney Thurgood Marshall recognized the importance of the Clarks' findings. As the consolidated school desegregation lawsuits were presented to the U.S. Supreme Court in *Brown v. Board of Education*, Kenneth Clark served as the NAACP's psychology expert. His findings were major evidence against segregation.

Clark continued as an academic and writer, focusing on Northern ghettos. He eventually became the first black tenured professor at City College in New York.

In 1983, Mamie Clark died. Like many African American activists in the movement, Clark became disillusioned in the mid-1980s, especially after the death of his wife. "It took me 10 to 15 years to realize that I seriously underestimated the depth and complexity of Northern racism," he said in 1984. "In the South, you could use the courts to do away with separate toilets and all that nonsense. We haven't found a way of dealing with discrimination in the North."

On May 1, 2005, Clark died from cancer. He was 90 years old.

1948

ORDER BY PRESIDENT TRUMAN DESEGREGATES ARMED FORCES

On this day in civil rights history, President Harry S. Truman signed Executive Order 9981 desegregating U.S. military forces.

Although not known as a civil rights president, Truman was in many ways one of the most sympathetic to the plight of African Americans and he was the first president to meet officially with the NAACP. In 1946, he called for a committee on civil rights. One year later the committee issued its report, recommending "to end immediately all discrimination and segregation based on race, color, creed, or national origin in . . . all branches of the armed services."

Photo courtesy of Library of Congress

President Harry S. Truman

Truman responded by sending a special civil rights proposal to Congress. He proposed a far-reaching program, including an antilynching law, a Fair Employment Practices Commission, a Civil Rights Commission, and immediate desegregation of the armed forces. He was years ahead of his time, and the measures quickly became bogged down in Congress. Southern Democrats bolted their party and formed the so-called Dixiecrats, nominating South Carolina segregationist Strom Thurmond as their candidate to oppose Truman's reelection. Faced with disarray within his party, Truman backed off on the proposals.

On June 29, labor leader A. Philip Randolph threatened a black boycott of the military if Truman did not desegregate. Under mounting political pressure while also dealing with the emerging Cold War with the Soviet Union, Truman considered his options. Then, in a bold, surprise move, Truman desegregated the military by executive order rather than waiting for approval of an amendment. Liberals, conservatives, radicals, blacks, and whites were stunned by the decision.

The order states: "It is hereby declared to be the policy of the President that there shall be equality of treatment and opportunity for all persons in the armed services without regard to race, color, religion, or national origin."

The simple, straightforward language was unambiguous. The armed forces were soon fully integrated. Truman's action was a huge victory for African Americans and gave impetus to the emerging civil rights movement.

Truman's other proposals were tabled; he would do little else for civil rights. But Executive Order 9981 was a landmark, laying the cultural precedent for future civil rights legislation.

— JULY 27 —

1898

QUEEN MOTHER MOORE BORN IN LOUISIANA

On this day in civil rights history, Queen Mother Moore was born in New Iberia, Louisiana. From her poor, uneducated roots she would go on to take part in civil rights for nearly a century, her career encapsulating the black liberation movements of the 20th century.

She was born Audley Moore to a family scarred by racism. Her grandfather had been lynched. She lost both of her parents when she was in grade school and dropped out to work as a hairdresser so she could take care of her sisters.

Her life changed when she happened to hear Marcus Garvey deliver a speech in New Orleans. Moore was hooked by the charismatic man and his back-to-Africa ideals. Inspired by Garvey, Moore left the South to travel around the United States looking for a community of free African Americans. She could not find one anywhere. Everywhere she went, poverty or segregation or oppression marred black communities. She finally moved to Harlem, where she became a leader in Garvey's Universal Negro Improvement Association.

From her new vantage point in Harlem, Moore became a militant pan-Africanist and black nationalist leader. She organized early rent strikes in New York, while also helping women's organizations. At the personal request of Mary McLeod Bethune, she became a member of the National Council of Negro Women.

She helped organize a protest for the Scottsboro Boys in 1931. After the Scottsboro case, she joined the Communist Party but soon left, feeling that the party did not understand the issues of black self-determination.

Moore was a committed antiwar and anticolonialist activist. In 1955, she began stumping for slavery reparations from the U.S. government. All the while she worked as a labor organizer. In the 1960s, she joined Malcolm X's short-lived Organization of Afro-American Unity.

During the 1970s, Moore was invited to tour Africa's newly independent nations and visited Nigeria, Uganda, and Tanzania, among others. It was in 1972, during her visit to Ghana, that she was dubbed "Queen Mother"; the nickname stuck.

In 1995, she made her last public speech at the Million Man March. The Queen Mother died in 1997 at age 98.

— JULY 28 —

1917

10,000 PARADE IN SILENT NEW YORK PROTEST

On this day in civil rights history, the NAACP staged a silent parade of over 10,000 marchers down Fifth Avenue in New York.

The march was a protest of a race riot in St. Louis that killed more than 40 African Americans. The marchers, dressed in dark suits and white dresses, walked with stoic dignity down the street in silence, carrying posters that read, "Thou Shall not Kill," and "Mr. President, Why Not Make America Safe for Democracy?"

The incident they were protesting was a dark stain on the Midwest and on the American consciousness.

In the Great Migration of the early 1900s, thousands of Southern blacks migrated to Northern cities looking for jobs and better lives. In St. Louis, these questing African Americans found the same segregation and racial violence they were fleeing.

The particular 1917 violence began when corporations in St. Louis tried to break white union strikes with imported black workers. The results were disastrous. A rumor began to circulate that blacks in the city were planning a massacre on the Fourth of July. On May 28, union members, after meeting with city representatives, began prowling the streets, beating black pedestrians with sticks and fists.

The black community responded in kind. Two white police officers were killed in a shooting, giving the white populace the pretense they needed. On July 2, white mobs beat black citizens all across the city, pulling them from streetcars, from their homes, or just off the street. The mobs used stones, metal pipes, guns, and fists. Setting fire to black homes, angry whites lay in ambush as the choking victims fled their burning houses. Blacks were lynched in the streets, hung from lampposts, shot, stabbed, and bludgeoned. Dozens were left to die in the bloody gutters. It was a massacre.

The death toll was set officially at 40, though some have claimed as many as 200 African American casualties. Some 7,000 blacks fled from the city, never to return.

The silent protest a few weeks later in New York was a sorrowful missive to President Woodrow Wilson, who had ignored the NAACP's calls for action to stop lynchings and white-mob massacres. Wilson did not listen. Two years later, the 1919 riots of "Red Summer" would once again bring racial violence to the forefront of America's domestic problems.

— JULY 29 —

1942

FELLOWSHIP OF RECONCILIATION PROTESTS WWII

On this day in civil rights history, the Fellowship of Reconciliation protested U.S. entry into World War II.

Decades earlier, as Europe headed for inevitable conflict in 1914, an international cabal of pacifists met in Switzerland to discuss ways to avoid the coming World War I. War began before the conference ended, however, and the various pastors and ministers dispersed back to their homes. Leaving the conference, a German theologian and a British Quaker decided to create an organization of unity despite their countries' pledges of war against each other. The Fellowship of Reconciliation was born.

In 1915, A. J. Muste, Jane Addams, and Norman Thomas, with 65 other pacifists, founded the American branch of FOR as a protest to the U.S. entry into World War I. From the beginning, FOR was a Christian pacifist organization devoted to the cessation of war. This was always FOR's primary and essential goal.

The organization's early activity included a conscientious-objector program and pro-labor actions that temporarily aligned FOR with the American Federation of Labor. FOR was a focal point for early leftist activity.

In 1940, Muste led FOR's campaign against American involvement in World War II. FOR also campaigned for the release of Japanese Americans interned in California.

In 1942, FOR staffers James Farmer and George Houser, under the guidance of Bayard Rustin, formed the Congress of Racial Equality as a civil rights-centered affiliate. CORE emulated Gandhian nonviolent revolution and Henry David Thoreau's model of civil disobedience. While FOR remained involved in antiwar and pacifist causes, CORE became a major civil rights organization and led the first freedom ride in 1947.

In the 1950s, FOR led protests against the Korean War and became a target of the House Un-American Activities Committee.

In 1955, FOR staffer Glen Smiley traveled to Montgomery to help with the Montgomery bus boycott, where he met Martin Luther King Jr. and Ralph Abernathy. FOR also sponsored workshops on nonviolence throughout the South.

In the late 1960s, FOR focused on the national obsession of the Vietnam War. In the 1980s and 1990s, FOR worked on various antiwar activities. With affiliates in more than 40 countries, it remains a thriving interfaith pacifist organization.

— July 30 —

1866

Race Riot Disrupts Louisiana Constitutional Convention

On this day in civil rights history, a race riot broke out at the Louisiana State Constitutional Convention.

During Reconstruction, white Southerners seethed and schemed. They had lost the War, were being occupied by their enemies, and worst of all, now had to live side-by-side with their former chattel slaves.

Where Southern whites still had governmental influence, they began to enact Black Codes, the early segregation laws. Where they lacked control, in communities large and small across the South, resistant whites formed insurrectionary groups as part of a conspiracy to restore their pre-war position of privilege.

Meanwhile, Radical Republicans worked at state and federal levels to implement a new social structure that would accommodate the newly freed slaves and hopefully ameliorate the harsh conditions and racial strife that threatened the peace.

President Andrew Johnson, a Tennessean who was sympathetic to the "Southern way of life," favored a lenient, localized policy toward the South. He did not want to interfere with the mechanisms—legal, social, or otherwise—of the individual states.

In Louisiana, white Republicans responded by reconvening the Louisiana Constitutional Convention, led by Governor James Madison Wells. They planned to insert into the state's constitution universal male suffrage. Twenty-five legislators were in attendance, along with a few hundred supporters, mostly African American war veterans.

Outside the meeting hall, a disruption broke out between opponents and supporters of the Republican convention. In the confusion, former Confederates attacked the convention with pistols, rifles, and swords. Whites also randomly attacked African Americans around the city, most of whom had nothing to do with the convention.

The legislators tried to flee but were pursued. Some raised white flags of surrender and were promptly shot. Federal troops arrived too late. In the aftermath almost 40 were dead, more than 100 wounded. Police, many of whom had participated in the carnage, rode through the streets in wagons disposing of the bodies.

This incident is described in history books as a riot, but that seems to be a misnomer. U.S. Army General Philip Sheridan, the post-war commander of the Louisiana district, said in his report: "It was not a riot. It was an absolute massacre by the police."

The incident was also a coordinated attack on Reconstruction politics and revealed the weakness of President Johnson's leadership for rebuilding the nation.

— JULY 31 —

1921

NATIONAL URBAN LEAGUE LEADER WHITNEY YOUNG BORN

On this day in civil rights history, Whitney Young Jr. was born in Kentucky. He served in the military during World War II and returned to the States ready to tackle the broad problems of race and prejudice. Young studied social work in college, becoming dean of the school of social work at Atlanta University in 1954. Later he became Georgia state president of the NAACP.

In 1961, Young became executive director of the National Urban League and oversaw a drastic increase in its membership, funding, and prestige. The NUL had up to that point been a mostly philanthropic organization, but Young pushed it toward greater activism. Under his direction, the NUL sought better housing, better education, and more employment opportunities. Many of his ideas became part of President Lyndon Johnson's "Great Society" plan of American reforms.

In 1963, Young was a key organizer of the March on Washington for Jobs and Freedom and was one of the few chosen to speak. His remarks focused on economic inequality and the plight of urban blacks. African Americans, he said, "must march from the congested, ill-equipped schools . . . from a present feeling of despair and hopelessness . . . to renewed faith and confidence."

Young participated personally in many of the other major civil rights demonstrations of the 1960s, including the Selma-to-Montgomery March. But as the head of a national civil rights organization, he was also involved in much behind-the-scenes strategizing and lobbying.

Young recognized that although direct action and civil disobedience were effective tools to win public support, someone must direct government policy. He felt that all the protests in the world meant little if no new laws were drafted or no reforms were implemented. And he argued that jobs were as important as the right to vote.

Young spent much of his energy working with corporations and financial institutions to open up jobs and career paths for African Americans. Thus Young worked inside the system as a crucial bureaucratic counterpoint to other activists.

Young was enough of an insider to serve as an adviser to presidents Kennedy, Johnson, and Nixon on race matters. In 1968, President Johnson awarded Young the Medal of Freedom.

In March 1971, while vacationing in Nigeria, Young drowned while swimming. He was 50 years old.

This day in August

— AUGUST 1 —

1834

ENGLAND OUTLAWS SLAVERY IN ITS COLONIES

On this day in civil rights history, England outlawed slavery throughout the colonies of its vast world empire.

From the Ottoman Empire to the African kingdoms to the new world, slavery was a worldwide phenomenon. England, France, and Portugal all operated huge slaving operations in the Caribbean and South America. In England proper, slavery was formally abolished in the late 1700s. But profitability and practicality justified the maintenance of large slave-owning colonies.

The islands of Jamaica, Trinidad, and others were converted into huge sugar and tobacco plantations. England could well afford to abolish slavery at home as it raked in the profits from slavery abroad.

Antislavery activists in England, however, worked to eliminate the practice throughout the empire. The leading antislavery advocate was William Wilberforce, a social reformer and member of the English Parliament who proposed an abolition law in the House of Commons every year. Wilberforce finally got an 1807 law passed that forbade any British subject to transport slaves. Slavery persisted in England's colonies, but England would no longer participate in the trading of human lives.

France outlawed slavery in 1794, only to have the practice reinstalled in 1802 by Napoleon, who also brought back the "Code Noir," a collection of statutes similar in effect to Jim Crow segregation ordinances in the 20th-century United States. In 1808, the United States outlawed the importation of slaves, but by this point there were enough slaves to make the institution self-sustaining to the end of the Civil War.

William Wilberforce

In 1827, England passed a law that declared all slaving was piracy and was punishable by death. Finally, in 1834, slavery was abolished throughout the British Empire. Freed slaves were placed in an apprentice system (abolished four years later), while their former owners were compensated for the loss of their property.

Abolitionists in England then turned their attention to outlawing slavery in other nations and to lobbying the British government for policies that sanctioned slave-holding countries. London became a center for antislavery groups, including Anti-Slavery International, which operates to this day.

1924
NOVELIST JAMES BALDWIN BORN

On this day in civil rights history, writer James Baldwin was born in Harlem.

Most famous for his novels—*Go Tell It on the Mountain, Giovanni's Room,* and *Another Country*—Baldwin also became involved with the civil rights movement in the late 1950s and early 1960s. He spent time with Medgar Evers in Mississippi before Evers was killed, and he visited Selma.

The 1963 publication of his incendiary book-length essay on American racial politics, *The Fire Next Time,* propelled him to the center of the movement. The work was met with instant acclaim, he met with Robert Kennedy, and he was on the cover of *Time.*

James Baldwin

The book's first part is a letter to Baldwin's young nephew, telling of the dismal state of racial matters in the United States and the obstacles that will hinder the nephew's prospects as he grows up. It is a sad, stark piece of writing, detailing the distress and damage done by racism to both blacks and whites in America.

The second part of the book details Baldwin's childhood on the streets of Harlem, his conversion to white Christianity, and the rise of black nationalism. Two or three years before the black power militants broke off from the mainstream civil rights movement, Baldwin correctly predicted the paradigm shift in the African American community, from a philosophy of nonviolence toward a more militant stance. "The real reason nonviolence is considered to be a virtue in Negroes," he wrote, "is that white men do not want their lives, their self-image, or their property threatened."

Baldwin's title for the book intimates that a final judgment awaits the white power structure that refuses to acknowledge the dark stain of America's history. He linked religion, imperialism, capitalism, and American foreign policy into a holistic set of problems the United States must answer or face annihilation. "We human beings now have the power to exterminate ourselves; this seems to be the entire sum of our achievement."

The book sold well and it shocked readers across the country. Unaffiliated with any civil rights organization, Baldwin eventually phased out of the movement, but his oblique involvement in many ways ruined him as a novelist. He would never recapture the passion of his early novels or find the same audiences for them.

— AUGUST 3 —

1967

WILLIAM KUNSTLER AND OTHER LAWYERS FORM THE CCR

On this day in civil rights history, William Kunstler worked with other lawyers in the first year of the Law Center for Constitutional Rights, later the Center for Constitutional Rights. The CCR would become one of the most important legal organizations for the civil rights movement.

Born in New York on July 7, 1919, Kunstler graduated from Yale University and served in the Army from 1941 to 1946. He began a legal career in the late 1940s, a hard-working, Jewish, left-wing attorney. He then joined the ACLU.

In 1961, Kunstler traveled to Jackson, Mississippi, to offer moral support to Jack Young, a black ACLU lawyer working in the Deep South. While visiting, Kunstler witnessed the first freedom riders being mistreated while being arrested. The experience changed the course of his life. Kunstler began working in civil rights cases. He was involved in the formation of the Lawyers Constitutional Defense Committee in 1962.

In 1964, he became director of the ACLU. Kunstler and others worked in Mississippi during Mississippi Freedom Summer, Kunstler as general counsel for the Council of Federated Organizations, the umbrella organization that included SNCC, SCLC, CORE, and the NAACP.

Kunstler became convinced that a private organization was needed to work solely on civil rights cases. In 1966, Kunstler, with Morton Stavis, Arthur Kinoy, and Ben Smith, created the Center for Constitutional Rights. As both ACLU director and founding partner of the CCR, Kunstler took part in many famous civil rights cases. Through the 1960s and 1970s, he defended H. Rap Brown, Stokely Carmichael, Angela Davis, and Malcolm X, among others. He served as special counsel for the SCLC while also handling free speech and obscenity cases for Lenny Bruce and Abbie Hoffman, among others.

In 1968, Kunstler took his most famous case, defending the "Chicago Eight," the eight activists charged with inciting a riot at the Chicago National Convention. The defendants were found not guilty.

In 1995, Kunstler died of a heart attack. He was 76.

— August 4 —
1962
Stanley Levinson Advises the SCLC

On this day in civil rights history, Stanley Levinson worked as a close adviser and fund-raiser for the Southern Christian Leadership Conference.

Levinson, a New York Jew, entered the movement as a friend of Bayard Rustin. In 1957, Rustin, Levinson, and Ella Baker formed In Friendship, a fund-raising organization to help the burgeoning civil rights movement in the South. Levinson, Rustin, and Baker all went on to play important roles in the movement and with the SCLC. Levinson also became a close friend and adviser to Martin Luther King Jr.

Although he was a strong fund-raiser and dedicated activist, Levinson's earlier membership in the American Communist Party eventually became a divisive issue among civil rights leaders.

Historically, there was a supportive bond between African Americans and American Jews. Both were victims of persecution and discrimination. The NAACP was partly founded by Jews, as was the Urban League. Many of the freedom riders and Freedom Summer volunteers were Jewish. And Jewish money, raised by In Friendship and other groups, helped maintain the movement. Often aligned with progressive, labor, and leftist causes, American Jews found themselves allied with the civil rights movement against common foes. In the 1930s and 1940s, Northern Jewish professors made up the majority of teachers in black colleges, themselves partially funded by Jewish philanthropists. Many significant Jewish figures played prominent civil rights roles, including Marvin Rich, Kivie Kaplan, and Julius Rosenwald, among others.

Levinson worked as a speechwriter, accountant, and general logistician, all for free. He provided expertise, support, connections, and talent. But along with Jack O'Dell, another SCLC worker, and Bayard Rustin, Levinson was under the close scrutiny of the FBI, whose officials believed he was a Soviet agent. J. Edgar Hoover began targeting Levinson in his surveillance of the SCLC, using the alleged communist link as a pretense to bug King's house (approved by Attorney General Robert Kennedy). Other civil rights leaders wanted King to sever ties with Levinson, fearing negative publicity, if released, could undermine the movement. President John F. Kennedy even met privately with King on this issue. King stuck by his friend, demanding proof of the innuendoes against Levinson.

Levinson remained close with King throughout the major campaigns of the 1960s, all the way to King's death in 1968.

— AUGUST 5 —

1920

CENTRAL FLORIDA LYNCHINGS FORESHADOW ROSEWOOD

On this day in civil rights history, four African American men were removed from a central Florida jail and lynched for allegedly raping a white woman.

Although technically not the starting point of what is now called the Rosewood Massacre, the incident is included in the chronology of events identifying the racial problems in the area. Nine more deaths occurred in the next two years.

On New Year's Eve 1922, a huge Ku Klux Klan meeting was held in Gainesville, Florida. The KKK paraded through the streets in full hooded regalia, with ominous signs that read, "First and Always—Protect Womanhood."

The next morning, Fannie Taylor, a white woman in nearby Sumner, claimed that an unidentified black man raped her. The police arrested a suspect named Aaron Carrier. News of the attack began to circulate. By late afternoon a white mob captured, tortured, and killed a black man named Sam Carter. Two days then passed quietly.

"Harpers Weekly" illustration of lynching

On January 4, 1923, however, a mob attacked the black town of Rosewood, a country hamlet of 25 to 30 families. The mob approached Aaron Carrier's house, and after a standoff, killed his family and burned their house. The mob then began burning homes and churches. Blacks fled in terror through the swamp and surrounding woods, trying to hide. Some were shot in the back as they ran. Hundreds of whites, many affiliated with the Klan, flocked to the area, joining in the carnage. African Americans were lynched, burned, shot, and beaten to death. Law officers did not stop the violence.

Eventually, most of the Rosewood residents escaped to Gainesville by train, leaving behind their possessions and in some cases their dead relatives.

By January 7, Rosewood was deserted. Several hundred whites returned to the empty town and burned it to the ground, leaving ashes and utter destruction. Today only a small green marker and a few discarded bricks stand as evidence that people ever lived there.

On February 11, 1923, a Florida grand jury opened an investigation into the Rosewood mob violence, but a few days later found insufficient evidence to continue. In 1993, the state of Florida began a new investigation of the massacre and in 1994, the Florida senate voted to pay reparations to the survivors and their families.

— AUGUST 6 —
1965
VOTING RIGHTS ACT SIGNED INTO LAW

On this day in civil rights history, President Lyndon Johnson signed into law the Voting Rights Act of 1965. The Act abolished literacy tests, poll taxes, and other impediments to African American voter registration.

The Selma-to-Montgomery marches and the violence they prompted earlier that year brought the country's attention to the plight of disenfranchised Southern blacks. Two days after "Bloody Sunday," Johnson sent this bill to Congress. He recognized a shift in the national mood and used his political acumen and vast persuasive powers to push the Voting Rights Act through both houses.

Negro voters turn out at Cardoza High School in Washington, D.C.

Southern Democrats argued that voting was a state-sponsored privilege, not a federally endowed right. State Democratic parties in the South held that they were private political organizations, not subject to the oversight of the federal government, and could bar blacks from voting in Democratic primaries. But as the South was a one-party state, this strategem effectively barred blacks from voting at all. Finally, there was the problem of at-large elections, where white politicians drew district lines so that minority votes were spread so thinly that minority-preferred candidates could never win.

The Voting Rights Act addressed all these problems. And as with the Civil Rights Act of 1964, the U.S. attorney general was given the power to send examiners to inspect problem counties and if necessary to register new voters. Most controversial of all, in the states and counties that did not meet certain standards, any alteration of voting procedures at the state or local level required advance federal approval.

The bill states: "No voting qualification or prerequisite to voting, or standard, practice, or procedure shall be imposed or applied by any State or political subdivision to deny or abridge the right of any citizen of the United States to vote on account of race or color."

Southern states challenged the bill's constitutionality, but the U.S. Supreme Court upheld the law.

African American voting numbers swelled quickly throughout the South. As blacks began to make their numbers felt at the ballot box, Southern politicians had to adapt. The bill was another enormous victory for the movement.

— AUGUST 7 —

1904

DIPLOMAT RALPH BUNCHE BORN

On this day in civil rights history, Ralph Bunche was born in Detroit. Orphaned at age 13, Bunche moved to Los Angeles, where he graduated from high school and college. He then earned a PhD in government from Harvard University, and in 1930 he began teaching at Howard University.

At Howard, Bunche wrote scholarly papers and civil rights pamphlets and contributed to research for what would become the landmark 1944 sociological study by Gunnar Myrdal, *An American Dilemma: The Negro Problem and Modern Democracy*. He also found time to serve on President Franklin D. Roosevelt's "Black Cabinet," an informal but influential advisory group.

An old football injury prevented Bunche from fighting in World War II. Instead, he worked as an analyst in the Office of Strategic Services, the precursor to the CIA. In 1947, Bunche was named chief of the U.S. State Department's Africa section.

From this position he became involved with the United Nations and was director of the Department of Trusteeship and Information for the Non-Self-Governing Territories from 1947 to 1954, where he worked on the decolonization process in Africa.

Ralph Bunche

Photo courtesy of Library of Congress

In 1949, Bunche negotiated an armistice between Israel and Palestine, an accomplishment that earned him the Nobel Peace Prize. He was the first person of color so honored. During the Cold War, Bunche mediated conflicts in India, Pakistan, Cyprus, and Egypt. Bunche was the progenitor of sorts of international peacekeeping. He also helped form the International Atomic Energy Agency.

Throughout his career, Bunche was an ardent supporter of the civil rights movement at home and abroad. International work kept him too busy to serve in leadership positions in any of the major civil rights organizations, but he took part in many seminal events, including the 1965 Selma-to-Montgomery March. Black leaders in the U.S. sometimes criticized Bunche for his focus on international affairs, but this view ignores his substantial contribution to the movement as an adviser to the NAACP and the Urban League, and the important role he played in multiple peace and decolonization movements.

In 1968, he became the undersecretary-general of the United Nations. He died in New York in 1971.

— August 8 —
2005
Pioneering Publisher John Johnson Dies

On this day in civil rights history, publisher and pioneering businessman John H. Johnson died of heart failure at age 87.

Born into poverty in Arkansas City, Arkansas, Johnson and his mother moved to Chicago when he was a child, after his father died in a mill accident. He started a publishing venture with a $500 loan he secured with his mother's furniture as collateral. Using *Reader's Digest* as his model, he published *Negro Digest*, using subscriptions to pay for the printing costs. In November 1945, Johnson released his first issue of *Ebony*. Six years later, he launched *Jet*.

At the time, black newspapers were fairly common, but magazines for black audiences were nonexistent. White advertisers were not interested in advertising their products in black media, so Johnson formed his own line of mail-order cosmetics and advertised the beauty products in his magazines. Johnson is credited for single-handedly creating the black media market and for fostering black consumerism. He eventually broke the color barrier and drew white advertisers, which opened the door for white investments into black businesses.

From his first earned dollar, Johnson was a big success, an African American mogul with the Midas touch. *Ebony* gained the largest circulation of any black-owned magazine in the world. *Ebony* and *Jet* eventually reached a combined readership of more than three million. In 1982, Johnson was named to Forbes's list of richest Americans.

Although filled with entertainment and celebrity gossip, *Ebony* also published serious news stories. In 1955, Johnson published photos of the mutilated body of Emmett Till. Many civil rights workers later referred to the *Ebony* photographs as a primary influence for their involvement and activism in the movement. In the 1960s, Johnson brought widespread attention to the Southern civil rights movement, as well as enhanced the celebrity of Malcolm X, Martin Luther King Jr., and other black leaders. Some critics argue that Johnson could have done more with his influence and wealth to advance the movement. But his magazines devoted substantial room to civil rights causes, while also building a positive cultural foundation for African Americans.

— AUGUST 9 —
1948
WHITE JOURNALIST DISGUISES SELF AS BLACK

On this day in civil rights history, journalist Ray Sprigle published his account of living undercover as a black man in the Deep South.

Sprigle was a Pulitzer Prize–winning journalist for the *Pittsburgh Post Gazette*. In 1938, he had become nationally known when he cracked the story that Supreme Court Justice Hugo Black had once been a member of the Ku Klux Klan. A few years after the end of World War II he hit upon an idea for a great story about race issues in the South.

With the help of the NAACP, Sprigle decided to live as a black man in the South. But how to pass for African American? He consulted chemists and cosmeticians about the problem but the chemical solutions were dangerous or too permanent. He finally tanned for three weeks and shaved his head and mustache to pass as a light-skinned African American. At age 61, Sprigle boarded a train to Georgia as a black man. He traveled around the back roads of Georgia, talking with poor farmers and wage laborers.

The resulting articles were titled, "I was a Negro in the South for 30 days" and ran for two weeks, detailing the sad and frustrating existence of the Southern black. The first article began, "I ate, slept, traveled, lived Black. I lodged in Negro households. I ate in Negro restaurants. I slept in Negro hotels and lodging houses. I crept through the back and side doors of railroad stations. I traveled Jim Crow in buses and trains and street cars and taxicabs. Along with 10,000,000 Negroes I endured the discrimination and oppression and cruelty of the iniquitous Jim Crow system."

Sprigle's articles revealing his adventures, thoughts, and observations about racism and segregation were controversial and incendiary. In summary, Sprigle called for an end to Jim Crow, for abolishment of the sharecropping system, and for immediate universal suffrage.

Time and *Newsweek* both ran pieces about Sprigle and his journey. Fifteen major newspapers syndicated the stories. People all over the Northeast read his riveting account.

Sprigle published the articles as a book, *In the Land of Jim Crow,* to disappointing sales. In 1957, Sprigle died in a car accident.

— AUGUST 10 —

1962

ALBANY MOVEMENT DRAGS TO A CLOSE

On this day in civil rights history, the Albany movement officially ended after nine months of campaigning, with little progress made. It was a rare and frustrating defeat for Martin Luther King Jr.'s strategy of nonviolent resistance.

The problem was that the police chief in Albany, a small city in central Georgia, wouldn't give civil rights marchers enough dramatic violence to resist against. Chief Laurie Pritchett managed to restrain his officers, and the city's white leadership—for the most part—kept in check the thugs who attacked demonstrators in other places.

King and the Southern Christian Leadership targeted Albany for a major campaign against segregation, but without visible confrontations, the campaign could not develop media coverage or significant momentum. And without the outside pressure of public opinion, local segregation practices continued.

Even when King was arrested and tried to go to jail, as he did in early July when he returned to Albany to face a fine resulting from earlier protesting, he was outmaneuvered. Deciding to serve his time rather than pay the fine, King publicly announced his intent to stay in jail for the full 45-day sentence. On July 10, he entered jail, but just two days later was released, his fine having been paid by the city.

African Americans in Albany were growing restless. With no gains and no dialogue with the city, they felt they were losing a long war of attrition. Violence broke out on July 26. The next day, a prayer vigil was held in front of city hall, and again King and Ralph Abernathy were arrested. But it was all part of a cycle of protest, arrest, then release. The white establishment appeared to be dedicated to public safety and order, while the protesters appeared to be outside agitators and rabble-rousers.

Chief Pritchett's shrewd handling of the protesters had handed the civil rights movement its first real defeat.

The reasons for the Albany campaign's failure are complex. "Human beings with all their faults and strengths constitute the mechanism of a social movement," King said. "They must make mistakes and learn from them, make more mistakes and learn anew. They must taste defeat as well as success, and discover how to live with each."

He knew his next campaign would have to target a city where the entrenched racists would attack, thus revealing the wrongs of segregation to the outside world. Conveniently, the Reverend Fred Shuttlesworth invited King to help jump-start a Birmingham campaign. He felt that Police Commissioner Eugene "Bull" Connor could be counted on to deliver the crisis the movement needed. King agreed, and the Albany campaign's failure would result in the Birmingham campaign's success.

— AUGUST 11 —
1965
WATTS RIOT ERUPTS IN LOS ANGELES

On this day in civil rights history, a six-day riot broke out in the urban ghetto of Watts, Los Angeles.

Just south of the heart of Los Angeles, one of the richest cities in the wealthiest country in the world, the Watts community was a festering pit of drugs, prostitution, and petty crime. Up to 1948, it was the only neighborhood where working-class blacks could live in rigidly segregated Los Angeles. Decades of police brutality had eroded African American trust in white city government.

The riot began when a man was pulled over for erratic driving. A crowd gathered and watched as the police eventually used batons on the driver, his brother, and their mother. The police fled with the three blacks while the crowd stayed and began harassing traffic. When more police returned to disperse the crowd, rioters threw rocks, bottles, and pipes. Looting began. Guns appeared. Fires broke out around the neighborhood.

Demonstrators push against a police car

As black smoke billowed across Watts, a television helicopter filmed the destruction and broadcast the images across the country.

On Saturday, August 14, the National Guard was called in with tanks, snipers, and machine guns. A curfew and checkpoints were established. Slowly, the riot dissipated and by the 17th, the incident was over and the Guardsmen left.

But 34 (mostly black) were dead, more than 1,000 were injured, and property damage totaled $100 million. Speaking in Paris shortly afterwards, Martin Luther King Jr. said of the outbreak: "This was not a race riot. It was a class riot."

Watts became a powerful symbol for urban neglect, but worse riots were to come. In 1967, a wave of rioting hit major U.S. cities like Detroit, Atlanta, and New Jersey, leading President Lyndon Johnson to establish the Kerner Commission to investigate the causes. The commission ultimately cited inadequate housing, high unemployment, poor living conditions, and black frustration with lack of economic and political opportunity as the sparks that set off the rioting.

But the findings did little to help the Watts community. After the riots, the smoldering heap of Watts was mostly left to rot. The Guardsmen left, and little was done to cool the rage of the beleaguered community.

— August 12 —
1875
Mississippi Plan Disenfranchises Many

On this day in civil rights history, fallout from the "Mississippi Plan" spread to other Southern states, marking the beginning of the end of Reconstruction and widespread disenfranchisement for African Americans.

The Civil War resulted in catastrophic destruction in the South. Nearly half of the farming machinery was destroyed, cities like Richmond and Atlanta were burned to ash, close to half of the livestock had been killed, and one of four military-age males lay dead. The social and economic infrastructures were gone.

The North emerged from the war an industrialized region running on full steam, while the South had nothing left. Localized corruption in the military-installed governments in the South led to widespread bitterness. And the psychological damage of a prolonged, horrific war left generations slightly deranged.

Worst of all, the freed slaves, considered as subhuman by some Southern whites as a justification for keeping them in bondage, were now sharing government positions and equal status. Southern Republicans, referred to as "scalawags," and Northerners, called "carpetbaggers," were unpopular with the defeated whites and ex-Confederates. As blacks began to be elected to state positions and the Republican government remained in power due to the new black voters, whites sought to strike back.

The Mississippi Plan was a systematic attack. Democratic rabblerousers disrupted Republican rallies and meetings, often with the barrel of a gun. "Rifle Clubs" began to patrol voting stations, harassing and sometimes killing black voters. Meanwhile, white Republicans were threatened with social, physical, and economic reprisals. Many switched back to the Democratic Party.

The Mississippi Plan worked. Democrats regained power in the South and began working toward total disenfranchisement of black voters. Poll taxes, literacy tests, physical intimidation, and diluted black voting blocs through redistricting were the tools used as white Democratic lawmakers remade the new South in the old one's image.

Soon the South was a solid Democratic voting bloc whose power held President Rutherford B. Hayes and his successors in thrall. Jim Crow segregation was swept under the rug and ignored; the South was on its own.

— AUGUST 13 —

1911

ACTIVIST JOURNALIST ETHEL PAYNE BORN IN CHICAGO

On this day in civil rights history, Ethel Payne, "First Lady of the Black Press," was born in Chicago, Illinois.

Payne studied journalism at Northwestern University, but eventually got a job as a USO Army club hostess in Japan. She kept a journal of her experiences of racism and prejudice in the army and handed her reflections to a journalist back in the states. Her diary came across the desk of the *Chicago Defender*, and in 1951 she was offered a full-time job. She became one of the most famous African American journalists in America.

The *Defender* was America's most influential black newspaper. As an on-location reporter, Payne covered many of the biggest stories of the modern civil rights movement, including the Montgomery bus boycott, the Central High School crisis in Little Rock, and the Selma-to-Montgomery March. Her stories were read by hundreds of thousands of African Americans across the country.

In 1954, she became chief of the *Defender*'s Washington bureau. She was the first black woman to become an accredited White House correspondent (Payne competed with Alice Dunnigan, another black female reporter working in Washington).

Payne was famous for her tough, uncompromising questions, which often put presidents and other politicians on the spot. She challenged President Dwight Eisenhower so many times that he finally stopped calling on her at his press conferences.

In the 1960s and 1970s, Payne also wrote about liberation movements and revolutions in the African colonies. She traveled to Vietnam, reporting on black soldiers in Southeast Asia.

Fearless, tireless, and talented, Payne discarded the notion of objectivity where civil rights and race relations were concerned. The issues were too important, she decided, to maintain a veneer of impartiality. In the 1970s, she became the first black woman to be employed by a national radio and television network. In the 1980s, Payne used her prestige to campaign for the release of South Africa's Nelson Mandela.

She worked up until her death on May 28, 1991, still freelancing for black papers and magazines across the country. She was 79.

— AUGUST 14 —

1965

SEMINARIAN JONATHAN DANIELS JAILED IN ALABAMA

On this day in civil rights history, Jonathan Daniels, a white Episcopal seminarian from New Hampshire, was jailed in Hayneville, a small town in the rural county between Selma and Montgomery.

Daniels had come South that spring to take part in the the Selma-to-Montgomery March and had stayed in the area to help with voter registration in Lowndes County. Although predominantly black and just 20 miles from the state capital, Lowndes was a poor Black Belt farming county and had zero registered black voters.

During a voting rights demonstration, Daniels and several others were arrested and locked up in the Lowndes County jail in Hayneville, the county seat. Six days later, on August 20, Daniels and his companions were suddenly released from jail.

Outside the courthouse on a hot summer day, they pondered what to do next and decided to cross the street and enter a small store to buy soft drinks. Inside the store, a white man, Tom Coleman, was armed with a shotgun. Coleman was a reserve sheriff D5s deputy and the son of the Lowndes County superintendent of schools.

Coleman ordered the group to leave, then uttered a curse at and pointed his gun toward Ruby Sales, a Tuskegee Institute student.

Daniels pulled the young African American woman back and stepped in front of her just as Coleman fired; the blast killed Daniels instantly. A second shot then struck the Reverend Richard Morrisroe, a white Catholic priest from Chicago who was trying to protect another young black student, Joyce Bailey. Neither Sales nor Bailey was injured. Morrisroe spent six months in the hospital and two years in therapy before he could walk again. Coleman was subsequently acquitted by an all-white jury of all charges related to the murder of Daniels and the maiming of Morrisroe.

In 1991, the Episcopal Church recognized Jonathan Myrick Daniels as one of 15 modern-day martyrs of the church, and August 14, the day of his arrest, is observed in his memory. Ruby Sales, the student whose life was spared by Daniels's D5s sacrifice, decided to attend Episcopal Theological Seminary and eventually founded a Washington, D.C., mission dedicated to Daniels.

— AUGUST 15 —

1935

BIRTHDATE OF VERNON JORDAN

On this day in civil rights history, future lawyer, activist, and power broker Vernon Jordan was born in Atlanta.

Jordan spent his childhood in the segregated South, but he attended college at Depauw University in Indiana. He graduated in 1957.

Three years later Jordan earned his law degree from Howard University Law School and immediately began a clerkship with a civil rights law firm in Atlanta, working for attorneys David Hollowell and Horace Ward. Jordan was their law clerk when Hollowell and Ward represented Charlayne Hunter and Hamilton Holmes in desegregating the University of Georgia in 1961.

Jordan escorted Hunter and Holmes when they entered the campus for the first time. An angry white crowd yelled and threatened violence. With his arm around Hunter, Jordan pushed his way through the mob.

In 1961, he became the Georgia field secretary of the NAACP, working with regional director Ruby Hurley. In 1961, Hurley and Jordan became involved in the SCLC's Albany campaign.

In the mid-1960s, Jordan became head of the Voter Education Project and was a delegate to President Lyndon Johnson's White House Conference on Civil Rights. In 1970, he served as president of the United Negro College Fund, and from 1972 to 1981, he was president of the National Urban League. Increasingly, his stature and influence grew within both the civil rights leadership and within the white establishment of politics, government, and business.

Vernon Jordan

In 1980, in Fort Wayne, Indiana, he was shot by a white supremacist sniper who was targeting black victims. Jordan survived the attack, but resigned from the Urban League.

Entering the 1980s, Jordan left the nonprofit sector and became a well-known Washington power broker. He remained active in politics and was an outspoken critic of presidents Carter, Reagan, and George H. W. Bush. In the 1990s, by now rich and very influential, Jordan became a close personal friend and legal adviser to President Bill Clinton. He reportedly was offered but refused the position of attorney general. Jordan later became mired in the alleged coverup of Clinton's Monica Lewinsky scandal.

In 2001, he published his acclaimed autobiography, *Vernon Can Read.* In 2005, Jordan attended the Bilderberg Conference, the elite annual meeting between European and American businessmen and politicians. He is a partner in the New York investment firm Lazard Frere & Company.

— AUGUST 16 —
1963
'FREEDOM VOTE' REGISTERS RURAL POOR IN MISSISSIPPI

On this day in civil rights history, "Freedom Vote" registered blacks in the poor counties of Mississippi.

By this point, SNCC and the NAACP had both been active in Mississippi for several years, but little progress had been made toward abolishing total segregation and voting discrimination within the state. White resistance was too strong and Mississippi was too dangerous a place for the systematic desegregation activities that had worked in other states.

In 1962, the NAACP joined with CORE, SNCC, the SCLC, and local groups to form the Council of Federated Organizations (COFO), an umbrella alliance created by and placed under the control of SNCC field organizer Bob Moses.

COFO's first major campaign was the 1963 "Freedom Vote." The idea was the brainchild of Allard Lowenstein, a Northern Democratic Party activist. Instead of placing African Americans across the state at risk of physical reprisals for trying to vote in whites-only Mississippi elections, COFO would hold a mock election.

This would minimize confrontation with violent white supremacists while revealing blacks' desire to vote and the implicit danger preventing them from doing so, along with the hypocrisies of Southern politics. "Freedom Party" candidates Aaron Henry and Edwin King were placed on mock ballots against the Republican and Democratic candidates for governor and lieutenant governor.

Bob Moses decided that the best way to accomplish the Freedom Vote was to utilize willing white students from America's most prestigious universities. This was a calculated move. The federal government would be more likely to offer protection to the white college students from middle America, just as the national media would be more likely to cover the story. Dozens of white students came to Mississippi to help with "Freedom Vote," going door-to-door in black neighborhoods to prepare for the election. White police and thugs harassed and arrested many of the Freedom Vote volunteers, but on election day more than 90,000 African Americans voted for the Freedom Party candidates, who in the mock election won the ticket. The project was a huge success.

COFO decided on an even more ambitious Mississippi campaign for the next year. It would be called Freedom Summer.

— AUGUST 17 —

1906

SECOND NIAGARA CONFERENCE ORGANIZES FOR CIVIL RIGHTS

On this day in civil rights history, delegates to the historic 1905 Niagara Conference reconvened, this time at Storer College in Harpers Ferry, West Virginia. The meeting consolidated efforts by W. E. B. Du Bois and others to create a new civil rights movement for full equality, thus rejecting the accommodationist stance of Booker T. Washington. The Niagara Movement insisted that accepting separate but equal policies, as Washington preached, was a strategic mistake for African Americans.

Ironically, Washington's influence with white business leaders and journalists was so great at that point that he was able to use his connections to suppress coverage of the Niagara Conference. Except for publications controlled by Niagara members, only a few of the nation's newspapers carried news of the conference. Nevertheless, the Niagara Movement significantly undercut Washington's standing within the African American community, and was a precursor to the 1909 founding of the NAACP.

Male delegates on the
Storer College campus

"The battle we wage is not for ourselves but for all true Americans," Du Bois said to his fellow partipants. He urged African Americans to involve themselves in every level of American society. The statement issued during the conference reads, in part:

"We will not be satisfied to take one jot or tittle less than our full manhood rights. We claim for ourselves every single right that belongs to a freeborn American, political, civil and social; and until we get these rights we will never cease to protest and assail the ears of America.

"In detail our demands are clear and unequivocal. First, we would vote; with the right to vote goes everything: Freedom, manhood, the honor of your wives, the chastity of your daughters, the right to work, and the chance to rise, and let no man listen to those who deny this."

The document called for an immediate end to all discrimination in public accommodation, for blacks and whites to be able to associate with each other if they chose, and for equal enforcement of laws against "rich as well as poor; against Capitalist as well as Laborer; against white as well as black."

Over the next few years, the Niagara members would tirelessly promote these objectives. Their organization, however, never gained widespread membership, and within a few years Du Bois turned his energies to the new NAACP.

— AUGUST 18 —
1906
NIAGARA ROLE ILLUSTRATES WOMEN'S CHALLENGES

On this day in civil rights history, women took an active part in the second Niagara Conference held at Harpers Ferry, but one might not know it from some records of the event.

Note the photo for August 17 that shows the assembled conference attendees—all male. The statement released at the conference was in the name of "the men of the Niagara Movement" and demanded nothing "less than our full manhood rights" and called for "full manhood suffrage."

There was nothing unusual in this. The leaders of the Niagara Movement—some of the leading African American intellectuals of the day—were simply products of their time. It would be another 14 years before U.S. women—white or black—gained the right to vote with the ratification of the 19th Amendment.

Women at the 1907 Niagara Conference

African American women in the civil rights movement sometimes had to struggle against two foes: the overall society and laws that discriminated against them as blacks, and the tendency of even their closest male colleagues in the movement to push them to secondary roles. Yet women were always present in the movement, organizing, writing, protesting, going to jail, and leading by example if not by authority.

Ironically, in the case of the Niagara Movement, its originators—W. E. B. Du Bois, John Hope, Monroe Trotter, and others—held a secret meeting to develop their strategy in the home of Mary Burnett Talbert, a prominent Buffalo, New York, activist and suffragette. But when the meeting actually took place, the invitations went to businessmen, and the attendees were 29 men.

Women were at the 1906 meeting, however. Those who took part included Gertrude Wright Morgan, Mrs. O. M. Waller, Mrs. H. F. M. Murray, Mollie Lewis Kelan, Ida D. Bailey, Sadie Shorter, and Charlotte Hershaw.

— AUGUST 19 —
1938
NATIONAL LAWYERS GUILD

On this day in civil rights history, the National Lawyers Guild continued its second year of operation.

Founded in 1937 as an alternative to the segregated American Bar Association, the National Lawyers Guild was the first racially integrated legal association. The NLG was composed of lawyers, legal workers, law students, and legal organizations. The NLG's stated aim was "to eliminate racism; to safeguard and strengthen the rights of workers, women, farmers, and minority groups; to maintain and protect our civil rights and liberties in the face of persistent attacks upon them; to use the law as an instrument for the protection of the people, rather than for their repression."

In the late 1930s, the NLG helped organize the United Auto Workers and the Congress of Industrial Organizations, two of the major labor organizations in the United States. The activist NLG was dedicated to social and economic justice, was strongly pro-labor, and vigorously supported President Franklin D. Roosevelt's New Deal. With its fingerprints on so many organizations, the NLG became a powerful legal entity. In fact, the NLG was chosen as one of the few nongovernmental organizations to represent the United States at the formation of the United Nations.

The NLG's core beliefs placed it at the legal epicenter of the American left in the middle of the 20th century. NLG lawyers represented the "Hollywood Ten," the leftist screenwriters and directors who were tried by the House Un-American Activities Committee for alleged communist ties, and the Rosenbergs, the Jewish couple accused, tried, and executed for passing American nuclear secrets to the Soviet Union. Because of their various legal campaigns, the NLG was labeled subversive and became a primary target of HUAC.

As the civil rights movement got under way, the NLG opened law offices in the South to provide legal support. NLG worked on hundreds of civil rights cases. In the late 1960s, the NLG provided legal counsel to the antiwar and student groups.

The NLG remains at the vanguard of American leftist politics and is involved with the Center for Democratic Communications, the National Immigration Project, and the National Police Accountability Project, among other groups and projects.

1831

NAT TURNER PLOTS HIS REBELLION

On this day in civil rights history, Nat Turner prepared for the slave rebellion that would become the most famous of the slave uprisings. Turner himself would gain mythic status as a hero to blacks and abolitionists and a scourge to slave-holding whites.

Nat Turner was born into slavery in Virginia around 1800. He was a religious child, prone to visions, prophecy, and solitary talks with God. The devout child grew into an odd, intense man. His visions became well-known amongst other slaves. By the age of 21, Turner was known as "the prophet," and was a minor leader.

Photo courtesy of Library of Congress

Sensationalized illustration of the rebellion

In February 1831, Turner witnessed a solar eclipse. He took it as a sign that God wanted him to lead a slave revolt. He picked Independence Day, July 4, as the date when he would act. But Turner became ill, and his revolution was postponed. The sun turned odd colors on August 13, which Turner took as a second sign. The time for freedom was nigh.

In the early morning hours of August 21, Turner and six other slaves crept through the woods to their master's house. They broke in and killed the entire family as they slept. They then rode on horseback from house to house through the Virginia countryside, murdering every white person they found and collecting more recruits and weapons as they went. Soon Turner was at the helm of an armed 40-man force. Over two days, the insurrectionists killed more than 50 white slave owners and family members.

By midday of August 22, white militiamen scattered Turner's forces in a series of skirmishes. Turner escaped into the woods, while most of his force was captured or killed. Hysteria gripped the white populace. Roving mobs hunted down and lynched blacks, as many as 200 in total, most of whom had nothing to do with the revolt. The manhunt for Turner continued for almost two months before his capture on October 30.

While in prison, Turner "dictated" his story to his court-appointed trial lawyer, Dr. Thomas Gray, who later published the account as *The Confessions of Nat Turner*, the veracity of which is disputed by historians to this day.

On November 5, Turner was tried, found guilty, and sentenced to death. Six days later, he was hanged. His body was skinned and cut into pieces that were kept as memorabilia. Unsure how to respond to the danger of further revolts, Virginia lawmakers considered abolishing slavery altogether, but a more repressive reaction of controls and laws was implemented.

— AUGUST 21 —
1966
CIVIL RIGHTS LEADERS APPEAR ON 'MEET THE PRESS'

On this day in civil rights history, several major black leaders of the 1960s met on a 90-minute special of television's "Meet the Press." This would be the first and only time the major leaders would appear on television together.

Floyd McKissick of CORE, Stokely Carmichael of SNCC, Whitney Young of the National Urban League, Roy Wilkins of the NAACP, Martin Luther King Jr. of SCLC, and James Meredith, famous for his "March Against Fear" of two months earlier, all took part in the live debate and discussion over the future of the movement.

NBC newsman Edwin Newman acted as the moderator, with Rowland Evans asking questions.

The fractious group of leaders attempted to portray a unified front, but Carmichael's "black power" speech one month earlier had signified the coming division. Wilkins, and to a lesser extent King, had immediately and publicly criticized the new trend. Having replaced James Farmer as the director of CORE at the beginning of 1966, McKissick appeared to be leaning toward more militancy. SNCC was already merging with the growing antiwar movement, while King was busy with the fledgling Chicago campaign.

Young and Wilkins represented the conservative arm of the movement, McKissick and Carmichael the radicals. King was in the middle.

The leaders were civil to each other, if terse, as they discussed racial issues, the Voting Rights Act, and the state and future of the movement. They also spoke about the Vietnam War, black military recruitment, and the nascent peace movement.

The most contentious issue was the role of nonviolence. King denounced violence of any kind, including riots, as self-defeating. McKissick responded that nonviolence was "a thing of the past." CORE workers, he said, would from this point on defend themselves.

The television show ended with little drama. Behind the scenes, however, the different groups were on divergent paths, and all knew it.

— AUGUST 22 —
1989
BLACK PANTHERS' COFOUNDER KILLED BY STREET THUG

On this day in civil rights history, Huey Newton, the cofounder and leader of the Black Panther Party, was shot and killed on the streets of Oakland by a young drug dealer over a trivial dispute. It was a sad ending to a potentially great man.

Entering the 1970s, U.S. counterculture organizations were coalescing around resistance to the war in Vietnam, and the Black Panther Party seemed poised to inherit some part of civil rights leadership. With rising membership in the late 1960s, a high profile, and charismatic leaders, the BPP was as likely as any other group to become a voice for African Americans.

So what happened to the Black Panther Party?

First, the COINTELPRO operations against the BPP took their toll. Well-publicized murder trials undermined the organization's legitimacy. Many leaders were sentenced to jail, while others, including Newton and Eldridge Cleaver, fled the U.S. to live in exile for a time. The organization eroded from within.

Membership began drying up. As the vestiges of segregation fell and the vote was obtained, the issues became more complex. Many saw the civil rights movement as over, and public attention moved on. People wanted a new cause.

And there were major divisions within the Panthers. Vast ideological differences erupted between east and west coast factions and between militant and moderate voices. In 1969, Stokeley Carmichael left the group. In 1971, Cleaver and Newton expelled each other from the Party, which splintered into minor factions. Newton proclaimed himself the "Supreme Servant of the People." Meanwhile, Cleaver worked with guerilla cells in Algeria, trying to spark an international revolution.

In the late 1970s and early 1980s, Newton and Cleaver both became addicted to drugs, despite the Panthers' official line against drug use. Cleaver eventually bested his addiction, but Newton's led him into crime. The year of his death Newton was convicted of embezzling Panther funds.

The BPP had wanted too much, too soon, too militantly. Ultimately, the Panthers could not overcome fears about black rage, which prevented the Party from gaining mainstream political viability. But for a time the Panthers offered at least the concept of an alternative, progressive, community-based approach to African American issues.

— AUGUST 23 —
1964
SEGREGATIONIST MISSISSIPPI DELEGATION CHALLENGED

On this day in civil rights history, the national media reported the story of the Mississippi Freedom Democratic Party's efforts to unseat the all-white regular Mississippi delegation to the Democratic National Convention.

By the end of Freedom Summer, volunteers had registered thousands of new black voters in Mississippi, but these black voters were unable to participate in Mississippi's segregated Democratic Party primaries. The newly formed MFDP thus elected and sent 68 delegates of their own to the DNC in Atlantic City. Delegates included civil rights leaders Aaron Henry, Fannie Lou Hamer, Victoria Gray, and Ed King, among others, but most were former sharecroppers with little formal education. But they were veterans of what had amounted to a war with violent white supremacists in Mississippi, and their determination showed on their faces.

The presence of the MFDP was an embarrassment to the national Democratic Party and to President Lyndon Johnson, who was seeking his party's nomination for reelection. His campaign needed the support of both the civil rights voters and the moderate white Southern Democrats. Here at his most important hour was a gaggle of loud Southern blacks seeking to disrupt the machinery that guaranteed his reelection.

Fierce backroom negotiating took place at the convention. Finally, the MFDP was given a chance to present its case before the Credentials Committee on August 22. In proceedings broadcast across the country, the MFDP laid out the reasons why it should replace the regular Mississippi delegates.

MFDP attorney Joseph Rauh guided the presentation. "Are we for the oppressor or the oppressed?" he asked. He called on many of the MFDP delegates to speak, but the witness the nation remembers was Fannie Lou Hamer. She detailed her life as a sharecropper and her travails in trying to vote. Then, in horrifying detail, she recounted a savage beating she took at the hands of Mississippi police.

"All of this is on account we want to register, to become first-class citizens, and if the Freedom Democratic party is not seated now, I question America, is this America?" she thundered.

— AUGUST 24 —
1964
JOHNSON ADMINISTRATION NEGOTIATES WITH MFDP

On this day in civil rights history, negotiations continued between the Mississippi Freedom Democratic Party (MFDP) and the Democratic Party leaders seeking to contain potential damage to the reelection bid of President Lyndon Johnson.

The MFDP's presence placed both the national Democratic Party and President Johnson in a vulnerable position. Johnson responded by dispatching Vice President Hubert Humphrey and Senator Walter Mondale to mediate. Other civil rights leaders such as Bayard Rustin, James Farmer, and Martin Luther King Jr. were brought in and a series of compromises was proposed.

Photo courtesy of Library of Congress

President Lyndon Johnson

Southern white Democrats threatened to pull their support from Johnson. Republican presidential nominee Barry Goldwater was already appealing to many Southern whites, as he promised a scaled-down government that would not interfere with the inner workings of the states, thereby leaving segregation alone. Johnson could ill afford to lose the Southern electoral votes he would need to defeat Goldwater.

Bargaining continued. The MFDP pushed for a roll-call vote that would publicly expose the national Democrats who failed to support them. But Johnson utilized his political clout to kill any pro-MFDP efforts.

The final compromise offered the MFDP was two at-large delegate seats and a promise to correct the segregated Mississippi primaries before the 1968 elections. SNCC was disgusted by the offer. King and others urged the MFDP to take the symbolic victory.

Fannie Lou Hamer summed up the MFDP's reaction: "We didn't come all this way for no two seats." The MFDP rejected the Democratic Party's offer and staged a sit-in at the convention in protest.

The MFDP actions represented one of SNCC's finest hours—a bold gambit of coalition-building that almost paid off and an example of real black political power. But its failure in many ways spelled the end of the organization, as its members could no longer agree on the coalition-integrationist platform of the mainstream civil rights groups. Too many had been hurt. There had been too many betrayals. "After Atlantic City," SNCC staffer Cleveland Sellers said, "our struggle was not for civil rights, but for liberation." Many in SNCC began leaning toward a more militant approach.

— AUGUST 25 —
1967
J. EDGAR HOOVER LAUNCHES COINTELPRO

On this day in civil rights history, FBI Director J. Edgar Hoover began the Counter-Intelligence Program (COINTELPRO) against communist, African American, and antiwar organizations. The program was intended to "divide, conquer, and weaken" and "expose, disrupt, misdirect, or otherwise neutralize the activities of black nationalist . . . organizations." It would also gather information about the KKK, the Weathermen, and other "extremist" groups.

The FBI had a long history of spying on the movement. From the beginning Hoover was convinced that black groups like the NAACP, SCLC, and SNCC were saturated with communist agents. SCLC phones were tapped and undercover agents infiltrated the organization as far back as 1958. As time passed and Martin Luther King Jr. became better known, Hoover fixated on him. In a 1964 press conference, Hoover called King a "notorious liar."

Hoover loosed the entire arsenal of the FBI against groups like the Black Panthers, the NAACP, and SNCC. Phones were tapped, offices were burglarized, illegal substances were planted. False letters were sent to various leaders with intent on widening the rift between different factions.

COINTELPRO also discredited civil rights groups in the national media. Fake literature was distributed that misrepresented various groups' beliefs or methods. Working with local law enforcement, members of different groups

J. Edgar Hoover

were arrested for minor offenses or on trumped-up charges. Agents spread rumors, preyed on paranoia, even called relatives of suspects with warnings and threats.

There were more than 300 COINTELPRO operations against different groups, but the major target was the Black Panthers. "The Black Panther Party . . . represents the greatest threat to internal security of this country," Hoover said. The FBI turned the BPP leadership against each other. All its high-ranking members were imprisoned or driven into exile.

COINTELPRO was effective and its activities partially explain why there is still so much misinformation about different figures in the movement. In the early 1970s, a watchdog group exposed COINTELPRO and myriad superficial reforms followed. But the shadow agency's covert operations did not immediately end.

— AUGUST 26 —
1966
CHICAGO CAMPAIGN ENDS INCONCLUSIVELY

On this day in civil rights history, Martin Luther King Jr., members of the SCLC, CCCO, and Chicago Mayor Richard Daley, with his aides, held a summit at the Palmer House to agree over protesters' demands, avoid violence, and save face for those involved with the Chicago campaign.

King was the public image of an increasingly large and fractious SCLC. Hosea Williams, Andrew Young, James Bevel, Ralph Abernathy, and Bernard Lee were just a few of the large personalities that clashed behind closed doors. The CCCO was a separate organization with its own personnel—Al Raby, John McDermott, and Edwin Berry, among others—who brought their own set of demands to the table. And Daley represented the bureaucrats, judges, and private businesses, all with their own agendas.

Photo courtesy of Library of Congress

Chicago campaign strikers

For months tension had built as the SCLC led marches into white neighborhoods to demand fair housing. The Illinois governor had called in the National Guard after a few sporadic outbreaks of small-scale violence. A temporary injunction limiting the size of marches and protests was held over the civil rights organizations' heads, which they in return used as leverage with the threat of a mass march into the Cicero neighborhood.

One goal of the summit meeting was to hash out a plan to end the discriminatory housing practices of the Chicago Real Estate Board and its myriad private members. After many hours of discussion, an 11-page agreement was reached. Daley promised stricter enforcement of the city's housing and building code ordinances and improvements in the construction of public housing.

King ended the meeting with cautious but congratulatory remarks: "Now, we don't want to threaten any additional marches, but if this agreement does not work, marches would be a reality. . . . I think now we can go on to make Chicago a beautiful city, a city of brotherhood."

The Cicero march was called off. But many Chicago African Americans felt betrayed by the SCLC compromise with the city; in the eyes of many, the leadership of the movement had sold out.

It remained to be seen whether Daley would keep his promises, but in the summer of 1966, the SCLC's experiment of the Chicago campaign was over.

— AUGUST 27 —
1963
W. E. B. Du Bois Dies in Ghana

On this day in civil rights history, on the eve of the March on Washington, W. E. B. Du Bois died in Accra, Ghana. One of the most influential African Americans who ever lived, he was no longer a U.S. citizen.

Du Bois lived almost a century and his life spanned from Reconstruction to the flowering of the civil rights movement he had helped make possible. After his early work articulating "the problem of the color line," calling together the Niagara Conference, cofounding the NAACP, founding and editing *The Crisis,* and more, Du Bois began to distance himself from the movement as he grew older. Impatient for change, he fell out with his former colleagues and despaired of the American Dream and the hope for full black integration into American society.

He turned increasingly toward Pan-Africanism, labor issues, and worldwide economic inequality. When he criticized the acting president of the NAACP, he was officially rebuked, and in 1934, Du Bois left the organization he had helped create.

He returned to teaching at Atlanta University until his antiwar sentiments made him unpopular and he was asked to leave. In the early 1950s, Du Bois publicly rejected capitalism, calling it an untenable economic system.

In 1961, disillusioned with the United States and after flirting with Marxism for almost 50 years, Du Bois officially joined the Communist Party. He traveled to Ghana to work on the *Encyclopedia Africana,* but was refused reentry into America. In response he renounced his U.S. citizenship.

Du Bois felt betrayed by his nation. "In my own country, for nearly a century," he wrote, "I have been nothing but a nigger."

In the twilight of his years, Du Bois despaired over the plight of people of color everywhere. He had lived a long life, but saw little hope for the future. The Cold War was in full effect. The civil rights movement, which he helped begin, seemed stuck in a rut and no longer had use for him. "Wed with truth," he wrote, "I dwell beyond the veil."

In art and literature and music, truth and beauty reign supreme; color means nothing. It is here, alongside Langston Hughes, James Baldwin, Zora Neale Hurston, and Richard Wright that Du Bois probably best belongs.

— AUGUST 28 —
1963
MARCH ON WASHINGTON; 'I HAVE A DREAM' SPEECH

On this day in civil rights history, the March on Washington for Jobs and Freedom brought more than 250,000 people to the nation's capital, making it the largest political rally in U.S. history up to that time. The principal organizers were Bayard Rustin and A. Philip Randolph. SNCC, the NAACP, the SCLC, the Urban League, and CORE all participated in the planning. Labor unions such as the United Auto Workers also took part.

Arriving by bus, train, car, and plane, the thousands upon thousands of people opposed to segregation assembled on the National Mall in front of the Lincoln Memorial. They carried banners, sang, and clapped, caught up in the euphoria of the historic day.

March on Washington, D.C.

Along with the ordinary citizens were celebrities such as Charlton Heston, Ossie Davis, Marlon Brando, Sammy Davis Jr., Sidney Poitier, Lena Horne, Paul Newman, Harry Belafonte, Josephine Baker, Marian Anderson, Rosa Parks, Daisy Bates, Diane Nash, Mahalia Jackson, and Bob Dylan, among others.

A. Philip Randolph, Roy Wilkins, Whitney Young, and John Lewis all delivered speeches. But it was Martin Luther King Jr.'s day. He delivered the closing address, his famous "I have a dream" speech, perhaps the single most remarkable oration in U.S. history. In part, he said:

"... In a sense we've come to our nation's capital to cash a check. When the architects of our republic wrote the magnificent words of the Constitution and the Declaration of Independence, they were signing a promissory note to which every American was to fall heir. . . . It is obvious today that America has defaulted on this promissory note, insofar as her citizens of color are concerned. Instead of honoring this sacred obligation, America has given the Negro people a bad check, a check which has come back marked 'insufficient funds.' . . . We refuse to believe that there are insufficient funds in the great vaults of opportunity of this nation. And so, we've come to cash this check, a check that will give us upon demand the riches of freedom and the security of justice . . . And when this happens, when we allow freedom to ring, when we let it ring from every village and every hamlet, from every state and every city, we will be able to speed up that day when all of God's children, black men and white men, Jews and Gentiles, Protestants and Catholics, will be able to join hands and sing in the words of the old Negro spiritual: 'Free at last! Free at last! Thank God Almighty, we are free at last!'"

— AUGUST 29 —
1955
EMMETT TILL MURDERED IN MISSISSIPPI

On this day in civil rights history, 14-year-old Emmett Till was missing after being taken at gunpoint the day before from his uncle's home on the outskirts of Money, Mississippi. His mutilated body was found two days later in the Tallahatchie River.

Emmett Till lived in Chicago and had come to Mississippi with his cousin, Curtis Jones, to visit their great-uncle Mose Wright. On August 24, Jones and Till had borrowed Wright's car to drive to the local store. Till was dared by some local boys to go inside and talk to the woman running the store, Carolyn Bryant. When Till was leaving the store, he either said, "Bye, baby" or whistled at her.

Four days later, Carolyn's husband, Roy Bryant, and his half-brother, J. W. Milam, came to Mose Wright's house in the middle of the night. They had a flashlight and a gun. They forced Wright to lead them to Till's room, and they ordered him to get dressed and come with them. Wright begged for them only to whip him, but they led Till away at gunpoint.

Search parties were sent out and Till's mother was notified in Chicago. Three days later, Till's body was discovered in the Tallahatchie River. The body was weighed down with a 70-pound cotton gin fan that had been tied around his neck with barbed wire. His face was so badly mutilated that the only way Wright could identify him was by a ring the youth had been wearing.

His mother, Mamie Till Mobley, decided to have an open-casket funeral for Till. She wanted the world to see what had been done to her son because of an insignificant insult to a white woman in Mississippi. Fifty thousand people attended the funeral. *Jet* magazine ran photos of Till's disfigured face. His death caused widespread outrage and awakened the nation to the dark side of "the Southern way of life."

— AUGUST 30 —
1901
BIRTHDATE OF NAACP DIRECTOR ROY WILKINS

On this day in civil right history, future NAACP Executive Director Roy Wilkins was born in St. Louis.

After graduating college, Wilkins worked as a journalist for various newspapers in the Midwest. He wrote against segregation, with particular emphasis on the evils of lynching. In 1931, Wilkins moved to New York and joined the staff of the NAACP, where his talent and drive were quickly noticed. One year later, Wilkins replaced W. E. B. Du Bois as editor of the NAACP magazine, *The Crisis.*

Photo courtesy of Library of Congress

Roy Wilkins

When Walter Francis White died in 1955, Wilkins succeeded him as executive director of the NAACP. He would remain in the position for 22 years, during almost the entire modern civil rights movement, from *Brown v. Board* to the death of Martin Luther King Jr. He was one of the most important and powerful black leaders of the era, one of the "Big Six" alongside A. Philip Randolph, King, Whitney Young, John Lewis, and James Farmer.

The NAACP was by the 1960s a moderate voice, led by older African Americans who were not quite in touch with the angry black youth. The NAACP favored lawsuits and lobbying over direct action. Where SNCC and the SCLC actively looked to create crises, the NAACP preferred to work in the courts. Systematic legal precedents and federal intervention were the long-term strategy; mass action, boycotts, and the like were to be used as a last resort.

The NAACP's position as the oldest and most experienced black organization but with a more conservative stance on political issues placed it often at loggerheads with the younger, more militant SCLC, CORE, and SNCC.

Still, Wilkins and the NAACP played a crucial role in many of the era's biggest events, including his speech at the 1963 March on Washington, which Wilkins helped organize. He also participated in the 1965 Selma-to-Montgomery March, and the 1966 March Against Fear. During his tenure in office he advised presidents Kennedy, Johnson, Nixon, Ford, and Carter.

He died September 9, 1981. His autobiography was published one year later.

— August 31 —
1955
Till's Body Found in Mississippi

On this day in civil rights history, the mutilated body of Emmett Till was found in the Talla-hatchie River. Till's death and subsequent discovery signified the brutality of Southern segregation unlike any other murder before it.

When lawmen pulled Till's body from the river, his face was crushed, one of his eyes was missing, and cuts lacerated his body. Till's body was taken in by the sheriff, but Till's mother, Mamie Till Mobley, insisted the body be transported to Chicago for a proper burial. Mobley opened the casket on the train platform to insure it was her son. "Lord, take my soul," she proclaimed, then fainted.

A media frenzy followed. A photo of the dead boy was published in *Jet* magazine, and other media outlets followed. Mobley arranged for an open-casket funeral, intent on shoving her son's pointless death into the face of his killers. On September 3, the funeral parlor opened the service. The wake was attended by thousands of people and lasted three days. Reporters snapped photos and placed stories in black newspapers all over the country. Donations to the NAACP and other organizations skyrocketed. Mamie Till Mobley used her status as a bereaved mother to push for justice, traveling around the country giving talks on the injustices of the segregated South.

Till's lynching was only one of many thousands over the years, but his was unique because he was accused—justly or unjustly—of no crime but merely of innocently violating a social custom of segregation. And he was only 14, still a child.

With Till's ghastly visage in newspapers and magazines across the country, no one could any longer argue that they were ignorant of the brutal race relations in the Deep South.

Till's murder shocked the country and served as a galvanizing force for the next generation of civil rights activists, many of them teenagers at the time but who in their 20s would come to prominence as members of SNCC and other civil rights organizations.

This day in

September

— SEPTEMBER 1 —
1926
ARIZONA OPENS HIGH SCHOOL FOR BLACKS

On this day in civil rights history, Phoenix Colored High School opened its doors to its all-black students for the first time. Arizona, like other places in the West, provided a safe haven to adventurous African Americans looking to escape the widespread violence and oppression of the Deep South. But racial discrimination followed the migrating blacks, to California, to Washington, and to Arizona.

Segregation was institutionalized in the Arizona territory in 1909—over the veto of then Governor Joseph Kibbey—three years before Arizona was admitted into the Union as a state. In 1948, NAACP activists picketed segregated lunch counters in Phoenix. Arizona citizens prided themselves that racially motivated violence was virtually nonexistent in the state. But Arizona remained segregated, as politicians stalled and equivocated, until the 1960s, when CORE and SNCC began sit-in campaigns. Even then, it took the Civil Rights Act to achieve full integration.

Cotton was Arizona's main crop until the mid-1950s. The fieldwork fell to underpaid African Americans, Hispanics, and American Indians; Arizona had a vested interest in keeping its minority populations at work in the cotton fields. Still, the children of these fieldworkers attended school. Until 1926, Phoenix's African American students attended the same high school as whites, but in a "colored" section in the basement. At first this constituted a handful of students, but soon the colored section did not have enough room.

PCHS, like other black schools, was underfunded, understaffed, and mostly left to its own devices. But the dedicated teachers of PCHS worked hard to foster learning, while the under-equipped sports teams began experiencing success. In 1943, the school was renamed in honor of George Washington Carver. Despite obsolete equipment and a lack of funding, Carver High School offered a quality education with qualified teachers. After the 1954 *Brown* ruling, Carver High was closed, and its students attended the same public high school that black students had been kicked out of almost thirty years earlier.

Despite CHS's successes, it was abandoned for many years. The Carver High buildings are now being renovated as a black cultural history museum.

— September 2 —
1957
KKK Kidnaps, Castrates Birmingham Man

On this day in civil rights history, in one of the most despicable chapters in a sick era, Edward Judge Aaron was kidnapped and mutilated by members of the Ku Klux Klan.

The KKK and its various offshoots grew enraged as the civil rights movement gained momentum in the late 1950s. As the integration of schools in Little Rock, Arkansas, was making headlines in the country's newspapers, a group of Klansmen in Alabama decided to make a statement.

Photo courtesy of Library of Congress

KKK parade without hoods

The Alabama Kluxers were further enraged by the agitating of Birmingham's Fred Shuttlesworth, a fearless preacher who appeared impervious to threats and even outright attacks. Led by Joe Pritchett, the exalted cyclops (president, more or less) of a local KKK chapter, a group of Klansmen began prowling the back roads of Alabama for a victim. "We just wanted some nigger at random," one of the men said later. They found their unfortunate victim in an unaware black man named Judge Aaron.

Aaron was walking home on a desolate back road when six hooded Ku Klux Klansmen kidnapped him. Shoving him into a deserted shack, the attackers stripped Aaron of his clothes and then castrated him with a razor blade. The Klansmen then poured turpentine on his wounds to maximize his suffering, but unintentionally saving his life because the turpentine stopped his bleeding. The Klansmen taunted Aaron, boasting that they would give similar treatment to any black who attempted integration. They left him to die, but Aaron survived.

The ghastliness of the incident horrified most Alabamians, even some of those opposed to integration. Police began an investigation and soon made a few arrests.

Pritchett, the undisputed leader of the KKK gang, was arrested and charged with mayhem. In November, an all-white Birmingham jury found him guilty. The white Alabama judge gave Pritchett the maximum allowable sentence of 20 years. "This is one of the worst things ever to come before my bench," he said.

Unfortunately, the arrest and conviction of KKK leader Pritchett, and general outrage over Aaron's treatment, did little to discourage Birmingham-area Klansmen from other acts of violence in the coming years. KKK members were involved in scores of beatings, crossburnings, arsons, bombings, and similar incidents from the 1950s through the mid-1960s, including an attack on freedom riders in 1961 and the deaths of four children in the 1963 bombing of the Sixteenth Street Baptist Church.

— SEPTEMBER 3 —
1895
CIVIL RIGHTS LAWYER CHARLES HAMILTON HOUSTON BORN

On this day in civil rights history, future civil rights attorney Charles Hamilton Houston was born in Washington, D.C.

After a studious childhood, Houston graduated from Amherst College in 1915, the only black student in his class. He taught English at Howard University for two years before serving as an infantry lieutenant in World War I. During the war, he encountered hatred and violence from his white fellow soldiers. "I made up my mind," he wrote, "that I would never get caught again without knowing my rights; that if luck was with me, and I got through this war, I would study law and use my time fighting for men who could not strike back. . . My battleground is in America, not France."

In 1919, Hamilton returned home shortly before "Red Summer"—a vicious cycle of 25 race riots in U.S. cities. In the fall of 1919, Hamilton entered Harvard University Law School, where he became the first African American chosen for the *Harvard Law Review*. In 1924, Houston began teaching law classes at Howard University Law School. He was a hard-nosed perfectionist who insisted on excellence. He eventually became dean.

In the early 1930s, Houston began trying cases for the NAACP, often with the help of his star pupil, Thurgood Marshall. In 1934, Houston was the primary architect of what would be the NAACP legal focus for the next 20 years—ending public school segregation. To do this, he decided, the NAACP should focus on the "equal" half of "separate but equal."

In 1935, he went to work for the NAACP full-time.

Houston's goal was to try cases that would result in legal precedents that over time would end discrimination. Other segregation cases would be tried as they arose, but the NAACP focused on education lawsuits. Houston began with cases against states with no black professional schools, where black students had been barred from whites-only programs. Soon he had set precedents in Maryland and Missouri.

Houston worked tirelessly for his cause, laying the groundwork for the long-term NAACP strategy. But the endless 18-hour workdays took their toll. Houston began to weaken in the late 1940s. On April 22, 1950, Houston died from a heart attack, four years before the NAACP's greatest victory in *Brown v. Board*.

Thurgood Marshall carried on Houston's work.

— September 4 —
1957
National Guard Blocks 'Little Rock Nine'

On this day in civil rights history, nine black students were blocked by the Arkansas National Guard from entering Little Rock's Central High School, thus setting in motion the first significant test of the federal government's resolve to enforce school desegregation.

Following the 1954 *Brown* decision, black students in eight states, including some in Arkansas, successfully enrolled in previously all-white schools. But that November segregationist Orval Faubus was elected governor of Arkansas. The following year, the U.S. Supreme Court issued its second *Brown* decision, calling for schools to integrate with "deliberate speed," but setting no deadline. Nonetheless, the Little Rock school board adopted a plan to gradually desegregate Central High School, beginning with the admission of 17 black students in the fall of 1957. Meanwhile, Faubus was elected to a second two-year term, and in the spring of 1957 he pushed through the Arkansas legislature four bills intended to block integration and limit the activities of the NAACP in the state.

LITTLE ROCK CENTRAL HIGH

RAY   ROBERTS   PATTILLO   THOMAS   WALLS

MOTHERSHED   BROWN   ECKFORD   GREEN

The Little Rock Nine

On August 27, Faubus testified to a state court judge that integration would lead to violence, and the judge enjoined the black students from enrolling at Central High. Three days later, the NAACP went to federal court and successfully blocked the state court order. Then, on September 2, Faubus said he had activated the Arkansas National Guard to keep order, and the local school board asked the black students to stay home. But U.S. District Judge Ronald N. Davies ordered the school board to proceed with the desegregation plan.

On September 4, nine black students attempted to enroll at Central High School anyway, and were blocked by the National Guard. Over the next few weeks, the issue was confined mostly to state and federal courtrooms as lawyers for Faubus, the NAACP, and the school board battled over the impasse.

Photo courtesy of Associated Press

— SEPTEMBER 5 —

1838

FREDERICK DOUGLASS ESCAPES FROM SLAVERY

On this day in civil rights history, after a harrowing escape, Frederick Douglass spent his first day as a free man in New York City. He was 20 years old.

The future leader of the abolitionist and African American movement was born in February of 1818, a slave to a Maryland plantation. A bright and driven young man, Douglass taught himself to read and write, and at the age of 13 was reading abolitionist tracts to other slaves.

Douglass was hired out as a caulker to a Baltimore shipyard in 1836. The job allowed Douglass a limited measure of freedom and a pittance of wages. In his free time he joined the East Baltimore Mental Improvement Society—a club for freed blacks—and met Anna Murray. The two began a relationship.

Frederick Douglass

Murray shared her savings with Douglass, helping him acquire forged sailor's papers. On September 3, 1838, Douglass dressed in a red sailor's shirt and boarded a train in Baltimore headed to Wilmington, Delaware. He did not match the man described in his identification papers, but the conductor did not pay close attention and Douglass was off. From Wilmington, Douglass got on a steamboat headed for Philadelphia. Worried that he might still be caught and brought back to Maryland, he took another train to New York City, arriving on September 4. As he stepped off the train, Douglass was elated by his newfound freedom. "Anguish and grief, like darkness and rain," he later wrote, "may be depicted, but gladness and joy, like the rainbow, defy the skill of pen or pencil." He woke up on September 5 a free man.

Ten days later, Anna Murray joined him and the two were married.

Douglass entered the fray as a fiery abolitionist. In 1841, he became friends with William Lloyd Garrison and later began writing for Garrison's paper, *The Liberator*. He began to tour, giving antislavery speeches across the North.

In 1845, Douglass published the *Narrative of the Life of Frederick Douglass, an American Slave*, and then took refuge in Europe out of fear for slave hunters. He remained in Europe until 1847, touring Ireland and England. Ellen and Anna Richardson, two English women, bought his freedom, allowing him to go home without fear of arrest. At 28, Douglass returned to the United States.

— SEPTEMBER 6 —

1848

FREDERICK DOUGLASS ELECTED CONVENTION PRESIDENT

On this day in civil rights history, fiery abolitionist and former slave Frederick Douglass was elected president of the Black National Convention in Cleveland, Ohio.

After two years in exile, Douglass returned to the United States as a free man and became even more active than before in the antislavery movement as a speaker, writer, and activist. In 1848, in addition to being elected president of the convention, he was also the only speaker at the Seneca Falls women's conference; he began operating a safe house in Rochester, New York, for escaped slaves in the Underground Railroad; and he met John Brown for the first time.

Douglass became close friends with abolitionist William Lloyd Garrison. Douglass's paper, *The North Star,* sold well, with the motto: "Right is of no sex—Truth is of no color—God is the Father of us all, and we are all Brethen." In the years leading up to the Civil War, Douglass became the most famous, or infamous, black man in America. In 1851, Garrison and Douglass had a falling out over the direction of the movement that left them bitter enemies for a decade before they reconciled.

In 1859, John Brown invited Douglass to join his raid on Harper's Ferry but Douglass refused.

During the war, Douglass delivered speeches in support of the Union, President Lincoln, and the enlistment of black soldiers, issuing his famous pamphlet, "Men of Color, to Arms." His sons, Lewis and Charles, were two of the first black men to enlist.

After the war, Garrison wanted to disband the American Anti-Slavery Society, considering the matter concluded. Douglass responded: "Slavery is not abolished until the black man has the ballot." Douglass continued his pursuit of racial justice, and in 1868, Douglass campaigned for Ulysses Grant. Grant, in turn, enacted many civil rights protections for African Americans.

But the failure of Reconstruction and the rise of Jim Crow segregation brought on profound disillusionment in Douglass. In 1882 his wife Anna Murray, who had been so instrumental in his attainment of freedom, died.

On February 20, 1895, Douglass spoke at the National Council of Women in Washington, D.C. He received a standing ovation. Later that evening, he died of a heart attack. He never knew his exact birth date, but he was approximately 77.

On this day in civil rights history, prominent black artist Jacob Lawrence was born in Atlantic City, New Jersey.

Lawrence's parents had moved North with thousands of other black families in the early part of the 20th century. When he was 13, his family settled in Harlem.

In the 1930s, the Harlem Art Workshop opened as one of many New Deal programs. Lawrence began taking classes there and Charles Alston, a graduate student from Columbia, became his mentor. Lawrence learned how to draw and paint, and Alston immediately recognized the young man's talent.

Lawrence portrayed the struggles of African Americans through everyday activity: ironing, reading, walking down the street. He referred to his style as "dynamic cubism." He devised a way to tell stories through series of small paintings. By age 23, he had created five cycles of paintings: the stories of John Brown, Harriet Tubman, Frederick Douglass, Haitian revolutionary Toussaint L'Ouverture, and his most famous, the Migration of the Negro.

Lawrence, partially influenced by the critic and scholar Alain Locke, recognized the Great Migration as a seismic cultural, economic, and spiritual event. African Americans, fleeing poverty, racism, and violence, had left the rural South to live in the Northern cities. Determined to get his material right, Lawrence spent months at the New York Public Library researching the Great Migration.

Jacob Lawrence

Photo courtesy of Library of Congress

The resulting 60-panel work tells the story of the Great Migration—from the Deep South to the industrialized North—through images of hope, courage, and dignity. The cycle of paintings was sold to prominent American museums. Lawrence's career was established.

In the 1940s, he said of his paintings' relationship to the outside world: "We don't have a physical slavery, but an economic slavery. If these people, who were so much worse off than the people today, could conquer their slavery, we can certainly do the same thing. . . . I am not a politician. I'm an artist, just trying to do my part to bring this thing about."

As the movement gathered momentum in the late 1950s and early 1960s, Lawrence, by then wholly accepted into the art world, focused his paintings on civil rights themes.

In 1970, Lawrence was granted a professorship at the University of Washington. He died 30 years later, on June 9, 2000. He was 82.

On this day in civil rights history, Ruby Bridges, who would become a national symbol of school desegregation, was born in Mississippi.

She was the oldest child of Abon and Lucille Bridges, who worked as sharecroppers on a plot of land with her grandparents. They decided to move to the city for better work and better opportunities for their children. They relocated to New Orleans where Abon worked as a gas station attendant and Lucille worked a variety of night jobs.

Legal wrangling over school desegregation continued across the South, despite the 1954 *Brown v. Board* decision. In New Orleans, a federal judge declared that on November 14, 1960, the city's public schools would have to desegregate. Ruby and five other students were chosen as the first black students to attend white schools. Two of the six students refused, while the other three attended a different public school across town.

Ruby would attend William Frantz Public School alone.

The morning of November 14, federal marshals drove Ruby and her mother to school. After parking the car, two marshals walked in front of her, two behind. She held her mother's hand while a crowd of angry whites yelled threats and threw trash. Artist Norman Rockwell later commemorated that scene and Ruby with his painting, "The Problem We All Live With."

As she crossed the threshold, Ruby Bridges became the first black child in Louisiana to attend a white school. She spent the day in the principal's office.

The next day, U.S. marshals again walked Ruby to the school door. The crowd was still outside, but the school was empty. White parents had taken their children out of the school; the white teachers refused to teach. Ruby attended class alone, taught by Barbara Henry. Teacher and pupil spent the odd year together, just the two of them in the empty classroom.

While Ruby attended class, riots erupted across the city. Her grandparents were kicked off their farm; her father lost his job; threats were made against the family.

But there were also donations, offers of assistance, and general support from across the country. The next year, Mrs. Henry was not rehired to teach, and Ruby did not see her for 35 years.

In 1999, Ruby, by then a married mother of four, founded the Ruby Bridges Foundation to help teach diversity and promote tolerance. The organization's slogan: "Racism is a grown-up disease. Let's stop using kids to spread it."

— September 9 —
1957
Civil Rights Act of 1957 Enacted

On this day in civil rights history, the Civil Rights Act of 1957—the first civil rights legislation since Reconstruction—was passed.

Paul Douglas, a Democratic senator from Chicago, worked in the 1950s to enact sweeping changes in the U.S., including open housing, better public transportation, and equal rights for all. More specifically, Douglas and other liberal senators wanted minorities to be protected by federal judges and the U.S. attorney general, not by all-white Southern juries.

A bill was proposed to create an agency that would protect minority rights. President Eisenhower publicly supported the measure but debate was fierce. Southern Democrats despised what they saw as federal interference in states' rights, but wanted to maintain the Democratic majority in the Senate. Thus some Southern Democrats were willing to pass a weak civil rights bill to appease the integrationists.

Senate Majority Leader Lyndon Johnson feared the bill's potential to split his party, so he sent the measure to a committee headed by Mississippi Senator James Eastland, where it was watered down.

On the Senate floor, Southern Democrats led by Strom Thurmond thought the bill was still too strong and filibustered against it. More amendments followed, until eventually it passed. The bill offered federal recourse to those denied the vote, but left the burden on them to prove they had been disenfranchised. The bill did create the U.S. Civil Rights Commission within the Department of Justice.

Most, including President Eisenhower, considered the bill a failure. Ralph Bunche said he would have preferred no bill at all to the lip service of this one. Still, the new law was a first step, breaking eight decades of federal silence on the civil rights issue.

The bill's passage also helped consolidate Lyndon Johnson's influence in the Democratic Party.

— September 10 —
1936
Southern Tenant Farmers Union Builds
Coalition of Interracial Activists

On this day in civil rights history, the Southern Tenant Farmers Union continued to build its constituency across the South.

Founded in 1934 in Tyronza, Arkansas, the STFU was a biracial labor organization of sharecroppers, tenant farmers, minor land owners, and day laborers. The STFU's purpose was to collectively bargain with the big planters.

Sharecroppers worked someone else's land for a percentage of the crop. The landowner supplied a house, oftentimes little more than a shack, and a store where the sharecropper could buy necessities on credit. By year's end, the sharecropper often owed the landowner more money than his percentage of the crop had earned. To pay off the debt, the sharecropper was forced to work another year. The resulting cycle of poverty gripped much of the southern United States from the end of slavery up to World War II. Many sharecroppers were poor whites, but many others were ex-slaves or the descendants of ex-slaves. Stuck in the labyrinth of sharecropping, sometimes held in place by fraudulent accounting on the part of landowners, the sharecroppers lived as indentured servants, tied to a small parcel of land.

Under President Franklin Roosevelt's New Deal, the Agricultural Adjustment Administration was established. In the throes of the Great Depression, the AAA decided that drastic measures were needed to stimulate the economy. Despite food shortages across the country due to unemployment and low wages, the AAA paid farmers not to farm, hoping to increase the demand for, and therefore the price or food. The AAA paid landowners government checks not to farm their land. Some landowners, however, did not pass along the funds to sharecroppers. The STFU was formed in part to help poor farmers collect some of the government money. It grew into a strong agricultural labor union with the slogan "Land for the landless."

The first executive director of the STFU was H. L. Mitchell, a socialist and small-business man who would go on to serve as president of the STFU's successor, the National Farm Labor Union.

The STFU was interracial from the start, welcoming blacks as equals. This radical stance on race and economics had repercussions. STFU members were harassed and often confronted with violence.

In 1937, the U.S. government approved limited loans to sharecroppers so they could buy their own land.

— September 11 —
1913
'Lift Ev'ry Voice and Sing' Popularized

On this day in civil rights history, African Americans embraced James Weldon Johnson's poem "Lift Ev'ry Voice and Sing." The words were set to music by his brother, John. In 1900, on Lincoln's birthday, Johnson, as principal of the Stanton School in Jacksonville, Florida, had the choir sing the song. Soon it became a mainstay in black churches and schools. In 1920—the same year James Weldon Johnson became NAACP executive secretary—the NAACP made "Lift Ev'ry Voice and Sing" the Negro national anthem.

Lift ev'ry voice and sing, 'Til earth and heaven ring,
Ring with the harmonies of Liberty;
Let our rejoicing rise, high as the list'ning skies,
Let it resound loud as the rolling sea.
Sing a song full of the faith that the dark past has taught us,
Sing a song full of the hope that the present has brought us;
Facing the rising sun of our new day begun,
Let us march on 'til victory is won.

Stony the road we trod, bitter the chastening rod,
Felt in the days when hope unborn had died;
Yet with a steady beat, have not our weary feet
Come to the place for which our fathers sighed?
We have come over a way that with tears has been watered,
We have come, treading our path through the blood of the slaughtered,
Out from the gloomy past, 'til now we stand at last
Where the white gleam of our bright star is cast.

God of our weary years, God of our silent tears,
Thou who has brought us thus far on the way;
Thou who has by Thy might, led us into the light,
Keep us forever in the path, we pray.
Lest our feet stray from the places, our God, where we met Thee,
Lest, our hearts drunk with the wine of the world, we forget Thee;
Shadowed beneath Thy hand, may we forever stand,
True to our God, true to our native land.

James Johnson

On this day in civil rights history, high school students in Little Rock, Arkansas, stayed home because Governor Orval Faubus had closed all the city's public high schools rather than allow integration to continue.

Faubus just could not leave the Little Rock school situation alone. His actions in 1957 had provoked the Central High School crisis, which resulted in several days of rioting and eventually the deployment of federal troops by President Dwight Eisenhower.

Photo courtesy of Library of Congress

Teenager doing homework by the TV

After peace was restored, however, the rest of the 1957–58 school year proceeded reasonably normally. At the end of the spring term, Ernest Green became the first African American to graduate from Central High.

However, over the summer of 1958, Faubus and the Arkansas legislature pushed the Little Rock school board to shut down the city's three white high schools and one black high school. Students and teachers simply had to sit out a year.

But gradually white parents in the community began to speak out against the segregationists and joined with black parents to try to get the schools reopened on a nonsegregated basis. By 1959 they had succeeded, and students and teachers gradually returned to the classrooms. Among the students reentering Central High were Carlotta Walls and Jefferson Thomas, two of the "Little Rock Nine."

One of the white parents who worked for the reopening of the schools was Sara Alderman Murphy. Over the next few years, she decided that her city was really "two communities that did not communicate or know enough about each other to solve problems together." She began an interfaith, interracial women's group that began leading frank discussions of racial issues at civic and women's clubs and in churches.

Over time, Little Rock's white parents accepted school desegregation. In 1997, Central High School observed the 40th anniversary of its desegregation crisis. By this time, the school had 2,000 students and had been recognized as one of the nation's best high schools by college-admission counselors. Central High has also been listed as a National Governors' Association Model School, one of only two such schools in Arkansas.

— September 13 —
2000
Black Mayor Elected in Selma, Alabama

On this day in civil rights history, James Perkins was elected the first black mayor of Selma, Alabama. He replaced Joe Smitherman, a 70-year-old politician who came to office six months before the 1965 Selma-to-Montgomery marches began.

Smitherman became famous as the segregationist mayor of Selma during the period when local police attacked civil rights marchers on "Bloody Sunday" and minister James Reeb was beaten to death on a Selma street by white thugs.

After the passage of the Voting Rights Act and after civil rights organizations had left Selma, African Americans achieved a voting majority in the city. Yet Smitherman astonishingly won reelection nine more times, for a total of 38 years in office. Voter apathy accounts for some of Smitherman's longevity, as well as multiple black candidates running simultaneously and splitting the black vote. Smitherman was also wily, and he had some black support.

Perkins, a Selma businessman, ran against Smitherman three times. His campaign slogan for 2000 was "Joe's Gotta Go." The NAACP and SCLC both decided to get involved with Perkins's campaign, which would be occurring on the 35th anniversary of the Selma demonstrations and the passage of the Voting Rights Act. President Bill Clinton had already made a visit to Selma in March on the "Bloody Sunday" anniversary.

When the polls closed August 22, Smitherman had a 300-vote lead over Perkins and several other challengers, not enough to win without a runoff. African Americans in the little city responded with rallies, marches, and parades. Martin Luther King III and Fred Shuttlesworth came to give speeches in favor of Perkins. Students from predominantly black colleges volunteered in Perkins's campaign. The spirit of the 1960s seemed alive again.

In the runoff, Perkins received 57 percent of the vote. Selma, the symbol of the drive for black voting rights, had finally elected an African American to its highest office. Perkins received only a few hundred white votes, yet in victory he declared, "We will make Selma the Mecca of reconciliation."

Smitherman retired from politics. Like George Wallace, he apologized for his earlier segregationist policies while entering the political graveyard.

In 2004, Perkins was reelected. One year later, Smitherman died.

— SEPTEMBER 14 —

1921

BIRTHDATE OF CONSTANCE BAKER MOTLEY

On this day in civil rights history, Constance Baker Motley was born in New Haven, Connecticut.

At a young age, Motley wanted to be an interior decorator. Fortunately for the civil rights movement, she later chose a career in law instead. Motley's parents could not afford to send her to college, however, so she took a job with New Haven's National Youth Administration, a New Deal agency.

Motley's talents won her the attention of Clarence Blakeslee, a wealthy white philanthropist. Impressed with Motley's drive and intelligence, Blackslee offered to pay for her schooling. She took him up on the offer and enrolled at Fisk University in Nashville, Tennessee.

Her first-hand experiences with segregation in the South left a deep impression on her and she transferred to New York University, where she graduated in 1943 with a degree in economics. Shortly thereafter, she enrolled in the Columbia University Law School, where she met Thurgood Marshall. During her senior year, Marshall hired her as a clerk with the NAACP Legal Defense Fund. After graduation and admission to the bar, she became an NAACP lawyer.

From 1945 to 1964, Motley worked on all the major NAACP desegregation case—including *Brown v. Board, Swain v. Alabama,* and James Meredith's suit against the University of Mississippi—with Marshall and Charles Hamilton Houston, among others. After Houston's death in 1950 and Marshall's appointments a decade later as U.S. solicitor general and then Supreme Court justice, Motley stepped out of their shadows to become the NAACP's lead trial attorney. She won nine of ten Supreme Court cases she handled as chief counsel.

In 1964, Motley entered politics and won a seat in the New York state senate. She was the first African American woman to serve in that legislative body, where she worked on the passage of civil rights bills and the creation of low-income housing.

On January 25, 1966, President Lyndon Johnson appointed Motley as the first African American woman federal judge. She remained on the bench for two decades, reaching senior judge status in the 1980s.

In 1993, Constance Baker Motley was admitted into the National Women's Hall of Fame.

— September 15 —
1963
Sixteenth Street Baptist Church Bombed

On this day in civil rights history, a bomb exploded in the basement of Sixteenth Street Baptist Church, while Sunday school was in session. Eleven-year-olds Denise McNair and Cynthia Wesley and fourteen-year-olds Addie Mae Collins and Carole Robertson were killed instantly. Dozens of others were injured.

Birmingham had been under a reign of terror for years, as dozens of racially motivated bombings had taken place, earning one neighborhood the nickname "Dynamite Hill." The SCLC's Birmingham campaign had ended a few months earlier with a very public success for the movement through the Birmingham accords. In response, the KKK conspired to strike back.

Before the dust from the explosion had settled, riots broke out across the city as news of the tragedy spread. Angry African Americans pelted rocks at passing cars and at police. Police fired shotguns into the air and killed a sixteen-year-old boy. A white teenager was killed in a suburb outside of town in a racially motivated incident. A city-wide catastrophe loomed.

Photo courtesy of Birmingham Public Library

The damaged church

Martin Luther King Jr. and other SCLC members sped to Birmingham. King called for federal help, saying Birmingham was in "a state of civil disorder . . . . The Negro community is about to reach a breaking point."

Ultimately, the bombing became both a rallying point and a point of division for the movement. Some would point to the blast as the moment they lost faith in America, while others used the four girls' deaths as inspiration to work harder to end racism.

At a funeral service three days later, King delivered the eulogy. "These children—unoffending, innocent, and beautiful—were the victims of one of the most vicious and tragic crimes ever perpetrated against humanity . . . my friends, they did not die in vain. God still has a way of wringing good out of evil. And history has proven over and over again that unmerited suffering is redemptive. The innocent blood of these little girls may well serve as a redemptive force that will bring new light to this dark city."

No other act of white terrorism during the civil rights era aroused more ire across the country. The pressure it brought helped change the climate that had supported segregation in the South.

The bombing was unsolved until the late 1970s, when one Klansman was convicted. A second round of investigations in the late 1990s convicted two others.

On this day in civil rights history, Justice Hugo Black spent his last full day on the nation's highest court.

Born in February 1886 in a small wooden farmhouse in Harlan, Alabama, Black graduated from the University of Alabama Law School in 1906. He embarked on a legal career in Birmingham, working in various capacities as an attorney until he joined the army during World War I. He served one year, without seeing any combat. Black returned to Birmingham to work again in private practice and became a highly successful plantiff's attorney.

Photo courtesy of Library of Congress

Hugo Black

He specialized in winning large verdicts on behalf of blacks and poor whites against the large "big mule" corporate interests of the day, notably the railroads and the steel and coal companies. A devout Baptist and a Sunday school teacher, Black was a tee-totaler and gained a statewide reputation during Prohibition as a special prosecutor of bootleggers.

In 1921, Black defended a Klansman accused of murdering a priest. Black built the defense around unabashedly racist appeals to the all-white jury. Two years later, Black was inducted into the Klan, resigning a few years later. The KKK was commonplace in Alabama and in fact across the nation in the mid-1920s; Black was among many elected officials who belonged to it.

In 1926, Black was elected to the U.S. Senate, where he served for 11 years. Black was a vigorous supporter of President Franklin D. Roosevelt and the New Deal. Roosevelt nominated Black for the Supreme Court in 1937. Despite his earlier KKK membership, he was confirmed. On the court, Black was a fierce protector of free speech, freedom of the press, and individual liberties. Until the arrival of Chief Justice Earl Warren, appointed by President Dwight Eisenhower in 1952, Black was often a liberal dissenter from the court's rulings. But on the Warren court, Black's opinions were part of a majority. Over the next two decades Black helped reshape the nation.

Black sided with civil rights causes in almost every case before the court. Black's legal philosophy was centered in the Bill of Rights, and he believed the Constitution applied equally to all citizens, regardless of race, creed, or gender. Thus he strongly supported school desegregation, voting rights, privacy rights, freedom of speech and religion, the right to counsel, and so on. His rulings extended the Bill of Rights to the states and blocked segregationists from hiding behind states' rights.

On September 17, 1971, Black retired from the court. He died eight days later.

— SEPTEMBER 17 —

1866

MARY BURNETT TALBERT BORN IN OHIO

On this day in civil rights history, NAACP activist and suffragette Mary Burnett Talbert was born in Oberlin, Ohio.

In 1887, Talbert became the first African American high school principal in Arkansas, at Union High School in Little Rock. In 1891, Talbert married and moved to Buffalo, New York. The move shifted her education career into social activism.

In Buffalo, she joined a number of civic and Christian societies, including the Phyllis Wheatley Club of Colored Women, which in 1900 organized a protest demanding a Negro exhibit at the Pan-American Exposition. She became a well-known figure in women's rights and antilynching circles, and associated with Mary White Ovington and Mary McLeod Bethune, among others.

Talbert was a lifelong women's rights activist. In 1911, she became a charter member of the Empire Federation of Women's Clubs, serving as president from 1912 to 1916. "It should not be necessary to struggle forever against popular prejudice," she wrote, "and with us as colored women, this struggle becomes twofold, first because we are women and second, because we are colored women." She was later elected president of the National Association of Colored Women. In 1920, she served as a delegate to the International Council of Women in Norway.

In 1905, Burnett invited W. E. B. Du Bois, William Monroe Trotter, John Hope, and 27 others for a secret meeting to discuss a new organization. This seed grew into the Niagara Movement and, later, the NAACP.

Talbert was deeply involved with the NAACP from the beginning. She gave speeches, wrote articles for *The Crisis*, and toured the country in support of equal rights.

She served many years on the NAACP national board of directors and as vice president and for several years as its director. She was later awarded the Springarn Medal, the NAACP's highest honor.

Entering the 1920s, Talbert campaigned for the antilynching bill, while also working for prison reform.

By her death at age 57 in 1923, she was an international figure, though today she is largely unknown. A tiny gravestone and a small historical marker are the earthly remains of this remarkable woman's achievements.

— September 18 —
1895
Booker T. Washington Proposes 'Atlanta Compromise'

On this day in civil rights history, Booker T. Washington delivered the "Atlanta Compromise" speech at the Cotton States and International Exposition in Atlanta. With an accomodationist solution to the South's racial tensions, Washington's controversial and still-debated speech is one of the most noteworthy in American history.

Washington's solution to the South's "Negro problem"—widespread poverty and degradation, and few educational institutions, for example—was to encourage African Americans to become

Photo courtesy of Library of Congress

Booker T. Washington

proficient in practical, mechanical labor. Blacks, he argued, would prosper in American society in proportion to their hard work. Self-reliance was the key; blacks should accept segregation as a fact of life and build their own communities and institutions, as Washington himself had done at Tuskegee Institute. Equality would eventually take place if African Americans made themselves indispensable to everyday life. Whites and blacks could "be as separate as the fingers, yet one as the hand in all things essential to mutual progress."

But whites needed to help their African American brethren, by trusting them with jobs, by giving them a chance to prove their worth. Mostly though, he urged blacks to: "'Cast down your bucket where you are.' Cast it down, making friends in every manly way of the people of all races, by whom you are surrounded."

He received a standing ovation and was heralded as a major moral leader in turn-of-the-century America. But as much as the white media lauded his speech and ideas, black intellectuals began criticizing him. Ida Wells-Barnett declared that Washington ignored the perils of the racially striated society and erased any debt that America owed its oppressed black citizenry.

Washington's most vocal critic was his former friend W. E. B. Du Bois, who began calling him "the Great Accommodator." Washington was popular with whites, Du Bois argued, because he told them what they wanted to hear. Washington praised American society and eased white fears of racial retaliation, while misleading his own people into lives of second-class servitude. To Du Bois, the Atlanta Compromise speech represented a conservative, unenlightened, and naïve view of race and power politics.

The Atlanta Compromise created a schism in the African American community: followers of Du Bois on one side, of Washington on the other. The dueling visions would haunt the civil rights movement well into the 20th century.

— SEPTEMBER 19 —
1955
ALL-WHITE JURY ACQUITS MURDERERS OF EMMETT TILL

On this day in civil rights history, the trial of Roy Bryant and J. W. Milam for the murder of Emmett Till began in Mississippi.

The trial began just two weeks after Till's body was found. Reporters, photographers, and the curious packed the tiny Mississippi courtroom during the proceedings.

The evidence against Bryant and Milam was strong. Six eyewitnesses testified to the pair taking the boy from his uncle's home shortly before the projected time of death, along with other, more damning testimony.

But just as the nation had erupted in anger at Till's murder, so did Mississippi whites rally around the two defendants. Five defense attorneys volunteered their services and a defense fund was raised. During the trial, the defense used familiar tactics: Don't let outsiders tell white Mississippians how to run our lives. The racially charged defense worked. Despite the overwhelming evidence and their own admission that they kidnapped the boy, Bryant and Milam were found not guilty. An all-white jury came back with the verdict after less than two hours of deliberation.

African Americans held protest rallies in Cleveland, Boston, Chicago, New York, and other cities. Outside the South, newspapers editorialized against the verdict. And around the globe, the United States that proclaimed itself the freest country in the world looked hypocritical, oppressive, and undemocratic, even as it was locked in a Cold War with the Soviet Union.

Bryant and Milam went free, but their story did not end here. Two months after the verdict, the author William Bradford Huie paid the two men to tell him their stories, which they did because, having been acquitted, they could not be prosecuted again. In chilling detail, the two men said they had intended to scare Till into compliance with local racial customs. But Till refused to acknowledge that he had done anything wrong and then refused to beg for mercy, so they killed him.

Bryant and Milam were later charged with kidnapping, but again were found not guilty. Both men are now dead, but new evidence has recently come to light that others might have been involved or might have concealed their guilt. As of 2005, the U.S. Department of Justice had reopened the Till murder case.

— September 20 —

1664

Maryland Passes First Miscegenation Law

On this day in civil rights history, Maryland passed the first miscegenation law banning interracial marriage in the United States.

Early in the European settlement of North America, the distinction between slaves and indentured servants was not so great. Slaves could own property, marry whom they chose, and after a time, many were granted their freedom. Indentured servants were a more common source of labor than slaves. Only a few hundred slaves were in Maryland before 1680.

As time passed and African slavery became more widespread, both laws and customs became more restrictive. Slaves came to be regarded as simple-minded, then subhuman, and finally as property. The impetus for Maryland's ban of interracial marriage revolved around the offspring. What legal status should a person of mixed race be afforded?

The early miscegenation laws were a step in the reduction of persons of African descent to the status of chattel property. Other states followed in Maryland's footsteps. Soon, every colony—and after independence, every state—regulated interracial marriage, though the laws did not prevent white slave owners from coupling with female slaves.

Maryland also barred slaves from owning property and made it illegal for owners to emancipate slaves. Interestingly, in the west, miscegenation laws applied to Mexicans and to American Indians. A sexual caste system was in place.

During Reconstruction, Radical Republicans overturned some miscegenation laws. But then the Black Codes emerged to limit all interaction between blacks and whites, and socially, one aspect of Jim Crow segregation was to maintain the "purity" of the white race. White supremacy held that nonwhites were genetically inferior. Worse, many whites argued, mixed-race marriages were against God's will, unnatural, and predicated on illicit sexual depravity.

By Reconstruction's end, miscegenation laws were back in force in much of the nation. In some states, the penalties were draconian, both legally and extra-legally. Offenders faced long prison terms, plus they risked being beaten or lynched.

In 1958, Richard Loving, a white man, and Mildred Jeter, a black woman, got married in Washington, D.C. When they returned to their home state of Virginia, they were arrested. A nine-year legal battle ensued. In 1967, the Supreme Court declared miscegenation laws unconstitutional, siding in favor of the interracial couple.

Alabama was the last state to abolish miscegenation laws . . . in 2000.

— September 21 —
1905
Atlanta Life Insurance Company Founded

On this day in civil rights history, Alonzo Herndon, a former sharecropper, founded the Atlanta Life Insurance Company.

Herndon belonged to the first generation of post-Civil War black entrepreneurs, who fostered capitalism blended with racial self-help. They were activist businessmen who used their ideas to help their communities and themselves.

Herndon operated a barbershop in downtown Atlanta and saved his profits. His barbershop was destroyed in the 1905 Atlanta race riots. He responded by opening the Atlanta Life Insurance Company, with his first insurance office on "Sweet Auburn" Avenue, just down the street from Ebenezer Baptist Church (later pastored by Martin Luther King Sr.).

Herndon's new company offered a few simple policies for life, work, and health insurance. He envisioned a mutually beneficial operation, where customers' claims would be paid promptly, while ALIC could serve as a beacon for other black-owned businesses. In the process, Herndon would make money for himself. The plan worked, and by 1909 he had more than 20,000 policyholders. By 1927, Herndon was the wealthiest African American in Atlanta. Herndon died that year and his son Norris took over and continued to build the company.

The ALIC and other black-owned insurance companies—Mississippi Life, Standard Life, North Carolina Mutual, and National Benefit Life, to name a few—later played a key role in the civil rights movement. Like black pastors and black funeral home directors, black insurance agents were among the few black workers of the era whose economic wherewithal could not be threatened by white employers.

Black insurance agents could not lose their jobs or be kicked off a white-owned farm for agitating for civil and voting rights. The agents were also out in the black community daily, going door-to-door, and they thus became important conduits of information about civil rights activity.

The ALIC supported strikes, protests, and marches in the greater Atlanta area. In the 1950s and 1960s, ALIC posted bail for jailed protesters, offered employment to blacks fired due to their civil rights involvement, and provided numerous support operations including printing.

Today, ALIC remains one of the leading African American stock-owned insurance companies in the nation.

— SEPTEMBER 22 —
1906
ATLANTA RACE RIOT

On this day in civil rights history, the worst violence in a series of race riots occurred in Atlanta.

After being burned to the ground during the Civil War, Atlanta was rebuilt during Reconstruction as the center of Southern commerce. Black businesses and colleges also found success there as part of a large, thriving black community. But a series of small race riots occurred from the late 1890s to the early 1900s. Dozens of blacks were lynched during this time period.

The worst of the riots occurred in 1906 as cultural forces aligned with political expediency to turn Atlanta into a tinderbox. First, a dramatization of Thomas Dixon's *The Klansman*, featuring troupes of black-face actors threatening the purity of helpless white women, became popular. Second, white resentment grew toward black business successes. Finally, Hoke Smith, paradoxically a progressive reformer and a virulent segregationist, was elected governor of Georgia. As governor, Hoke enacted harsher Jim Crow laws.

Smith's election roused angry whites to action. Smith ran on a race-baiting segregationist platform, inflaming tensions with fiery racist invective. His election was a sign of white anger toward blacks. Meanwhile, a newspaper circulation war prompted "yellow journalism" stories of masses of black rapists prowling the Atlanta streets. The made-up stories were believed. In mid-September a story involving black harassment of white women caught the imagination of angry white men. Shortly after Hoke's election, white mobs formed to attack the black section of town.

On Peachtree Street, Atlanta's main downtown thoroughfare, white mobs savagely beat black pedestrians and bootblacks with fists and clubs. Racial violence also broke out in Five Points, the business center of Atlanta at the time. Rioters, unsatisfied with attacking black businesses near white areas, decided to invade and burn black neighborhoods.

The rioting lasted three days. Officially, at least 15 people were killed, although the number was probably higher. Hundreds were wounded. Police did little to protect Atlanta's black community, and actually aided the white mobs by disarming blacks.

Martial law was declared to quell the violence.

— September 23 —
1863
NAACP Cofounder Mary Church Terrell Born

On this day in civil rights history, Mary Church Terrell was born in Memphis, Tennessee. Her parents, both former slaves, had become successful through canny business decisions and provided their daughter with a first-class education. She became an early activist and women's suffragette and by her death in 1954 was one of the most-respected civil rights leaders in the nation.

Terrell could speak Italian, French, and German and was one of the first African American women to earn a degree. This was the first of a lifetime of firsts. She was the first African American woman appointed to the District of Columbia Board of Education. She lectured on racial matters and belonged to dozens of activist organizations over her lifetime, and would live through the end of the Civil War, Reconstruction, the rise of Jim Crow, the formation of the NAACP, two world wars, and the milestone litigation that would ultimately jumpstart the modern civil rights movement.

In 1892, she founded the Colored Women's League. In 1896, with Josephine Ruffin, Terrell merged CWL with the National Federation of Afro-American Women into the National Association of Colored Women. Terrell was its first president. She proved to be an adept political organizer.

In 1909, Terrell was a founding member of the NAACP, along with Mary White Ovington, Ida Wells-Barnett, and other influential women activists and progressives.

She spent the coming years involved in the international movement for women's rights, often wowing audiences with quadra-lingual speeches. She received honorary doctorate degrees from Howard University and Wilberforce and Oberlin colleges.

Mary Church Terrell

Photo courtesy of Library of Congress

She published her autobiography, *A Colored Woman in a White World*, in 1940.

In 1949 she became the first African American woman to be invited to the American Association of University Women.

In her eighties, Terrell led her own successful three-year campaign to desegregate Washington, D.C.'s eateries, using protests, sit-ins, and boycotts, along with legal action.

She died in Maryland at age 90, but had lived to see the *Brown v. Board* decision.

— SEPTEMBER 24 —
1957
MOB PREVENTS 'LITTLE ROCK NINE' ENTRY TO SCHOOL

On this day in civil rights history, police in Little Rock, Arksansas, were unable to keep order as a mob of more than a thousand angry whites gathered outside Central High School to protest the entry of the black students who have come to be known as "the Little Rock Nine."

The students were Ernest Green; Melba Pattillo Beals; Elizabeth Eckford; Gloria Ray Karlmark; Carlotta Walls LaNier; Terrence Roberts; Jefferson Thomas; Minnijean Brown Trickey; and Thelma Jean Mothershed Wair.

The "Little Rock Crisis" had been brewing for several weeks since Governor Orval Faubus used the Arkansas National Guard to circumvent a federal judge's order that the black students be admitted to the previously all-white school. On September 20, the judge ordered the state to stop interfering, and Faubus responded by withdrawing the National Guardsmen, thus clearing the way for the mob to overpower the local police force.

On September 24, President Dwight Eisenhower dispatched 1,200 troops with the 101st Airborne Division to restore order and ensure that the black students were allowed to enroll, which they did on September 25, under armed escort. Meanwhile, U.S. military vehicles patrolled Little Rock streets.

The crisis was temporarily over. On October 12, more than 6,000 Little Rock residents, both black and white, held a day of prayer for their city, although the next morning the white segregationists were back outside Central High protesting the black students inside. Some white students also did what they could to make the nine blacks miserable. Later, Elizabeth Eckford would say: "Some of the [Central High] students I'd known since I was ten years old, who were white, were afraid to speak to me in school. It's true there were only about 50 students who were actively harassing us. But some of those other students were cooperating in that violence through their silence."

Day by day, however, things calmed down, and on November 27, the U.S. Army troops withdrew from Little Rock.

On May 25, 1958, Ernest Green became the first African American to graduate from Central High. He and the eight other blacks had endured much harassment and pressure, but they had completed the year.

— SEPTEMBER 25 —
1957
TROOPS PATROL LITTLE ROCK AS STUDENTS ADMITTED

On this day in civil rights history, more than a thousand U.S. soldiers kept order in the streets of Little Rock so the black students known as the "Little Rock Nine" could enter Central High School.

The troops, members of the 101st Airborne Division, were dispatched to Little Rock after Governor Orval Faubus had withdrawn the Arkansas National Guard—thus letting white mobs take over—rather than have the guardsmen protect the students.

In response, President Dwight Eisenhower reluctantly declared martial law and sent in the federal soldiers. Not since Reconstruction had the U.S. military been used in a Southern city to enforce a federal judge's order (the earlier order to desegregate Central High School), but Eisenhower said he felt he had no other choice.

He gave a televised address to the nation on September 24, saying: "At a time when we face grave situations abroad because of the hatred that communism bears toward a system of government based on human rights, it would be difficult to exaggerate the harm that is being done to the prestige and influence and indeed to the safety of our nation and the world. Our enemies are gloating over this incident and using it everywhere to misrepresent our whole nation. We are portrayed as a violator of those standards which the peoples of the world united to proclaim in the Charter of the United Nations."

Eisenhower

Eisenhower's actions were predictably sharply condemned by Southern governors and other politicians. South Carolina Senator Olin Johnston, a former two-term governor of his state, went so far as to suggest that Faubus send the Arkansas National Guard back in to battle the U.S. soldiers.

Other national leaders praised Eisenhower. Oregon Senator Wayne Morse said "every American citizen who believes in the supremacy of the American Constitution under a system of government by law should support President Eisenhower in the civil rights crisis" and added that the president's use of federal force at Little Rock "is a constitutional and needed exercise of his presidential duty."

With the troops in place, the students enrolled and peace gradually returned to the streets. By late November, the last members of the 101st Airborne had left Little Rock.

— SEPTEMBER 26 —
1899
COMPOSER WILLIAM DAWSON BORN

On this date in civil rights history, African American composer William Dawson was born in Anniston, Alabama. His orchestras performed at the White House and on national and international stages, calling attention to slave, folk, and protest music and thus to the plight of black Americans.

At the age of 13, Dawson ran away from home and entered Tuskegee Institute, where he supported himself through manual labor. He left Tuskegee in 1921 to attend the Horner Institute of Fine Arts, playing the trombone. He received his master's degree from the American Conservatory of Music.

Dawson was a composer from a young age. His first pieces were for the violin, cello, and piano. His chamber music was interesting, but he became famous for his variations on Negro spirituals. Dawson moved away from the European tradition of music by examining his African roots and the songs of lament sung by slaves. Dawson was soon a recognized expert on the Negro folk music tradition.

In 1931, Dawson returned to Tuskegee to form the School of Music, where for the next 25 years he conducted the 100-voice Tuskegee Choir. Two years after it began, the Tuskegee Choir was a big attraction at the grand opening of Radio City Music Hall in New York City. The choir performed Dawson's original choral pieces for President Franklin Roosevelt in the 1930s.

In 1934, Dawson's "Negro Folk Symphony" premiered to worldwide attention, with the Philadelphia Symphony Orchestra, directed by Leopold Stokowski, performing the groundbreaking work. Incorporating his knowledge of African American music, Dawson infused slave and protest songs with African rhythms. He was soon a famous international conductor and composer.

While continuing his work with Tuskegee, Dawson rearranged the "Negro Folk Symphony" after visiting West Africa in 1952. He maintained until the end of his life that he was not a "black composer"; music to Dawson was a color-free place, devoid of racism and discrimination.

In the late 1960s, Dawson was invited as a guest conductor around the country, including the Kansas City Philharmonic Orchestra, the Nashville Symphony Orchestra, and the Baltimore Symphony Orchestra.

He died on May 4, 1990.

— SEPTEMBER 27 —

1822

HIRAM REVELS BORN IN NORTH CAROLINA

On this day in civil rights history, future U.S. senator Hiram Revels was born in Fayetteville, North Carolina, a rare free black man in a slave state.

Early on, Revels worked for his brother, learning to be a barber. After his brother's death in 1843, Revels ran the barbershop himself. But he decided to get an education and left in 1844 to attend a Quaker school in Liberty, Indiana, and later Knox College in Galesburg, Illinois. Revels was soon ordained as a minister and began preaching to congregations in Ohio, Tennessee, Indiana, Kentucky, Missouri, and Kansas. He worked with the African Methodist Episcopal Church, an active and important denomination in the larger African American community.

When the Civil War began in 1861, Revels worked in Maryland to rally the state to the Union side. He also recruited African Americans in Missouri, where he served as a combat chaplain. He worked as a recruiter and military chaplain during the war, serving as provost marshal of Vicksburg, Mississippi, during the Union siege.

By war's end, Revels settled in Natchez, Mississippi, where he joined the Methodist Episcopal Church and was soon the presiding elder. In 1868, Revels served on the Natchez city council as alderman. Two years later he was elected to the U.S. Senate as a Republican, the first African American to serve in the Senate (filling the seat held by Jefferson Davis before the Civil War).

Hiram Revels

Photo courtesy of Library of Congress

Revels served one year before returning to Mississippi. During his time as senator he introduced several bills, and spoke eloquently about the readmittance of the Southern states into the Union, and the long road toward reconstruction.

Upon his return, Revels was named president of Alcorn College, the first African American college in Mississippi. He served as president for many years, and retired in 1882. During this time he also served as the interim Mississippi secretary of state in 1873.

In retirement, Revels continued his religious work as a preacher and his political campaign work. He died in January 1901 of a stroke while attending a church service in Aberdeen, Mississippi.

In 1953, *The Autobiography of Hiram Rhoades Revels Together with Some Letters by and about Him* was published.

— September 28 —
1868
'Negro Hunt' Results in Massacre in Opelousas

On this day in civil rights history, the Opelousas massacre occurred in Louisiana, one of the worst outbreaks of racial violence during Reconstruction.

Located in central Louisiana, Opelousas, a small town named after an Indian tribe, was the capital of the state for a brief period in 1862 when Baton Rouge fell to Union control. It is the third-oldest city in Louisiana, a former French trading outpost, the chosen home of Alamo hero Jim Bowie, and the seat of St. Landry Parish.

The yoke of Reconstruction was difficult to bear for the recently defeated white Southerners. Their society lay in ruins and they were occupied by the army that had devastated them. The Knights of the White Camellia—a secret order similar to the Ku Klux Klan—formed in response to the occupation and engaged in terrorism and intimidation toward blacks and carpetbagging whites. The White League followed in the Knights' footsteps, forming the nucleus of white-sponsored terror in Louisiana. The League hated Republicans and Northerners, but they hated blacks the most.

The violence in Opelousas began when three whites beat up newspaperman Emerson Bentley. Bentley was editor of a Republican paper and a teacher with the Freedman's Bureau. Local blacks responded to help Bentley. In the resulting fight, 12 black men were arrested. Late that night, they were taken out of the jail and hanged.

Emboldened, marauding whites, many of them ex-Confederate veterans and White Leaguers armed with pistols, rifles, and hunting dogs, began to scour the surrounding countryside on a "Negro hunt." African Americans fled into the surrounding swamp areas and were hunted down like animals. When the sun came up the next morning, hundreds of blacks were dead. No one knows exactly how many were murdered, but most sources say between 200 and 300.

Today, Opelousas is a struggling Deep South town with an African American majority and with 38 percent of citizens living below the poverty line. In May 2000, Opelousas was named the Zydeco capital of the world.

On this date in civil rights history, the *Booker T. Washington,* a World War II Liberty ship, was launched at Wilmington, Delaware. It was the first major U.S. oceangoing ship to be named in honor of an African American, and it was the first to go to sea under command of a black captain and with an integrated crew whose ethnic backgrounds represented 17 nationalities.

The ship was christened by opera diva Marian Anderson. Later, 16 more Liberty ships (of 2,700 total) were commissioned and named for African Americans—including Frederick Douglass, George Washington Carver, Paul Laurence Dunbar, John Hope, James Weldon Johnson, and Harriet Tubman—but the crew and officers of the Washington took pride in being the first.

Marian Anderson christening "Washington"

Built in Los Angeles, the *Booker T. Washington* displaced 10,500 tons. Under Captain Hugh Mulzac's command, it made 22 voyages during the war years as a troop-transport ship, ferrying more than 18,000 troops to Europe and the Pacific.

After World War II, the ship hauled coal for the Luckenbach Steamship Company under the command of another black officer, Captain James H. Brown Jr. It was scrapped in 1969.

Among the ship's officers during World War II was the U.S. protest poet John Beecher, who wrote a book about the ship's experiences, *All Brave Sailors: The Story of the* S.S. Booker T. Washington.

— SEPTEMBER 30 —

1962

JAMES MEREDITH ENROLLS IN OLE MISS

On this day in civil rights history, a deal was struck between segregationist Mississippi Governor Ross Barnett and U.S. Attorney General Robert Kennedy to allow the enrollment at the University of Mississippi (Ole Miss) of its first African American student, James Meredith.

This followed an 18-month-long court battle and a protracted negotiation during which Barnett privately pledged cooperation but publicly proclaimed that Mississippi would never yield to federal force. Finally, Barnett ran out of legal maneuvering room and on the evening of September 30, federal marshals secretly escorted Meredith onto the Ole Miss campus.

Photo courtesy of Library of Congress

Arriving on campus

When his presence became known, a mob of some 2,000 angry whites, whipped up by Barnett's public rhetoric, surged onto the campus, overwhelming the marshals and other security guards assigned to protect Meredith. Throughout that night and into the next day, the guards were assaulted with rocks, Molotov cocktails, bottles, bricks, and guns. Tear gas wafted across the scenic campus as the battle raged. Finally, President Kennedy sent federal troops to restore order, but not before two people had been killed and 160 injured, including 28 federal marshals who suffered gunshot wounds.

In the end, the protests subsided, and Meredith attended classes and graduated two years later. He described his experiences in a 1966 book, *Three Years in Mississippi*.

Meredith went on to become an unusual civil rights hero. In 1966, he staged a one-man "March Against Fear" from Memphis, Tennessee, to Jackson, Mississippi, to encourage other blacks to exercise freedom of thought and movement. This march was interrupted when he was shot by unknown assailants along a lonely stretch of highway. Other civil rights leaders, including Martin Luther King Jr. and Stokely Carmichael took up his march and Meredith recovered from his injuries. In later years, Meredith renounced civil rights, embraced conservative causes, and often managed to confound both his supporters and his enemies.

This day in October

— OCTOBER 1 —

1964

CORE ARREST KICKS OFF FREE SPEECH MOVEMENT

On this day in civil rights history, police arrested Jack Weinberg for passing out CORE pamphlets on the University of California–Berkeley campus. The arrest kickstarted the free speech movement and is noted by many as the beginning of the student movements of the 1960s.

During the summer of 1964, the Berkeley campus CORE office worked hard to raise awareness of and enlist volunteers for the civil rights movement. But student radicals, frustrated by lack of success in the movement, projected their anger onto the UCB administration, which responded by cracking down on protests on campus, which inflamed the students to further action.

At the time, any political activity on campus was a violation of UCB rules. School officials announced they would enforce these regulations and barred any political activity of any kind on campus.

On October 1, Jack Weinberg defied the order. He set up a table and began passing out CORE leaflets. He was arrested and the leaflets confiscated. But as Weinberg was being taken away in a police car, a crowd of some 3,000 students blocked its path. For 36 hours, Weinberg sat in the car while students gave speeches and held an impromptu rally. Weinberg was eventually released and the charges dropped.

But UCB brought charges against some students involved in the protest. Students responded by organizing a huge sit-in in Sproul Hall, one of the main administration buildings. The sit-in and consequent protests and marches almost shut the campus down. Solidarity developed among the Berkeley students—Republicans and Democrats, radicals and conservatives—who formed a broad coalition to fight for students' rights. Some tenured professors began protesting with the students.

Student Mario Savio emerged as the spokesman of the free speech movement, and on December 3, 1964, he gave its most famous oration about the necessity for opposition to "the operation of the machine."

On January 3, 1965, a new chancellor partially gave in to student demands. The steps of Sproul Hall could be used for political activity for a few designated hours each day.

Although it began as a platform for academic freedom and free speech, the free speech movement had a generally utopian focus that was antiwar, pro-feminist, and pro-civil rights. The Berkeley antiwar movement evolved from the free speech movement, as did the multitudinous leftwing student organizations that defined the campus in the late 1960s.

— OCTOBER 2 —
1963
SAVANNAH DESEGREGATES

On this day in civil rights history, the people of Savannah, Georgia, experienced their first full day of desegregation.

One of America's oldest cities and relatively undamaged in the Civil War, Savannah sits on the east coast of Georgia and is the embodiment of Southern grace, charm, and gentility.

Like everywhere else in the South, of course, Savannah was segregated and had no plans to change. Six years after *Brown v. Board*, Savannah's public schools remained segregated. Theaters, restaurants, lunch counters, and all public places were divided into two unequal classes.

Army veterans Westley W. Law and Hosea Williams took the lead in desegregating Savannah. In 1950, Law became a member of the NAACP National Board of Directors and later president of the Savannah NAACP chapter. In 1959, he began pushing for change through direct action.

In 1960, activists began a sit-in campaign at the city's lunch counters. For months, students and activists would sit at lunch counters and refuse to leave until they were served. In response, the protesters were thrown out or arrested. Law saw the need to capitalize on this momentum and three years of direct action followed. Black activists were engaged in all manner of protests, including attempts to desegregate the whites-only beaches, and "play-ins" where black and white kids would play basketball and other sports in segregated public parks, along with boycotts and marches. African Americans lined the streets with posters denouncing segregation. Meanwhile, dozens of black parents filed suit against Savannah's public schools.

Savannah's reputation as a peaceful, progressive place was threatened, and the city began to buckle under the negative publicity.

A series of widespread night marches in late 1963, combined with a city-wide boycott on segregated businesses, eventually broke Savannah's intransigence. On October 1, Savannah officially desegregated its lunch counters, theaters, and restaurants. The debate over Savannah's public schools would continue, but Law, Williams, and the hundreds of brave Savannah citizens had won a huge victory.

The desegregation of Savannah was unique. Relatively little violence occurred during the years of protest and civil disobedience, and both sides seemed ready to move toward the future. The rest of the South did not respond so delicately.

AMERICAN FRIENDS SERVICE COMMITTEE, FRIENDS OF CIVIL RIGHTS, WAGES PEACE DURING WARTIME

On this day in civil rights history, the American Friends Service Committee aided conscientious objectors in World War I. The Quaker-led AFSC would grow into a powerful pacifist and civil rights organization, befitting the Quakers' long tradition as ardent champions of freedom.

Quakers came to the New World a persecuted minority, only to face continued harassment. Massachusetts Puritans, determined to stamp out what they saw as religious heresy, arrested Quakers and confiscated their property. But the Quakers, also known as the Religious Society of Friends or the "children of light," persevered, becoming a small but vocal minority for peace and brotherly love.

Quakers were among the first abolitionists and in 1688 formed one of the first antislavery societies. Quakers' belief in egalitarianism far exceeded any other group's vision at the time; they were early advocates for women's rights, fair treatment of American Indians, and the immediate abolition of slavery. By 1776, the Quaker religion forbade the ownership of slaves. In the 1800s, Quakers served as organizers, conductors, and providers of safe houses for the Underground Railroad.

A Quaker letter to Lincoln

By the 20th century, the Religious Society of Friends had cemented its place in progressive circles as devoted pacifists and social reformers.

In 1917, the American Friends Service Committee was formed to help Quakers and other conscientious objectors avoid being drafted into World War I as soldiers; instead, they offered their services as ambulance drivers and medics in war zones.

After the end of World War I, the AFSC quickly became a humanitarian organization, providing relief aid to war-torn Europe. In the 1930s, the AFSC provided aid in the Spanish Civil War, and in World War II its volunteers worked in various humanitarian capacities, such as feeding the hungry in famine zones.

At home, the AFSC organized community-centered projects and worked for better housing and improved labor conditions. The AFSC was an early ally of the civil rights movement, and many members of the Fellowship of Reconciliation and CORE were Quakers, including Bayard Rustin.

In 1947, the AFSC was awarded the Nobel Peace Prize.

In the 1950s, the AFSC publicly supported Martin Luther King Jr. and sent members into the South on the freedom rides. They also became stalwarts of the peace movement.

Although never exclusively a civil rights organization, the AFSC worked as a tireless advocate while providing logistical support to the movement.

— October 4 —
1943
H. Rap Brown/Abdullah al-Amin Born in Louisiana

On this day in civil rights history, H. Rap Brown was born in Baton Rouge, Louisiana.

A student at Southern University when the sit-ins began in 1960, Brown was an early member of the Student Nonviolent Coordinating Committee. He soon became a full-time activist and in 1966 became SNCC's Alabama project director. After Stokeley Carmichael left SNCC in 1967, Brown became its national director.

Brown entered the civil rights movement as a pacifist dedicated to nonviolence. But by the late 1960s, years of frontline activism had made him a hard-line militant. "Violence is as American as cherry pie," he famously said. In 1968, Brown left SNCC and became minister of justice in the Black Panther Party.

Brown speaking
at press conference

Brown was imprisoned several times in the late 1960s and he made the FBI's ten most-wanted list after he evaded capture on charges of inciting a riot. In 1969, Brown expressed his feelings of persecution in a widely read autobiography, *Die, Nigger, Die.*

In 1971, Brown engaged in a shootout with New York City police. He was shot and arrested, then convicted of armed robbery and sentenced to 15 years in Attica Prison (that year, the Attica prison riot left 40 dead).

In prison, Brown converted to Islam, changing his name to Jamil Abdullah al-Amin. He began preaching for peace, speaking out against drugs, gambling, and violence of any kind. Paroled in 1976, Brown became a spiritual leader for the National Ummah, one of the largest U.S. Muslim groups. Al-Amin began community-building, opening mosques in low-income areas.

He opened his own grocery store in Atlanta's low-income West End community. Years passed, with Al-Amin remaining a devout Muslim cleric and community activist.

In 2000, two sheriff's deputies appeared at Al-Amin's store with an arrest warrant for a minor theft charge. According to later court testimony, Al-Amin opened fire on the two officers with an automatic rifle, injuring both. Prosecutors charged that while deputy Ricky Kinchen lay bleeding in the street, Al-Amin unloaded three bullets into his chest, killing him. During his trial, Al-Amin's lawyers claimed his innocence, saying his arrest was a case of mistaken identity combined with government persecution. In March 2003, Al-Amin was sentenced to life in prison without parole. The ruling is under appeal.

— OCTOBER 5 —

1928

CORE, SNCC ACTIVIST JAMES FORMAN BORN IN CHICAGO

On this day in civil rights history, James Forman was two days old after being born in Chicago, Illinois, the day before.

Forman spent much of his childhood with his grandparents in Mississippi. After school and four years in the military, Forman enrolled at the University of Southern California.

Forman became a writer for the *Chicago Defender* and in 1958 was in Little Rock to cover the continuing story of school desegregation at Central High School. Two years later, he joined the Congress for Racial Equality. While working for CORE in 1961, he was jailed with the freedom riders. Impressed by their passion and commitment, he moved south to join SNCC.

He was a decade older than most other SNCC staffers, and his organizational strengths quickly won recognition. From 1961 to 1965, Forman was SNCC's executive director. Under his and John Lewis's leadership, SNCC became a respected civil rights organization, sitting alongside SCLC and the NAACP as the major groups doing grass-roots organizing in the South. SNCC was edgier, younger, more aggressive, and more reckless.

Forman oversaw SNCC's expansion into voter registration projects in Mississippi, Georgia, and Alabama. Forman's efficiency kept the organization intact. He helped raise funds and organize logistics of transportation, housing, and food for field workers and bail for those arrested. Under his watch, the Albany campaign, the 1963 March on Washington, Mississippi Freedom Summer, and the Selma campaign all occurred.

Forman was not as committed philosophically to nonviolence as Lewis or the reverends at SCLC. He considered nonviolence an effective tool in the fight against segregation, but felt that self-defense was necessary. At the time, for this and other reasons, Forman was considered a militant voice within the movement, and he gave a number of fiery speeches, including the one in March 1965 where he threatened to knock the legs off the table of democracy if blacks couldn't sit at that table.

But in 1966, Forman, along with John Lewis, was purged from the organization he had helped build. Stokeley Carmichael, Ruby Doris Robinson, and H. Rap Brown edged Forman out of SNCC for not being militant enough. SNCC then fired all of its white members, and soon imploded from internal conflict and lack of support.

Forman wrote several books in the 1970s, while working for antipoverty and urban renewal programs. On January 10, 2005, James Forman died of cancer. He was 76.

— OCTOBER 6 —

1917

ACTIVIST FANNIE LOU HAMER BORN IN MISSISSIPPI

On this day in civil rights history, Fannie Lou Hamer was born to sharecropping parents, the youngest of their 20 children. She grew up in poverty and worked on a plantation, first with her family and later with her husband, Perry Hamer.

In August 1962, however, Hamer heard James Bevel of the SCLC give a sermon in Ruleville, Mississippi, calling for brave African Americans to register to vote. Hamer was the first to volunteer; the decision altered the course of her life and ultimately made her famous.

Fannie Lou Hamer

For her effort to register to vote, she and her family were promptly evicted from their sharecropper home.

SNCC activists Bob Moses and Charles McLaurin then recruited Hamer to travel around the South telling about her experiences. Though uneducated, Hamer was a charismatic speaker—a large woman with a large voice that packed emotion into the old spirituals she sang wherever she went.

On the way to a SNCC conference in June 1963, Hamer was jailed with a number of other activists in Winona, Mississippi, where she was systematically beaten over the course of an entire night. The assault was so savage she spent over a month in recovery.

Hamer returned to work afterwards, though, organizing and campaigning during the Freedom Vote and later during Mississippi Freedom Summer. But Hamer's greatest moment came during the 1964 Democratic National Convention, when, as vice chair of the Mississippi Freedom Democratic Party, she testified on live television to the brutality and inhumanity of Southern racists.

"I am sick and tired of being sick and tired," she said. "Is this America, the land of the free and the home of the brave where we have to sleep with our telephones off the hooks because our lives be threatened daily because we want to live as decent human beings—in America?"

The MFDP failed at the DNC to unseat the white Mississippi delegation, but the nation was watching and listening. Hamer pressed on. She ran for Congress twice and in 1968 attended the Democratic National Convention as a member of that previously all-white Mississippi delegation. She criticized the Vietnam War.

Hamer spent the rest of her life working in various grassroots programs, including the Poor People's Campaign. She died on March 14, 1977, in Mound Bayou, Mississippi.

— OCTOBER 7 —
1967
KILLERS OF THREE CIVIL RIGHTS WORKERS TRIED

On this day in civil rights history, 18 men were put on trial for federal charges of conspiracy to commit the 1964 murders of Andrew Goodman, James Chaney, and Michael Schwerner in Mississippi; there had been no convictions for the murders in state courts.

The judge assigned to the case was William Cox, well-known for his racist leanings. One of the 12 white jurors was a self-professed former Klan member. The prospect of a guilty verdict did not look good.

The chief prosecutor was John Doar. The FBI had accumulated lots of evidence, but the brunt of the case rested on the shoulders of James Jordan, who had been present at the killings, turned state's evidence, and was placed in the FBI's protective custody. Two other Klan informants, Delmar Dennis and Wallace Miller, also testified during the trial.

Doar presented a sharp case that the Klan had carried out a well-planned assassination of the three SNCC activists, with the deaths ordered by KKK leaders Sam Bowers and Edgar Ray Killen. The lead murderer was Wayne Roberts, while a dozen other Kluxers helped arm the killers, abduct the victims, and then hide the bodies. The nervous Jordan gave damning testimony about the details of the murder and the events leading up to it.

The defense appealed to the racist beliefs of the jury, relying on prejudice and stereotype. The resulting verdict was better than many observers had hoped for but was still sad and unjust.

Seven of the men, including Bowers, Roberts, and Sheriff's Deputy Cecil Price, were found guilty of conspiracy to commit murder. The others, including Killen and Sheriff Lawrence Rainey, were acquitted. Judge Cox handed down light sentences—the longest was ten years. Deputy Price, who had helped to cold-bloodedly murder three men, was paroled after just four years in prison.

"They killed a nigger, one Jew, and a white man—I gave them all I thought they deserved," Cox said later.

The federal government then considered the case closed. The state of Mississippi, however, would revisit the case three decades later.

— October 8 —
1963
'Dynamite Bob' Chambliss Acquitted in Birmingham

On this day in civil rights history, Robert Chambliss was found not guilty of the murder of four victims in the Sixteenth Street Baptist Church bombing in Birmingham, Alabama.

As evidence would show, Klansman Chambliss worked with at least three other men—Bobby Frank Cherry, Thomas Blanton, and Herman Cash—when he planted the 19 sticks of dynamite in the church.

The resulting deaths of four girls spurred President John F. Kennedy and later President Lyndon Johnson to pass the Civil Rights Act of 1964.

There were many killers and thugs in the Klan terrorist apparatus, but this wanton destruction of children in a church was a shocking example of premeditated racially motivated violence. Blacks, whites, civil rights leaders, and average citizens across the nation all wanted justice. It would be years before they would get it.

Chambliss (nicknamed "Dynamite Bob" for his alleged role in many bombings in Birmingham) was identified by witnesses as being at the scene of the crime near the time of the incident. When arrested, he was charged with murder and possession of more than 100 sticks of dynamite without a permit. The jury found him not guilty of the four murders, but did fine him $100 and sentence him to six months in prison on the other charges.

In 1974, a young prosecutor, Bill Baxley, who had been in law school at the time of the bombing, was elected attorney general of Alabama. Baxley reopened the case. His investigators requested FBI files on Chambliss and discovered much evidence that had not been used in the original trial. The FBI, it seemed, had suppressed evidence. Chambliss was retried by Baxley in 1977 and this time was convicted. He was 73. He refused to cooperate with the authorities, however, and did not name those who had worked with him. In 1985, Chambliss died in prison.

But the odyssey for justice was not over. The FBI announced on May 17, 2000, that the Sixteenth Street Baptist Church bombing had been the work of a KKK splinter group named the Cahaba Boys. Chambliss and Cash had died, but Cherry and Blanton were still alive. The state pressed charges and new trials were held. Both Blanton and Cherry were convicted. Cherry died in prison in November 2004.

— OCTOBER 9 —
1950
TEXAS ACTIVIST JUANITA CRAFT TRAINS A GENERATION

On this day in civil rights history, Juanita Craft continued to work with black youths in Dallas, training a whole generation of Texas activists.

Craft was born in Round Rock, Texas, in 1902. When she was 16, her mother died after a white hospital denied her treatment for tuberculosis. Craft then moved to Dallas and worked as a maid at the Adolphus Hotel.

In 1935, she joined the NAACP, becoming its Dallas membership chairwoman in 1942; three years later, she was named the NAACP Texas field organizer.

Dallas had fewer blacks than many Southern cities, but African Americans still made up close to 20 percent of the city's population. All of Texas, including Dallas, also had a large Mexican American population. Segregation was a fact of life for both ethnic groups. African Americans and Mexican Americans were excluded from public office, public schools, and public places. They were kept separated from each other as well; Texas cities had distinct white, black, and Mexican neighborhoods. Three separate school systems existed.

As field organizer, Craft formed more than 150 NAACP chapters. She traveled all over the state as a recruiter, often in the face of harassment and personal danger. In 1944, Craft was the first African American woman to vote in Dallas County; she was also the first black woman to be deputized to collect poll taxes. That year she began to help with the integration of the University of North Texas, and later the University of Texas Law School.

In 1946, Craft was appointed youth council adviser to the Dallas branch of the NAACP. She proved an excellent organizer and motivator of black youth, and soon other branches were following her example. She trained a generation of future black leaders, using her house as a school and recreation center.

As the movement began to take form in other cities in the South during the 1960s, Craft led sit-ins, boycotts, protests, and marches in the Dallas area; the youth council conducted much of the actual protesting. Craft emerged as a powerful local figure. Partially through her influence, Dallas avoided the racial violence that marked the era in so many cities.

Over her career, she met with presidents Kennedy, Johnson, Nixon, and Carter. She received numerous awards for her 50 years in the movement, including the Eleanor Roosevelt Humanitarian Award.

She died in 1985, at age 83.

— OCTOBER 10 —
2003
MINNESOTA MONUMENT REMEMBERS LYNCHING VICTIMS

On this date in civil rights history, a monument dedicated to three victims of lynching was unveiled in Duluth, Minnesota, in an attempt by the rust belt city to redress a grim page in its history.

In June 1920, the Duluth police incarcerated Elmer Jackson, Elias Clayton, and Isaac McGhie. Accused of raping a white woman, the three black circus workers waited in the dark while an enormous white mob formed outside the prison. The mob broke down the front door and held an impromptu "trial." Found "guilty," the three men were dragged from their cells into the street and beaten severely. Thousands watched as the three men were then hung from a lamppost in downtown Duluth. Photographers took photographs of the cheering crowd; later postcards of the grisly scene were circulated. The bodies were buried in unmarked graves.

Two months later, 19 men were indicted for their parts in the murders. A few were found guilty of inciting a riot and were sentenced to less than five years in prison. The rest went free.

The city's collective role in the murders festered in the minds of the black community, while the unspoken guilt was passed along to the next generations of whites. Around Duluth, the topic was taboo.

The story remained mostly ignored until the publication of *They Was Just Niggers* in 1979 (republished in 2000 as *The Lynchings in Duluth*). Duluth newspapers published articles on the mostly forgotten crime titled "Duluth's Lingering Shame." Duluth citizens formed a committee to face the past and admit the city's role, and plans were made to erect a plaque dedicated to the victims. In 2001, a small memorial service was held for the three men, and headstones were made to denote their passing.

Duluth Mayor Gary Doty and the rest of the city became involved. The plaque turned into an enormous wall. At the unveiling, prominent Duluth members apologized for their ancestors' roles in the killings. Huge letters marking the sidewalk in front of the monument read: "Compassion."

The monument stands as a new step in race relations in Duluth and across Minnesota, and as an example of America returning to face the widespread terrorism that marked the decades between Reconstruction and the civil rights movement.

— OCTOBER 11 —
1884
ELEANOR ROOSEVELT BORN

On this day in civil rights history, Eleanor Roosevelt—niece to President Theodore Roosevelt, future first lady of the United States, and lifelong activist for civil and human rights—was born in New York City.

In 1905, Eleanor married her cousin, Franklin Delano Roosevelt, both committed Democrats. They had six children together. In World War I, Franklin served as assistant secretary of the Navy while Eleanor worked as a Red Cross nurse.

In 1921, Franklin fell ill with polio. He would never regain full use of his legs. Eleanor nursed him back to health and encouraged him to reenter politics.

Mrs. Roosevelt became friends with Mary McLeod Bethune and Walter White and became a champion of civil rights. A committed women's rights suffragette, she also joined the League of Women Voters. When her husband was elected president in 1932, Mrs. Roosevelt became the most politically active first lady in U.S. history. She traveled around the country and abroad, campaigning for various progressive issues. She held press conferences, live radio broadcasts, and had a syndicated opinion column titled, "My Day."

In 1939, when the Daughters of the Revolution refused to allow Marian Anderson to sing in Constitution Hall, Roosevelt helped organize a performance for her at the Lincoln Memorial. That same year she also defied segregation in the South when she pointedly placed her chair in the aisle between the white and colored seating sections at Birmingham's Municipal Auditorium during the Southern Conference for Human Welfare.

Eleanor Roosevelt

Photo courtesy of Library of Congress

And in 1941, she showed her support for the Tuskegee Airmen by taking a flight in a training airplane piloted by one of the black instructors. Roosevelt pleaded with her husband to take a firm stand on civil rights, but, scared of losing the support of Southern Democrats, FDR remained aloof and did not give his support to an antilynching bill.

After FDR died, Mrs. Roosevelt remained a committed activist and was chairperson for the United Nations Committee on Human Rights. She helped draft the Universal Declaration of Human Rights. At the UN on December 10, 1948, she called the Declaration "the international Magna Carta of all mankind." She remained involved in national and international affairs throughout the 1950s. She never stopped pushing for civil rights.

On November 7, 1962, Eleanor Roosevelt, called by President Harry Truman "the first lady of the world," died from complications of tuberculosis. She was 78.

— October 12 —
1875
Penn School Imparts Knowledge to Freed Slaves

On this day in civil rights history, the Penn School in South Carolina was teaching freed slaves to read, write, and do arithmetic.

Founded in 1862, the Penn School, named after William Penn, was part of the Port Royal Experiment, a Quaker-led philanthropic venture to help educate ex-slaves on the South Carolina Sea Islands who were freed at the beginning of the Civil War. The school's founders, Laura Towne and Ellen Murray, taught in a one-room schoolhouse on St. Helena Island. But the students were so excited about learning that they quickly outgrew their meager classroom, and the Penn School started to grow. More teachers arrived, including Charlotte Forten, the first African American teacher in the program.

With its white and black staff, the Penn School was one of the first interracial facilities in the South.

Murray and Towne worked on St. Helena Island for 40 years as teachers, organizers, and administrators. In 1900, the school became more trade-oriented, changing its name to the Penn Normal, Industrial and Agricultural School, following the Booker T. Washington example of teaching self-sufficiency. The new Penn School taught cobbling, carpentry, and other practical skills.

In 1949, the school closed, but it remained a community-focused institution as the Penn Community Services Center.

In the 1960s, the Penn Center, tucked away in relative isolation and safety, was chosen by the SCLC as a training site, retreat center, and base of strategic planning. Here Martin Luther King and his lieutenants planned many SCLC campaigns.

In 1974, the Penn Center was designated a historic landmark. Nowadays, the Penn Center's mission mostly focuses on the preservation of Geechee, or Gullah—the hybrid of African, European, and American culture similar to the Creole—through art, film, and the written word. It remains an important cultural and educational institution.

— OCTOBER 13 —
1961
KENTUCKY CIVIL RIGHTS COMMISSION FIGHTS THE GOOD FIGHT

On this day in civil rights history, the Kentucky Commission on Civil Rights continued to work toward integration.

The first state whose constitution institutionalized slavery, and a border state during the Civil War, Kentucky at one point had two rival governments, as half of the state aligned with the Confederacy and fought the other half, which remained loyal to the union.

In 1914, the NAACP opened a branch in Louisville to protest lynching and racial violence. It immediately began to work against housing ordinances that maintained rigidly segregated neighborhoods. Louisville grew into one of America's largest cities.

As World War II wound down, Kentucky proved to be progressive by Southern standards. In 1948, the Kentucky public library desegregated. One year later, the University of Kentucky admitted black students to its graduate schools. And in 1950, hospitals across the state were integrated after an African American youth was denied medical treatment and died.

But public places remained segregated. In 1960, CORE students began to hold demonstrations and sit-ins at lunch counters, department stores, and movie theaters, while the SCLC held a rally for a voter-registration drive. That same year, the Kentucky legislature created the Kentucky Commission on Civil Rights "to continue fair treatment, to foster mutual understanding and respect among, and to discourage discrimination against any racial or ethnic group of its members." The KCCR prohibited discrimination in state employment. A series of fairly progressive governors mostly controlled civil rights–related violence in the turbulent era.

In 1961, a boycott called "Nothing New for Easter" was enacted against white businesses that remained segregated.

The major obstacle in Louisville, and Kentucky at large, was housing. Activists began to focus on the issue, pushing for a bill in the state legislature.

In the biggest event in Kentucky's movement, in 1964, Martin Luther King Jr., Mahalia Jackson, Wyatt Walker, Ralph Abernathy, and Jackie Robinson, among others, led a demonstration of more than 10,000 people in Frankfurt, the state capital, in support of a public-accommodations bill.

In 1966, Kentucky passed the Kentucky Civil Rights Act, called by King "the strongest and most important comprehensive civil rights bill passed by a Southern state." Kentucky went on to pass fair-housing laws. Kentucky later struggled with school-busing issues in the 1970s, but the state never suffered as much violence or resistance to the movement as most other states in the South.

— OCTOBER 14 —
1998
CONFEDERATE FLAG CONTROVERSY IN SOUTH CAROLINA

On this day in civil rights history, debate continued over the Confederate flag that adorned the South Carolina state capitol. African Americans wanted the flag taken down; many white South Carolinians wanted it to remain.

The largely symbolic struggle has its roots in the history of South Carolina, stained by slavery, warfare, and oppression. South Carolina served as a major entry point for incoming Africans shipped across the Atlantic as slaves. South Carolina was also the first state to secede from the Union, and was where the Civil War officially began.

Flag incites controversy

At the turn of the 20th century, South Carolina elected "Pitchfork Ben" Tillman as governor. Tillman was a progressive candidate in some ways, but he was a vehement racist and white supremacist who enacted harsh Jim Crow laws across the state. He said in a famous speech, "We of the South have never recognized the right of the Negro to govern white men, and we never will. We have never believed him to be equal to the white man, and we will not submit to his gratifying his lust on our wives and daughters without lynching him."

Strom Thurmond carried on this virulent tradition, first as governor of the state and later as senator.

In 1962, the all-white South Carolina legislature voted to place the Confederate Flag at the top of the capitol building, in defiance of the civil rights movement. At the time, South Carolina civil rights leaders, such as Joseph De Laine, were more concerned with equal protection under the law than with the flag. But in the 1990s, NAACP state president James Galman called for its removal. The state lawmakers refused. In 2000, the National Urban League, PUSH, and the NAACP called for a tourism boycott of the state until the flag came down. The boycott worked. Conventions, meetings, and athletic events were relocated. In April, lawmakers voted to take the flag down, amidst pro- and anti-flag protests.

The issue remains contentious. The flag was moved to another prominent location, where it waves to this day. In the 2004 presidential election, the issue was a question in the debates.

A similar controversy occurred in Georgia, where the state flag contained a portion of the Confederate flag; in Alabama, where the rebel flag flew over the capitol until it was removed in the 1990s; and in Mississippi, where the Ole Miss nickname was the Rebels and the Confederate battle flag was waved wildly at football games starred in by black players, the flag was gradually removed.

— OCTOBER 15 —

1966

BLACK PANTHER PARTY OFFICIALLY ORGANIZED

On this day in civil rights history, the Black Panther Party officially came into being.

The organization was the brainchild of Bobby Seale and Huey Newton, two burgeoning black intellectuals in Oakland, California. The original name was the Black Panther Party for Self Defense, which the founders took from the Lowndes County Freedom Organization, a black political party in central Alabama that used a black panther as its ballot symbol.

Unveiling a radical manifesto for the new organization and a call to self-determination, Newton and Seale began recruiting around Oakland for members. Their 10-point plan demanded full employment for African Americans; decent, affordable housing; a fair and balanced education; universal exemption from military service; an end to police brutality; release of all black prisoners; and "land, bread, housing, education, clothing, justice, and peace." Seale was the public speaker, Newton the writer and thinker, and they proved to be effective partners. Membership in the BBP swelled in just a few years to thousands.

Widespread dissatisfaction over the slow pace of integration in the United States led many black youths to embrace the self-empowerment and black pride the BPP offered. African Americans were tired of waiting for decent jobs, decent housing, and fair pay. To urban blacks, the nonviolent message of the SCLC rang hollow. In contrast, the Panthers' message was that freedom would never be granted by the oppressor; it had to be taken by force.

Black Panther convention

The BPP was a combination of paramilitary group and political party. Its leaders gave themselves titles like Minister of Defense and Minister of Education. The high-ranking members of the BPP eventually included Newton, Bobby Seale, James Forman, Eldridge Cleaver, David Hilliard, George Mason Murray, Stokely Carmichael, Elaine Brown, Angela Davis, and H. Rap Brown.

The Black Panthers would go on to experience a brief but explosive history, complete with community programs and progressive ideas but also with ideological infighting, gunfights with police, and high-profile criminal trials.

— OCTOBER 16 —

1995

'MILLION MAN MARCH' IN D.C.

On this date in civil rights history, upwards of 900,000 African Americans, mostly men, held a rally in Washington, D.C., that had been promoted as "the Million Man March." The name stuck.

Black organizations struggled in the mid-1990s. The NAACP suffered from a controversy over mismanaged funds, SNCC and the Panthers were long gone, SCLC was trying to find new leadership and a new role for itself, no one was quite sure what Jesse Jackson's PUSH stood for, and no strong leader had emerged in the 25 years since Martin Luther King's death to take his place. Yet as the recent Rodney King riots in Los Angeles had shown, there was still deep racial division in the United States.

The Million Man March was the brainchild of Nation of Islam leader Louis Farrakhan. Originally a militant racist and a zealous follower of Elijah Muhammad, Farrakhan in the mid-1990s softened his speeches and began to focus more on community-building. His march was conceived to combat the negative images of blacks in the media, confront the crisis of urban black living, and bring together hundreds of thousands of black men to commit themselves to work for the betterment of their communities.

On the appointed day, black men from all walks of life—bankers, lawyers, gang members, and blue-collar workers—traveled to Washington from across the country. It was a spiritual, positive event, and one of the largest rallies in U.S. history.

White politicians distanced themselves from the event, mostly because they were wary of Farrakhan's controversial history. The success of the march temporarily bolstered the Nation of Islam's profile in the African American community.

Speakers during the day's events included Cornel West, Isaac Hayes, Jesse Jackson, Maya Angelou, Queen Mother Moore, M. C. Hammer, Rosa Parks, Stevie Wonder, and Farrakhan. Other civil rights leaders attending included C. V. Smith, Al Sharpton, Wyatt Walker, and Martin Luther King III. The energetic tone of the day and the absence of violence left the organizers calling the event a triumph, a return to the glory days of the movement.

However, many women activists, including Myrlie Evers-Williams and Angela Davis, felt slighted by the male-centric event. A Million Woman March took shape, and on October 25, 1997, more than 500,000 women, mostly African American, took part in a day of unity and celebration in Philadelphia. Maxine Waters, Sister Souljah, and Winnie Mandela were among the day's speakers.

— OCTOBER 17 —

1960

DEPARTMENT STORES INTEGRATE LUNCH COUNTERS

On this day in civil rights history, Woolworth, Grant, Kresge, and McCrory announced they would desegregate their lunch counters and department stores across the country, after student-led protests crippled their businesses.

In February 1960, students in Greensboro, North Carolina, and later in Nashville, Tennessee, embarked on a "sit-in" campaign to desegregate lunch counters in their cities. The first four black students to participate in the first sit-in—Ezell Blair Jr., David Richmond, Joseph McNeil, and Franklin McCain—formed the Student Executive Committee for Justice and began recruiting more students for what was becoming a campaign. The strategy was simple. Black and white students would sit at the whites-only lunch counter and order coffee and food, refusing to leave until they were served. The first sit-in protesters were assaulted, humiliated, or arrested, but soon hundreds of students were taking their place.

Although it began as a student movement, other civil rights organizations quickly recognized the momentum of the sit-in campaign. At the end of February 1960, CORE and the SCLC called for a nationwide boycott of Woolworth's stores (Woolworth was targeted because it had the most stores at that time). All over the country, picket lines formed in front of Woolworth stores. The issue soon spread beyond simple segregation; protesters demanded that blacks be given jobs in the national chains.

The protest spread to Kress department stores, Grant's and Kresge's dime stores, and McCrory's clothing outlets. Direct action combined with an economic boycott proved an effective tool. Negative publicity combined with the boycott and the picketing resulted in slipping profits. In response, Woolworth and the others issued an announcement: they would integrate all of their stores.

Unlike the municipal governments in the South, the white businesses quickly saw the wisdom in integration and followed through with their promises. Segregation would continue on a local business level, but the national entrepreneurs exorcised public discrimination from their companies.

— OCTOBER 18 —

1945

PAUL ROBESON RECEIVES SPRINGARN MEDAL

On this day in civil rights history, actor-activist Paul Robeson received the Springarn medal from the NAACP.

Born in Princeton, New Jersey, in 1898, Robeson graduated high school with honors in 1915. Granted an athletic scholarship, he attended Rutgers University, where he distinguished himself on the field as a football All-American, and in the classroom where he was Phi Beta Kappa and class valedictorian.

"Othello" with Paul Robeson

Robeson had proven he could do just about anything as he moved to Harlem after graduating. He enrolled at Columbia University Law School and was one of the first African Americans to get a law degree from the prestigious university. Athlete, lawyer, and scholar, Robeson reportedly could speak in 20 languages. But poised on the brink of a promising legal career, Robeson was drawn to the stage.

He got a few small parts here and there, including a prominent role in the historic 1922 musical *Shuffle Along*. Soon he was acting in numerous productions, and his deep, strong voice made him a well-known singer of spirituals. With his newfound fame, Robeson entered the movie business, acting in a number of early films, such as *Show Boat* and *The Emperor Jones*.

In the early 1930s, Robeson and his family moved to England, where he became a renowned stage actor and movie star, as well as a popular bass singer. He returned to the United States in 1939, immediately joining leftist political movements—including the Council on African Affairs, with W. E. B. DuBois, and the American Communist Party. Outspoken and undaunted, Robeson used his fame to criticize American policy, both abroad and at home. As a regular visitor to the Soviet Union, Robeson became enthralled by the possibilities of Soviet-style communism.

His politics made him a target in the 1950s for the House Un-American Activities Committee. He was blacklisted by Hollywood, investigated by the FBI, and had his passport revoked. In 1958, when his passport was reinstated, he moved back to England.

In 1961, after praising the Soviet Union with increasing alacrity and attacking any of its critics with invective, Robeson tried to commit suicide in a Moscow hotel room. He survived to return to live in the United States, where he suffered from severe depression for the rest of his life.

In 1976, Paul Robeson died. He was 77.

— OCTOBER 19 —

1936

ACTIVIST, ORGANIZER JAMES BEVEL BORN IN MISSISSIPPI

On this day in civil rights history, James Bevel was born in Ittabena, Mississippi.

After serving in the military, Bevel landed in Nashville, Tennessee, enrolling in the American Baptist Theological Seminary. In Nashville, Bevel came under the leadership of James Lawson, who led workshops in nonviolent resistance. Lawson trained a core group of dedicated students, including Bevel, John Lewis, Diane Nash, and Marion Barry, among others. In 1960, they began participating in the student sit-in movement.

Bevel married Diane Nash, and the two formed a dynamic duo for the movement. In 1961, when the first freedom rides were halted by violence in Alabama, Bevel and Nash were key to restarting them.

Bevel joined the staff of the SCLC in the early 1960s, and risked his life to register voters in the Mississippi Delta and elsewhere. Bevel was a passionate public speaker and a fearless, larger-than-life activist. He was soon one of Martin Luther King Jr.'s most trusted advisers.

Bevel's shining moment in the movement was in 1963, when he arrived in Birmingham to help Fred Shuttlesworth and King in the stalled Birmingham campaign. While the various factions debated strategy, Bevel led the "Children's Crusade" that captured the attention of the media and steered the campaign to victory.

The next year, Bevel, Nash, and James Orange began working on a voter project called the Alabama campaign that led to the Selma-to-Montgomery March.

Bevel played an important role in many of the biggest SCLC campaigns: the 1963 March on Washington, the 1965 Selma-to-Montgomery March, the 1966 Chicago campaign, and in 1968, the Memphis sanitation workers strike and the Poor People's Campaign. Near the end of the 1960s, Bevel also became involved in the antiwar movement in opposition to the Vietnam war.

Nash and Bevel eventually divorced, but they have two children together.

Bevel left the SCLC in 1969. He founded the Making of a Man clinic in 1970, and in the 1980s he founded Students for Education and Economic Development. He is currently pastor of a multidenominational church in Chicago.

— October 20 —
1933
Scottsboro Cases Removed from Judge Horton's Court

On this day in civil rights history, the cases of the Scottsboro Boys were removed from the docket of Judge James Horton, and reassigned to a judge less likely to be a maverick from the 1933 standards of Alabama justice.

Horton had offended the sensibilities of Alabama's other white judges, white prosecutors, white jurors, white lawmen, and white citizens in these cases when, on June 22, 1933, he had set aside the rape conviction of Scottsboro Boy Haywood Patterson because he was convinced the case against Patterson was a lie.

Horton presided over that earlier trial and had seen the all-white jurors disregard overwhelming testimony supporting Patterson's innocence. In addition, Horton knew that additional exculpatory evidence had been suppressed by the prosecution. So in response to defense attorney Sam Liebowitz's motion for a new trial, Horton stunned his fellow white citizens of north Alabama by vacating Patterson's death sentence and ordering a retrial.

The next year, Horton was defeated for reelection and his career as a judge was over.

Meanwhile, Alabama officials reassigned the Scottsboro Boy cases to a different judge, William Callahan, who presided over a November 1933 retrial. In his instructions to the jury at the close of the case, Callahan told them they were to presume as a matter of law that no white woman in Alabama would voluntarily have sex with a black man.

Predictably, Patterson was again convicted and again sentenced to death, as was Clarence Norris, the next of the nine defendants to be retried. The other seven cases were then put on hold pending the appeals for Patterson and Norris.

The U.S. Supreme Court heard the appeals on February 15, 1935. One of the defense arguments was that blacks were excluded from juries in Alabama, thus denying black defendants their constitutional rights to a trial by a jury of their peers. Liebowitz argued that jury rolls introduced at trial and allowed as evidence by Judge Callahan had been forged. He brought in the rolls and a magnifying case and presented them to the Supreme Court justices, who one by one examined the documents. Observers reported that disgust and disbelief were apparent on the faces of the justices.

A few weeks later, in *Norris v. Alabama,* the Supreme Court declared Alabama's jury selection system to be unconstitutional and again reversed the convictions of Haywood and Norris.

New trials were set for 1936.

— OCTOBER 21 —
1955
MARY LOUISE SMITH ARRESTED FOR BUS-SEATING VIOLATION

On this day in civil rights history, Mary Louise Smith, an 18-year-old black woman, was arrested for refusing to give up her seat on a Montgomery City Lines bus to a white passenger. This was, of course, six weeks before Rosa Parks was arrested for the same offense.

In fact, African American riders were often involved in incidents on the buses. For various reasons, none before Parks became the rallying point for a mass boycott of the buses. Smith did not, partly because her father insisted that she pay her fine and drop the matter. In February 1956, however, after the bus boycott had failed to win even modest compromises from white city officials, attorney Fred Gray filed a federal lawsuit challenging the entire system of segregation on the buses. Mary Louise Smith then became one of the plaintiffs in that case, *Browder v. Gayle*. On May 11, 1956, Smith took the witness stand. Gray's law partner, Charles Langford, questioned her about her arrest the previous October, and she responded:

"Well, this particular incident took place on Highland Avenue bus. I was sitting on the bus side reserved for 'white and colored.' I was sitting behind the sign that said for 'colored.' At this partiular moment a white lady got on the bus and she asked the bus driver to tell me to move out of my seat for her to sit there and he asked me to move three times. And I refused. So he got up and said he would call the cops. And he asked me move. And I told him, 'I am not going to move out of my seat. I am not going to move anywhere. I got the privilege to sit here like anybody else does.' So he say I was under arrest, and he took me to the station."

Langford: "What happened after that?"

"Well, they arrested me and they kept me in jail for about two hours or more longer, and then they charged me five dollars and cost of court."

Langford: "You are a Negro and you were required to move from that seat to allow a white woman to sit down?"

"That's right."

Langford: "Would you ride the buses again [the boycott was then in effect] if the laws were changed?"

"I would ride provided we had no segregation on the buses."

On June 5, the judges listening to Smith's testimony ruled in her favor by a 2–1 vote. On November 13, the U.S. Supreme Court upheld the lower-court ruling, and on December 20, U.S. marshals served city officials with an injunction barring further segregation on the city buses. On December 21, Martin Luther King Jr., Rosa Parks, and other boycott leaders again boarded the city buses. And so did Mary Louise Smith.

— October 22 —
1859
John Brown's Revolt Crushed

On this day in civil rights history, John Brown lay wounded in a Virginia jail, his revolution a failure.

Born in Connecticut in 1800, Brown was a staunch abolitionist from the beginning. As a young man, he began a series of businesses, finding his most success with a tannery. But in 1831, he fell on hard times. Soon he was struggling with debt. During this period, many of his children died from dysentery and other illnesses.

John Brown

Faced with bankruptcy, Brown abandoned business and became a revolutionary. His antislavery fervor brought him into abolitionist circles. He met all the major abolitionist figures of the era, including Harriett Tubman, Frederick Douglass, Henry David Thoreau, Ralph Waldo Emerson, and William Lloyd Garrison. Rail-thin with stern eyes and wild hair, Brown was a scary, inspiring figure—a zealot with nerves of steel.

Brown's early plan involved establishing a mountain fortress in the Allegheny Mountains, waging guerilla raids onto plantations, and returning to the base with new recruits culled from the freed slaves.

In 1856, however, he went west where he and his sons killed five pro-slavery settlers in Kansas. Brown's guerilla action was in response to the killings of antislavery settlers by pro-slavery forces. Brown became a national figure and a wanted criminal. One year later he traveled secretly in the North, raising funds for his next campaign.

His plan was daring but touched with madness. He would raid a federal arsenal and use the weapons to supply slaves who would revolt, inspired by his brilliance. He put the word out and expected thousands to heed his call; only 21 men did.

On October 16, Brown and his small band, including three of his sons, descended on the town of Harper's Ferry. They quickly captured the armory and gathered hostages. A firefight between Brown's raiders and local militiamen broke out. By the morning of the 18th, the U.S. government had dispatched troops, led by Lt. Col. Robert E. Lee.

Brown and a few of his men barricaded themselves inside a small engine house. Lee gave Brown a last chance to surrender: "Are you ready to surrender, and trust the mercy of the government?"

"No," he replied, "I prefer to die here."

Marines broke down the door. In the fighting, Brown was stabbed through his torso, but he was captured alive.

— OCTOBER 23 —

1948

JESSE LEROY BROWN BECOMES FIRST BLACK NAVAL AVIATOR

On this day in civil rights history, Jesse LeRoy Brown earned his wings as a naval aviator, becoming the U.S. Navy's first black pilot.

Earlier that year, President Harry Truman had desegregated the military with his Executive Order 9981. Some in the military leadership disliked what they saw as social meddling from their civilian commander-in-chief. But the armed forces grudgingly followed orders.

There were pockets of segregation, however, that were difficult to pierce. The officer barrier was one; blacks struggled at the beginning to become ranking officers. Flying was another. Despite the success of the Tuskegee Airmen in World War II, many white officers held the bigoted view that black pilots could not be as good as white pilots in combat.

Jesse LeRoy Brown, born in Hattiesburg, Mississippi, in 1926, enlisted in the Naval Reserve in 1946. His dream was to fly. Brown was the only black cadet to enter flight school in Pensacola, Florida, alongside 100 white applicants.

Like other African Americans in the military, he encountered racism from fellow soldiers and apathy from the command. If a black man wanted to fly in the Navy, he would get no help. Brown responded by excelling and was one of only six in his cadet class to graduate. In 1948, he was granted his wings, and one year later won his commission as ensign.

In Korea, the United States and the Soviet Union each occupied half of the conquered country after World War II. Both superpowers installed governments friendly to their policies. In 1948, the United Nations tried to oversee popular elections, but the Soviet Union refused to honor the results. Communist North Korea, headed by General Secretary Kim Il Sung, invaded South Korea in June 1950. The United States, joined by 15 UN member countries, sent troops to the region, led by U.S. Army General Douglas MacArthur. The Korean War had begun. As it was the first conflict after Executive Order 9981, it would be the first war fought by a desegregated U.S. military.

Brown flew an F4U-4 Corsair jet during the Korean War. Flying in the Chosin campaign at the end of 1950, Brown was hit by strafing fire and crashed to his death. He was posthumously awarded the Distinguished Flying Cross, and in 1973, a U.S. warship was named in his honor.

1947

DU BOIS SPEAKS TO UNITED NATIONS ON COLONIZATION ISSUES

On this day in civil rights history, W. E. B. Du Bois addressed the United Nations on behalf of the NAACP and of blacks living across the globe.

Du Bois organized a petition to call attention to the socioeconomic problems facing colonized peoples all over the world. He titled his petition: "Statement on the denial of human rights to minorities in the case of citizens of Negro descent in the United States of America and an appeal to the United Nations for redress."

Photo courtesy of Library of Congress

Du Bois

Leaders in Africa and parts of Asia offered their support. U.S. policymakers, uneasy over the nation's reputation abroad in the new war against communism, were understandably worried. Leveraging for influence against the Soviet Union in Latin America, Asia, and Africa, the United States' leadership did not want to appear oppressive at home.

The Cold War had a chilling effect on the civil rights movement. The FBI continually harassed leftist civil rights leaders. But presidents Truman, Eisenhower, Kennedy, Johnson, and Nixon were all engaged in a covert war, and thus needed to eliminate the appearances of racism in U.S. society. Meanwhile, the Soviet Union used Jim Crow segregation and racial violence in the U.S. in much of their propaganda.

The U.S. presidents tried to balance the risk of angering white Southern voters with civil rights actions against the risk of losing international support if they ignored civil rights issues. The presidents thus correctly saw the civil rights movement as a threat to pro-democracy perceptions that the United States worked so hard to foster abroad.

The Cold War, then, both hurt and helped the movement. It helped by applying another level of pressure on the president and his cabinet, while also guaranteeing international attention to domestic confrontations involving SCLC, CORE, SNCC, and NAACP. But anti-communist hysteria was used against the civil rights organizations.

Other leaders followed Du Bois's lead, attempting to use international law to curb racism at home. In 1951, Paul Robeson accused the United States of practicing genocide against African Americans through slavery and segregation and asked the UN to intercede, calling for reparations. Malcolm X also made appeals to the UN.

The United States successfully avoided UN sanctions. But each time an African American spoke out against the U.S. government to the international community, the nation lost credibility in world opinion.

— OCTOBER 25 —

1958

YOUTH MARCH FOR SCHOOL INTEGRATION IN D.C.

On this day in civil rights history, A. Philip Randolph, Jackie Robinson, Coretta Scott King, and Harry Belafonte led the first youth march for integrated schools in Washington, D.C.

After the momentous ruling of *Brown v. Board*, the NAACP recognized that Southern schools would not desegregate without a fight. But the mainstream media was framing the discourse unfairly, portraying the NAACP and other civil rights organizations as either a very vocal minority or worse, under the control of communist agents.

Randolph, who more than any contemporary leader knew how to harness the power of mass protests, came up with the idea of a march of black and white students to combat this smear against the movement. Randolph envisioned a coalition of students from all over the country to march on Washington to submit a resolution to President Dwight Eisenhower. Randolph asked Bayard Rustin and Frank Crosswaith to be the organizers.

The march was also intended to show that middle America supported integration. The NAACP became involved. Flyers and letters began to circulate.

Older citizens support youth march

More than 10,000 students participated. Colleges, church groups, and civic organizations responded with gusto. The demonstration, led by Belafonte, began near the White House. Thousands of students paraded down Constitution Avenue to the Lincoln Memorial. Eisenhower refused to meet with the youth delegation, but the rally went on. Coretta Scott King spoke in her husband's absence:

"There is a unique element in this demonstration; it is a young people's march. You are proving that the youth of America is freeing itself of the prejudices of an older and darker time in our history. . . . Keep marching and show the pessimists and the weak of spirit that they are wrong. Keep marching and resist injustice with the firm, nonviolent spirit you demonstrated today. . . . The future belongs, not to those who slumber or sleep, but to those who cannot rest while the evil of injustice thrives in the bosom of America. The future belongs to those who march toward freedom."

The march brought students and young people into the movement. Another march was planned for spring of the following year.

On this day in civil rights history, Mahalia Jackson, one of the greatest gospel singers, was born in New Orleans. Her voice and spirit eventually would inspire the civil rights movement.

She grew up in the historic "Black Pearl" neighborhood of New Orleans, surrounded by the city's blossoming jazz and rhythm and blues. From almost the time she could walk and talk, Jackson sang at Mount Moriah Baptist Church.

In 1927, Jackson moved to Chicago. She worked as a laundress but also continued singing in Baptist churches. Soon, she was touring churches all over the country, belting out her inimitable music while shaking her body and shouting and clapping her hands. She began singing with the Johnson Brothers, one of the earliest professional gospel groups.

Photo courtesy of Library of Congress

Mahalia Jackson

A decade later, Jackson started her solo career with Decca Records and then with Apollo Records and had a few modest successes. In 1948, she hit the big time with her record, "Move On Up a Little Higher." She was soon an international star, a favorite with white and black audiences. She won awards in France and Norway. She played Carnegie Hall.

Jackson's mainstream success earned her a radio show and a new record deal with Columbia Records. But she stuck with Christian gospel music, refusing to sing secular songs. She saw her career as mission work. "Anybody that sings the blues is in a deep pit, yelling for help," she once said. Although she did not sing jazz or blues, she incorporated their styles into her gospel music.

She sang at many important events, including the inauguration of President John F. Kennedy and the 1963 March on Washington for Jobs and Freedom, where she sang an old Negro spiritual from slavery times. She also regularly sang at fundraising rallies.

In 1968, she sang at the funeral of her friend, Martin Luther King Jr.

As time passed, gospel's popularity waned and Jackson's career declined. She retired from music in 1971 and died a year later in Chicago from heart failure. More than 50,000 people attended her funeral.

— OCTOBER 27 —

1924

BIRTH OF RUBY DEE, PARTNER TO OSSIE DAVIS

On this day in civil rights history, actress and civil rights campaigner Ruby Dee was born. A distinguished actress, Dee shared a lifetime of activism and one of Hollywood's greatest love stories with her husband, actor Ossie Davis. From their first meeting in 1946, the two maintained a loving marriage while hurdling social, artistic, and racial barriers.

Dee and Davis were both well-recognized actors and members of the NAACP, CORE, SNCC, and SCLC. A sign of their significance to the movement was their selection to be co-masters of ceremony at the 1963 March on Washington. They were friends with both Martin Luther King Jr. and Malcolm X.

Ruby Dee

In February of 1965, Davis delivered the eulogy for the slain Malcolm X: "Malcolm had stopped being a Negro years ago. It had become too small, too puny, too weak a word for him. Malcolm was bigger than that. Malcolm had become an Afro-American, and he wanted—so desperately—that we, that all his people, would become Afro-Americans, too . . . And we will know him then for what he was and is—a prince—our own black shining prince!—who didn't hesitate to die, because he loved us so."

In 1968, Davis delivered a second eulogy, this time for King.

Of course, Dee and Davis were among many black celebrities to participate in the movement. Nat King Cole, Sam Cooke, Mahalia Jackson, Jackie Wilson, Nina Simone, Josephine Baker, Jerry Butler, John Coltrane, and Curtis Mayfield, among others, were all vocal supporters and ardent fundraisers. Sammy Davis Jr. singlehandedly raised hundreds of thousands of dollars for civil rights work. Dick Gregory was shot, arrested, and incarcerated while taking part in sit-ins, protests, and marches. Sidney Poitier and Harry Belafonte were almost killed by the Klan.

Like their white counterparts, black entertainers risked much by involving themselves, and many times wanted to be even more involved than they were. Dee and Davis played crucial roles in the movement.

In February 2005, America lost one of its wisest voices when Ossie Davis died of a heart attack. He was 87. Ruby Dee, now in her 80s, continues in his absence. Their joint autobiography was published in 2000.

— October 28 —
1859
John Brown Convicted, Hanged

On this day in civil rights history, John Brown underwent his second day of trial on charges of treason, murder, and conspiring with slaves. His wounds from the battle at Harper's Ferry were serious enough that at times he had to lie down in the courtroom.

Despite an impressive array of lawyers who put up a spirited defense, Brown was doomed and he knew it.

The stoic Brown attended the trial and seemed calm and collected. After prosecution and defense completed their cases, he gave a closing statement:

"If it is deemed necessary that I should forfeit my life for the furtherance of the end of justice and mingle my blood further with the blood of my children and with the blood of millions in this slave country whose rights are disregarded by wicked, cruel, and unjust enactments, I say, let it be done."

On November 2, Brown was found guilty and sentenced to be hung one month later.

For the month of November, Brown dominated the national discourse. Abolitionist forces coalesced around his cause. Brown wrote many letters from his cell, declaring his unwavering belief in the rightness of his cause. There were rumors of a planned rescue attempt, but Brown deflected such talk, saying he chose to remain in custody.

On the morning of December 2, Brown readied himself to die. "I, John Brown," he wrote that morning, "am now quite certain that the crimes of this guilty land will never be purged away but with blood."

More than 2,000 spectators assembled as Brown kissed a slave child on the way from his cell and walked calmly to the gallows. He thanked his executioners (including guard John Wilkes Booth) and was hanged.

Brown's failed raid and subsequent martyrdom accelerated the course toward civil war. North and South recognized in the other divergent and intractable interests and values. To protect itself from other abolitionist crusaders, the South began forming militias that later would become the Confederate Army. The abolitionists, meanwhile, pushed harder for the end of slavery.

In the South, Brown was considered a madman; in the North, he was called a hero.

— October 29 —
1969
Supreme Court Shuts Door on Integration Delays

On this day in civil rights history, the U.S. Supreme Court ruled again on the issue of school desegregation, in the case *Alexander v. Board of Education,* or *Brown* III.

Despite *Brown* I and II, Southern schools remained mostly segregated. In some cities, it was de facto segregation that left public schools divided along color lines due to residential patterns. And most Southern states had refused to cooperate. Enforcing or applying the *Brown* ruling appeared impossible. The states blamed the counties. The counties passed the blame to the local school boards. The bureaucratic web of "all deliberate speed" appeared to be impenetrable. "It means slow," NAACP attorney Thurgood Marshall later said.

Only a handful of public schools integrated in the late 1950s. The Southern states' intransigence continued into the late 1960s. It became clear that public school integration would not happen without stricter guidelines.

Jack Greenberg argued the *Alexander* case for the NAACP Legal Defense Fund, aided by James Nabrit, Norman Amaker, Melvyn Zarr, and Charles Black Jr.

After hearing the arguments, the Supreme Court, with Thurgood Marshall now a justice, declared that "no person is to be effectively excluded from any school because of race or color." The ruling required immediate desegregation. The stalling tactics of many Southern school boards would no longer be tolerated and dual school systems had to be abolished at once.

With their legal options exhausted, hold-out school districts finally complied. For a few years in the early 1970s, school desegregation finally was achieved in most areas. For the most part, the process went smoothly.

Still, the Supreme Court did not outline the explicit ways in which school districts could or should integrate. The justices left the process up to the states. In many districts, the court orders prompted controversial forced busing in an effort to counterbalance white flight to the suburbs. Meanwhile, thousands of private so-called "seg academies" sprang up in Southern school districts where the public schools would have been predominantly black after merger.

Over the next two decades, resegregation occurred due to the combined effects of residential patterns, increased private school enrollments, the curtailment of busing, and a withdrawal of federal emphasis on desegregation.

The problems of race, public education, and equality did not disappear, as civil rights advocates had hoped. At the beginning of the 21st century, some school districts, especially in the South, were almost as segregated as they were in the 1950s.

— October 30 —

1959

Juanita Stout, Pioneering Pennsylvania Judge, Completes First Week on the Bench

On this day in civil rights history, Juanita Stout finished her first week as the first African American female judge of the Common Pleas Court in Philadelphia. It was one of many pioneering steps in a remarkable legal career.

Born in Wewoka, Oklahoma, in 1919, Stout grew up in a segregated town with a segregated educational system. Upon graduating from high school, she left Oklahoma to attend an accredited university, finally settling on the University of Iowa, where she earned an art degree. She returned to Oklahoma and began teaching music in high schools. But she developed a desire to study law and enrolled at Indiana University, earning her JD degree in 1948. She moved east to begin her law career, passing the Pennsylvania bar exam in 1954. She joined the district attorney's office in Philadelphia as an assistant DA and was promoted to chief of appeals, pardons, and paroles.

A talented and effective lawyer, Stout was appointed to a judgeship in the Philadelphia municipal courts. Her sharp legal mind and her commitment to upholding the law soon earned her widespread respect. She was recognized as a judge who was tough on crime but who tempered her verdicts with wisdom and compassion.

In 1963, President John F. Kennedy appointed Stout as special ambassador to the Kenya Independence Celebration. She later toured other African countries delivering speeches.

As a citizen, lawyer, and judge, Stout received numerous awards, including Outstanding Woman Lawyer of the Year in 1965 and the AFL-CIO's Good Citizen Award in 1971. She heard hundreds of cases from the bench and had only a handful overturned in the appellate courts.

In 1988, Stout was named to the Pennsylvania Supreme Court, the first African American woman to achieve such an important legal position.

She died on August 21, 1998. She was 79.

— OCTOBER 31 —

1981

ANDREW YOUNG SERVES AS ATLANTA MAYOR

On this day in civil rights history, Andrew Young served his second day as mayor of Atlanta.

Born March 12, 1932, in New Orleans, Young attended Howard University before heeding the call to the ministry. In 1955, he received a divinity degree from Hartford Theological Seminary in Connecticut.

Shortly afterwards, Young began a pastorship in Marion, Alabama. Young began to preach a blend of social activism, brotherly Christianity, and Gandhian pacifism, encouraging his church members to register to vote. In Marion, he also met his future wife, Jean Childs. He met a fellow young preacher, Martin Luther King Jr., around this time, and the two became friends.

In 1957, Young left Alabama to live in New York. But as the civil rights movement began to mobilize, he realized his place was in the South. He became involved in the movement in the early 1960s and by 1964 was executive director of the Southern Christian Leadership Conference.

Andrew Young

Photo courtesy of Library of Congress

As a member of SCLC, Young took part in many of the era's major civil rights events, as organizer, speaker, and frontline activist. He was one of King's best friends and most trusted advisers.

In 1964, Young helped draft the Civil Rights Act and one year later lobbied for passage of the Voting Rights Act of 1965.

In 1968, Young was on the balcony of the Lorraine Motel in Memphis when King was shot and killed.

After King's death, Young entered mainstream politics as a Democrat, embarking on an esteemed political career. He ran for Congress in 1972 and won, becoming the first black congressman from Georgia since Reconstruction. In 1976, President Jimmy Carter appointed Young as the U.S. ambassador to the United Nations. He was fired from his post in 1979, however, when he met with the Palestinian Liberation Organization, contrary to Carter's foreign policy. In 1981, Young received the Congressional Medal of Honor and that same year was elected mayor of Atlanta, a post in which he served until 1990.

Young continues to work for human rights causes and is cochair of Good Works International. He has written several books about his experiences.

This day in

November

— NOVEMBER 1 —
1961
FIRST PROTEST ACTION IN ALBANY MOVEMENT

On this day in civil rights history, SNCC operatives Cordell Reagon and Charles Sherrod tested the federal law by trying to patronize the segregated bus facilities in Albany, Georgia. The two young African Americans fled when they met police in the station, but their tentative action was the beginning of the Albany movement.

A few months earlier, three SNCC workers had moved into Albany to prepare for a voting rights campaign. Albany was chosen for this effort because it had a large African American population and a nucleus of middle-class blacks to help support a base of operations. Sherrod, Reagon, and Charles Jones began recruiting new SNCC members among the black high school and college students of the small city.

But the local chapter of the NAACP bristled at the newcomers' activities. The NAACP was the most conservative of the civil rights organizations, while SNCC was the most radical. Reagon and Sherrod, young men in their 20s, were viewed by the older NAACP members as inexperienced and unwelcome. Infighting and egotism threatened to choke any chance at unity.

The main question was who would be in charge, and the inability to answer this may have led to the eventual ruin of the Albany campaign.

False starts and petty squabbling characterized the early stages of the campaign. Without a unified front or even recognized leadership, the disparate personalities floundered while trying to organize a city-wide campaign.

The Albany movement may illustrate better than any other civil rights event the internal disagreements over how to conduct the movement. SNCC believed in youth, in long-term voter drives and education campaigns, while striving for local African American community-building. SNCC was nonhierarchical, uncompromising, and aggressive. The NAACP believed in patient legal battles, drawing the federal government into the proceedings with selected legal cases. The NAACP often agreed to stop protests for short periods of time while the governing body deliberated. And, most importantly, the NAACP wanted to run the movement without the intrusion of inexperienced youths.

— November 2 —
1910
The NAACP Launches 'The Crisis'

On this day in civil rights history, the NAACP, under the editorial leadership of W. E. B. Du Bois, began its first full day of work on its publication *The Crisis*.

Du Bois declared the magazine's intent in his first editorial: ". . . to set forth those facts and arguments which show the danger of race prejudice, particularly as manifested today toward colored people. . . . its editorial page will stand for the rights of men, irrespective of color or race, for the highest ideals of American democracy, and for reasonable but earnest and persistent attempts to gain these rights and realize these ideals."

In its persistent editorial call for action, *The Crisis* followed in the advocacy footsteps of William Lloyd Garrison's *Liberator* and Frederick Douglass's *North Star*, while also serving as an arts journal and scholarly publication.

By 1920, *The Crisis* had more than 100,000 readers. The publication offered current affairs, reviews, poems, art and photography, and stories, along with antilynching essays and political-call-to-arms pieces. During the Harlem Renaissance and later, dozens of the best African American writers, including Langston Hughes, Jean Toomer, James Weldon Johnson, Charles Chestnut, and Countee Cullen, were published in *The Crisis*, guided by the genius of literary editor Jessie Fauset.

The publication was the voice of the NAACP, but it was mostly a sounding board for Du Bois's powerful, logical attacks against discrimination, inequality, and—turning his scrutinizing eye toward other African Americans—accommodation with segregation. This was fine while Du Bois and the NAACP were philosophically aligned. In 1934, however, Du Bois broke with the mainstream NAACP message by advocating black separatism. The NAACP board rebuked him, and in the subsequent fallout Du Bois resigned.

Roy Wilkins was named his successor. Wilkins oversaw the magazine for over a decade, working with writers like Robert C. Weaver, Chester Himes, and Margaret Walker before becoming acting executive director of the NAACP in 1949 and full-time executive director in 1955.

The magazine continued with James Ivy as the managing editor. Ivy retired and was replaced by Henry Lee Moon in 1966. *The Crisis* remains in print, a bimonthly publication.

— NOVEMBER 3 —
1979
KLANSMEN, NAZIS GUN DOWN FIVE IN GREENSBORO, N.C.

On this day in civil rights history, Ku Klux Klansmen and Nazis killed five people in North Carolina, in what would become known as "the Greensboro Massacre."

Weeks earlier, the Workers' Viewpoint Organization had planned an anti-Klan rally to be held in Morningside Homes, a black housing project in Greensboro. In the late 1970s, the WVO, a biracial organization, helped textile unions in North Carolina negotiate better working conditions. The WVO grew out of the civil rights and antiwar movements of the late 1960s as activists sought to continue their work in the post-civil rights era.

Under WVO auspices, poor black and white textile workers built a coalition to improve their situation. On occasion, the KKK threatened the union leaders and, as an act of defiance, the WVO planned a rally against the Klan. The activists were also planning to announce the new name of their organization: the Communist Workers' Party.

The so-called "Death to the Klan" rally was to be a combination social protest, political gathering, and economic declaration. Learning of the event, members of the KKK and the American Nazi Party, both then active in middle North Carolina, planned a competing anti-communism event.

The anti-Klan rally began around 11 a.m. Soon afterwards, carloads of Klansmen and Nazis disrupted the rally. Television news cameras were present, and their film of the incident showed the armed Klansmen and Nazis getting out of their cars and, with guns drawn, approaching the anti-Klan parade, targeting members of the Communist Workers Party and firing point-blank at them. The entire incident lasted only a few minutes. At the end, five leaders of the rally lay dead—Caesar Cauce, Mike Nathan, Sandi Smith, Bill Sampson, and James Waller—with ten injured.

Survivors of the attack alleged a conspiracy, and with good reason. The local police, who were warned of the potential for trouble, were suspiciously absent at the time of the attack. Informants in the Klan had relayed information about the potential attack, but no one had done anything about it. In the subsequent state and then federal trials, however, the murderers were found not guilty on all charges. In a civil trial, the City of Greensboro paid some of the survivors a settlement without admitting any wrongdoing.

The Greensboro Massacre caused a national outrage and led to the formation of the National Anti-Klan Network (later the Center for Democratic Renewal). Some 100 civil rights, church, labor, and community organizations joined in the network. In the summer of 2004, Greensboro launched the Greensboro Truth and Reconciliation Commission to investigate the incident.

— NOVEMBER 4 —

1999

HEROINE OF CENTRAL HIGH CRISIS DIES

On this day in civil rights history, Daisy Bates, who in 1957 was at the center of the school desegregation battle, died in Little Rock.

Bates was born in Huttig, Arkansas, in 1914, and was victimized by Southern justice early on when her mother was killed by three local whites who were never prosecuted. The death ruined her father, who left her with family friends and disappeared. The people raising her, whom she thought were her parents, were just friends of her biological parents.

Photo courtesy of Library of Congress

Protesting school desegregation

In 1942, she married insurance agent and part-time journalist L. C. Bates. Together they founded the *Arkansas State Press,* which published scathing editorials on segregation and racially motivated violence. Their paper was the major voice for African Americans in Arkansas, and it began making inroads against police brutality and egregious discriminatory practices. Daisy served as one of the main writers, and in L. C.'s absence, as editor of the paper. Her dedication and talent brought her into activist circles, and in 1952, Bates was elected president of the Arkansas branch of the NAACP.

Bates played a crucial role—organizing, planning, and orchestrating—in the 1957 desegregation of Little Rock's Central High School. Governor Orval Faubus called out the National Guard to prevent the students from entering, resulting in days of chaos and violence. President Dwight Eisenhower then federalized the National Guard and occupied Little Rock until the crisis passed.

Afterwards, Bates's paper closed. She moved to Washington, D.C., serving on the Democratic National Committee and later as a staffer of one of President Lyndon Johnson's antipoverty programs. In 1962, she published her book, *The Long Shadow of Little Rock,* detailing her life in the movement and the critical Little Rock days, with a foreword by Eleanor Roosevelt.

She suffered a stroke in 1965 and returned to Arkansas in 1968.

As time passed, she became more and more recognized as a hero. Bates revived the *Arkansas State Press* in the 1980s. In 1988, her memoir was reissued and won an American Book Award, the only reprint ever to be so honored. In the late 1980s, Little Rock opened Daisy Bates Elementary School. Finally, a state holiday was named in her honor.

— NOVEMBER 5 —

1991

CLARENCE THOMAS, CONTROVERSIAL SUPREME COURT JUSTICE, GETS ACCUSTOMED TO THE JOB

On this day in civil rights history, Clarence Thomas, the second African American to serve on the Supreme Court, began his second month as an associate justice.

Born on June 23, 1948, Thomas grew up in segregated Savannah, Georgia, where he was raised Catholic by his grandparents. Early on he was impressed by his grandparents' work ethic and self-reliance, and as a young man he read Ayn Rand and absorbed her libertarian philosophy.

In 1974, Thomas graduated from Yale Law School. Afterward, he came across the black conservative economist Thomas Sowell, who further led him toward a philosophy based on free-market capitalism and self-reliance. He soon became an up-and-coming member of the Republican Party.

In 1981, Thomas was appointed assistant secretary in the U.S. Department of Education Office of Civil Rights under President Ronald Reagan. One year later he became chair of the U.S. Equal Employment Opportunity Commission, where he served until 1990, when President George H. W. Bush nominated him to the Supreme Court to replace the retiring Thurgood Marshall.

Thomas's nomination put black organizations in a tough spot. The NAACP and the Urban League both campaigned against him. In a highly publicized nomination hearing, former coworker Anita Hill accused Thomas of sexual harassment. After much debate, Thomas was confirmed by the Senate.

Thomas's performance on the bench has been much as was expected; he has pleased states' rights conservatives and angered liberals and civil rights organizations. With fellow Justice Antonin Scalia, Thomas has anchored the extreme conservative end of a conservative court. Thomas follows, however, less the neoconservative than the libertarian philosophy. Although the descendent of slaves and a beneficiary himself of affirmative action, Thomas argues that blacks in America have to stand alone; welfare, affirmative action, and the like, to Thomas's thinking, damage the African American community by robbing it of gumption and drive. He has consistently voted against cases that would benefit black causes.

Thus Thomas has, in the eyes of many, come to embody everything that is wrong with the federal government at the dawn of the 21st century. Critics say he ignores history by generalizing from his own particular success.

In 2005, Thomas turned 57. He promises to be on the court for a long, long time.

1983

CIVIL RIGHTS LEGEND BOB MOSES UNLOCKS THE SECRETS OF HIGHER MATH FOR INNER-CITY STUDENTS

On this day in civil rights history, former SNCC leader Bob Moses fine-tuned a teaching initiative that would become the Algebra Project.

Born in New York in 1935, Moses taught math in New York for three years before he joined SNCC in 1960. He served as SNCC's Mississippi field secretary and as codirector of the Council of Federated Organizations in the most dangerous places and during the most dangerous times of the civil rights movement. He was one of the principal architects of Mississippi Freedom Summer.

Moses often applied uniquely creative thinking to civil rights issues, such as when he helped craft the Mississippi Freedom Democratic Party's attempt to unseat the state's Democratic regulars at the 1964 Democratic National Convention. Moses was a mainstay of the movement—a critical thinker and a talented mass organizer—and one of the bravest members of SNCC.

In 1966, however, SNCC elected Stokely Carmichael as its national chairman. As Carmichael began calling for "black power," Moses saw the new direction of the organization and resigned from his post. He moved to Tanzania, where he worked with the Ministry of Education. In 1976, Moses returned to the United States to get his PhD at Harvard.

In 1982, Moses was awarded a five-year MacArthur Foundation "genuis fellowship." A teacher at heart, Moses returned to teaching in Cambridge, Massachusetts, where he recognized a disturbing trend. Black and Latino students—all inner-city students, in fact—were not learning math. A shocking 73 percent of black high school seniors tested below grade levels in the subject. Moses understood the correlation between decent math scores and college acceptance, and between high math scores and good-paying jobs in technology and industry. He saw that technical professions were essentially closed to inner-city students, especially minority students, mainly due to inadequate math education.

The Algebra Project, now almost two decades old, began as an inner-city initiative in which teachers would use real-world situations, such as bus and subway schedules, to teach students abstract mathematics.

The Algebra Project is a huge success, now operating in more than 20 cities, including Atlanta, Boston, and Chicago. Moses currently teaches math at a high school in Mississippi.

— NOVEMBER 7 —

2001

LOUIS FARRAKHAN, INCENDIARY RELIGIOUS LEADER, RECUPERATES FROM SURGERY

On this day in civil rights history, Nation of Islam minister Louis Farrakhan recovered after emergency surgery to combat cancer.

The Nation of Islam began in 1930 when Wallace Fard, a mysterious figure, began holding religious meetings in Detroit. The NOI now reveres Fard as divine. He altered the traditional five pillars of Islam with a new black-centered cosmology combined with a Marcus Garvey–inspired black nationalism. In this new mythology, Africans were the only people in an earthly paradise before a power-mad black scientist unleashed a diabolical race of white demons into the world. The demons became the white race.

Fard began to garner followers in the Detroit area. His number one pupil was Elijah Muhammad, who took over the organization in 1934 and greatly expanded it; Fard who by this time had disappeared. In the crumbling urban cities of the North, NOI offered independent schools for children, community centers, and other social programs, while preaching black pride.

In 1952, Malcolm X joined the NOI, quickly becoming Muhammad's rising young star; two years later, Louis X became another recruit. (The "X" that most of the NOI members adopted represented their lost African surnames.) Malcolm X was a dynamic speaker, preaching self-sufficiency and self-defense. In the early 1960s, he and the NOI offered a volatile counterpoint to the nonviolent philosophy of the SCLC and early SNCC (NOI's black nationalism was a precursor to the Black Panther Party). Many African Americans heeded the NOI call.

In 1961, Malcolm X met with the KKK to discuss a separate black state within America. The organizations found that they had something in common: The NOI agreed with the Klan's beliefs on miscegenation.

Malcolm X broke with the Nation of Islam before he was murdered in 1965. Ten years later, Elijah Muhammad passed away. The organization fell to his son but soon was usurped by Louis X, who began calling himself Louis Farrakhan. Farrakhan continued in the separatist vein. NOI's membership and influence began to dwindle, but a core group of devotees continued to push for the NOI cause.

In the early 1990s, Farrakhan, though still controversial and extreme, began to soften his rhetoric, and in 1995 he served as the principal organizer of the Million Man March.

In 2005, after recovering from his bout with cancer, Farrakhan called for a ten-year-anniversary Millions More rally, which was held October 15 and was attended by a smaller but still-enthusiastic crowd.

On this day in civil rights history, Nicholas Katzenbach and John Doar continued to enforce the Constitution from their positions within the U.S. Justice Department.

Born in Philadelphia in 1922, Katzenbach graduated from Yale Law School in 1947. After receiving a Rhodes Scholarship to Oxford, he returned to the States to practice law and teach as an associate professor at his alma mater.

In 1961 he joined the Justice Department's Office of Legal Counsel, and was soon assistant attorney general. In this capacity he helped oversee the desegregation of the University of Mississippi by James Meredith in 1962 and the desegregation of the University of Alabama by Vivian Malone and James Hood in 1963. The next year he worked to secure passage of the 1964 Civil Rights Act. A staunch believer in civil rights, Katzenbach was matched in dedication by his colleague in the Justice Department, John Doar, who was born in 1921 in Minneapolis.

Photo courtesy of Library of Congress

Malone and Katzenbach

As assistant attorney general in the civil rights section of the Justice Department, Doar worked on many important civil rights cases from 1960 to 1967, crucial years in the movement. A hardworking, serious man, Doar worked closely with many civil rights groups in Mississippi, including the SCLC, SNCC, and the NAACP. He took it upon himself to prosecute the murderers of Schwerner, Goodman, and Chaney in the "Mississippi Burning" trials, as well as later the murderers of Viola Liuzzo.

While Doar remained a federal presence at the front lines of the Deep South movement—as mediator, prosecutor, and investigator—Katzenbach was promoted in 1965 by President Lyndon Johnson to the office of attorney general after Robert Kennedy left to run for the Senate. As attorney general, Katzenbach, with Doar's input, helped draft the 1965 Voting Rights Act.

Katzenbach soon came into conflict with FBI Director J. Edgar Hoover over the unauthorized wiretaps and other covert activities aimed against civil rights leaders. After just one year, Katzenbach resigned, stating he could no longer do his job due to "Hoover's resentment of me."

Katzenbach and Doar went into private practice after leaving the Justice Department at the end of the 1960s. They are both still practicing law.

— NOVEMBER 9 —

1968

SINGER JAMES BROWN GIVES MOVEMENT TO THE MOVEMENT

On this day in civil rights history, James Brown performed his new single, "Say it Loud, I'm Black and I'm Proud."

Born in 1933 in South Carolina, Brown worked a variety of odd jobs in his youth and served a stint in prison. He was poor and uneducated, but he was also driven and talented and soon he discovered music.

Brown was a dynamic act, touring the "chitlin' circuit"—the all-black music, comedy, and entertainment venues in the segregated South—the majority of the year. Like his contemporaries Ray Charles and Little Richard, Brown was a larger-than-life, raucous figure on stage, fusing blues and bop and early rock into the magic of soul. Soon Brown had a laundry list of monikers: "Mr. Dynamite," "The Hardest Working Man in Show Business," "Soul Brother Number One," and "The Godfather of Soul," among others. Entering the early 1960s, Brown was sleek, sexy, and popular; he was also moving away from pure entertainment due to his blossoming social consciousness.

Brown's commitment to black causes first manifested in positive songs. In 1966, Brown visited the wounded James Meredith, who was shot at the beginning of his one-man "March Against Fear." This brought Brown into civil rights circles, and soon he was playing benefit shows, including a special concert for the SCLC.

In 1968, after lending his voice against the riots breaking out across the country after Martin Luther King Jr.'s death, Brown recorded "Say It Loud—I'm Black and I'm Proud," a black-pride anthem that became one of the main protest songs of the era, despite the fact that Brown eschewed militant black separatism. That same year, President Lyndon Johnson invited Brown to the White House. Seen often on magazine covers and heard constantly on the radio, Brown emerged as an important social and cultural figure.

Entering the 1970s, Brown became the pioneer of funk. He wrote the soundtracks to a number of blaxploitation films, including *Black Caesar*. He continued to support black causes.

A singer, songwriter, producer, and unparalleled entertainer, Brown as a musician bridges the gap between soul and funk, and later between funk and hip-hop. His personal life, like those of many musicians who rose from poverty and ignorance, was plagued with problems, including drug addiction, marital infidelities, and money crises. But through all his trials, Brown has remained a beacon of black pride and a musician-activist of the first order.

— NOVEMBER 10 —
1963
MALCOLM X SPEECH

On this day in civil rights history, Malcolm X delivered one of his most famous speeches at the Northern Negro Grass Roots Leadership Conference in Detroit.

The Northern Negro Leadership Conference excluded black nationalists from its membership, so the Northern Negro Grass Roots Leadership Conference was formed as an alternative. Malcolm X was the main speaker at the two-day event.

"As long as the white man sent you to Korea, you bled," he said. "He sent you to Germany, you bled. He sent you to the South Pacific to fight the Japanese, you bled. You bleed for white people, but when it comes to seeing your own churches being bombed and little black girls murdered, you haven't got any blood. You bleed when the white man says bleed; you bite when the white man says bite; and you bark when the white man says bark. I hate to say this about us, but it's true. How are you going to be nonviolent in Mississippi and Alabama, when your churches are being bombed, and your little girls are being murdered, and at the same time you are going to get violent with Hitler, and Tojo, and somebody else you don't even know? . . . If violence is wrong in America, violence is wrong abroad. If it is wrong to be violent defending black women and black children and black babies and black men, then it is wrong for America to draft us and make us violent abroad in defense of her."

This was vintage Malcolm. He criticized the entire concept of nonviolent resistance. He continued:

"Revolution is bloody, revolution is hostile, revolution knows no compromise, revolution overturns and destroys everything that gets in its way. And you, sitting around here like a knot on the way, saying, 'I'm going to love these folks no matter how much they hate me,' No, you need a revolution. Whoever heard of a revolution where they lock arms, singing 'We Shall Overcome?' You don't do that in a revolution. You don't do any singing, you're too busy swinging."

With such speeches, Malcolm X served as a counterpoint to Martin Luther King Jr.'s message of a "beloved community" that would be ushered into existence through nonviolent protest. As Du Bois and Washington had a half century earlier, the two civil rights leaders became symbols of the two major strains of 1960s black thought.

— NOVEMBER 11 —
1964
AMELIA BOYNTON APPEALS FOR SCLC
TO JOIN SELMA PROTEST

On this day in civil rights history, Amelia Boynton personally appealed to Martin Luther King Jr. to bring the SCLC to Selma to get involved in the ongoing voter-registration campaign.

Boynton and her husband, S. W. Boynton were prominent in Selma's black community and were leaders of the Dallas County Voters League, which met in the office of their insurance agency.

Since the 1950s the Boyntons had been working with a handful of other Selma African Americans to encourage black citizens to register to vote. Their efforts had been slow going, frustrated at every turn by white voting officials, who used arcane rules, inconvenient and limited registration hours, and often outright harassment and persecution to discourage new applicants as well as the DCVL members who recruited them.

In the early 1960s, federal officials began enforcing some provisions of the Civil Rights Acts of 1957 and 1960, including in Dallas County and Selma. Then in 1963 SNCC activists had come to Selma and joined with the DCVL to step up registration efforts. Hostile white officials had gotten a local judge to enjoin mass meetings in the community, however, and by 1964 the voter registration efforts seemed to be stalled.

Then, according to historian Mills Thornton in his book *Dividing Lines,* Amelia Boynton took the opportunity of being at an SCLC staff retreat in Birmingham to urge King to add his and the SCLC's presence to the civil rights activities in Selma.

Thornton wrote, "For SCLC, a campaign in Selma had two great virtues: it would focus upon precisely the issue that the organization now most wished to emphasize, voting rights, and it would build upon a strong existing local foundation in the Voters League."

King aide C. T. Vivian returned to Selma with Boynton and immediately began talking to local leaders. Then he reported favorably to the SCLC staff in Atlanta, where planning for a "Selma crusade" began in earnest.

In Selma, there were turf issues to work out with SNCC, but before long staff members of both civil rights groups were working regularly with the DCVL and other members of the local black community.

The stage was being set for the events in the spring of 1965 that would culminate in the Selma-to-Montgomery march and lead to the passage of the 1965 Voting Rights Act.

— NOVEMBER 12 —
1964
FIFTH CIRCUIT FEDERAL JUDGES ENFORCE THE LAW

On this day in civil rights history, federal judges were in the thick of the legal maneuvering that brought about a fundamental transformation of the nation, particularly the South.

Consider that in 1950 the South was completely and rigidly segregated by a system of customs and laws. By 1970, some of the customs remained, but the segregation laws had been totally swept away. Much of this astonishing change occurred in the courtrooms presided over by the judges at the district and appellate levels in the states of Georgia, Florida, Alabama, Mississppi, Louisiana, and Texas—the old Fifth U.S. Judicial Circuit (since subdivided), with headquarters in Atlanta.

Of the judges on the Fifth Circuit Court of Appeals, four led the way on civil rights issues: Chief Judge Elbert P. Tuttle in Atlanta, Richard T. Rives in Montgomery, John Minor Wisdom in New Orleans, and John Robert Brown in Houston. Three of the four were Republicans appointed by President Dwight Eisenhower.

These judges took the precedent established by the Supreme Court in 1954—overturning the 1896 *Plessy* doctrine of "separate but equal"—and extended it to every aspect of Southern life. During the key years of the movement, according to historian Jack Bass (whose book *Unlikely Heroes* portrays the "Fifth Circuit Four"), the Supreme Court issued relatively few civil rights decisions, preferring to affirm major Fifth Circuit rulings without hearings, thus sending a clear signal to the courts below. Bass said the Supreme Court "believed that desegregation law shaped by Southern judges would be more acceptable to the South."

Whether this is true is debatable, but it was effective. Southern states tried every tactic imaginable to evade or postpone desegregation. But the Fifth Circuit kept hammering the states with the due-process and equal-protection clauses of the 14th Amendment until finally school superintendents and legislatures and governors had no place else to hide.

Bass says the judges "extended the reach of *Brown* with landmark decisions on school integration, voting rights, employment discrimination affecting both blacks and women, rights of prison inmates and the mentally ill, and jury discrimination."

The Fifth Circuit judges were hearing appeals of decisions made by the District Court judges below them, and of those, two particularly stand out: Frank M. Johnson Jr. in Montgomery, and J. Waites Waring in Charleston. Both made numerous rulings that were extremely unpopular with whites in their home communities but were received by blacks as proof that God and the federal courts were on their side, at last.

— NOVEMBER 13 —
2000
LAURIE PRITCHETT, KING FOIL IN ALBANY, DIES

On this day in civil rights history, former Albany, Georgia, chief of police Laurie Pritchett died. Dubbed the "white knight" of the segregationists, Pritchett was a cagey antagonist to Martin Luther King Jr. and the SCLC.

During the Albany movement of late 1961, Pritchett learned from others' mistakes and enacted a strict policy of nonconfrontational law enforcement. When the Albany campaign began, he countered every move of the protesters with elegant precision. He understood the one weakness of the nonviolent movement: It required violent response to harness public opinion and galvanize the federal government to action. Unlike Birmingham's Bull Connor, Pritchett did not allow violence to erupt. Instead, he patiently arrested African American protesters for violating loitering injunctions and parading without a license. By arresting protesters not under the segregation laws, which could be struck down in court, but instead under the umbrella of protecting the public order, Pritchett sidestepped an important issue.

When African Americans began entering Albany's jails en masse, Pritchett bused certain high-profile people to other jails around the state while ensuring they stayed unharmed. Along with Albany mayor Asa Kelley, Pritchett publicly shaped the discourse by offering some concessions while quietly continuing segregationist policies. Pritchett further employed a canny series of fines that taxed the civil rights organizations just as much as the jailed protesters taxed the public coffers.

Like other civil rights campaigns, the Albany campaign was expensive. The prolonged peace, peppered by nonviolent arrests and fines, drained the resources of the civil rights organizations that wanted to continue with other campaigns. Albany became a bureaucratic mire. Operating with patience and resolve, Pritchett figured that without drama the movement would eventually fade; the media would leave and the agitators would go elsewhere.

He was right. Without achieving significant gains and with minimal violence, the Albany movement sputtered and eventually died.

Despite his cleverness, Pritchett was ultimately on the wrong side of history; his short-term victories were in defense of a sick, immoral system. The movement learned from Pritchett and put that knowledge to good use in the next big campaign, and one of its biggest successes: the Birmingham movement of 1962–63.

— NOVEMBER 14 —
1960
LANDMARK VOTING DISTRICTS CASE DECIDED

On this day in civil rights history, the U.S. Supreme Court decided the case of *Gomillion v. Lightfoot*, establishing an important precedent in the voting rights of African American citizens. The case originated in 1957, when the Alabama legislature passed Act 140 to redefine the boundaries of the city of Tuskegee, in Macon County.

This action was one of many taken by the Alabama legislature in the 1950s in resistance to legal challenges to segregation.

Tuskegee is home to the famous Tuskegee Institute (now Tuskegee University) and to a large Veterans Administration hospital that was established to care for black military veterans. Both institutions thus had large contingents of well-educated African American professionals who had become registered voters. Macon County and the city of Tuskegee both had majority-black populations, and local whites feared that increased black voter registration would lead to eventual black control of city offices. They thus sought to minimize the number of blacks eligible to vote in city elections, and local legislators used Act 140 to change the city boundaries from a square to a 28-sided polygon. This bill passed without debate and unanimously in the all-white legislature.

The new boundaries managed to exclude from the city limits no white voters but all but four or five black voters, thus denying Tuskegee's African American citizens not only access to the ballot box but to fire and police protection and to street improvements and other municipal benefits.

Dr. C. G. Gomillion, leader of the Tuskegee Civic Association, asked attorney Fred Gray (who had already won the Montgomery bus boycott case) to file a federal lawsuit to have the gerrymandering declared unconstitutional. After three years of legal maneuvering in the lower courts, the case reached the U.S. Supreme Court. Attorney Gray argued the case in May 1959, and a year later the court ruled in his favor.

Justice Felix Frankfurter wrote the majority opinion striking down Act 140 as a violation of the constitutional protections against unequal treatment. Frankfurter wrote, "When a legislature thus singles out a readily isolated segment of a racial minority for special discriminatory treatment, it violates the Fifteenth Amendment."

The fears of local whites about black control came true. With the gerrymandering undone, and following the passage of the 1965 Voting Rights Act, the majority-black population of Tuskegee and Macon County gradually elected blacks to most major local offices. In 1970, attorney Gray was himself elected to the Alabama legislature.

— NOVEMBER 15 —
1945
HARRY MOORE LAUNCHES FLORIDA VOTER REGISTRATION

On this day in civil rights history, Harry Tyson Moore began a massive voter registration drive in Florida, forming the Progressive Voters' League. It would prove to be an enormous success, but at the price of his life.

Compared with other states, not much is written about the movement in Florida, despite a massive Klan presence in the central part of the state, a bus boycott similar to Montgomery's in Tallahassee in 1956, and racially motivated lynchings throughout the state. Although white resistance to integration was far less in Florida's political system, thanks largely due to moderate governor LeRoy Collins, there was still backlash.

Moore was a teacher when he learned about the NAACP in the early 1930s, and he used his influence to begin the first Brevard County branch. But the NAACP was decentralized and lacked power at the time. To rectify this, Moore established the first state conference and organized Florida's NAACP chapters into one unit in 1941. He served as the first president and immediately began stretching the organization.

When the Supreme Court in *Smith v. Allwright* declared segregated political primaries to be unconstitutional, Moore saw his chance to balance the scales of power.

Harry Moore (r), John Milton (l), and Mrs. Milton

Photo courtesy of Library of Congress

"The fact is," he said as he kicked off his voter registration campaign, "that practically every city, county, and state official in Florida is selected in the Democratic primaries. In order to help select these officials, Negroes must vote in the Democratic Primaries."

The Progressive Voters' League slogan was "A voteless citizen is a voiceless citizen." Moore attacked the problem with zeal, proving to be an effective campaigner. In 1940 there were fewer than 20,000 registered black voters in Florida. In one year the PVL had doubled the number, and by 1950 there were more than 110,000 African American Florida voters, more than 30 percent of those eligible in the state. This was 50 percent higher than in any other Southern state.

Moore's success, however, earned him enemies. On Christmas night 1951, a bomb exploded underneath Moore's bedroom, killing Moore and his wife, Harriett. He was 46. The FBI investigated the killings, but closed the case when the two lead suspects died of natural causes while evidence was being collected.

— November 16 —
2000
Activist Hosea Williams Dies

On this day in civil rights history, outspoken activist Hosea Williams died in Atlanta, after a three-year battle with cancer.

Born in Atapulgus, Georgia, in 1926, Williams was raised by his grandparents until he left home at age 14. He enlisted in the army during World War II, where he served in an all-black unit under General George S. Patton. He won the Purple Heart and was hospitalized for a year after being the only survivor of a German bombing run. Returning to the U.S., Williams earned his high school diploma in his early 20s and later received bachelor's and master's degrees in chemistry from Morris Brown College and Atlanta University.

His career seemed set.

But one day he drank from a whites-only water fountain and was severely beaten by a white mob. Doctors predicted he would die from his injuries, but he survived. Leaving the hospital, he turned his considerable energies to the civil rights movement.

Williams first joined the NAACP, but was more attracted to SCLC's direct action. In 1963, he became part of Martin Luther King Jr.'s SCLC staff. Uncompromising and opinionated on every topic, Williams knocked heads with many of the other staffers, most notably with program director Randolph Blackwell. But Williams was also fearless and tireless; he was arrested more than 100 times during his civil rights career. Beatings, jail cells, harassment—none deterred Williams.

Despite animosity between Williams and other staffers, Williams soon became head of the SCLC voter education division. He began devising a massive voter registration project, nicknamed SCOPE, which was an SCLC version of Mississippi Freedom Summer.

In 1965, Williams was with SNCC's John Lewis at the head of the column that crossed the Edmund Pettus Bridge in Selma, Alabama, on what became known as Bloody Sunday. The demonstrators were beaten and teargassed by sheriff's deputies and state troopers. Williams was left with a fractured skull and a concussion.

Williams was with King in the Chicago and Memphis campaigns. After King's death, Williams became involved in Georgia politics, winning terms on the Atlanta City Council and in the Georgia General Assembly. In 1987, in his 1960s, Williams led a widely publicized march into Forsyth County, a predominantly white suburb of Atlanta which had a long reputation for racism and discrimination.

On this day in civil rights history, SNCC, the NAACP, and local activist groups put aside their differences and formed the Albany movement, a coalition designated to bring change to the Deep South city of Albany, Georgia. The Albany movement represented a shift in civil rights strategy, having as its aim the total and immediate desegregation of an entire city. This lofty goal allowed the participants to plan demonstrations in every aspect of Albany life, but it proved vague and overly ambitious.

Leaders of the campaign included Charles Sherrod, Marion Page, C. B. King, Ruby Hurley, William Anderson, and others. James Forman of SNCC and Vernon Jordan of the NAACP agreed with the overall intent, although neither organization quite agreed on how the campaign should be run or who exactly should run it.

Threatening a boycott of white businesses and the bus system, sit-ins at the parks, libraries, and lunch counters of the city, and mass protests, the Albany movement spokesmen asked the city commission to establish a biracial board to address desegregation issues. The six-member commission refused to negotiate. James Forman then led a group of freedom riders into Albany, where they were promptly but politely arrested by Police Chief Laurie Pritchett. In response, the people of Albany began to march. African Americans stopped patronizing white businesses and stopped riding the Albany buses.

Within a few weeks, no one had been beaten by the restrained Albany police, but more than 500 protesters were in jail. Pritchett's tactics of nonviolent law enforcement were working. The Albany movement was stalling, and the leadership knew it. SNCC, NAACP, and SCLC were never on the same page. Different factions, including local African Americans, made backroom deals with the city's administration, often at the expense of other groups' actions.

A decision to invite Martin Luther King Jr. and the SCLC entourage was made. King answered the call, and soon arrived in Albany. But the tactics of low-key oppression adopted by local officials in response to the nonviolent demonstrations proved to be a difficult challenge for civil rights workers. Change, it appeared, would come slowly and undramatically to Albany.

— November 18 —
1797
Sojourner Truth Born

On this day in civil rights history, approximately, Sojourner Truth, one of the most famous abolitionists and suffragettes, was born a slave in Ulster County, New York. Her given name was Isabella Baumfree. Like most slaves, she never knew her exact birth date.

Baumfree was sold to different owners during her childhood. In 1827, New York State abolished slavery and she moved to New York City and began working as a domestic servant for a number of religious communes.

Photo courtesy of Library of Congress

Sojourner Truth

In 1843, Baumfree had a vision. She changed her name to Sojourner Truth and walked across Long Island and Connecticut, preaching the gospel. She joined the Northampton Association of Education and Industry, a pacifist, abolitionist, utopian community in Massachusetts. In Northampton, she met Frederick Douglass, William Lloyd Garrison, David Ruggles, and health buff Sylvester Graham, among other important abolitionist figures.

In 1846, the community disbanded but Truth remained in Massachusetts and with the help of her neighbor, Olive Gilbert, she wrote *The Narrative of Sojourner Truth, a Northern Slave*, which was published in 1850.

Although functionally illiterate, Truth became a popular orator. Her rhythmic cadence and strong, booming voice boosted campaigns for the abolition of slavery and for women's rights. "Where did your Christ come from?" she asked in one of her many speeches. "From God and a woman! Man had nothing to do with Him."

In 1855, the second edition of her autobiography featured an introduction by Harriet Beecher Stowe. Truth worked with Elizabeth Cady Stanton and Lucretia Mott, among other famous suffragettes.

When the Civil War began, Sojourner Truth began recruiting black men to fight for the Union, while also working to get supplies to black regiments. After the Emancipation Proclamation, she moved to Washington, D.C., to work with the National Freedman's Relief Organization. She met with President Lincoln.

After the war, she moved to Battle Creek, Michigan. In 1870, while campaigning for a "Negro State" in the West, she met with President Grant.

On November 26, 1883, Sojourner Truth, 86 years old as far as anyone knows, died in her home. A monument to her honor was unveiled in Michigan in 1999.

— NOVEMBER 19 —

1962

LEROY JOHNSON ELECTED TO GEORGIA STATE SENATE

On this day in civil rights history, LeRoy Johnson served in the Georgia state senate as the first African American elected to Georgia's top legislative body since 1862.

Born in Atlanta in 1928, Johnson graduated from Morehouse College, earned a master's degree from Atlanta University, and then a law degree from North Carolina School of Law. Johnson returned to Atlanta where he began working as the first black man employed by the U.S. Attorney's office in the fifth judicial district.

Atlanta was the institutional center of the civil rights movement and had a "New South" reputation. It boasted several leading historically black colleges and a thriving black middle class whose businesses were centered along "Sweet Auburn" Avenue. But racial problems plagued Atlanta. Race riots in 1906 left many dead. The Great Depression in the 1930s exacerbated racial tensions.

But Atlanta was also the home of Coca-Cola, which provided jobs and through the leadership of chairman Robert Woodruff helped stabilize local politics. When the civil rights movement got underway in the late 1950s, Atlanta's civic and business leaders avoided the violence that plagued many other parts of the South, fostering Atlanta's reputation as "the city too busy to hate." With new businesses choosing Atlanta as a base, the city became the largest city and most powerful business center in the South.

From his position in the U.S. Attorney's office, Johnson became a well-known figure. While the civil rights movement fought to desegregate the South, Johnson ran for the 38th district senate seat in Fulton County, which included Atlanta. Johnson defeated three opponents and in 1962 became the first black Georgia state legislator since Reconstruction.

In 1969, Johnson became the first African American to be named chairman of a Georgia senate standing committee, as he chaired the powerful judiciary committee.

In 1974, Johnson left the senate and politics. He served on the trustee board of Ebenezer Baptist Church, the church where Martin Luther King Sr. and Jr. preached.

As of 2005, Johnson was still practicing law in his birth city of Atlanta.

— NOVEMBER 20 —
1866
HOWARD UNIVERSITY FOUNDED

On this day in civil rights history, Howard University was founded in Washington, D.C., by congressional charter. Much of its initial funding came from the Freedman's Bureau.

Black colleges existed as early as 1837 to educate freed slaves. After the Civil War and during Reconstruction, dozens of black universities began to appear. The nation as a whole was expanding its educational opportunities and public land grant colleges were created. However, most of the publicly supported state college systems were segregated. Most blacks enrolled in private institutions run by religious groups.

Photo courtesy of Library of Congress

Founders Library at Howard University

Because of segregation, almost every leading black figure from Reconstruction to the mid-20th century studied in black institutions, such as Howard, Fisk, Alabama State, Morehouse, Xavier, Spellman, Southern, and Bethune-Cookman, to name just a few.

Most of the private schools focused on the humanities until Booker T. Washington's success at Tuskegee Institute led to a shift toward a pedagogy of practicality. With blacks' access to white-collar and professional occupations severely limited, Washington argued that African Americans should learn practical things in college—how to build a house, fix a car, till the soil—thereby ensuring they would have a trade and could make a decent living.

Others disagreed. W. E. B. Du Bois, for example, deplored the movement away from intellectualism. These critics also lamented that many black colleges were led by white or Jewish administrators. Not until 1926, for instance, did Howard University have its first black president, Mordecai Johnson.

Howard played a significant role in the civil rights movement. Howard Law School Dean Charles Hamilton Houston and his star pupil, Thurgood Marshall, would go on to form the nucleus of the NAACP legal campaign that brought down Jim Crow segregation. Marshall, Constance Baker Motley, Jack Greenberg, and others used Howard as a base to plan their final legal strategy for the landmark *Brown v. Board* case.

Ironically, their success against segregation may have weakened their mother institutions. As segregation barriers in higher education fell, black student enrollment expanded in previously white schools. Some historically black colleges and universities have closed and others struggle today for funds. However, despite dwindling enrollments, the surviving HBCUs remain as cultural centers of black scholarship and thought.

JACK GREENBERG, CIVIL RIGHTS LAWYER

On this day in civil rights history, Jack Greenberg, along with other NAACP Legal Defense Fund (LDF) lawyers, prepared for various desegregation cases that would eventually be combined under *Brown v. Board of Education*.

One year after graduating from Columbia Law School in 1948, Greenberg, a young Jewish lawyer, joined the NAACP as a legal counselor. He would continue in this capacity until 1984, playing an integral role within the NAACP Legal Defense Fund.

LDF became a separate organization in 1957, but it had operated autonomously within the NAACP since its inception in 1940. The unit was organized to fight segregation in the courts, case by case.

Charles Hamilton Houston and Thurgood Marshall were the primary architects of LDF, but many other lawyers played crucial roles, including Greenberg, William Henry Hastie, Constance Baker Motley, and Wiley Branton, among others. LDF provided legal assistance to almost every major civil rights case, from the many school cases to the Montgomery bus boycott, to Martin Luther King Jr.'s jailing in Birmingham, to the restoration of Muhammad Ali's boxing license.

In the beginning, LDF focused on integration, mostly of public schools. In 1954, Greenberg was a member of the team that argued and won the *Brown* case. In 1961, Thurgood Marshall left the LDF to become a federal judge, and Jack Greenberg was named director-counsel in his place. Greenberg stayed in this position until 1984, overseeing the NAACP's legal work through the dramatic years of the 1960s and 1970s. He argued 40 cases before the U.S. Supreme Court.

In 1984, he left LDF to teach at Columbia Law School, where he eventually became dean. Ten years later, he published his memoir, *Crusaders in the Courts,* retelling the vital role the LDF lawyers played in the movement.

In 2001, President Bill Clinton awarded the Presidential Citizens Medal to Greenberg. He remains active in many human rights and civil rights organizations.

— November 22 —
1963
President John F. Kennedy Assassinated

On this day in civil rights history, President John F. Kennedy was assassinated in Dallas, Texas. Although remembered as one of America's best and brightest who brought a new style of American politics, Kennedy's administration was beset by indecision on civil rights issues.

Elected over Richard Nixon in 1960, Kennedy began his presidency promising to end racial segregation while supporting a new era of progressive liberalism. But in 1961, under Kennedy's command, the United States was involved in the failed Bay of Pigs invasion of Cuba and then in the Cold War Cuban missile crisis standoff with Soviet Premier Nikita Khrushchev. Kennedy also increased U.S. involvement in Vietnam and supported dictators in Latin America to oppose communism.

Photo courtesy of Library of Congress

President and Mrs. John F. Kennedy, Gov. John Connally and wife

On the domestic front, Kennedy, along with his brother, Attorney General Robert Kennedy, danced around civil rights issues. Kennedy was personally sympathetic to civil rights, and he met with civil rights leaders and helped form the Voter Education Project. But he also refused to risk his political clout to fully endorse the movement and was reluctant to interfere with state affairs.

Like Eisenhower before him, Kennedy responded to crises by deploying the National Guard, in quelling rioting over the freedom riders in Alabama and James Meredith's integration of the University of Mississippi. But in the first half of his term, he did not lead the nation on moral issues pertinent to the civil rights movement. After the 1963 Birmingham campaign, however, Kennedy began to focus more strongly on the discrimination faced by blacks in the South. He had sent a civil rights bill to Congress before his death.

Near the end of 1963, Kennedy began touring the country, gearing up for his reelection campaign. In Dallas on November 22, the presidential motorcade traveled slowly down Main Street toward the Texas School Book Depository. Kennedy, his wife Jacqueline, and Texas Governor John Connally and his wife were waving at the crowds when sniper fire injured Connally and fatally wounded Kennedy. The accused assassin, Lee Harvey Oswald, was shot and killed two days later. Dozens of conspiracy theories still rage about the killings.

With Kennedy's assassination, the civil rights movement lost an ally who was just beginning to grow into his role.

— NOVEMBER 23 —
1963
C. T. VIVIAN, FEARLESS STAFFER FOR SCLC

On this day in civil rights history, the Reverend C. T. Vivian continued his first year as a member of the SCLC national staff. An early proponent of Gandhian nonviolence and civil disobedience and a strong organizer, Vivian was well suited for the role.

Born in Howard, Missouri, in 1924, Cordy Tindell Vivian as a young boy moved with his mother to Macomb, Illinois. After graduating from Western Illinois University, Vivian worked for the Carver Community Center in Peoria in 1947. He led a successful movement to desegregate Peoria's cafeterias.

Vivian left Illinois to enter ministerial studies at the American Baptist College in Nashville, where he met James Lawson in 1959. Lawson's tireless community activism and workshops on nonviolence soon brought Vivian fully into the civil rights movement. Vivian founded the Nashville Christian Leadership Conference, a local offshoot of the SCLC, and became involved with the burgeoning student movement led by John Lewis, Diane Nash, and Bernard Lafayette. Vivian helped organize the first sit-ins in Nashville in 1960.

One year later, Vivian served as a replacement freedom rider, after the CORE-sponsored freedom ride was interrupted by assaults by violent racists. In 1963, he joined the SCLC, where he became a trusted aide to Martin Luther King Jr.

Vivian played important roles in the Birmingham, St. Augustine, Selma, Chicago, and Memphis campaigns, working as a planner, logistician, and frontline protester. Vivian became an international figure in 1965, when he was punched in the mouth by Selma Sheriff Jim Clark in front of news cameras and photographers, after confronting Clark over his racism and his disrespect for American democracy.

In 1969, Vivian published *Black Power and the American Myth*, an early book on the civil rights movement. Throughout the 1970s and 1980s, he worked for various civil rights groups, including the Black Action Strategies and Information Center, the Center for Democratic Renewal, and the Southern Organizing Committee Education Fund, among other black organizations.

Vivian continues to speak across the country, still carrying the banner of peace, love, and integration. He also works as a consultant for corporations seeking to improve their race relations and/or internal diversity.

— NOVEMBER 24 —

1830

MARION, ALABAMA, HOME OF CIVIL RIGHTS WOMEN

On this day in civil rights history, the small town of Marion in west Alabama was newly incorporated and facing its unusual future significance in the struggle against segregation.

Named for Revolutionary War hero Francis Marion, the town is the county seat of Perry County, in the heart of the rich agricultural "black belt." Slaveowners flocked into the area and built plantations and established schools. Judson College, once the country's fifth largest women's college, opened in Marion in 1838. Marion Military Institute, the oldest military prep school in the country, is also located there. A black college that was moved to Montgomery and is now Alabama State University also began in Marion.

By the mid-1960s, a century after Emancipation, and after mechanization had replaced many black workers in the cotton fields, Marion and Perry County continued to have a majority black population. Yet none of the black citizens could vote.

In 1965, Marion was one of the locus points for James Bevels's Alabama Project to register black voters. After SCLC staffer James Orange was arrested in Marion, a night march was planned for February 17. During the march, local youth Jimmie Lee Jackson was shot and killed by an Alabama state trooper. Outrage over Jackson's death led directly to the Selma-to-Montgomery March, which galvanized Congress to pass the Voting Rights Act.

Another remarkable thing about Marion, however, is the coincidence that three of the leading civil rights figures in U.S. history married wives who grew up in Marion. Coretta Scott King, Juanita Jones Abernathy, and Jean Childs Young, the wives of Martin Luther King, Ralph Abernathy, and Andrew Young respectively, all were born and grew up in or around Marion.

Besides playing an active role in the movement, Juanita Abernathy served in numerous civic organizations. Jean Childs Young worked as an organizer in the 1970s and was a noted educator. And Coretta Scott King was often beside her husband during the movement and has carried on his legacy since his death.

These three women suffered deaths of loved ones, bombing and shooting attacks on their homes, endless crises, financial woes, and the accompanying stress of living on the front lines. They also raised families. Each recognized their husband's importance to the movement, and worked in a supportive role. Each sacrificed much of their relationship to the larger cause.

— November 25 —
1955
ICC Outlaws Segregation on Interstate Buses

On this day in civil rights history, the U.S. Interstate Commerce Commission outlawed segregation on interstate buses, though it would take years for the ruling to be enforced.

Created in the Grover Cleveland administration by the Interstate Commerce Act of 1887, the ICC was the first regulatory agency in U.S. history. The ICC was intended to rein in the railroad industry, where a few rich businessmen with their rail monopolies were fleecing small farmers and local businesses. The ICC worked to stabilize prices and end discriminatory business practices of corporations involved in what amounted to large-scale theft.

The ICC was relatively powerless, however, until President Theodore Roosevelt expanded its powers. In the 20th century, the ICC also took charge of trucking lines, bus lines, water freight carriers, and pipelines, making it a major agency in the government and an important regulatory commission.

In charge of regulating commerce and travel between states, the ICC became involved in the civil rights movement first tangentially and later as an agent for change.

In 1942, Thurgood Marshall used the ICC clause as the main thrust of his argument in the landmark *Irene Morgan v. Virginia* case, the first court ruling against the separate-but-equal doctrine. Though narrowly defined and thus easily circumvented, the ruling in the case paved the way for the later challenges involving segregated travel on all carriers.

In 1955, the ICC banned segregation on buses that traveled across state lines. In the South, however, the law was not enforced. The freedom riders of 1961 decided to test the law—and the Kennedy administration's commitment to enforcement of civil rights—by traveling in biracial groups on buses through the Deep South states.

As a result, in 1962, the ICC banned segregation in bus terminals and lunch counters in bus stations. The two rulings together had widespread consequences in ending Jim Crow segregation.

In the 1970s and 1980s, Congress deregulated many industries while creating new agencies to oversee aspects of commerce, trade, and business. The ICC soon became irrelevant and in 1995 was abolished.

— NOVEMBER 26 —

1960

SNCC FORMATION SHIFTS MOVEMENT TACTICS

On this day in civil rights history, the Student Nonviolent Coordinating Committee continued to grow, after its creation in April.

The dramatic, immediate impact of the student sit-in movement, which began in February 1960, caused many in the civil rights movement to want to harness the momentum and the spirit of the next generation.

SNCC arose out of a two-day youth conference organized at Shaw University in April. SCLC staffer Ella Baker sponsored the meeting and it was funded with an $800 grant from SCLC. Early SNCC leaders included John Lewis, Marion Barry, Bob Moses, Diane Nash, James Bevel, James Forman, Charles McDew, and Julian Bond; there were many others.

SNCC made the more established civil rights groups nervous. SNCC was aggressive and at times reckless, fiery, and often uncompromising, but it was also spirited, inventive, and dedicated, tapping into the huge reservoir of earnest college kids looking for something to believe in. SNCC workers were disciplined nonviolent activists; many of the early leaders had trained in James Lawson's workshops on nonviolence.

The group was involved in all the major civil rights activities of the 1960s, from the 1963 March on Washington, where John Lewis delivered the most stringent criticism of the Kennedy administration's lack of progress in the civil rights arena, to Freedom Summer in Mississippi, to the Selma-to-Montgomery March, to name just a few.

SNCC sought to be a grassroots, egalitarian organization. It was effective, if sometimes unwieldy. The older leaders of SCLC, most of them ministers, had mixed feelings for SNCC, while the NAACP seemed to look down on the youngsters.

But the SNCC activists made themselves a necessity for civil rights campaigns. They supplied many of the frontline registrars, activists, and protesters, laying the groundwork and infrastructure for the SCLC preachers to capitalize on in many of their campaigns.

In 1966, SNCC imploded. Stokely Carmichael replaced John Lewis as national director, while dozens of other key staffers, including Bob Moses, left the organization. SNCC purged itself of its white membership. Carmichael then popularized the phrase "Black Power," charting the future of the organization. SNCC discarded nonviolent resistance for self-defense, and then later advocated revolutionary tactics. Carmichael left to be replaced by H. Rap Brown.

By the close of the 1960s, SNCC had sputtered to an end. The premiere student group, the precursor to the student antiwar movement, and one of the most important U.S. civil rights organizations simply disappeared.

— NOVEMBER 27 —
1943
CORE PIONEERS CIVIL RIGHTS ACTIVITY

On this day in civil rights history, the Congress of Racial Equality developed its segregation-fighting techniques and worked to attract new members. Although overshadowed by SNCC and SCLC in later years, CORE was in many ways the pioneering civil rights organization.

CORE grew out of the mostly Quaker Fellowship of Reconciliation. Founded by James Farmer, Bayard Rustin, George Houser, and Berniece Fisher, among others, CORE at first operated as a localized grassroots organization. Houser, a white Chicago student, was co-leader of the group, establishing the organization's multiracial message of tolerance, respect, and integration.

Unlike the Fellowship of Reconciliation, however, CORE was not purely a pacifist organization, but rather was an organization that would use nonviolence to achieve its goal of integration. CORE's leaders believed that widespread civil disobedience, in the vein of Henry David Thoreau and Mohatma Gandhi, would be a powerful weapon against segregation.

In 1942, almost 20 years before the student sit-in movement began, CORE organized a series of sit-ins.

In April 1947, CORE sent a biracial group of bus riders into the South in an effort to challenge segregation across interstate lines. This would become known as the first freedom ride. A decentralized mostly volunteer organization, CORE decided to strengthen itself as a national organization. Farmer was elected its first national director in 1953.

After the 1960 sit-ins in Greensboro and Nashville, CORE remobilized. In 1961, CORE, with Farmer at the helm, decided to revive the freedom rides concept.

During the 1960s, CORE was one of the big three civil rights organizations in the South, alongside SNCC and SCLC. CORE played an integral part in the 1963 March on Washington, Mississippi Freedom Summer, and other key events.

James Farmer led CORE through most of the early 1960s successes. But in 1966, as the movement began to split into bickering factions, Farmer left the organization, disillusioned with the black power direction. He was replaced by Floyd McKissick, who would do away with the nonviolent philosophy altogether. Like SNCC, CORE also ceased to be a multiracial organization.

In 1968, McKissick was replaced by Roy Innis, who continues to run the organization today.

— November 28 —
1960
Novelist Richard Wright Dies

On this day in civil rights history, novelist Richard Wright died. His writing inspired many in the movement.

Wright was born to illiterate sharecroppers in Roxie, Mississippi, in 1908, on a plantation near Natchez. When his father abandoned his family, Wright and his mother and brother moved to Jackson. Wright attended a segregated high school and was stung by the miserable conditions African Americans were living in.

He published his first short story in 1924. In 1927, he moved to Chicago and worked as a postal clerk. When the Great Depression hit, he worked a variety of jobs, and became involved with the Communist Party. He began publishing articles for the *Daily Worker*.

In 1937, he moved to New York and a year later published a collection titled *Uncle Tom's Children*. He was awarded a Guggenheim Fellowship and with that money was able to finish his one undisputed masterpiece, *Native Son*.

Native Son follows Bigger Thomas, a black man from the Chicago slums who begins working for a wealthy white family, falls in with a group of communists, and accidentally commits a murder. Thomas is locked into a pattern of others' creation; his lack of education, society's low expectations, and unwritten social codes have resulted in a doomed life. Whether he tries to do good or ill, he does not have a chance. The novel is a harsh, uncompromising meditation on race and politics, revealing the brutal social controls held in place by white America. *Native Son* sold 250,000 copies on its initial publication.

While he was writing it, Wright knew that *Native Son* was going to be different: ". . . no one would weep over it . . . it would be so hard and deep that they would have to face it without the consolation of tears." Few novels of the 20th century match it.

In 1946, Wright moved to Paris to live free from the institutionalized racism of America; James Baldwin and Chester Himes followed in his footsteps. Wright became friends with Albert Camus and Jean Paul-Sartre, and his writing took on greater existentialist dimensions, but most critics agree that his work suffered from the disconnection to his home country.

Wright died from a heart attack in Paris in 1960. He was 62.

— NOVEMBER 29 —
1908
CONGRESSMAN ADAM CLAYTON POWELL JR. BORN

On this day in civil rights history, future congressman Adam Clayton Powell Jr. was born in Connecticut. His father preached at New York's Abyssinian Baptist Church, the largest Protestant congregation in the United States at the time, and Powell spent much of his youth in the big city.

During the Great Depression, Powell moved to Harlem and became a popular community organizer of rent strikes and mass protests, as well as boycotts of white businesses that refused to hire blacks. In 1937, Powell succeeded his father as pastor of Abyssinian and began a career as an activist preacher, pushing for reforms from the pulpit while using his position in the community to enter politics.

In 1944, Powell was elected to Congress from New York's 22nd district, which included his hometown of Harlem. As one of only two blacks in Congress (with William Dawson), Powell fought against segregation and pushed for stronger social legislation. And he agitated the Southern members of the Democratic Party, who hated sharing the same room with him.

Powell was elected to 11 consecutive terms, and with each new term gained seniority and prestige. In 1961, Powell became chair of the House Education and Labor Committee. From here he helped raise minimum wages, worked to improve educational standards, and helped the disabled. After years of effort, he became one of the more powerful men on Capitol Hill.

But Powell's success came at a price. The decades of power politics made him difficult, egotistical, and manipulative. As a high-profile public African American, he attacked Martin Luther King Jr. and A. Philip Randolph, among others, and had a personal vendetta against Bayard Rustin. He criticized other black leaders so often that he was not invited to speak at the 1963 March on Washington, despite his stature.

Eventually he was damaged by campaign finance scandals and he lost his seat in 1970 to Charles Rangel. In his last days, Powell spent his days fishing in the Bahamas, while drinking the evenings away at a bar called The End of the World.

On April 4, 1972, he died. More than 100,000 mourners filed past his coffin during the Harlem funeral.

— NOVEMBER 30 —

1924

BIRTHDATE OF SHIRLEY CHISHOLM

On this day in civil rights history, groundbreaking educator and politician Shirley Chisholm was born in Brooklyn, New York.

Chisholm's parents were from Barbados and Ghana, and Chisholm spent much of her childhood in Barbados, attending classes in the British school system, far away from the tainting prejudice that scarred many American black children. She returned to the United States to attend high school. In 1949, Chisholm graduated from Brooklyn College. She went on to earn a master's degree from Columbia University and then spent ten years as a director and later consultant of large daycare systems.

Chisholm

In 1964, Chisholm ran for the New York state legislature and won. Four years later, she ran for the House of Representatives and was elected to U.S. Congress as a Democrat; she defeated James Farmer, civil rights leader and founder of CORE, who ran as a Republican. Chisholm was the first black woman elected to Congress.

Chisholm shocked Congress when, as a freshman, she demanded reassignment after being placed on the House Forestry Committee. She was reassigned to the Veterans' Affairs Committee. Chisholm earned a reputation as a strong liberal opposed to militarism and was soon on the Education and Labor Committee.

In 1969, Chisholm became a founder of the Democratic Select Committee, which became the Congressional Black Caucus. In 1972, she made history with a strong bid for the Democratic presidential nomination. George McGovern eventually defeated her. But her campaign gave her a platform to push for the issues she believed in, including civil rights.

During her tenure, Chisholm worked for increased spending for education, a higher minimum wage, and better health care, while tirelessly stumping for the needs of inner-city residents. In 1982, she retired from Congress.

She went on to teach at the university level and lecture. She published two books, *Unbought and Unbossed* and *The Good Fight*.

On January 1, 2005, after several strokes, Chisholm died in her home in Florida. She was 80 years old. "She was a woman of great courage," Jesse Jackson said at her funeral.

This day in

December

— December 1 —
1955
Rosa Parks Arrested on Montgomery Bus

On this day in civil rights history, Rosa Parks was arrested for defying segregated seating laws on a Montgomery, Alabama, city bus. Her arrest triggered the Montgomery bus boycott, and many view Parks as the "mother of the 20th century civil rights movement" in the United States.

On the afternoon of December 1, Parks left her job as a seamstress in the Montgomery Fair department store in downtown Montgomery, ducked into a drugstore for a small purchase, then boarded the Cleveland Avenue bus for the one-mile ride to her home.

The bus was almost full, and Parks took a seat in the first row of seats in the "colored" seating section. At the next stop, white passengers were waiting to board, but there were no more seats in the "white" section. As bus drivers were empowered to do under local custom and city ordinance, driver J. F. Blake ordered Parks and the three other blacks sitting beside her to stand so the whites could sit down. Three complied; Parks sat silently. When she continued to refuse the bus driver's command, he got off the bus and called the police. Shortly officers Fletcher May and Dempsey Mixon arrived, arrested Parks, and took her to the police station for booking.

Parks then called her mother, who contacted local civil rights leader E. D. Nixon, who sought to learn the charges against Parks. Police officials would not tell him anything, so Nixon called local white attorney Clifford Durr. Durr and his wife Virginia, the sister-in-law of Supreme Court Justice

Sheriff's booking photo of Rosa Parks

Photo courtesy of Associated Press

Hugo Black, went with Nixon to the jail, where Nixon pledged his home as security on Parks's bond, and she was released. She was to appear in Montgomery municipal court on Monday, December 5, to face the charges against her.

Over the years, Parks, a quiet, dignified woman, has been quoted as saying "tiredness" was the reason for her refusal to give up her seat. But there was more than physical tiredness behind her actions. She was the secretary of the local NAACP chapter, had attended integrated workshops at the Highlander Folk Center in Tennessee, and was well aware of previous arrests of other Montgomery women on charges similar to hers.

— DECEMBER 2 —
1955
WOMEN'S POLITICAL COUNCIL FORCES BOYCOTT ISSUE

On this day in civil rights history, word of the arrest of Rosa Parks spread rapidly through the African American community in Montgomery.

At Alabama State College, the Women's Political Council, under the leadership of Professor JoAnn Robinson, wrote and began mimeographing thousands of copies of a flyer urging a Monday boycott of the City Lines bus company. The WPC members worked in secret, because they were risking their jobs by using college equipment to print the flyers. Although Alabama State was a black college, it was under the control of the state of Alabama, and the state's policies were completely in support of segregation.

Students talk to reporter at Alabama State

When they completed their work, the WPC members fanned out across the city delivering the boycott flyers within the black community. Meanwhile, E. D. Nixon had been phoning other black leaders and a meeting was arranged to discuss the situation. The meeting was to be Friday evening, December 2, at the Dexter Avenue Baptist Church, whose young pastor was the Reverend Martin Luther King Jr.

By the time the 75 ministers and other leaders assembled, sentiment for a boycott had already been so stirred up by the flyers, that there was little choice but to follow the WPC's lead. A few committees were created and another meeting was set for Monday night to review the results of Parks's pending court hearing and whether the boycott had been effective.

Then everyone waited.

The members of the WPC were motivated both by a strong sense of civic responsibility and by personal experience. Even though they were professional women and among the most educated citizens in Montgomery, almost all of them one time or another had been the victims of mistreatment on the city's buses.

Robinson would later write a memoir in which she told how she had boarded an almost empty bus in 1949 and taken a seat near the middle, only to have the bus driver stop the bus and come back to her seat and tell her gruffly that she was too close to the front of the bus and would have to move back. Afraid of being physically assaulted by the driver, she chose instead to leave the bus. Her experience was all-too familiar to many black women in Montgomery.

Months before Parks's arrest, Professor Robinson had presented a statement to the Montgomery city commission requesting changes in the bus sytem, including more courtesy from white drivers toward their black patrons. The request had gone unanswered by city officials.

— DECEMBER 3 —

1955

REPORTER'S 'SCOOP' OF BOYCOTT HELPS SPREAD THE WORD

On this day in civil rights history, Joe Azbell, city editor of the *Montgomery Advertiser*, wrote the story that would appear in Sunday morning's edition warning that local Negroes were planning to boycott the city bus system.

The story was just what black leader E. D. Nixon had hoped for when he called Azbell to meet him at the train station Friday afternoon if he wanted a good story. Nixon, a Pullman porter as well as the local NAACP leader, had spent Thursday evening bailing Rosa Parks out of jail, then that evening and Friday morning calling black ministers to alert them and to ask to come to a meeting Friday afternoon to discuss the situation. Nixon wouldn't be at the meeting, because he was leaving beforehand on a train run, which is why he asked Azbell to meet him at the station.

By this time, JoAnn Robinson's flyer calling for a Monday bus boycott was already circulating in the black community, and Nixon gave Azbell a copy of it.

The flyer read, in part: "Don't ride the bus . . . Monday, December 5 . . . Another Negro woman has been arrested and put in jail because she refused to get up out of her seat on the bus and give it to a white person. . . This must be stopped . . . The next time it may be you or you or you . . . Come to a mass meeting Monday at 7 p.m. at Holt Street Baptist Church for further instructions."

Nixon anticipated that Azbell would want the "scoop" for a sensational story that would get the attention of the white community, which was already worked up about racial issues in the aftermath of the 1954 *Brown* ruling of the U.S. Supreme Court, as well as other cracks in the segregation wall. But Nixon was also counting on Azbell's story to help get the word out to the black community.

Sure enough, Azbell's story in the *Advertiser* on Sunday morning, December 4, 1955, did both. And the story also helped motivate city officials to send out motorcycle cops to trail buses through black neighborhoods in case anyone tried to "intimidate" blacks from riding the bus on Monday morning.

The heavy police presence, of course, instead of reassuring black bus riders, made them even more likely to stay off the buses and thus avoid any potential for trouble with the police, who were at this time all white and not known for their sympathy with the black community.

Both men are now dead, but Nixon had a long, friendly relationship with Azbell, who eventually became an aide to Alabama Governor George C. Wallace. In the 1960s, Azbell wrote a scurrilous book, *The Riotmakers*, which attacked civil rights activists and claimed to "expose the vicious and violent campaigns of hate waged by these individuals and groups and against the South and the white people."

— December 4 —
1967
Poor People's Campaign Announced by SCLC

On this day in civil rights history, Martin Luther King Jr. announced the Poor People's Campaign.

King left the Chicago campaign intent on broadening his impact, while struggling with profound weariness. The burden of leadership and his hectic schedule were taking their toll.

His speeches more and more denounced the widespread greed he found inherent in the capitalist system: "Large segments of America still suffer from a repulsive moral disease. . . . America's greatest problem and contradiction is that it harbors 35 million poor at a time when its resources are so vast that the existence of poverty is an anachronism." While the U.S. military budget ballooned with the costs of fighting in Vietnam, little money was being spent fixing problems at home. King began to see militarism, racism, joblessness, and poverty as linked in a vicious cycle of crass American neocolonialism, propped up by greed. It was time to rewrite the nation's history of profit-driven abuses.

Poor People's March

"Our emphasis," he said, "should shift from exclusive attention to putting people to work to enabling them to consume." And later, "A radical redistribution of power must take place."

He no longer saw the civil rights movement as only encompassing blacks.

He conceived a new March on Washington that would call the nation's poor to squat in the capital, disrupting the city's day-to-day operations until the U.S. government met their needs. He was dreaming of civil disobedience on an unprecedented scale—"to dislocate the functioning of a city." In King's mind, protests would happen simultaneously in other major urban areas. The march was planned for late April 1968. The goals included:

1. $30 billion had to be earmarked for antipoverty efforts.
2. The government had to guarantee an annual income for all citizens.
3. The government had to build at least 500,000 low-income housing units.

King had difficulty winning support for his new campaign. The SCLC was divided. Some staffers and board members wanted the organization to stay with traditional race-based civil rights activities; others supported King's antiwar and antipoverty efforts. Still others felt the plan was too ambitious and was destined for failure.

As April came around, a sanitation workers' strike in Memphis materialized and King decided to go there to speak on the workers' behalf.

— DECEMBER 5 —
1955
BUS BOYCOTT BEGINS IN MONTGOMERY, ALABAMA

On this day in civil rights history, Rosa Parks was convicted in Montgomery municipal court for violating segregation laws on a local bus four days earlier. Her conviction was expected, and the local black community was already in vigrous preparation of an unprecedented protest of her arrest and the larger issues involved.

A one-day boycott of the buses in protest of Parks's arrest had been called over the weekend for the morning of her trial. Local black leaders got up early and watched anxiously as the buses began running. To their delight, practically no blacks were on the buses; the boycott was working beyond their hopes.

Attorney Fred Gray argued on Mrs. Parks's behalf but to no avail; she was quickly convicted and fined $10 and court costs by Judge John Scott. Gray announced that he would appeal.

That afternoon, some 16 black leaders, who had responded on Friday to E. D. Nixon's call for a meeting to discuss the Parks situation, reconvened in the basement of the Dexter Avenue Baptist Church and organized the Montgomery Improvement Association; Dexter's pastor, the Reverend Martin Luther King Jr., 26, was elected as president, the Reverend L. Roy Bennett as vice president, and all those present as an executive committee. The Reverend Ralph D. Abernathy, 29, was named head of a committee to draft resolutions to be presented at a mass meeting that evening.

Reverend Abernathy

Photo courtesy of Library of Congress

The mass meeting had already been called for in the flyer prepared and distributed over the weekend by the Women's Political Council. The meeting was to be at 7 p.m. at Holt Street Baptist Church. By the appointed hour, the church was packed, and loudspeakers were set up so the thousands standing outside could hear the proceedings.

For most present, it was their first time to hear King speak, as he had been Dexter's pastor and in Montgomery for only a short time. He presided over the meeting, gave an eloquent and powerful summation of the grievances behind the boycott, presented the resolutions prepared by Abernathy's committee, and asked the audience if they wanted to continue the boycott indefinitely until the bus company met a short list of demands for better service to the black community.

The crowd enthusiastically responded, and the Montgomery bus boycott was underway.

— December 6 —

1935

National Council of Negro Women Formed

On this day in civil rights history, or the day before, Mary McLeod Bethune formed the National Council of Negro Women. After years struggling as both an African American and a woman, Bethune decided that a national women's organization was needed in the ongoing struggle for equal rights for African Americans. Early on, she had discovered that even in progressive organizations, women were often shunted to the side.

Photo courtesy of Urban Educator

President Dorothy Height

As a separate but related issue, women did not gain the right to vote in the United States until 1920. The two causes had much in common but never quite congealed into a unified movement. (Similarly, the plight of American Indians was not taken up by African American organizations, nor do Latinos and blacks work closely together. Malcolm X, after his journey to Mecca, realized the problem of racism in America was multifaceted and global: economic and racial, based on centuries of exploitation, division, and class. Martin Luther King Jr. was moving to a similar territory, when he was killed.)

The National Council of Negro Women grew out of Bethune's desire to see unity within rights causes. An adviser to four presidents, Bethune formed the NCNW, replacing the older National Association of Colored Women, to speak and act for African American women in national and international affairs. Eleanor Roosevelt attended the first meeting, as did future NCNW president Dorothy Height.

Although women played a crucial part in the formation of the NAACP and other organizations, as the civil rights movement entered the 1950s and 1960s, women were excluded from many leadership decisions and positions. There is ample evidence of this, but one notable example is that no woman spoke at the 1963 March on Washington. Despite the substantial contributions made by women such as Fannie Lou Hamer, Ella Baker, Dorothy Height, Daisy Bates, and countless others from abolitionism through the 1960s, the place of women in the movement is problematic. Except for SNCC, the civil rights organizations were mostly hierarchical and patriarchal, reflecting the same conservative white man-centric establishment they challenged.

NCNW is still active. Its community-based approach was implemented early on, and the NCNW operates as a research and advocacy group, with more than four million members worldwide. Its emphasis has always been on women of color, so it is no surprise that the organization now focuses much of its attention on issues affecting women in parts of Africa.

— DECEMBER 7 —

1977

JOSEPH LOWERY LEADS SCLC

On this day in civil rights history, Joseph Lowery, colleague to Martin Luther King Jr. and Ralph Abernathy, and with them a cofounder of the SCLC, continued his work as the organization's new president.

Born in Huntsville, Alabama, in 1921, Lowery spent his adolescence in Chicago before returning to Huntsville to finish high school. In Alabama, he lived under the hard edge of segregation and resolved to fight it. After graduating from high school, Lowery studied at Knoxville College, then earned his divinity doctorate from the Chicago Ecumenical Institute. In 1950, he moved to Mobile, where his first preaching job was at Warren Street United Methodist Church.

In Mobile, Lowery became the head of the Alabama Civic Affairs Association, an early civil rights organization that worked to desegregate Alabama's public places.

In 1957, Lowery was one of the organizers of the SCLC and was elected vice president. He remained in the organization throughout the late 1950s and 1960s, playing important roles in the major SCLC events.

Even after the civil rights movement began to dissipate in the late 1960s and early 1970s, Lowery remained a steadfast activist. In 1977, he succeeded Ralph Abernathy as SCLC president and filled the post for 20 years. During the late 1970s and the 1980s, he worked to free Nelson Mandela and end South African apartheid.

In 1978 and 1979, Lowery led a campaign in north Alabama to protest the suspicious arrest of a retarded black youth—later cleared of the charges—in connection with the rapes of several white women. A march in this protest was attacked on May 26, 1979, by some 125 armed Ku Klux Klansmen; Lowery and his wife narrowly avoided being shot in the incident. A lawsuit filed as a result of the incident later bankrupted one of the three major KKK organizations.

Lowery was also a cofounder of the Black Leadership Forum, a coalition of advocacy groups, and he served as the group's president after Benjamin Hooks and Vernon Jordan.

In 1997, Lowery retired from the SCLC. He continues to speak around the country, remaining an active presence in politics. In 2001, Clark Atlanta University established the Joseph E. Lowery Institute for Justice and Human Rights. At his 84th birthday party in 2005, attended by Shirley Franklin, Andrew Young, and former Georgia governor Roy Barnes, Lowery challenged the 800 guests to register more voters.

Lowery is married to Evelyn Gibson Lowery, a fellow activist.

— DECEMBER 8 —
1886
AMERICAN FEDERATION OF LABOR FOUNDED

On this day in civil rights history, the American Federation of Labor (AFL) was founded by Samuel Gompers in Columbus, Ohio. Trade unions have a long and mostly supportive history with respect to African American interests.

From its inception, the AFL was a pragmatic union that favored solving immediate problems over long-term political change. The AFL began as a progressive organization on the issue of race, refusing to grant charters to unions that barred black members. But when the AFL merged with the International Association of Machinists, some of IAM's segregationist policies were adopted. As the 20th century began, the AFL became more conservative.

Photo courtesy of Library of Congress

Samuel Gompers votes

As blacks migrated from the South to the North in huge numbers, they looked for employment in the booming industrial centers. These African American workers joined local unions and craft guilds, such as the Congress of Industrial Organizations (CIO), which guaranteed them certain wages and offered protections from the type of exploitation they had suffered in the South. With union protection, many African Americans began earning decent wages for the first time in their lives, allowing many to enter the lower-middle to middle classes.

The AFL and most other unions were always politically left of center. After World War I, the AFL became a stronghold for the Democratic Party. This placed the new black activists in the same camp as the majority of prolabor workers. In the South, however, the opposite was true: Many white unionists rejected the progressive politics of the national AFL.

In 1955, the AFL merged with the more progressive CIO to form the AFL-CIO, led by George Meany and Walter Reuther. As the civil rights movement got under way in the 1960s, the AFL-CIO and most other labor unions were supportive, especially by pushing for civil rights legislation within the Democratic Party.

The epitome of black labor and civil rights activism was A. Philip Randolph, president of the Brotherhood of Sleeping Car Porters and later vice president of the AFL.

— DECEMBER 9 —
1959
JAMES LAWSON LEADS NONVIOLENCE WORKSHOPS

On this day in civil rights history, approximately, James Lawson conducted workshops on nonviolent resistance in Nashville, laying the groundwork for the student movement and SNCC activism.

Born in Uniontown, Pennsylvania, in 1928, Lawson came from a family of Methodist ministers. In 1947, he joined the Fellowship of Reconciliation (FOR) and the Congress of Racial Equality (CORE). CORE organized scattered sit-ins in the North, with moderate success. FOR founder A. J. Muste and Howard Thurman were two of Lawson's early mentors.

In 1951, Lawson was sent to prison for refusing military service, as a conscientious objector during the Korean War. He served 13 months before being paroled.

After being released, Lawson traveled to India as a Methodist missionary in 1953, where he studied the nonviolent techniques of Gandhi.

He returned to the U.S. to study theology at Oberlin College in Ohio. At Oberlin, Lawson met Martin Luther King Jr., who convinced Lawson of the necessity of direct action in the South. "Come now . . . we don't have anyone like you in the South," King told him. Lawson heeded the call; he enrolled in Vanderbilt University in Nashville, and became the Southern director of FOR.

In Nashville, Lawson began conducting workshops in nonviolent civil disobedience techniques, funded by the local arm of the SCLC. He became a mentor to black college students in the Nashville area, including Marion Barry, James Bevel, Bernard Lafayette, Diane Nash, and John Lewis. Under Lawson's tutelage, in 1960 many of the students he taught in his workshops were pioneers of the sit-in movement and then helped found SNCC.

Vanderbilt expelled Lawson for his involvement in civil rights. Lawson later worked with SNCC and the SCLC, helping coordinate the 1961 freedom rides. In 1962, Lawson moved to Memphis to pastor a Methodist church. He worked as an activist in Memphis, preaching from the pulpit against the evils of militarism and segregation. He helped James Meredith put together his March Against Fear in 1966, and he was a major organizer of the 1968 strike by sanitation workers in Memphis. In fact, it was Lawson who invited King to participate in the strike in early 1968.

In 1974, Lawson moved to Los Angeles to pastor another Methodist church. Now retired, Lawson remains an advocate for prolabor and antiwar causes.

— December 10 —
1964
Martin Luther King Jr. Accepts Nobel Peace Prize

On this day in civil rights history, Martin Luther King Jr. became the youngest person to win the Nobel Peace Prize. Nobel committee chairman Gunnar Jahn said the award was presented because King was "the first person in the Western world to have shown us that a struggle can be waged without violence. He is the first to make the message of brotherly love a reality in the course of his struggle, and he has brought this message to all men, to all nations and races."

In accepting the award, King said, in part:

MLK receives Prize from Gunnar Jahn

"I accept the Nobel Prize for Peace at a moment when 22 million Negroes of the United States are engaged in a creative battle to end the long night of racial injustice. I accept this award in behalf of a civil rights movement which is moving with determination and a majestic scorn for risk and danger to establish a reign of freedom and a rule of justice.

"I am mindful that only yesterday in Birmingham, our children, crying out for brotherhood, were answered with fire hoses, snarling dogs, and even death. I am mindful that only yesterday in Philadelphia, Mississippi, young people seeing to secure the right to vote were brutalized and murdered. And only yesterday more than 40 houses of worship in the state of Mississippi alone were bombed or burned because they offered a sanctuary to those who would not accept segregation.

"I am mindful that debilitating and grinding poverty afflicts my people and chains them to the lowest rung of the economic ladder.

"Therefore, I must ask why this prize is awarded to a movement which is beleaguered and committed to unrelenting struggle; to a movement which has not won the very peace and brotherhood which is the essence of the Nobel Prize.

"After contemplation, I conclude that this award which I receive on behalf of that movement is profound recognition that nonviolence is the answer to the crucial political and moral question of our time—the need for man to overcome oppression and violence without resorting to violence and oppression."

— DECEMBER 11 —

1977

RANDALL ROBINSON ADVOCATES REPARATIONS FOR SLAVERY

On this day in civil rights history, Randall Robinson, as national director of TransAfrica, crafted the arguments he would use for reparations for slavery.

Born in Richmond, Virginia, in 1941, Robinson attended Norfolk State College in 1959 on a basketball scholarship. He later left Norfolk and earned a degree from Virginia Union University. He graduated from Harvard Law School in 1970.

In 1977, Robinson formed the TransAfrica organization to promote constructive relationships between the United States, Africa, and parts of the Caribbean. In the 1980s, Robinson became known as a foreign-policy expert as he worked to end South African apartheid and to free political prisoner Nelson Mandela. In 1994, Robinson staged a much-publicized 27-day hunger strike to protest U.S. foreign policy in Haiti.

In 2000, Robinson gained widespread attention with the publication of his best-selling book, *The Debt: What America Owes to Blacks*, which calls for U.S. reparations to African Americans. He says near the book's beginning: "As Germany and other interests that profited owed reparations to Jews following the holocaust of Nazi persecution, America and other interests that profited owe reparations to blacks following the holocaust of African slavery which has carried forward from slavery's inception for 350-odd years to the end of U.S. government-embraced racial discrimination—an end that arrived, it would seem, only just yesterday."

The Debt jump-started debate over reparations, though the issue is not new. During Reconstruction, the idea that the state would pay the recently freed black men and women was considered. W. E. B. Du Bois, Paul Robeson, and others called for reparations in the early 20th century.

Opponents argue that slavery happened a long time ago, that there have been other wronged ethnic groups, and that reparations already exist in the form of affirmative action.

Proponents ask for reparations not just for slavery but also for legalized segregation and point to the restitution made to the Japanese Americans interned during World War II. Finally, advocates of reparations argue that systematic white privilege and black neglect remain in place, resulting in continued economic and social disparity.

Robinson, meanwhile, decided to leave America to live in Kitts-Neru, the Caribbean birthplace of his wife. He chronicled his decision in another book, *Quitting America*.

— DECEMBER 12 —
1805
ABOLITIONIST WILLIAM LLOYD GARRISON BORN

On this day in civil rights history, fiery abolitionist William Lloyd Garrison was born in New-buryport, Massachusetts. He apprenticed to a printer at a young age.

In 1831, in Boston, Garrison founded *The Liberator* newspaper. Its masthead declared: "Our country is the world—our countrymen are mankind." Garrison wrote with moral gravitas and unequivocal clarity, attacking slavery, slave owners, and gradualists who advocated a slow emancipation. He criticized the South, the federal government, and the church.

A visionary social reformer, Garrison wanted to create a crisis that would end slavery. He believed abolition would be a transfigurative event, heralding a new age of Christian charity and democracy. His hero was British antislavery crusader William Wilberforce. Garrison demanded a society of total equals—he rejected any compromise for less. He also began campaigning for women's suffrage.

In 1832, Garrison helped form the New England Anti-slavery Society. By the end of 1832, *The Liberator* had several thousand subscribers, and Garrison, only 27, was one of the most influential and infamous abolitionists.

His fame came at a high price. The state of Georgia offered $5,000 for his arrest. In 1835, he was dragged by an angry mob through the streets of Boston. The mob planned to lynch him, but he was rescued and put in prison. Garrison was vilified, harassed, and impugned everywhere he went. Still, he persisted. He wrote in his column: "Talking will create zeal—zeal, opposition—opposition will drive men to inquiry—inquiry will induce conviction—conviction will lead to action—action will demand union—and then will follow victory."

As the abolitionist movement grew, Garrison became a focal point, meeting with John Brown, Frederick Douglass, Henry Ward Beecher, and every other major abolitionist and black figure.

Garrison and Douglass became friends but had a falling-out over the future of abolitionism and the U.S. Constitution, which Garrison thought was evil. In 1854, Garrison burned a copy of the Constitution in a public ceremony.

After the Civil War, Garrison continued to work for women's suffrage and civil rights. But in 1865, after the passage of the 13th Amendment, he ceased publication of *The Liberator*. He believed that his work was over.

He died May 24, 1879.

— DECEMBER 13 —
1903
ELLA BAKER BORN IN VIRGINIA

On this day in civil rights history, Ella Baker, influential member of the NAACP and the SCLC, and mentor of SNCC, was born in Norfolk, Virginia. This remarkable woman played an integral part in much of the 20th century effort to free African Americans from segregation.

She began work for progressive organizations in the 1930s when she became the first national director of the Young Negroes Cooperative League. In 1938, Baker began a career with the NAACP as a field secretary. She traveled across the South, recruiting and organizing local campaigns. In her travels she built up a network of grassroots activists that would later form much of the bedrock of the 1960s movement. In 1952 she became president of the New York NAACP chapter.

NAACP 35th Annual Conference, 1944

In 1957, Baker helped form the SCLC as one of its charter members and its first executive director. In 1960, she left, unhappy with the cult of personality she saw developing there. She had a less autocratic, more group-centered organization in mind. She would later say of SCLC, "The most important thing was, and still is in my mind, is to develop people to the point that they don't need a strong, savior-type leader."

Baker went to work for the YWCA and invited students to a youth leadership conference at Shaw University over Easter Weekend 1960. The conference was to help organize the students involved in the burgeoning sit-in movement. At the conference, the Student Nonviolent Coordinating Committee was formed under her tutelage. Baker began working for SNCC immediately. Baker was involved in all the SNCC actions during the 1960s, including voter-registration projects and the Mississippi Freedom Democratic Party, of which she played a central part.

Throughout her life, she was close to the center of the movement, serving in leadership positions at various times with the NAACP, SCLC, SNCC, and SDS.

She died on her birthday in 1986.

- DECEMBER 14 -

1930

CIVIL RIGHTS ATTORNEY FRED D. GRAY BORN

On this day Fred David Gray was born in a shotgun house in Montgomery. His father, a carpenter, died when he was two, and he was raised by his mother, a domestic servant; four of this remarkable woman's five children earned college degrees.

After graduating from Alabama State College, Fred Gray wanted to become a lawyer, but the only law school in Alabama did not admit African Americans. However, in compensation for denying professional training to blacks, the state would pay part of their expenses at schools in the North. Thus, Gray enrolled in Case Western Reserve Law School in Cleveland, Ohio. He was an outstanding student and on graduation was offered good positions with firms in Cleveland. But he had made a vow to himself to return to his native Alabama and "destroy everything segregated I could find."

After passing the bar exam in Alabama, Gray became one of two African American lawyers in Montgomery. He was 23 years old. His law practice was slow in the beginning, but he worked hard and began to join local black organizations, including the NAACP, where he met a young woman named Rosa Parks, who was a seamstress at a department store around the corner from his office. He also met a 25-year-old preacher named Martin L. King Jr.

When Rosa Parks was arrested December 1, 1955, for violating the local bus-segregation ordinance, Gray became her attorney. He was also the attorney for the Montgomery bus boycott that grew from Parks's arrest. Two months later he filed a federal court lawsuit challenging the segregation ordinance, and he represented Parks, King, and 86 other black leaders arrested for violating a century-old antiboycott law. He won all these cases, and Gray's legal victories and the Montgomery bus boycott are widely regarded as the flashpoint of the 20th-century civil rights movement.

Gray went on to fulfill his vow of destroying segregation wherever he found it. His lawsuits over the next two decades desegregated schools, colleges, police departments, housing complexes, recreation facilities, and more, setting legal precedents that changed not only his native Montgomery but the state and nation.

In 1970 he was elected to the Alabama Legislature, and in 2004, he became president of the once-segregated Alabama State Bar Association.

— DECEMBER 15 —
2003
STROM THURMOND'S FAMILY ACKNOWLEDGES HIS BLACK CHILD

On this day in civil rights history, the family of Strom Thurmond acknowledged that the late senator had an illegitimate black daughter. The announcement was the final chapter in a strange, racially charged odyssey of politics and family secrets.

Thurmond had a long and controversial political career. In 1947, he was elected governor of South Carolina in a campaign in which he gave incendiary speeches full of racist invective. One year later, he ran as the presidential nominee of the Dixiecrat Party. He said in a campaign speech: "I want to tell you, ladies and gentleman, that there's not enough troops in the army to force the Southern people to break down segregation and admit the nigra race into our theaters, into our swimming pools, into our homes, and into our churches."

In the subsequent election, Thurmond carried four states.

In 1954, Thurmond was elected to the U.S. Senate. He quickly established himself as a powerful figure and was a principal author of the Southern Manifesto, released in response to the *Brown v. Board* decision. In opposition to the 1957 Civil Rights Act, Thurmond delivered the longest individual filibuster in Senate history, speaking for 24 hours and 18 minutes. In an era of race-baiting demagogues, Thurmond was a champion.

Essie Mae Washington-Williams

Photo courtesy of Clemson University

In 1964, Thurmond switched political parties, a move that highlighted the shift then beginning of Southern white Democratic voters to the Republican Party.

However, like many other Southern politicians, Thurmond moderated his views during the 1970s as—thanks to legislation he had opposed—blacks began to vote in increasing numbers. In 1981, Thurmond became president *pro tempore* of the Senate.

In January of 2003, Thurmond retired from office after serving for almost 50 years, the longest-serving senator ever. He died six months later at age 100.

After his death, a strange story appeared. A 78-year-old black woman named Essie Mae Washington-Williams claimed that she was the illegitimate daughter of Thurmond and that they had maintained a secret familial relationship. "I never wanted to harm him," she answered when asked why she remained quiet until after his death. Thurmond's family then acknowledged that Washington-Williams was indeed Thurmond's daughter, born as the result of a 1920s affair with an African American maid in Thurmond's parents' home.

It was an odd end to Thurmond's racially charged political career.

— December 16 —

1961

Hundreds of Protesters Arrested in Albany, Georgia

On this day in civil rights history, Martin Luther King Jr. and Ralph Abernathy were arrested, along with hundreds of other demonstrators, in Albany, Georgia.

King, Abernathy, and SCLC Executive Director Wyatt Walker had arrived in the central Georgia city the night before in response to a call from local civil rights leaders to get involved with growing protests against segregation. SNCC workers had come to town a few months earlier to register black voters, and an impromptu sit-in on November 1 had led to a November 17 coalition between SNCC's "outside agitators" and older Albany NAACP leaders. That coalition kicked off marches and demonstrations that quickly escalated.

But the SCLC was not involved until King received the invitation to come down from Atlanta and give a speech. King and his colleagues came, he preached a sermon, and afterwards he realized he was committed to what would become known as the Albany movement. Then on December 16, King and the others marched and were promptly arrested.

Albany Police Chief Laurie Pritchett immediately had King and Abernathy bused separately to the Sumter County jail. Cut off from the other prisoners, King felt isolated. Walker decided to take command, but that unsettled the leaders of the SNCC/NAACP coalition.

A few days later, King and Abernathy appeared at trial. They were released in a compromise reached with local white officials. Part of the compromise, however, was a moratorium on the protests, and many who had been marching in Albany before the SCLC arrived were upset that their momentum would be lost.

Months of minor clashes, stalled protests, and broken promises followed. Albany's white officials and police did not respond with violence, so no dramatic news coverage resulted. Making matters worse, they succeeded in portraying SNCC, SCLC, and the NAACP as outside agitators and declared that until the outsiders left, the city would not deal with the issues of segregation. Of course, the white officials were the ones driving the issues in the first place. This circular sequence of events prevented real progress. And Chief Pritchett, with his clever passive resistance, shaped public opinion against the Albany movement.

King and the SCLC maintained a presence in Albany, though he left frequently for speaking engagements elsewhere. Larger issues seemed to be weighing on his mind. As long as Albany was the main SCLC issue, he would be hamstrung in other actions. Meanwhile, the resources of SNCC, SCLC, and the NAACP were being taxed. The Albany movement was beginning to look like a quagmire.

— DECEMBER 17 —
1965
PHOTOGRAPHERS SHAPED THE VIEW OF THE MOVEMENT

On this day in civil rights history, selected at random, images by photographers and television news cameramen shaped the world's reaction to the civil rights movement.

Across the many battle lines of the struggle, news photographers and freelance journalists were often present, sometimes risking their lives to deliver images of the movement to the world.

Photographers and journalists captured localized campaigns in the South, transmitting the hope and terror, the dismay and fear, the courage and passion—the raw emotion of the civil rights movement—to the rest of the United States, and the world. Their powerful images played a tremendous role in pulling the majority of white Americans into sympathy with the movement.

Without the stills and newsreel footage of Birmingham schoolchildren being blasted by powerful water hoses and attacked by police dogs, or the wrenching images of sheriff's deputies descending on peaceful marchers with horses, billy clubs, and tear gas in Selma, or the horror of blood streaming down the face of freedom rider James Zwerg in Montgomery, the majority of Americans would have paid little attention to civil rights protests. The photographs and news footage, however, were shocking and could not be ignored or denied. In large measure, the presence of journalists offered some protection to civil rights workers, and their images inflamed the indignation and outrage of the American public and were catalysts to the civil rights legislation of the 1960s.

Some of the key photographers were:

Spider Martin, working for the *Birmingham News,* who photographed the 1965 "Bloody Sunday" attack on marchers at the Edmund Pettus Bridge in Selma.

Danny Lyon, SNCC staff photographer, who captured many demonstrations and confrontations.

Charles Moore, who worked for the *Montgomery Advertiser* and later with *Life* magazine as a contract photographer. He covered Freedom Summer, James Meredith desegregating the University of Mississippi, the Birmingham campaign, and the Selma-to-Montgomery March.

Ernest Withers, a self-employed photographer, traveled with Martin Luther King, James Meredith, and other civil rights leaders. He was at many important events, including the desegregation of Little Rock and the Memphis Sanitation Workers Strike.

There were many others, including Matt Herron, Jack Moebes, and Harold Lowe.

— December 18 —

1912

Aviator Benjamin Davis Born

On this day in civil rights history, military hero Benjamin O. Davis Jr. was born in Washington, D.C., in the segregated capital of a segregated country.

His father, Benjamin O. Davis Sr., was a successful military officer in his own right, achieving the status of the first black U.S. Army general in 1940. Davis Jr. followed in his father's footsteps.

In 1932, Davis entered West Point Military Academy. He was ostracized by the white cadets in his four years there; he never had a roommate and ate his meals silently and alone. On graduation in 1936, he was commissioned a second lieutenant, becoming one of only two black officers in the Army, the other being his father.

Gen. Benjamin O. Davis (l)

Davis was eventually stationed in Tuskegee, where he taught military tactics to black military reservists. His career seemed permanently sidetracked.

In 1941, however, President Franklin Roosevelt ordered the creation of a black fighter-pilot squadron. Tuskegee was chosen as the training base. As the only black officer, Davis was picked to lead the experiment. Davis earned his pilot's wings and became commander of the all-black 99th Pursuit Squadron. He was later named commander of the 332nd Fighter Group, a larger all-black flying unit that became known as the Tuskegee Airmen.

From the beginning, the all-black squadron had its critics. A movement to remove the black pilots from duty compelled Davis to testify before General George Marshall. Davis's fighter pilots had been accused of performing poorly, but Davis argued that his squadrons in fact outperformed white squadrons, especially considering the black squadrons were understaffed and flew twice as much.

Exonerated of the charges, the 332nd ended the war as one of the most lauded fighter squadrons. The Tuskegee Airmen shot down more than 100 German planes and never lost a bomber they were escorting.

After WWII, President Harry Truman in 1948 desegregated the armed forces by executive order. Davis, by then a colonel, helped draft the Air Force plan for integration of its units. He was finally in a position to rectify the abuses he had suffered as a young man.

Davis went on to become chief of staff for American military forces in South Korea, and received nearly every major Air Force honor during his illustrious career.

In 1991, he published his autobiography, *Benjamin Davis, Jr.: American*.

He died July 4, 2002.

Photo courtesy of Library of Congress

— December 19 —
2002
Convictions Dismissed in Central Park Jogger Case

On this day in civil rights history, a New York judge dismissed the convictions of five young men—four black and one Latino—who served years in prison for a 1989 crime that new evidence showed they did not commit.

The case involved a 28-year-old white investment banker who was jogging in New York City's Central Park when she was assaulted, brutally beaten, and left for dead. The victim was in a coma for 12 days but recovered, although her memory was damaged in the attack and she was unable to help investigators with details such as descriptions or how many attackers there were.

The sensational nature of the crime and its brutality made national headlines and exacerbated racial tensions, particularly after it came out that the only evidence against the five defendants was their "confessions." They apparently were arrested because they had been roaming Central Park the night of the assault. Their supporters said the youths—ages 14 to 16 at the time—had been coerced into confessions; no forensic evidence linked them to the crime scene.

They were nonetheless convicted and served terms ranging from 6 to 11 years. Only one of the five was still in prison in 2002, when prosecutors announced that they had a new confession and a DNA match in the case from serial rapist Matias Reyes; DNA testing had not been available in 1989 when the five youths were tried.

Civil rights leaders had expressed concern about the trials and convictions of the five youths from the beginning, and the case had the overtones of so many criminal cases over the years involving sexual assaults on white women, after which the police rounded up the first or most-available black suspects they could get their hands on.

No one minimized the Central Park victim's suffering, but some pointed out that her violation would be made worse if the guilty went unpunished while innocent persons were convicted for the crime. And that apparently is just what happened.

This case is just one of many over the past decade in which DNA testing has cleared black men wrongly accused of rapes and murders while helping law enforcement to catch the ones who actually committed the crimes.

Better late than never, though there is no way of knowing how many innocents have been imprisoned or even executed over the years under similar circumstances where there was a rush to convict, especially in the case of white women victims of sexual assaults.

JULIAN BOND WORKS TO DISMANTLE SEGREGATION IN ATLANTA

On this day in civil rights history, approximately, Julian Bond helped mount a desegregation campaign in Atlanta.

Born in Nashville in 1940, Julian Bond was raised in an atmosphere of black intellectualism. His father, Horace Mann Bond, was the first black president of Lincoln University. Bond grew up in Pennsylvania.

In 1957, Bond enrolled at Morehouse College in Atlanta. He helped form the Committee on Appeal for Human Rights, an organization that staged sit-ins and boycotts and ultimately desegregated Atlanta. His activity brought him into student activist circles, a web that led to creation of the Student Nonviolent Coordinating Committee, of which Bond was a founder.

From 1961 to 1966, Bond was one of SNCC's most visible members, serving as its communications director and as editor of its newspaper, *The Student Voice*. He helped organize and lead desegregation marches and protests in Georgia during this time. In 1964, he participated in Mississippi's Freedom Summer.

In 1965, Bond was elected to the Georgia House of Representatives. His fellow congressmen refused to seat him, however, due to his opposition to U.S. activity in Vietnam. A lawsuit was filed, and ultimately the U.S. Supreme Court ordered Georgia to seat him. He went on to serve multiple terms. In 1968, at the Democratic National Convention, he became the youngest person nominated to become the vice presidential candidate of a major party.

Articulate, witty, and personally charming, Bond became a popular lecturer on college campuses and a frequent guest on television interview shows. On April 9, 1977, Bond even hosted *Saturday Night Live,* with Tom Waits as his musical guest. During the show, John Belushi played George Wallace, giving a speech on how to improve the South's image.

In the mid-1980s, Bond decided to seek the U.S. House of Representatives seat for the Atlanta district. His opponent was his old friend and fellow SNCC founder John Lewis. The campaign was hard and personal. In 1986, Lewis won, and Bond went into teaching, working at Harvard and the University of Virginia, among other universities.

In 1998, Bond was named chairman of the NAACP. He remains a vocal, public figure on the forefront of African American issues.

— December 21 —

1956

In Victory, Riders Return to Montgomery Buses

On this day in civil rights history, 381 days after they began boycotting the city buses in Montgomery, Alabama, African American riders returned on a new, nonsegregated basis. They were free to sit anywhere they chose at any time, thanks to a court order that had arrived the previous day from the U.S. Supreme Court.

The Supreme Court had upheld a 2–1 decision by the U.S. District Court in Montgomery that found bus segregation to be unconstitutional in light of the clear mandate of the 1954 *Brown v. Board* decision overturning the "separate but equal" doctrine. Montgomery city officials had appealed the lower-court ruling, but the Supreme Court affirmed the decision without a new hearing. That left the city of Montgomery with no choice but to end the "white and colored" seating policies that had led to the arrest a year earlier of Rosa Parks and had prompted the yearlong boycott.

It is noteworthy that it was the lawsuit in federal court, and not the boycott itself, that actually overturned segregation on the buses. Yet the boycott had sustained Montgomery's African American community through the months while the lawsuit was being filed, argued,

Boycott leaders take a symbolic ride

and decided. And it was the boycott that gave Martin Luther King Jr. a chance to develop his talents for leadership and oratory that would influence millions through the larger civil rights movement that followed.

For a time, there continued to be incidents on the buses as Montgomery's white and black passengers and the bus drivers got used to the new rules. In fact, the roguish elements in Montgomery reacted immediately to the desegregation with a new round of violence. Cars belonging to prominent African Americans were vandalized. Gunshots were fired at buses (seriously wounding one black woman), and on January 10 four black churches and two homes were bombed with dynamite. One black man was murdered in a separate incident, and there was another bombing on January 27 and an attempted bombing the same night at King's home.

If anything, Montgomery was suffering more racial tension than ever. But gradually the tension eased, and bus riding again became a matter of routine. Ironically, the city buses gradually resegregated themselves as changing housing patterns and increased automobile ownership removed most white passengers from the bus routes.

ARMED SERVICES DESEGRATES WOMEN'S BRANCHES

On this day in civil rights history, the U.S. Navy gained its first two black WAVES officers. Black women were barred from the WAVES (Women Accepted for Volunteer Emergency Service) until Mildred McAfee and Mary McLeod Bethune successfully lobbied Navy Secretary James Forrestal to change enrollment policies. Harriet Ida Pickens and Frances Wills were subsequently sworn in as the first two black WAVES officers.

U.S. military forces were mostly segregated throughout the war, to the frustration and bitter disappointment of the black men and women who fought for democracy for Europe only to be denied it in their own ranks and back at home.

President Harry Truman would eliminate segregation, quotas, and discrimination in the armed forces by signing Executive Order 9981 on July 26, 1948, but even before then some gains were made, though progress varied from branch to branch.

In January 1941, the Army opened its nurse corps to blacks but with a ceiling of only 56. In June 1941, President Franklin D. Roosevelt created the Fair Employment Practices Commission, and two years later an amendment to the Nurse Training Bill barred racial bias. Soon 2,000 blacks were enrolled in the Cadet Nurse Corps.

The quota for black Army nurses was eliminated in July 1944, and the Navy dropped its color ban in January 1945. On March 9, 1945, Phyllis Daley became the first black commissioned Navy nurse.

Navy recruitment poster

On January 6, 1948, Ensign Edith DeVoe was sworn into the Regular Navy Nurse Corps, becoming its first African American officer. In March 1948, First Lieutenant Nancy C. Leftenant similarly desegregated the Regular Army Nurse Corps.

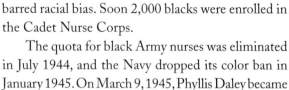

— DECEMBER 23 —

1867

BUSINESS MOGUL MADAME C. J. WALKER BORN

On this day in civil rights history, Madame C. J. Walker was born in Delta, Louisiana.

Walker grew up picking cotton in the sharecropping system. She lived a hard early life. At 7 she was orphaned. At 14, she was married. She gave birth to her daughter Lelia at 16. And at 20, she was widowed, her husband lynched by a white mob. After her husband's death, she moved to St. Louis, working as a laundress to keep food on the table. In her limited free time, she became involved in the National Association of Colored Women.

A freak accident left Walker bald. She became interested in hair tonics as a result. In 1905, she moved to Denver with only a few dollars in her pocket. But she met and married a newspaperman. She changed her name to "Madame," and opened Madame C. J. Walker's Manufacturing Company, selling tonics and cosmetics. She advertised in black newspapers across the country, while utilizing a door-to-door sales force. As her business grew, Walker started a college to train her salespeople, naming it Lelia College, after her daughter.

By 1917, she had the largest black-owned business in the United States and was the first female African American millionaire.

Walker employed thousands of African American women as commissioned sales representatives, women who otherwise would have worked as domestics. Walker gave generously to the NAACP, Tuskegee Institute, and Bethune-Cookman College. As an influential philanthropist, she met most of the civil rights figures of the time, including Ida Wells-Barnett, Mary McLeod Bethune, James Weldon Johnson, Booker T. Washington, A. Philip Randolph, and W. E. B. Du Bois.

The poor girl born to ex-slaves lived her last days in a 34-room mansion on the Hudson River in New York. "I am a woman who came from the cotton fields of the South," she said in a speech in 1912. "From there I was promoted to the washtub. From there I was promoted to the cook kitchen. And from there I promoted myself into the business of manufacturing hair goods and preparations. . . . I have built my own factory on my own ground."

On May 25, 1919, she died at age 52. Her daughter Lelia carried on the thriving family business.

i

— DECEMBER 24 —
1886
FIRST BLACK TOWN ORGANIZED

On this day in civil rights history, ex-slaves in central Florida began forming the town of Eatonville, Florida, which would become the first official black town in the United States.

Slavery in Florida was subtly different from slavery in other states. Infused with a Spanish sensibility, Florida allowed more freedoms to its slaves, who often mixed with indigenous American Indians. After the Civil War, slaves in Florida were freed. But the white slave-owners needed blacks, as they were the primary source of labor. Thus, like everywhere else in the agrarian South, ex-slaves went to work as sharecroppers and wage-laborers. Unsure of what to do or how to live, ex-slaves often signed unfair contracts. In 1866, the Union military commander of the Florida District called for a renegotiation of all contracts, as they were exploitative, amounting to slavery by another name.

Photo courtesy of Library of Congress

Zora Neale Hurston and friends in Eatonville

Near the end of Reconstruction, many African Americans in Florida remained near the plantations on which they had been slaves. But some migrated, looking for better work. Many ended up working on the huge citrus farms in Orange County, in the sweltering heat of central Florida.

Freed blacks worked in Maitland, a small town in Orange County, as domestics, citrus farmers, and day laborers. But the whites in Maitland did not like the shantytowns the poor African Americans were building around the city. The solution, proposed by Maitland mayor Josiah Eaton, was to sell the African American populace some nearby land where they could build their own town. Joseph Clark, an ex-slave, took the lead, purchasing a plot of land.

In August 1887, Clark and 26 other black men incorporated the town of Eatonville, named after Maitland's mayor. Newspapers around the country began commenting on the novel idea. Built and run by freed blacks, Eatonville began to thrive.

The small town spawned two celebrities: Deacon Jones, a professional football player, and Zora Neale Hurston, the acclaimed writer.

Eatonville remains a predominantly black town. Each year the city holds a Zora Neale Hurston arts festival.

— DECEMBER 25 —
2000
BIRTHDAY OF JESUS OBSERVED IN
AFRICAN AMERICAN CHURCHES

On this day in civil rights history, the birthday of Jesus is noteworthy for the importance of Christianity to African Americans and the history of Christianity and its relationship to slavery, segregation, and white supremacy.

Slaves arrived in the United States practicing voodoo, various animist religions, and Islam, but many converted to Christianity. Whites used Christianity to justify slavery, calling Africans the "cursed children of Ham," while also attempting to use the gospel as a platform for "love and obey thy master" teachings (later, segregationists would use the Bible to argue that God had ordained blacks to be a servant class, and white supremacists would argue an even darker vision that interpreted the Bible as proof that blacks, like Jews, were subhuman).

But the vision of a peaceful afterlife offered a sustaining message; slaves embraced the idea of the Promised Land, where earthly suffering was fleeting in the face of eternal love and delight.

African Americans formed their own churches as early as 1788, but after Emancipation black churches began to surface across the South, becoming the centers of social, economic, and intellectual life in black communities. As Jim Crow segregation and the peonage system set in, blacks continued to seek comfort in the balm of heaven.

Entering the 20th century, black preachers were among the few African Americans who had secure jobs not dependent on white employers. Black preachers thus had more freedom than others to push for equality and civil rights. Pastors like Vernon Johns and Martin Luther King Sr. began to preach the liberation struggles of Moses and the Jews, recasting African Americans as a persecuted people held in oppression by 20th-century Pharaohs. This new vision of Christianity—based on Jesus' radical rebelliousness—focused on setting the captives free, on ministering to the poor, on healing the sick, and on the equality of brotherly love. The Bible was no longer simply the promise of a better afterlife; now it was the justification for demanding equal rights now in the present.

Christian pastors formed the bedrock of the civil rights movement, and Christian churches became the centers of civil rights activity in the South. SCLC, FOR, CORE, and SNCC all celebrated Christian roots. Preachers, pastors, and ministers took on leadership roles. Utilizing Gandhi's nonviolent methods, the Christian pastors appealed to their antagonists' Christian virtue while stirring the black populace with images of Christ-ordained disobedience and an undercurrent of martyrdom.

Despite a 20th-century surge of black separatism that aligned more closely with Islam and other more Afrocentric belief systems, African Americans remain staunchly allied with the Christian faith.

— DECEMBER 26 —
1960
JAZZ MUSICIANS ISSUE CIVIL RIGHTS ALBUM

On this day in civil rights history, black and white jazz fans alike listened to the protest songs on the album *We Insist: Freedom Now.*

In 1958, tenor saxophonist Sonny Rollins recorded the first *Freedom Suite* with Max Roach and Oscar Pettiford. The album was the first extended instrumental protest piece. In his liner notes, Rollins said, "America is deeply rooted in Negro culture: its colloquialisms; its humor; its music. How ironic that the Negro, who exemplifies the humanities in his very existence, is being rewarded with inhumanity."

Jazz, blues, and later bop were all forms of musical protest from their beginnings. Musicians sang and played about the black American experience, sometimes mourning, sometimes celebrating, but always agitating. Black jazz musicians became angered over the white co-opting of black music for popular consumption. In reaction to this, many wanted to recast jazz in solely black terms: Nina Simone called it "black classical music"; Duke Ellington referred to it as "Negro music"; and Max Roach called it "great black music."

After being invited to commemorate the 100th anniversary of the Emancipation Proclamation, Roach, a trailblazing jazz drummer, decided to do a protest album of his own. Roach was an ardent supporter of the civil rights movement; he was outspoken, controversial, and uncompromising. In constructing his protest album, Roach wanted to connect the turmoil of American apartheid with the postcolonial struggles in Africa. Oscar Brown Jr. wrote the lyrics, and Roach's future wife, Abbey Lincoln, sang the vocals. The album was titled *We Insist: Max Roach's Freedom Now Suite.*

Other jazz musicians also issued protest songs and albums, including Charles Mingus's "Fable of Faubus" and Ornette Coleman's *Free Jazz,* among others. Throughout the 20th century, black musicians, especially jazz artists, worked in the protest vein, including Duke Ellington, Louis Armstrong, Billie Holiday (who popularized the antilynching song "Strange Fruit"), Charlie Parker, John Coltrane, Thelonius Monk, Dizzy Gillespie, and Nina Simone, among many, many others.

For decades before folk, rock, and blues became the popular forms of protest in the 1960s, the civil rights movement grooved on the sounds of the black jazz masters. The music was indispensable to black culture, black pride, and black progress.

— DECEMBER 27 —

1980

BARBARA JORDAN TEACHES

On this day in civil rights history, approximately, Barbara Jordan taught at the University at Texas after a distinguished political career.

Born in Houston in 1936, Jordan was raised the youngest daughter of a Baptist preacher. She graduated with honors from Texas State University in 1956, a member of Delta Sigma Theta sorority. She graduated from Boston University Law School in 1959, returning to Texas to open a law practice.

Jordan ran unsuccessfully for the Texas House of Representatives in 1962 and 1964. In 1966, however, her persistence paid off and she was elected to the Texas state senate. She was the first black female senator ever, and the first African American to serve in the Texas state senate since 1883.

In 1972, she ran for the U.S. House of Representatives and won, becoming the first Southern black woman to serve in Congress.

One year later, however, multiple sclerosis struck. Despite being confined to a wheelchair, she was reelected to the House of Representatives in 1974. As a member of the House Judiciary Committee, she gave a damning speech against Richard Nixon in his impeachment hearings, and in 1976 she was the keynote speaker at the Democratic National Convention. As the first African American to deliver the keynote at a national political convention, she said, "Let there be no illusions about the difficulty of forming this kind of a national community. It's tough, difficult, not easy. But a spirit of harmony will survive in America only if each of us remembers that we share a common destiny."

In a later speech, Jordan expressed the core of her political beliefs: "America's mission was, and still is, to take diversity and mold it into a cohesive and coherent whole that would espouse virtues and values essential to the maintenance of civil order. There is nothing easy about that mission, but it is not Mission Impossible."

She retired from politics in 1979 and began teaching at the University of Texas in Austin. She hid her physical pain from the public eye, but multiple sclerosis and later leukemia left her in great discomfort. In 1992, Jordan was again the keynote speaker at the Democratic National Conventions. Two years later, she received the Presidential Medal of Freedom.

She died January 17, 1996. She was 59.

— December 28 —
2004
First Black Secretaries of State

On this day in civil rights history, Condoleezza Rice prepared to take over the office of U.S. Secretary of State, recently vacated by Colin Powell.

From the 1960s to the 1990s, Powell had a distinguished military career, serving in South Korea, Vietnam (where he was almost killed by a booby trap), and the first war in Iraq.

After the success of Operation Desert Storm in 1992, Powell was immensely popular and was courted by both political parties after he retired from the military. In 2001, President George W. Bush named Powell as the first black U.S. Secretary of State. Powell was the lone moderate in Bush's neoconservative cabinet. The turbulent first term of Bush's presidency, with the 9/11 terrorist attacks and the subsequent wars in Afghanistan and Iraq, took its toll on Powell and his popularity. He was put in the uncomfortable position of defending U.S. policy decisions he did not personally agree with. In November 2004, after Bush won his second term, Powell resigned.

Rice, born the same year as *Brown v. Board* and trained as a concert pianist, was named his successor. Fluent in Russian and an expert on professional football and international affairs, Rice had a distinguished academic and business career before entering politics. Under George H. W. Bush, Rice was director of Soviet and East German Affairs; under George W. Bush, she was National Security Advisor. Rice was one of the most vocal supporters of the war in Iraq.

Rice is praised by supporters as a razor-sharp, no-nonsense thinker and politician. Critics contend she is a war-hungry imperialist, with her worldview colored by obsolete Cold War thinking. As an African American woman named the most powerful woman on earth by *Forbes* in 2005, Rice has no peers in American politics.

As with Clarence Thomas and Thomas Sowell, Rice's and Powell's conservative politics are criticized by many contemporary black leaders who charge them with supporting an agenda that hurts the majority of African Americans.

— DECEMBER 29 —

1910

MILDRED JEFFREY BORN

On this day in civil rights history, Mildred Jeffrey, a white woman who became a women's rights and civil rights activist and labor leader, was born in Alton, Iowa.

The oldest of seven children, Mildred McWilliams studied psychology at the University of Minnesota after graduating from Minneapolis Central High School. At the U of M, she joined the YWCA, a then-controversial organization in some quarters due to its support of integration, which included interracial dances.

In 1934, McWilliams earned a graduate degree from Bryn Mawr College. She began working for the Amalgamated Clothing Workers of America, and eventually she served as the educational director of the Pennsylvania Joint Board of Shirt Workers. In 1936, she married union organizer Homer Newman Jeffrey. Together they traveled around the country, organizing textile workers. They also became friends with Walter and Victor Reuther, the two brothers who formed the United Auto Workers in 1935. Jeffrey was the first woman to chair a UAW department. She developed a reputation as a tough labor organizer.

Working with unions and organized labor brought Jeffrey into the early civil rights movement. In the 1940s, she joined the NAACP. Like many activists of the era, she saw the importance of the confluence of labor, women, and minority groups. Jeffrey was an important organizer who dedicated her entire life to the three causes.

Jeffrey became a prominent member of the National Organization of Women, helping found the National Women's Political Caucus. In the 1960s, Jeffrey participated in many civil rights marches alongside Martin Luther King Jr. and James Meredith, among others.

In 1962, Jeffrey arranged for her daughter Sharon and her fellow University of Michigan students to use an AFL-CIO camp as a meeting ground. The students released the Port Huron Statement, the manifesto of what became Students for a Democratic Society.

After the civil rights movement ended, Jeffrey continued to work for labor and women's issues. "I'll retire when I die," she said when she was 70.

In 1999, she was awarded the Presidential Medal of Freedom by President Clinton.

On March 25, 2004, Jeffrey died of natural causes, surrounded by her family. She was 93. The labor leader had finally retired after a lifetime of service.

— DECEMBER 30 —
2005
STUDY SHOWS SCHOOLS TO BE RESEGREGATING

On this day in civil rights history, a study from the Harvard Civil Rights Project reverberated with those who cared to listen.

Founded in 1996, the HCRP devotes its considerable resources to policy analysis and research. In this study, released in September 2005, the HCRP analyzed public education in five Southern states: Georgia, Florida, North Carolina, Mississippi, and Louisiana. The findings were alarming.

Two prominent minority groups, African Americans and Latinos, now exist alongside the white majority. As of 2005, 70 percent of black and Latino students in the South attend schools that are technically segregated. Nine out of ten segregated schools operate in poverty-stricken communities. The dropout rate is much higher in segregated schools (often underfunded due to weakened tax bases), and the test scores are much lower. The high dropout rate feeds drug and other crime problems in already depressed areas. This often leads to fewer jobs and lower property values, which reinforce housing discrimination and gentrification.

While 75 percent of white students graduate on time, slightly more than 50 percent of minority students will graduate with a regular diploma. The reasons for this are myriad, including the rise of private schools and white flight to the suburbs. The end result: Wealthy suburban public schools are thriving while inner-city schools crumble.

The resegregation trend started in the mid-1980s as forced busing and other integration rules were at first relaxed and in many instances done away with all together.

Further complicating matters is President Bush's No Child Left Behind Act, which places the onus of maintaining test-score standards on school districts. If a district underperforms, federal money can be withheld. The problem is that lowest-income districts are most at risk of failing to reach the nationwide standard. Thus the areas that need the money the most are deprived of essential funding. And so the cycle continues.

Integrating the public schools was always about fairness and equality; equal education was the cornerstone to African American progress in U.S. society.

— DECEMBER 31 —
1919
'IF WE MUST DIE, LET IT NOT BE LIKE HOGS'

On this day in civil rights history, a New Year's Eve, African Americans may have paused to wonder just what their country stood for and whether they could hope that next year might be better. In the pages of this book—a year's worth of dates plucked somewhat at random from five centuries of history—we have seen drama, tragedy, comedy, defeat, courage, triumph, cruelty, perseverence, creativity, folly, despair, and hope.

If there is a miracle of the civil rights story in America, it is that blacks could maintain hope when at many points it must have been hard to come by.

Violence against individual blacks was an ever-present danger, but in the early 20th century, a pattern emerged of white mob violence against entire black communities. Some 26 race riots occurred in 1919 in such cities as Chicago; Washington; Charleston; Knoxville; Nashville; and Omaha. More than 100 blacks were killed; thousands were wounded and left homeless. Some of the underlying cause seemed to be white anger over increasing black competition for jobs and housing in industrial cities. In these riots, white mobs entered black neighborhoods, burned homes and businesses, and beat and killed blacks unlucky enough to be in the way. Sociologist-economist Gunnar Myrdal viewed these conflicts not as riots, but as mass lynchings.

In the coming decades, the impact of the riots would be felt in the intense effort by blacks and their white and Jewish supporters to improve social conditions and break down segregation. In short, the riots helped bring on the civil rights movement. More immediately, however, they produced what some called a militant "new Negro." The poet Charles McKay addressed this in his 1919 response to the riots:

> If we must die, let it not be like hogs
> Hunted and penned in an inglorious spot,
> While round us bark the mad and hungry dogs,
> Making their mock at our accursed lot. . . .
> Oh, Kinsmen! we must meet the common foe!
> Though far outnumbered, let us still be brave,
> And for their thousand blows deal one deathblow!
> What though before us lies the open grave?
> Like men we'll face the murderous, cowardly pack,
> Pressed to the wall, dying, but—fighting back!

And blacks did resist and some armed themselves to protect their communities. The question, though, was whether a minority could gather enough weapons to become truly safe in such a society. Part of the genius of Martin Luther King Jr. was that he showed how to use the one weapon that could prevail over superior force.

Index

DeLaughter, Bobby, 33
"deliberate speed" decision, 169
Delta Sigma Theta, 25
Dent, Tom, 94
Detroit race riots, 72, 226
DeVoe, Edith, 384
Diggs, Charles, 16
Dirksen, Everett, 204
Dividing Lines (Thornton), 341
Dixon, Thomas, 288
Doar, John, 305, 338
Dole, Bob, 30
Doty, Mayor Gary, 308
Douglas, Paul, 275
Douglass, Frederick, 39, 51, 66, 210, 271, 272, 374
Douglass, Stephen A., 78, 168
Du Bois, W. E. B., ix, vi, 20, 21, 56, 67, 79, 111, 213, 251, 261, 284, 322, 332, 350
Duluth, Minnesota monument, 308
Dyer, Leonidas, 87
Dylan, Bob, 162

e

Eastman, Crystal, 198
Eatonville, Florida, 386
Ebony magazine, 242
education and Peabody Fund, 50
Edwards, Charles Marcus, 215
Eisenhower, Pres. Dwight D., 127, 169, 275, 278, 290, 291, 334, 342
Ellington, Duke, 388
Ellison, Ralph, 189, 224

Emancipation Proclamation, 13, 78
England outlaws slavery in colonies, 235
Evers, Charles, 209
Evers, Medgar, 33, 85, 148, 182, 193

f

Fair Housing Act, 117
Fard, Wallace, 337
Farmer, James, 24, 142, 357
Farrakhan, Louis, 314, 337
Faubus, Gov. Orval, 180, 270, 278, 291, 334
Fauntroy, Walter, 172
Fellowship of Reconciliation (FOR), 231, 371
Female Anti-Slavery Society, 66
Fields, Evelyn J., 46
Fifteenth Amendment ratified, 47, 104
Fifth Circuit of Appeals, 342
Fisk University, 21
Florida
  Eatonville, 386
  elections of 2000, 178
Folsom, Big Jim, 180
FOR (Fellowship of Reconciliation), 231, 371
Forbes, George, 113
Forman, James, 90, 303, 347
Forsyth County, GA, 36
Fortune, Timothy Thomas, 37, 111, 174
Foster, Rube, 57

Fourteenth Amendment ratified, 211
Fourth of July, 206
France, slavery and, 235
Frankfurter, Justice Frank, 344
Franklin, Aretha, 25
Franklin, Benjamin, 120
Franklin, John Hope, 146
Frederick Douglass, 36
Free Southern Theater (FST), 94
free speech movement, 299
freedom rides, 142, 152, 158, 167
"Freedom Vote" in Mississippi, 250
Fugitive Slave Law, 59

g

Gandhi, Mahatma, 30
Garrison, William Lloyd, 66, 271, 374
Garvey, Marcus, 51, 97, 229
Germantown Quakers pass antislavery resolution, 62
Gibson, Althea, 164
Goldwater, Barry, 258
Goodman, Andrew, 191, 192, 305
Gore, Al, 178
Gormillion v. Lightfoot, 344
Granger, Gen. Gordan, 189
Grant, Pres. U.S., 47, 50, 130, 184
Gray, Fred D., 64, 68, 76, 149, 319, 344, 376
Great Migration, the, 72